Apostolic
Faith
Today

Apostolic Faith Today

A Handbook for Study

Edited by
Hans-Georg Link

Faith and Order Paper No. 124
WORLD COUNCIL OF CHURCHES, GENEVA

The cover photograph shows a detail from a mosaic in the chapel of the Ecumenical Centre, Geneva. The mosaic is a copy of an eleventh century original in Daphne, near Athens, and was given to the Centre by Patriarch Athenagoras of Constantinople.

Cover design: Michael Dominguez/WCC

ISBN 2-8254-0827-1

Printed in Switzerland

TO THOSE
WHO CONFESSED THE FAITH BEFORE US

TO THOSE
WHO CONFESS THE FAITH WITH US

AND TO THOSE
WHO WILL CONFESS THE FAITH AFTER US

IN THE POWER OF THE HOLY SPIRIT

God, Creator and Author of life,
warned anew of the threats to human survival,
we confess that the way we live and order society,
sets us against one another and alienates us from your creation,
exploiting, as though dead, things to which you have given life.
Separated from you we live in emptiness.
We long in our own lives
for a new spirituality of intention, thought, and action.
Help us to struggle to conserve the earth for future generations,
and free us to share together, that all may be free.

Kyrie eleison, Lord have mercy

God of Love,
who through Jesus Christ shares our suffering,
forgives our sins, and delivers from the bondage of oppression,
help us to desire and nourish in ourselves,
sustaining community with our brothers and sisters everywhere.
Give us courage to share suffering when it comes.
Restore to us the joy of resurrection,
that in the midst of situations we can hardly bear we may sing out:

Hallelujah, Praise be to you, O Lord

God of Hope,
whose Spirit gives light and power to your people,
empower us to witness to your name in all the nations,
to struggle for your own justice against all principalities and powers
and to persevere with faith and humour in the tasks
that you have given to us.
Without you we are powerless.
Therefore we cry together:

Maranatha, Come Lord Jesus

And grant that we may with one voice and one heart,
glorify and sing praise to the majesty of your holy Name,
of the Father, the Son, and the Holy Spirit.

Amen

Prayer from the Fifth Assembly of the World Council of Churches, Nairobi, 1975

CONTENTS

PREFACE

Baptism, Eucharist and Ministry, the convergence document of the Faith and Order Commission of the World Council of Churches, has given rise to unprecedented interest in the churches all over the world. It is encouraging to see how the outcome of an intensive ecumenical theological exercise is able to meet the concerns and aspirations of many people in the churches.

Towards the Common Expression of the Apostolic Faith Today, one of the new Faith and Order studies, is closely related to *Baptism, Eucharist and Ministry*. The mutual recognition of baptism and ministries, eucharistic fellowship and the common confession of the apostolic faith are all indispensable elements of the visible unity we seek. Confessing our faith together is both an act of praise and an expression of witnessing discipleship in the world. Yet such common confession needs to be undergirded by a mutual understanding of the fundamentals of our Christian faith. Do we agree on these fundamentals? And how can we together interpret, confess and apply them in continuity with those who believed before us, in order that they serve as the firm basis of Christian conviction, life, service and hope in today's complex and threatened world?

To attempt answers to these questions is the purpose of the Faith and Order study on the apostolic faith. We do hope that once again many people in the churches will accompany us in this step towards greater and deeper Christian unity. I am grateful to my colleague Hans-Georg Link who has with great care prepared this book. Other colleagues in the World Council of Churches have helped with translation, typing and editing the manuscripts and preparing the book for publication. A financial contribution from the Evangelische Landeskirche in Würtemberg, Federal Republic of Germany, has helped to keep the costs down. We are grateful to all who have in various ways contributed to this publication. May this common work lead to the common confession of the apostolic faith — for which this book provides witnesses, hope and encouragement.

Geneva   GÜNTHER GASSMANN
Easter 1985   Director of the Sub-unit on Faith and Order

Introduction
TOWARDS UNITY IN THE FAITH

Hans-Georg Link

I. The theme

"To call the churches to the goal of visible unity in one faith and in one eucharistic fellowship expressed in worship and in common life in Christ, and to advance towards that unity in order that the world may believe" — this is the primary task of the World Council of Churches, according to its Constitution.[1] The *raison d'être* of the WCC and the whole the ecumenical movement of the twentieth century is the recovery of unity among the divided Christian churches, a unity which from the very beginning has been conceived of as a visible[2] reality. According to the Constitution of the World Council of Churches, the unity to which it is to call the churches is, above all, unity in "one faith" centred in "one eucharistic fellowship". "Faith" here means both content and act, and consequently finds expression both in the celebration of worship and in daily life together.

This is the unity with which the modern ecumenical movement is concerned, the unity towards which it is to advance so that the world may believe: unity in the truth, embracing faith and life, celebration and action. The task of the World Council of Churches thus responds to the exhortation of the Epistle to the Ephesians "to maintain the unity of the Spirit in the bond of peace", an exhortation which the apostle justified by his reference to the common Lord and to faith in him: "*one* Lord, *one* faith, *one* baptism; *one* God and Father of us all, who is above all and through all and in all" (Eph. 4:3,5f.). The apostle's exhortation to unity and our present search for unity have the same roots, and to disregard this authority amounts to disobedience to the one Lord.

As early as 1910, unity in faith had become a dominant concern, which led to the creation of the Faith and Order Movement. That year the General Convention of the Protestant Episcopal Church in the USA, a member of the Anglican communion, invited "all Christian communions throughout the world which confess our Lord Jesus

---

● This text has been translated from the German by the WCC Language Service.

[1] Constitution III, 1; in *Breaking Barriers: Nairobi 1975*, official report of the Fifth Assembly of the WCC, Nairobi, 23 November-10 December 1975, ed. David M. Paton, London, SPCK, and Grand Rapids, Wm. B. Eerdmans, 1976, pp.317f. The description of the "aim" of the Faith and Order Commission in section 2 of the By-Laws of the Commission is very similar; *ibid*, p.402.

[2] It was from Anglicanism that the twentieth century ecumenical movement largely originated. Article 19 of the Thirty-Nine Articles already affirms: *Ecclesia Christi visibilis est coetus fidelium.*

1

Christ as God and Saviour" to a conference "for the consideration of questions touching Faith and Order".[3] That identified the decisive theme which runs like a golden thread through the story of the ecumenical movement of this century.

At their Third Assembly in New Delhi in 1961, the member churches of the World Council made this vision their own and gave it substance by declaring: "We believe that the unity which is both God's will and his gift to his Church is being made visible as all in each place who are baptized into Jesus Christ and confess him as Lord and Saviour are brought by the Holy Spirit into one fully committed fellowship, holding the one apostolic faith, preaching the one Gospel, breaking the one bread, joining in common prayer, and having a corporate life reaching out in witness and service to all." Here, too, the common faith is highlighted as the first mark of the ecumenical fellowship and indeed, for the first time, the formulation used is the phrase which has since become the key term: the one apostolic faith.

The Fifth Assembly of the World Council of Churches in Nairobi in 1975 returned to the theme and asked the member churches "to undertake a common effort to receive, re-appropriate and confess together, as contemporary occasion requires, the Christian truth and faith, delivered through the Apostles and handed down through the centuries".[4] The Sixth Assembly in Vancouver in 1983 reflected on the meaning of "a common understanding of the apostolic faith"[5] and the Faith and Order Commission was urged to continue giving top priority in the coming years to a study "Towards the Common Expression of the Apostolic Faith Today" as outlined in Lima in 1982 and to link this study closely to the reception process of the document on "Baptism, Eucharist, Ministry" which presupposes this common expression of the apostolic faith in our day.[6]

On his visit to the Ecumenical Centre in Geneva on 12 June 1984, Pope John Paul II referred explicitly to the importance of an agreement on the common Christian faith: "This", he said, "is a fundamental theological work, for unity in the profession of faith conditions the outcome of all the efforts made in common, while these efforts in their turn are an important means of progressing towards this unity in the faith... Our witness cannot be truly and completely common until we reach unity in the confession of the apostolic faith."[7]

The theme "unity in faith" has been increasingly explored in the twentieth century ecumenical movement from the very beginning. It is also one of the main missions of the World Council of Churches and has a central place in the current theological work of the Faith and Order Commission. The future of the ecumenical movement depends in large measure on achieving a common expression of the apostolic faith.

II. The history

To help us see where we are today "on the way to the common faith", which stations lie behind us and which are still ahead, it will be useful to survey the work so far accomplished — to which the documents assembled in this book bear witness.

---

[3] Joint Commission appointed to arrange for a World Conference on Faith and Order, *Faith and Order Series No.1*, 1910, p.4.
[4] *Breaking Barriers, op.cit.*, p.66.
[5] Report of Issue Group 2: "Taking Steps Towards Unity", in *Gathered for Life*, official report of the Sixth Assembly of the WCC, Vancouver, Canada, 24 July-10 August 1983, ed. David Gill, Geneva, WCC, 1983, p.48.
[6] *Gathered for Life, op.cit.*, p.253.
[7] *The Ecumenical Review*, Vol. 36, No. 4, October 1984, pp.440 and 442.

1. The Lambeth Quadrilateral

The first station on the long ecumenical way to the common faith can be located in the year 1888. Meeting at that time for their Third Lambeth Conference, the bishops of the Anglican Communion agreed on a four-point declaration based on a proposal and preliminary work by the Protestant Episcopal Church in the USA. This declaration, known as the Lambeth Quadrilateral, summarized the essential contents of the Christian faith as follows:

1. The Holy Scriptures of the Old and New Testaments, "as containing all things necessary to salvation" and as being the rule and ultimate standard of faith.
2. The Apostles' Creed, as the baptismal symbol; and the Nicene Creed as the sufficient statement of the Christian faith.
3. The two Sacraments ordained by Christ himself — baptism and the supper of the Lord — ministered with unfailing use of Christ's words of Institution, and of the elements ordained by Him.
4. The historic episcopate, locally adapted in the methods of its administration to the varying needs of the nations and peoples called of God into the unity of his church.[8]

In this declaration, of course, the essence of the Christian faith is stated in a formal and itemized manner rather than descriptively. It nevertheless provided from the outset a short and succinct initial basis for agreement within the worldwide Anglican communion as well as with other churches. In this respect, the Lambeth Quadrilateral may fairly be described as the most important document of nineteenth century efforts towards church unity. The Third Lambeth Conference of 1888 was also careful to point out its "readiness to enter into brotherly conference... with the representatives of other Christian Communions of the English speaking races, in order to consider what steps can be taken, either towards corporate Reunion, or towards such relations as may prepare the way for fuller organic unity hereafter".[9]

Taking the 1888 Declaration as its basis, the 1908 Lambeth Conference also spelled out its vision of the reunited "church of the future":

> We must set before us the Church of Christ as He would have it, one spirit and one body, enriched with all those elements of divine truth which the separated communities of Christians now emphasize severally, strengthened by the interaction of all the gifts and graces which our divisions now hold asunder, filled with all the fulness of God.[10]

It is permissible, therefore, to consider the summary of the "essentials" of the Christian faith in the Lambeth Quadrilateral of 1888 as the starting point for far-reaching endeavours for unity both within the Anglican Communion and beyond it.

2. The Faith and Order movement

a) That the same American Protestant Episcopal Church which had provided the impetus for the Lambeth Quadrilateral should also have been responsible for the emergence of the Faith and Order movement some twenty years later was certainly no accident. Strikingly enough, it was "at a morning celebration of the Eucharist" during the World Missionary Conference in Edinburgh in 1910 that the idea was born, as Charles Brent — the New York bishop of the Episcopal Church who was later to

---

[8] Lambeth Quadrilateral 1888. See *The Five Lambeth Conferences 1867-1908*, Randall T. Davidson ed., London, SPCK, 1920.
[9] Lambeth Conference 1888, *ibid.*, p.122.
[10] *Ibid.*, p.314f.

become its President — tells us.[11] It will always be to the credit of the Protestant Episcopal Church that it not only invited "all Christian Communions throughout the world which confess Our Lord Jesus Christ as God and Saviour" to a "Conference for the consideration of questions touching Faith and Order"[12] but also, at the same General Convention in *Cincinnati on 19 October 1910*, with Anglo-Saxon pragmatism, established a special Commission to spread the idea and to prepare for such a conference.[13]

Two other church bodies in the United States were holding their meetings at the same time as the Episcopal Church Convention. On 20 October 1910, the National Council of Congregational Churches in the USA sent a message to the Episcopal Church assembly informing it of its decision, "in view of possible fraternal discussions on church unity", to create a five-member commission to consider possible responses during negotiations with other denominations.[14] The day before, 19 October 1910, the Disciples of Christ approved a union plan which, among other things, called for "a catholic confession of faith" (e.g. that of Peter in the New Testament) in the interests of church unity.[15] The fact that three independent initiatives for church unity were taken at almost the same time in the October of 1910 is impressive testimony to the already widespread desire for a future united church of Jesus Christ at that time in the United States.

b) Three events *in the year 1920* made it the next important ecumenical station. In January 1920, the Ecumenical Patriarchate of Constantinople issued an Encyclical "Unto the Churches of Christ Everywhere" urging the creation of some form of league of churches similar to the recently founded League of Nations, and recommending, among other things, the convocation of "pan-Christian conferences" and an "impartial and deeper historical study of doctrinal differences".[16] Then, at the beginning of August 1920, the Anglican bishops assembled at the Lambeth Conference issued their "Appeal to all Christian People" for the reunion of Christendom, in which they had this to say on the question of faith:

> We cherish the earnest hope that all these Communions, and our own, may be led by the Spirit into the Unity of the Faith and of the knowledge of the Son of God... The faith cannot be adequately apprehended and the battle of the Kingdom cannot be worthily fought while the body is divided and is thus unable to grow up into the fullness of the life of Christ... The vision which rises up before us is that of a Church genuinely Catholic... within whose visible unity all the treasures of faith and order, bequeathed us as a heritage by the past to the present, shall be possessed in common and made serviceable to the whole Body of Christ.[17]

Finally, a preparatory conference on Faith and Order was held in Geneva from 12 to 20 August 1920, dealing mainly with the significance of Bible and Creed for a united church.[18] In his closing words at this conference, Bishop Brent, its chairman, said:

---

[11] See H. Sasse ed., *Die Weltkonferenz für Glauben und Kirchenverfassung, Lausanne 3-21 August 1927*, Berlin, Furche Verlag, 1929, p.48.
[12] See Joint Commission, *op. cit.*, p.4.
[13] *Ibid.*, p.5f.
[14] Sasse, *op.cit.*, p.7; R. Rouse & S. Neill eds, *A History of the Ecumenical Movement 1517-1948*, London, SPCK, p.408.
[15] Rouse & Neill, *op. cit.*, p.407f.
[16] C. Patelos ed., *The Orthodox Church in the Ecumenical Movement: Documents and Statements 1902-1975*, Geneva, WCC, 1978, p.40ff.
[17] Henry Bettenson ed., *Documents of the Christian Church*, London, Oxford University Press, 2nd ed. 1963, p.442f.
[18] Cf. especially the contributions by A. Scott and J.E. Roberts, in report of the preliminary meeting at Geneva, Switzerland, 12-20 August 1920, in "A Pilgrimage Toward Unity", *Faith and Order Series No. 33*, pp.54-72.

Through a long stretch of time controversy has burned with fierce flame in the churches, great and small, and has blackened and scorched many a fair subject. It is not extinguished yet. The spirit of controversy rejoices in dialectic victory — what a hollow triumph it is! — and gloates over a defeated foe. The spirit of conference is the slave of truth... The study of the Church as it exists in the mind of God, of what we mean by unity, of the sources of the Church's inspiration, of the best expression in language of a living faith, occupied the prayers and thoughts of the pilgrims during the conference and for a long time to come will continue to occupy them. Faith first and then Order...[19]

c) The question of the common faith was tackled by the First World Conference on Faith and Order in *Lausanne in 1927* in two work groups. One of these discussed "the Church's message to the world: the Gospel". Here it was a matter of producing an initial account of what according to the members of the conference constituted the content of the gospel: "The Gospel is the joyful message of redemption, both here and hereafter, the gift of God to sinful man in Jesus Christ." This first ecumenical effort, after many centuries of division, to formulate together the content of the gospel for the twentieth century world was given wide distribution under the title of the "Lausanne Message".

The other work group in Lausanne tackled "The Church's Common Confession of Faith". In 1923, a preparatory committee on this theme had already produced a report on the "faith of the reunited Church". The strikingly brief final report of this work group — the shortest of all the section reports at Lausanne — is similar in form to the Lambeth Quadrilateral but, alongside scripture and the ancient church creeds, also emphasizes the importance of "the spiritual experience of the Church of Christ" for the common Christian faith.

Finally, the common faith was also dealt with in the Preamble adopted unanimously by the Conference:

> We representatives of many Christian Communions throughout the world... united in the common confession of faith in Jesus Christ the Son of God, our Lord and Saviour, believing that the Spirit of God is with us, are assembled to consider the things wherein we agree and the things wherein we differ.[20]

The World Conference in Lausanne helped its members to realize as Christians, for the first time for centuries, that they were fundamentally united by the common confession of faith in Jesus Christ, despite all the differences of detail in faith and practice. This was the new "Lausanne spirit" to which appeal was frequently made.

d) In his closing words to the Lausanne conference, Bishop Brent pointed out that the task had only begun and the Conference was only a starting point.[21] Not surprisingly, therefore, the conference created a Continuation Committee consisting of over a hundred members, whose chief responsibility it was to prepare the next World Conference on Faith and Order, which met in *Edinburgh on 3 August 1937*. The substantial findings of the Edinburgh conference on the question of the common faith are mainly summarized in the report on "The Grace of Our Lord Jesus Christ" which begins with the words:

> With deep thankfulness to God for the spirit of unity which by His gracious blessing upon us has guided and controlled all our discussions on this subject, we agree on the following

---

[19] *Faith and Order Series No. 33*, p.92f.
[20] L. Vischer ed., *A Documentary History of the Faith and Order Movement 1927-1963*, St Louis, Missouri, Bethany Press, 1963, p.27; cf. pp.29, 33.
[21] H.N. Bate ed., *Faith and Order Lausanne 1927*, London, SCM, 1927, p.474.

statement and recognize that there is in connection with this subject no ground for maintaining division between Churches.[22]

The report deals mainly with questions of soteriology — the old theme of theological controversy between Catholics and Protestants. In addition to this, however, there are also brief statements on the word of God, the church and sacraments, which are dealt with at greater length in other reports of the conference. The conference in Edinburgh was courageous enough to address the implications of the theological agreements for the divided churches in their relationship with one another.

e) The Faith and Order Commission retained the right to convene its own world conferences even after it had become an integral part of the World Council of Churches. At the Third World Conference on Faith and Order in *Lund, Sweden, in 1952*, at a time of reconstruction and new beginning after World War II, the main concern was to ensure that faith in the one church of Christ should be translated into acts of obedience.

The "Word to the Churches" put the question therefore:

> Should not our Churches ask themselves whether they are showing sufficient eagerness to enter into conversation with other Churches and whether they should not act together in all matters except those in which deep differences of conviction compel them to act separately?[23]

For the first time, the understanding of the church, which was emerging more and more clearly as the real seat of ecumenical conflict, was at the centre of the theological discussions. The main report here is entitled, significantly: "Christ and His Church"; in other words ecclesiology is viewed from the standpoint of Christology. The report explains on the one hand:

> Because we believe in Jesus Christ, we believe also in the Church as the Body of Christ.

On the other hand, it recommends as of "decisive importance"

> that the doctrine of the Church be treated in close connection both to the doctrine of Christ and to the doctrine of the Holy Spirit.[24]

f) Of the reports of the Fourth World Conference on Faith and Order in *Montreal, Canada, in 1963*, the most fruitful for our question of approaches to the common understanding of the Christian faith is the one on "Scripture, Tradition and Traditions", which differentiates between Tradition, tradition, and traditions:

> By *the Tradition* (with a capital T) is meant the Gospel itself, transmitted from generation to generation in and by the Church, Christ Himself present in the life of the Church.

This report reflects the hermeneutical discussion of the fifties and sixties, notably in certain European countries. While providing helpful conceptual and methodological distinctions, the report represents not much substantial advance in the exposition of the content of the gospel. Its first section nevertheless concludes with the suggestion:

> Should not the very fact that God has blessed the Church with the Scriptures demand that we emphasize more than in the past a common study of Scripture whenever representatives of the various churches meet?

g) For one reason or another, since Montreal, there has not been a world conference on Faith and Order. But the Faith and Order Commission has continued

---

[22] Vischer, *op. cit.*, p.40ff.
[23] *Ibid.*, p.86. The so-called "Lund principle".
[24] *Ibid.*, p.92.

resolutely to pursue the question of the common understanding and confession of the one Christian faith. It did so, above all, in the study "Accounting for the Hope That Is In Us", initiated in 1971 and concluded *in 1978* at the plenary Commission meeting in *Bangalore, India*. The Bangalore statement "A Common Account of Hope" can properly claim to have synthesized the trinitarian faith in God, ecclesiology, eschatology and ethics ("Hope as the Invitation to Risk").

Since then the Commission has been working on the study project "Towards the Common Expression of the Apostolic Faith Today". Looking back, one could say that at each one of its main conferences since the first conference in Lausanne in 1927, the Faith and Order movement has contributed at least one more piece to the mosaic of our common understanding and confession of the Christian faith. The question of our unity in the faith will be one of the main themes at a Fifth World Conference on Faith and Order planned for 1988 or 89.

3. The assemblies of the World Council of Churches

"The World Council of Churches is a fellowship of churches which accept the Lord Jesus Christ as God and Saviour."[25] This was the original form of the Basis of the WCC in 1948. This Christological formulation originated in the resolution adopted by the Protestant Episcopal Church in October 1910. Even its very wording, therefore, bears the imprint of the Faith and Order movement. Since the World Council of Churches was founded, the Faith and Order movement has become part of an even wider "fellowship of churches". The assemblies of the World Council of Churches are unique crystallizing points for the ecumenical movement as a whole. Because of the way they focus on issues, these assemblies have made a special contribution to agreement on the common Christian faith.

a) The inaugural Assembly in *Amsterdam in 1948* took as its theme: "Man's Disorder and God's Design". After the devastating experiences of human "disorder" during World War II and in face of the distress rampant in the post-war world, there was a keener interest in "God's design" not only for the Christian family now drawing closer together, but also for the world as a whole. What the First Assembly had to say about God's "saving purpose" is particularly instructive in this connection.

b) The theme chosen for the Second Assembly in *Evanston, USA, in 1954* was "Christ — the Hope for the World". In this period, that of the Cold War, when the whole climate was poisoned by distrust and divisive trends between East and West, it was particularly important to bear witness to the worldwide unity in Christ in a torn world. The influence of the Lund theme, "Christ and His Church", was particularly evident in Evanston in the report on "Our Oneness in Christ and Our Disunity as Churches".

c) The importance of the Third Assembly in *New Delhi, India, in 1961*, on the theme "Jesus Christ, the Light of the World", was considerably enhanced by the fact that, for the first time, it was being held in a country of the third world, and by the fact that most of the Orthodox churches then joined the Council and the International Missionary Council became an integral part of it. This made possible an unprecedented expression of the wholeness of the Christian witness, which is evident in the famous New Delhi statement on unity. The influence of the expanded ecumenical fellowship was also

---

[25] See *The First Assembly of the World Council of Churches*, Amsterdam 1948, W.A. Visser 't Hooft ed., London, SCM Press, 1949, p.197.

reflected in the changes made in the Basis of the World Council. Since 1961, this has read as follows:

> The World Council of Churches is a fellowship of churches which confess the Lord Jesus Christ as God and Saviour according to the Scriptures and therefore seek to fulfil together their common calling to the glory of the one God, Father, Son and Holy Spirit.[26]

d) Whereas in New Delhi there was a broadening of the ecumenical movement, the Fourth Assembly in *Uppsala, Sweden, in 1968*, was dominated by the ecumenical movement's turning towards the world as a whole. Around the theme "Behold, I make all things new", the renewing power of the Holy Spirit was re-discovered. At the same time, during a period of student unrest, there was the reminder of the catholicity of the church and its responsibility for the world.

e) At the Fifth Assembly in *Nairobi, Kenya, in 1975*, the ecumenical world became acutely conscious of the rich cultural diversity of the churches. The apartheid problem of South Africa and the full participation of Christians from Latin America in the debates helped to make the theme "Jesus Christ Frees and Unites" astonishingly topical. In Nairobi the dimension of public confession as an indispensable aspect of the Christian faith was rediscovered.

f) The outstanding feature of the Sixth Assembly in *Vancouver, Canada, in 1983*, was the richness of the worship experience. The daily worship regularly attracted an unexpectedly large gathering of worshippers. Although it did not figure on the official agenda of the plenary sessions, the convergence statement "Baptism, Eucharist and Ministry", adopted at the plenary Commission meeting of Faith and Order in Lima in 1982, was the object of unexpectedly intense interest.[27] These two features were combined in the celebration of the Lima Liturgy, a eucharistic service based on the three convergence statements. The theme of the Sixth Assembly — "Jesus Christ — the Life of the World" — challenged the churches to wrestle with the forces threatening life, especially with militarism and injustice on a world scale. Among other outstanding features of this most recent Assembly were the worship service and the prayer vigil for peace and justice, and the drafting and adoption of the Statement on Peace and Justice.[28]

When we try to sum up the contribution made to the "common expression of the apostolic faith today" through the written statements of assemblies of the World Council of Churches, it seems permissible to speak, on the one hand, of a broadening (extensifying) of the faith and, on the other hand, of a deepening (intensifying) of the faith. The line of extensification runs from "God's Design" (1948) *via* "Our Oneness in Christ" (1954) and "Jesus Christ: the Saviour of the World" (1961) to "The Holy Spirit and the Catholicity of the Church" (1968). In other words, in the first four WCC assemblies, we find an implicit trinitarian unfolding of the Christian faith. The intensification, on the other hand, takes place in respect of contextualization and inculturation (1975) and also in respect of spirituality and ethics (1983). The last two assemblies have helped to anchor the trinitarian faith in new territory culturally and ethically.

---

[26] See *The New Delhi Report*, New York, Association Press, 1962, p.152.

[27] They were even referred to in the Assembly Message: "We especially thank God for the hope given to us by the 'Baptism, Eucharist, Ministry' document and seek widespread response to it." See *Gathered for Life, op. cit.*, p.2.

[28] *Gathered for Life, op. cit.*, pp.130ff.

4. The participation of the Roman Catholic Church

It is common knowledge that since the *Second Vatican Council* (1962-65) the Roman Catholic Church has taken a lively interest in the ecumenical movement. It not only adopted a new attitude to other churches in the Decree on Ecumenism[29] but also, in the Dogmatic Constitution on Divine Revelation, made it clear how fundamental a role holy scripture had come to play in its life too:

> The apostles preached, as Christ had charged them to do, and then, under the inspiration of the Holy Spirit, they and others of the apostolic age handed on to us in writing the same message they had preached, the foundation of our faith: the fourfold Gospel according to Matthew, Mark, Luke and John... All the preaching of the church, as indeed the entire Christian religion, should be nourished and ruled by sacred scripture.

It is astonishing to note how closely this 1965 Constitution coincides in substance with the 1963 Montreal statement on "Scripture, Tradition and Traditions".

This new ecumenical openness of the Roman Catholic Church also entailed *structural consequences* in its relations with the World Council of Churches. The Joint Working Group was established as early as 1965 for the study of jointly defined problems of importance for dialogue and cooperation.[30] To carry out this task an additional "special theological commission" was also appointed for a time. Moreover, since 1968 ten to fifteen Roman Catholic theologians have cooperated as full members of the Faith and Order Commission[31] "with the agreement of the Roman Catholic Church".[32]

In view of the question of *unity in the faith*, the Joint Working Group decided in 1975-76 to discuss the theme "The Unity of the Church" specifically from this standpoint. In June 1978 a first exploratory conference on this theme was held in Venice. Its findings were published as Faith and Order Paper No. 100 in 1980: "Towards a Confession of the Common Faith".[33]

From the beginning of the seventies, the Joint Working Group has been examining the possibilities of a common witness.[34] It was confirmed in this purpose by the Synod of Bishops in October 1974 which declared:

> In carrying out these things we intend to collaborate more diligently with those of our Christian brothers with whom we are not yet in the union of a perfect communion, basing ourselves on the foundation of baptism and on the patrimony which we hold in common. Thus we can henceforth render to the world a much broader common witness of Christ, while at the same time working to obtain full union in the Lord.[35]

---

[29] The WCC Basis is reproduced almost verbatim in §20 of the *Decree on Ecumenism* which adds: "We rejoice that our separated brethren look to Christ as the source and centre of ecclesiastical communion. Their longing for union with Christ impels them ever more to seek unity, and also to bear witness to their faith among the peoples of the earth." Cf. A. Flannery ed., *Documents of Vatican II*, Eerdmans, Grand Rapids, 1975, p.468.

[30] See the First Official Report of the Joint Working Group, 1966.

[31] Third Official Report of the Joint Working Group, 1971.

[32] Other areas of organized cooperation are the annual joint preparatory conferences for the Week of Prayer for Christian Unity, the Sodepax Commission (1968-1980), the regular participation of Roman Catholic observers and consultants in major WCC conferences, as well as the inclusion of a member of the RC Church in the WCC's programme staff. The Catholic Church is now represented on at least 25 regional or national councils of churches.

[33] Cf. also the Fifth Report of the Joint Working Group, *The Ecumenical Review*, Vol. 35, No. 2, 1983, pp.198ff.

[34] Cf. the study "Common Witness and Proselytism", *The Ecumenical Review*, Vol. 23, No. 1, 1971, pp.9ff.

[35] Quotes from *Breaking Barriers, op. cit.*, p.279.

Work on this was vigorously pursued in the Joint Working Group following the Nairobi Assembly and rounded off in 1981 in the document "Common Witness".

In this connection, we should also mention the efforts made by the Conference of European Churches and the Council of European Episcopal Conferences to give contemporary expression to the heritage of faith. Agreement was reached at the Second European Ecumenical Encounter in Løgumkloster, Denmark, in 1981 to undertake a common interpretation of the Nicene Creed. The result — "Our Credo — Source of Hope" — was approved at the Third Encounter in Riva del Garda, Italy, in 1984 and sent to the participant European churches. On this occasion an ecumenical service was also held in the Cathedral in Trent when all the participants recited together the Nicene-Constantinopolitan Creed in its original 381 version as an expression of the common heritage of faith.

When the Roman Catholic Church refused an invitation to the 1927 Lausanne Conference and excluded any participation in the founding assembly of the World Council of Churches in Amsterdam in 1948 there was bitter disappointment. Since the Second Vatican Council, however, it has actively engaged in bilateral and multilateral dialogues with other churches. The patient and persistent participation of Roman Catholic theologians in discussions on fundamental theological questions has contributed enormously to the ecumenical cause.

5. The study "Towards the Common Expression of the Apostolic Faith Today"

Encouraged by the experiences gained in producing "A Common Account of Hope" and by the work initiated by the Joint Working Group on the common faith, the Faith and Order Commission in *Bangalore in 1978* decided to concentrate on the actual requirements for the unity of the church:

   a) consensus in the apostolic faith;
   b) mutual recognition of baptism, the eucharist and the ministry;
   c) structures making possible common teaching and decision-making.[36]

The Commission thus followed the lead given by Lausanne 1927 to establish "The Church's Common Confession of Faith", strengthened now by decades of experience and enriched by many studies.

At the Commission's plenary meeting in *Lima in 1982*, an outline plan for the whole study project was proposed by a working group and adopted unanimously by the members of the Commission.[37] This plan explained the importance of the theme in general and of the Nicene Creed in particular for the ecumenical movement. It then developed the project in three stages: the recognition, explication, and confession, of the apostolic faith today. Finally, the recommendations set out the various tasks to be tackled by the Commission in the eighties which would help to translate the project into reality.

---

[36] The Common Expression of the Apostolic Faith, in "Sharing in One Hope, Bangalore 1978", *Faith and Order Paper No. 92*, Geneva, WCC, 1978, p.243. This order of priorities was accepted in Vancouver in the report of Issue Group 2, "Taking Steps Towards Unity", under the heading "Marks of Such a Witnessing Unity", cf. *Gathered for Life, op. cit.*, p.45.

[37] Cf. my essay "On the Way to the Expression of the Common Faith: Notes on the Faith and Order Commission's Study on the Apostolic Faith Today", *The Ecumenical Review*, Vol.36, No.3, July 1984, pp.278ff.

A start had already been made in 1978, a few months after the Bangalore conference, to concentrate on some detailed aspects of the theme. Firstly, two smaller conferences were held in *Schloss Klingenthal in Alsace*, concentrating on the *filioque* controversy between the Eastern and Western churches. Their findings were published in 1979 as the "Klingenthal Memorandum".

In 1981, the jubilee year of the adoption of the Constantinopolitan Creed sixteen centuries ago, in addition to a moving ecumenical service in the chapel of the Ecumenical Centre in Geneva, two consultations were held in Chambésy, near Geneva, and *Odessa*, which examined the ecumenical significance of the Creed of 381. In its recommendations, the Odessa report also requests official church responses to the Klingenthal memorandum and urges further detailed studies.

This took place two years later at a conference in *Rome* on the theme "The Apostolic Faith in the Scriptures and in the Early Church". The conference not only discussed the roots of the apostolic faith in the Jewish tradition but also the forms in which this faith found expression in the ancient church liturgies.[38] In its report, the conference stated succinctly:

> We are convinced that the relation of Church and Jewish people is an essential aspect of the apostolic faith, and that any convergence document must deal adequately with this relation.

After examining three individual aspects — the filioque problem, the relevance of the Nicene-Constantinopolitan Creed, and the biblical and ancient church roots of the common faith — the Standing Commission on Faith and Order decided at its most recent meeting in Crete in 1984 to attempt a comprehensive explication of the apostolic faith for our time with the help of the Creed of 381. A first stage in this process has been completed in three conferences, each of which considered one particular article of the Creed:

1. Kottayam (India), November 1984: on the Second Article — We believe in one Lord Jesus Christ.
2. Chantilly (France), January 1985: on the Third Article — We believe in the Holy Spirit, the Church and the Life of the World to come.
3. Kinshasa (Zaire), March 1985: on the First Article — We believe in the one God.[39]

Despite the considerable diversity of the participants at these conferences, it was possible at all three of them to reach a fundamental agreement on the explication of the Christian faith. They showed that in the foundations of their faith there are more common points binding Christians together than they realize. Using these three consultations as a basis, an attempt will now be made at the next plenary Commission meeting in Stavanger, Norway, in the summer of 1985 to produce a first draft of an agreed explication of the Christian faith.

To complete this survey, we add a brief note on tasks ahead in the context of this study project. An "agreed explication of the apostolic faith" for our time represents a new departure point for a consideration of an ecumenical *recognition* of the Creed of 381, such as was already envisaged in Lima 1982:

---

[38] Cf. the essays by M. Wyschogrod and G. Kretschmar in "The Roots of Our Common Faith: Faith in the Scriptures and in the Early Church", ed. H.-G. Link, *Faith and Order Paper No. 119*, Geneva, WCC, 1984, pp. 23ff., 107ff.
[39] Some papers of these conferences will be published separately.

Therefore, the World Council of Churches might ask the churches to recognize anew that integral unity of the Christian faith expressed in the Symbol of Nicea-Constantinople, to reconsider the status of their own teaching in its light, to affirm its content as the basis of more comprehensive church unity, and to strengthen its place in the liturgical life of the churches wherever necessary and possible under circumstances of pastoral responsibility.[40]

Given such agreement on the essential content of the Christian faith, it should also be possible to overcome the *excommunications* (anathemata) which the different churches have pronounced in the past.[41] This would involve for the churches reconsideration of "the status of their own teaching".

The more they come to evaluate their particular confessional traditions in the light of the Creed, the more they may learn to understand other traditions as expressing the same faith under different circumstances and in different situations.[42]

Finally, in view of the questions and challenges of our time it will be important to find new ways of *confessing* our Christian faith together.

This applies in the first place to community within the Church and among churches, a community of women and men across all barriers of races, classes and cultures. But it also extends to the human community at large, to its economic and political conflicts in the national as well as international context, because the Church witnesses to the kingdom of God, the goal of all human community.[43]

III. The documents

The present collection originates in a decision of the Faith and Order Commission in Lima. The idea was to produce, in connection with the study on the common expression of the apostolic faith today, a handbook containing texts "from Lausanne 1927 to Lima 1982 and outlines for further study".[44]

The underlying aim in producing this handbook has been in the first place to bring together the most important *multilateral texts* on the theme of the "common expression of the Christian faith today" from the beginning down to the present day. More specifically, there are now documents from the period from 1923 to 1984. They reflect the way in which the Faith and Order movement, the World Council of Churches, the Roman Catholic Church and other participants have contributed to this common theme, at the same time remaining faithful to their mission and their cause through these decades. Through all the diversity of times, occasions, themes and persons in the ecumenical chorus, the counterpoint, the confession of Jesus Christ as Lord and Saviour, is clearly audible. These documents communicate a living impression of the diversity and consequently the richness of the Christian faith. They also communicate something of the growing unanimity emerging in the progress of the ecumenical movement. Finally, they show how many important individual steps have been taken towards unity in faith in the seventy-five years since the World Missionary Conference in Edinburgh in 1910.

---

[40] Report of Working Group §15.
[41] A Roman Catholic-Evangelical Theological Commission has already been working on this for some years in the Federal Republic of Germany.
[42] Report of Working Group §27b.
[43] Report of Working Group §26f.
[44] Report of Working Group, Recommendation IV, 3 C.

A word on the *selection of documents* for this collection. In an area like this, it is impossible to be exhaustive. It was decided, instead, to let each of the three chief participants in the multilateral efforts towards unity in faith take the floor in turn: the Faith and Order movement or Commission, the World Council of Churches, and the Roman Catholic Church. Secondly, the statements selected had to be the most representative ones possible, which for the ecumenical movement meant in most cases those produced at conferences and assemblies. Thirdly, in the case of Faith and Order and the World Council of Churches at least, the selection should make quite clear the continuity of their concern with fundamental questions, so as to counter the myth of an initial golden age and subsequent decline of ecumenism. Finally, the texts selected should, as far as possible, be ones dealing with the whole and not just parts of the Christian faith, however important such parts might be.

Even on the basis of these criteria, other texts could have been substituted or added. It is readily admitted, therefore, that a very different collection of the "Various Documents of the Ecumenical Movement" could have been assembled than what is presented here.

One other comment on the "Basic Texts" may be in order. When it comes to rediscovering and re-examining our specifically Christian roots, no excuse need be given for starting with the three classical creeds of the ancient church. On the contrary, many will welcome the inclusion of these creeds at the very beginning — even in their original languages — as an excellent point of departure. But why include, it may properly be asked, texts which document the division of the churches in a collection which sets out to illustrate how the conflicts can, at least partially, be overcome? Three considerations governed the decision here. Firstly, the authors of these confessions did not, for the most part, regard themselves as communicating mere fragmentary aspects of the Christian faith but rather the faith in its wholeness and integrity. Secondly, the role of these confessions in the confessional churches, the Christian World Communions, and in the bilateral and even in the multilateral dialogues down to the present time, is a far from negligeable or merely negative. Thirdly, most of these confessions were composed in an irenical rather than polemical spirit,[45] and the reader must examine them closely to decide which predominates in them — the differences or the common ground.

This volume has been compiled for a *wide range of readers*: for all who are interested in the heart-beat of the ecumenical movement, whether they be lay people or theologians, ordinary members of congregations or clergy, individuals or groups, women or men (it is, alas, too indigestable and boring for children!).

As a supplement to the documents presented here, the reader is referred to the series "Confessing Our Faith Around the World",[46] the volume "Growth in Agreement",[47] as well as to the publications of Christian World Communions.[48]

---

[45] This applies, for example, to the *Confessio Augustana*, mainly the work of Melanchthon; so much so, indeed, that it elicited the famous comment of Luther that he himself "was unable to walk so delicately".
[46] This is a recent series of publications of the Geneva Secretariat of the Faith and Order Commission containing contemporary regional confessional statements: Vol.I, 1980; Vol.II, 1983; Vol.III Caribbean and Central America, 1984. The series is to be continued.
[47] It contains a collection of "Reports and Agreed Statements of Ecumenical Conversations on a World Level", 1931 to 1982, eds H. Meyer and L. Vischer, *Faith and Order Paper No. 108*, New York, Ramsey, and Geneva, WCC, 1984. This volume is the most important supplement to the present collection.
[48] E.g. *Called to Witness to the Gospel Today:* An Invitation from the General Council of the World Alliance of Reformed Churches, 1983. *The Debate on Status Confessionis: Studies in Christian Political Theology*, ed. E. Lorenz, Geneva, Lutheran World Federation, 1983.

We hope that the collection will be useful to parish groups, ecumenical associations, student seminaries, ministerial unions, etc., as a "quarry" for ecumenical discussions on "the heart of the matter". Its purpose is to promote dialogue on the centre of ecumenism, namely, the common confession of the Christian faith today, at as many different levels as possible. The material in the appendices is meant for groups and individuals who wish to share in promoting the project in one way or another. The Geneva Secretariat of the Faith and Order Commission warmly welcomes all contributions to the question of the common expression of the apostolic faith today.

A.
FOUNDATIONS

I.
Ancient Church

1. THE NICENE-CONSTANTINOPOLITAN CREED
Text of 381 A.D.

According to church tradition, this creed, known under various titles,[1] goes back to the Second Ecumenical Council in Constantinople in 381. On 25 October 451 it was included in the definition of doctrine at the Fourth Ecumenical Council of Chalcedon. It thus became the official Creed of the ancient undivided church. It is the only Christian creed, therefore, with a well-founded claim to ecumenicity and universal recognition. Born of the struggle against Arianism and the Pneumatomachi, it formulates the one true Christian faith.

The Creed spread rapidly in the East, firstly as a baptismal symbol and later also as part of the eucharistic liturgy. In the West, thanks to the decision of the Synod of Toledo in 589, it was officially introduced into the celebration of the Lord's Supper. Relations between the traditions of the Eastern and Western churches have been blighted down to our own day by the official insertion of the filioque *into the Third Article in the Western church in 1014.*

The Nicene-Constantinopolitan Creed is recognized — and in varying degrees used — by all three main Christian traditions today, Orthodox, Roman Catholic and Protestant. "It is thus one of the few threads by which the tattered fragments of the divided robe of Christendom are held together."[2]

The ecumenical status of this Creed is explained not only by its widespread use both confessionally and geographically but also by its affirmation of unity. Just as there is the one God and the one Lord Jesus Christ, so too there is only the one church whose life is rooted in the one baptism for the remission of sins.

As a mark of respect for the decisions of the councils of the ancient church and in fidelity to the original tradition, the text reproduced here is the original Greek version of the year 381 (together with an English translation).

● Greek text in *Enchiridion Symbolorum, Definitionum et Declarationum de Rebus Fidei et Morum*, eds H. Denzinger and A. Schönmetzer, 32nd ed., Freiburg, 1963, p.66, No. 150.
● English text in *Prayers We Have In Common*, agreed liturgical texts prepared by the International Consultation on English Texts, 2nd revised ed., Philadelphia, 1975, p.6.

---

[1] The following designations are common: Nicene Creed, Nicene Symbol, the Nicaenum, the Constantinopolitan Creed, the Constantinopolitanum, the Credo, the Ecumenical Creed. It is sometimes called "the Faith of the 150 Fathers".
[2] J.N.D. Kelly, *Early Christian Creeds*, Longmans, 1972, p.296.

Πιστεύομεν εἰς ἕνα Θεόν,
  πατέρα παντοκράτορα,
  ποιητὴν οὐρανοῦ καὶ γῆς,
  ὁρατῶν τε πάντων καὶ ἀοράτων·

καὶ εἰς ἕνα κύριον Ἰησοῦν Χριστόν,
  τὸν υἱὸν τοῦ Θεοῦ τὸν μονογενῆ,
  τὸν ἐκ τοῦ πατρὸς γεννηθέντα πρὸ πάντων τῶν αἰώνων,
  φῶς ἐκ φωτός,
  Θεὸν ἀληθινὸν ἐκ Θεοῦ ἀληθινοῦ,
  γεννηθέντα οὐ ποιηθέντα,
  ὁμοούσιον τῷ πατρί,
  δι᾽ οὗ τὰ πάντα ἐγένετο·
  τὸν δι᾽ ἡμᾶς τοὺς ἀνθρώπους καὶ διὰ τὴν ἡμετέραν σωτηρίαν
    κατελθόντα ἐκ τῶν οὐρανῶν
  καὶ σαρκωθέντα ἐκ πνεύματος ἁγίου
    καὶ Μαρίας τῆς παρθένου,
    καὶ ἐνανθρωπήσαντα,
  σταυρωθέντα τε ὑπὲρ ἡμῶν ἐπὶ Ποντίου Πιλάτου
    καὶ παθόντα καὶ ταφέντα
    καὶ ἀναστάντα τῇ τρίτῃ ἡμέρᾳ
    κατὰ τὰς γραφάς,
    καὶ ἀνελθόντα εἰς τοὺς οὐρανούς,
    καὶ καθεζόμενον ἐν δεξιᾷ τοῦ πατρός,
  καὶ πάλιν ἐρχόμενον μετὰ δόξης κρῖναι ζῶντας καὶ νεκρούς·
    οὗ τῆς βασιλείας οὐκ ἔσται τέλος·

καὶ εἰς τὸ πνεῦμα τὸ ἅγιον,
  τὸ κύριον καὶ ζωοποιόν,
  τὸ ἐκ τοῦ πατρὸς ἐκπορευόμενον,
  τὸ σὺν πατρὶ καὶ υἱῷ συμπροσκυνούμενον καὶ συνδοξαζόμενον,
  τὸ λαλῆσαν διὰ τῶν προφητῶν.
  Εἰς μίαν ἁγίαν καθολικὴν καὶ ἀποστολικὴν ἐκκλησίαν.
  Ὁμολογοῦμεν ἓν βάπτισμα εἰς ἄφεσιν ἁμαρτιῶν.
  Προσδοκῶμεν ἀνάστασιν νεκρῶν
    καὶ ζωὴν τοῦ μέλλοντος αἰῶνος. Ἀμήν.

We believe in one God,
  the Father, the Almighty,
  maker of heaven and earth,
  of all that is, seen and unseen.

Identifies immediately who it is we believe in - from the Scriptures.

We believe in one Lord, Jesus Christ,
  the (only) Son of God,
  eternally begotten of the Father,
  Light from Light, ✱
  true God from true God,✱
begotten, not made,
  of one Being with the Father. THESIS STATEMENT
  Through him all things were made.
  For us men and for our salvation
    he came down from heaven:
  by the power of the Holy Spirit
    he became incarnate from the Virgin Mary,
    and was made man.
  For our sake he was crucified under Pontius Pilate;
    he suffered death and was buried.
    On the third day he rose again
      in accordance with the scriptures;
    he ascended into heaven
      and is seated at the right hand of the Father.
  He will come again in glory to judge the living and the dead,
      and his kingdom will have no end.

discerns the Son - over & against Arianism

coexisted / Jesus was not made - he is begotten, birthed

always been together?

In order to say who God is it tells the story.

Never has been the Father w/o the Son, nor the Son w/o the Father

We believe in the Holy Spirit,
  the Lord, the giver of life,
  who (proceeds) from the Father.
  With the Father and the Son he is worshipped and glorified.
  He has spoken through the Prophets.
  We believe in one holy catholic and apostolic Church.
  We acknowledge one baptism for the forgiveness of sins.
  We look for the resurrection of the dead,
    and the life of the world to come. Amen.

mission

- people in

19

2. THE APOSTLES' CREED

The Apostles' Creed owes its name to the fact that it summarizes the essential content of the apostolic faith. The assumption that the twelve apostles were the joint authors of this Creed, widely held from the fourth century onwards, has no historical foundation.

The Apostles' Creed derives from a tripartite confession of belief, of Roman origin, already in use in the second century according to the evidence available, namely, the Old Roman Creed. It was developed in the struggle against Gnosticism, and its existence in the present form is documented only from the eighth century.

The Apostles' Creed is a creed of the Western church having its context in baptism and the liturgy of the word. It was originally quite unknown in the tradition of the Eastern church. Nowadays the Apostles' Creed is mainly in use in Protestant churches and to some extent also in the Roman Catholic tradition, whereas it has up to now officially not been used at all in the Orthodox churches.

The Apostles' Creed is liturgical and historical in character. It proclaims belief in the saving acts of the triune God in history and, with its Christological concentration, has affiliations with the oldest of the Christian credal formulas found in 1 Corinthians 15:3b-5a.

● Latin text in *Enchiridion Symbolorum, Definitionum et Declarationum de Rebus Fidei et Morum*, eds H. Denzinger and A. Schönmetzer, 32nd ed., Freiburg, 1963, p.28, No. 30.
● English text in *Prayers We Have In Common*, agreed liturgical texts prepared by the International Consultation on English Texts, 2nd revised ed., Philadelphia, 1975, p.4.

Credo in Deum
  Patrem omnipotentem,
  creatorem caeli et terrae,

et in Iesum Christum,
  Filium eius unicum, Dominum
    nostrum,
  qui conceptus est de Spiritu Sancto,
    natus ex Maria virgine,
  passus sub Pontio Pilato,
    crucifixus, mortuus et sepultus,
  descendit ad inferna,
  tertia die resurrexit a mortuis,
  ascendit ad caelos,
    sedet ad dexteram Dei Patris
    omnipotentis,
  inde venturus est
    iudicare vivos et mortuos.

Credo in Spiritum Sanctum,
  sanctam Ecclesiam catholicam,
  sanctorum communionem,
  remissionem peccatorum,
  carnis resurrectionem,
  et vitam aeternam. Amen.

I believe in God,
  the Father almighty,
  creator of heaven and earth.

I believe in Jesus Christ,
  his only Son, our Lord.
  He was conceived by the power of the
    Holy Spirit
    and born of the Virgin Mary.
  He suffered under Pontius Pilate,
    was crucified, died, and was buried.
  He descended to the dead.
  On the third day he rose again.
  He ascended into heaven,
    and is seated at the right hand of the
    Father.
  He will come again to judge the living
    and the dead.

I believe in the Holy Spirit,
  the holy catholic Church,
  the communion of saints,
  the forgiveness of sins,
  the resurrection of the body,
  and the life everlasting. Amen.

3. QUICUNQUE VULT
The So-Called "Athanasian Creed"

It is also known as the "Athanasian Creed". The name Quicunque vult *comes from the opening words of this Creed:* Quicunque vult salvus esse, ante omnia opus est, ut teneat catholicam fidem... *(whosoever will be saved, before all things it is necessary that he hold the Catholic Faith.) Although this Symbol was for long attributed to the church father, Athanasius, it never played any part in the tradition of the Eastern church. It is a didactic Latin poem of the Western church probably composed around the year 500 in southern France or Spain. Its theological parentage includes Augustine, Ambrose and Vincent of Lérins. Its use became widespread in the Carolingian period and was regarded in the thirteenth century by scholastic theologians as on a par with the Nicene Creed and the Apostles' Creed. It was also introduced into the monastic daily offices (prime in particular) and from there it passed into the morning prayer of the Anglican tradition on feast days. Like Luther, the Reformation Book of Concord of 1580 includes the Athanasian Creed among "the three main symbols or confessions of faith in Christ commonly used in the churches". In continental European Reformation churches, however, it did not assume much significance.*

The text consists of forty-two doctrinal statements. It summarizes the essence of the Western church doctrine of the Trinity (3-28), including the filioque *(23) and the two-natures Christology (29-37). The* Quicunque vult, *therefore, is not a doxological creed as is the Nicene-Constantinopolitan Creed, nor a narrative confession of faith like the Apostles' Creed, but rather an intellectual and theological exposition.*

● Text in *Book of Common Prayer, According to the Use of the Protestant Episcopal Church in the United States of America*, New York, 1976, pp.864f.

Whosoever will be saved, before all things it is necessary that he hold the Catholic
Faith.

Which Faith except everyone do keep whole and undefiled, without doubt he shall
perish everlastingly.

And the Catholic Faith is this: That we worship one God in Trinity, and Trinity in
Unity,

Neither confounding the Persons, nor dividing the Substance.

For there is one Person of the Father, another of the Son, and another of the Holy
Ghost.

But the Godhead of the Father, of the Son, and of the Holy Ghost, is all one,
the Glory equal, the Majesty co-eternal.

Such as the Father is, such is the Son, and such is the Holy Ghost.

The Father uncreate, the Son uncreate, and the Holy Ghost uncreate.

The Father incomprehensible, the Son incomprehensible, and the Holy Ghost
incomprehensible.

The Father eternal, the Son eternal, and the Holy Ghost eternal.

And yet they are not three eternals, but one eternal.

As also there are not three incomprehensibles, nor three uncreated, but one uncreated,
and one incomprehensible.

So likewise the Father is Almighty, the Son Almighty, and the Holy Ghost Almighty.

And yet they are not three Almighties, but one Almighty.

So the Father is God, the Son is God, and the Holy Ghost is God.

And yet they are not three Gods, but one God.

So likewise the Father is Lord, the Son Lord, and the Holy Ghost Lord.

And yet not three Lords, but one Lord.

For like as we are compelled by the Christian verity to acknowledge
every Person by himself to be both God and Lord,

So we are forbidden by the Catholic Religion, to say, There be three Gods,
or three Lords.

The Father is made of none, neither created, nor begotten.

The Son is of the Father alone, not made, nor created, nor begotten.

The Holy Ghost is of the Father and of the Son, neither made,
nor created, nor begotten, but proceeding.

So there is one Father, not three Fathers; one Son, not three Sons; one Holy Ghost,
not three Holy Ghosts.

And in this Trinity none is above, or after other; none is greater, or less than another;

But the whole three Persons are co-eternal together and co-equal.

So that in all things, as is aforesaid, the Unity in Trinity and the Trinity
in Unity is to be worshipped.

He therefore that will be saved must thus think of the Trinity.

Furthermore, it is necessary to everlasting salvation that he also believe rightly
the Incarnation of our Lord Jesus Christ.

For the right Faith is, that we believe and confess, that our Lord Jesus Christ, the Son
of God, is God and Man;

23

God, of the Substance of the Father, begotten before the worlds; and Man,
of the Substance of his Mother, born in the world;

Perfect God and perfect Man, of a reasonable soul and human flesh subsisting;

Equal to the Father, as touching his Godhead; and inferior to the Father,
as touching his Manhood.

Who although he be God and Man, yet he is not two, but one Christ;

One, not by conversion of the Godhead into flesh, but by taking of the Manhood into
God;

One altogether; not by confusion of Substance, but by unity of Person.

For as the reasonable soul and flesh is one man, so God and Man is one Christ;

Who suffered for our salvation, descended into hell, rose again the third day from the
dead.

He ascended into heaven, he sitteth on the right hand of the Father, God Almighty,
from whence he shall come to judge the quick and the dead.

At whose coming all men shall rise again with their bodies and shall give account
for their own works.

And they that have done good shall go into life everlasting; and they that have done
evil into everlasting fire.

This is the Catholic Faith, which except a man believe faithfully, he cannot be saved.

II.
Sixteenth and
Seventeenth Centuries

1. THE CREED
Second Main Section of Martin Luther's
Small Catechism, 1529

This is the second main section of Martin Luther's Small Catechism, 1529. The ignorance of basic tenets of the Christian faith which Luther discovered among ministers and the laity in the course of the Visitation of the Church of Saxony in 1527, led him to preach three series of simple sermons in 1528 and to publish his Small and Large Catechisms in 1529. "In setting forth this Catechism or Christian doctrine in such a simple, concise, and easy form, I have been compelled and driven by the wretched and lamentable state of affairs which I discovered lately when I acted as inspector... and though all are called Christians... they (nevertheless) live like the poor cattle and senseless swine, though, now that the Gospel is come, they have learnt well enough how they may abuse their liberty."[1] The purpose of the Small Catechism is to explain to "ordinary people" in simple language the five main elements of Christian teaching: the Ten Commandments, the Creed, the Lord's Prayer, baptism, and the Lord's Supper. The Small Catechism was included in the Lutheran Book of Concord of 1580 and, since then, has been an official part of the confessional documents of the Evangelical Lutheran Church. It is still in use as a basis for confirmation courses in many churches marked by the Lutheran tradition.

The Apostles' Creed was adopted by Luther from the medieval tradition of the Western church as an authoritative summary of the Christian faith. Instead of dividing it into twelve sections as in the scholastic tradition, he focuses on the original three articles of the Creed, thereby bringing out its trinitarian character. The special merit of Luther's treatment of the three articles is due not only to his vivid and memorable style but also to the sharpness with which he brings out the soteriological thrust of the credal clauses.

● Text in *The Book of Concord: the Confessions of the Evangelical Lutheran Church*, ed. T.G. Tappert, Philadelphia, (1959), 1979, pp.344f.

---

[1] Preface to the Small Catechism, in *Documents Illustrative of the Continental Reformation*, ed. B.J. Kidd, Oxford, 1911, p.205f.

The First Article: Creation

"I believe in God, the Father almighty, maker of heaven and earth."
What does this mean?

Answer: I believe that God has created me and all that exists; that he has given me and still sustains my body and soul, all my limbs and senses, my reason and all the faculties of my mind, together with food and clothing, house and home, family and property; that he provides me daily and abundantly with all the necessities of life, protects me from all danger, and preserves me from all evil. All this he does out of his pure, fatherly, and divine goodness and mercy, without any merit or worthiness on my part. For all of this I am bound to thank, praise, serve, and obey him. This is most certainly true.

The Second Article: Redemption

"And in Jesus Christ, his only son, our Lord: who was conceived by the Holy Spirit, born of the virgin Mary, suffered under Pontius Pilate, was crucified, dead, and buried: he descended into hell, the third day he rose from the dead, he ascended into heaven, and is seated on the right hand of God, the Father almighty, whence he shall come to judge the living and the dead."
What does this mean?

Answer: I believe that Jesus Christ, true God, begotten of the Father from eternity, and also true man, born of the virgin Mary, is my Lord, who has redeemed me, a lost and condemned creature, delivered me and freed me from all sins, from death, and from the power of the devil, not with silver and gold but with his holy and precious blood and with his innocent sufferings and death, in order that I may be his, live under him in his kingdom, and serve him in everlasting righteousness, innocence, and blessedness, even as he is risen from the dead and lives and reigns to all eternity. This is most certainly true.

The Third Article: Sanctification

"I believe in the Holy Spirit, the holy Christian church, the communion of saints, the forgiveness of sins, the resurrection of the body, and the life everlasting. Amen."
What does this mean?

Answer: I believe that by my own reason or strength I cannot believe in Jesus Christ, my Lord, or come to him. But the Holy Spirit has called me through the Gospel, enlightened me with his gifts, and sanctified and preserved me in true faith, just as he calls, gathers, enlightens, and sanctifies the whole Christian church on earth and preserves it in union with Jesus Christ in the one true faith. In this Christian church he daily and abundantly forgives all my sins, and the sins of all believers, and on the last day he will raise me and all the dead and will grant eternal life to me and to all who believe in Christ. This is most certainly true.

2. ARTICLES OF FAITH AND DOCTRINE
Part I of the Augsburg Confession
(Confessio Augustana, CA), 1530

*The German text of this confession of faith was read out at the Reichstag in
Augsburg on 25 June 1530, and then presented to the Emperor Charles V. Mainly the
work of Philip Melanchthon, it was signed by representatives of five German states as
well as by those of two imperial free cities, Nuremberg and Reutlingen. Its most
important models were the Schwabach Articles of the summer of 1529 (for the first
part) and the Torgau Articles of March 1530 (for the second part).*

The Confessio Augustana *is the basic confession of the German Reformation; in the
Book of Concord it is placed first after the creeds of the ancient church and at the head of
the written confessions of the Reformation. This sequence, as well as specific references
of substance (as in Article 1, for example), shows that the Augsburg Confession is meant
to be seen in continuity with the creeds of the ancient church, and specifically with the
Nicene-Constantinopolitan Creed. Today it forms part of the doctrinal basis of over a
hundred Lutheran churches or churches influenced by Lutheranism. It is also part of the
official constitution of the Lutheran World Federation.*

*There are two parts to the Confession: Part I (Articles I-XXI) presents the
Reformation understanding of the Christian faith, while Part II (Articles XXII-XXVIII)
examines specific points of conflict.*

Preface

I. Articles of faith and doctrine

I-III	*The triune God*
IV-VI	*Justification and sanctification*
VII-VIII	*The church*
IX-XIII	*The sacraments*
XIV-XVI	*Church and state*
XVII-XXI	*Individual themes (Christ's return, free will, origin of sin, faith and works, veneration of the saints)*

II. Controversial Articles on corrected abuses

XXII-XXVIII	*Lord's Supper, priests, mass, confession, customs, monastic vows, bishops*

*Like almost all the sixteenth century confessions of faith, the Augsburg Confession
is clearly a doctrinal statement whose proper place is not in Christian worship but in
catechetical instruction. Composed in an unpolemical style, its purpose was to show*

that Reformation teaching was orthodox and in accord with the faith of the church throughout the ages, as is stated at the conclusion of Part I:

> *Since this teaching is grounded clearly on the Holy Scriptures and is not contrary or opposed to that of the universal Christian Church, or even of the Roman Church (in so far as the latter's teaching is reflected in the writings of the Fathers), we think that our opponents cannot disagree with us in the articles set forth above.[1]*

The purpose of the Confessio Augustana, *therefore, is not to be the foundation document of a separate confession but rather to help maintain the unity of the church. Its limits are indicated by the deliberate silence on important disputed points, such as the papal office, and by the radical repudiations voiced in many of the Articles (e.g. 1,2,5,8,9,12,16,17) especially in respect of Anabaptist Protestantism.*

The Preface to the Augsburg Confession appeals to "a general, free, and Christian Council".[2] In the form then requested, however, this Council has not yet been held. We reproduce here Part I of the Augsburg Confession.

● Text in *The Book of Concord: the Confessions of the Evangelical Lutheran Church*, ed. T.G. Tappert, Philadelphia, (1959), 1979, pp.27-48.

I. God

We unanimously hold and teach, in accordance with the decree of the Council of Nicaea, that there is one divine essence, which is called and which is truly God, and that there are three persons in this one divine essence, equal in power and alike eternal: God the Father, God the Son, God the Holy Spirit. All three are one divine essence, eternal, without division, without end, of infinite power, wisdom, and goodness, one creator and preserver of all things visible and invisible. The word "person" is to be understood as the Fathers employed the term in this connection, not as a part or a property of another but as that which exists of itself.

Therefore all the heresies which are contrary to this article are rejected. Among these are the heresy of the Manichaeans, who assert that there are two gods, one good and one evil; also that of the Valentinians, Arians, Eunomians, Mohammedans, and others like them; also that of the Samosatenes, old and new, who hold that there is only one person and sophistically assert that the other two, the Word and the Holy Spirit, are not necessarily distinct persons but that the Word signifies a physical word or voice and that the Holy Spirit is a movement induced in creatures.

II. Original Sin

It is also taught among us that since the fall of Adam all men who are born according to the course of nature are conceived and born in sin. That is, all men are full of evil lust and inclinations from their mothers' wombs and are unable by nature to

---

[1] *The Book of Concord, p.47.*
[2] *Ibid.*, p.27.

have true fear of God and true faith in God. Moreover, this inborn sickness and hereditary sin is truly sin and condemns to the eternal wrath of God all those who are not born again through Baptism and the Holy Spirit.

Rejected in this connection are the Pelagians and others who deny that original sin is sin, for they hold that natural man is made righteous by his own powers, thus disparaging the sufferings and merit of Christ.

III. The Son of God

It is also taught among us that God the Son became man, born of the virgin Mary, and that the two natures, divine and human, are so inseparably united in one person that there is one Christ, true God and true man, who was truly born, suffered, was crucified, died, and was buried in order to be a sacrifice not only for original sin but also for all other sins and to propitiate God's wrath. The same Christ also descended into hell, truly rose from the dead on the third day, ascended into heaven, and sits on the right hand of God, that he may eternally rule and have dominion over all creatures, that through the Holy Spirit he may sanctify, purify, strengthen, and comfort all who believe in him, that he may bestow on them life and every grace and blessing, and that he may protect and defend them against the devil and against sin. The same Lord Christ will return openly to judge the living and the dead, as stated in the Apostles' Creed.

IV. Justification

It is also taught among us that we cannot obtain forgiveness of sin and righteousness before God by our own merits, works, or satisfactions, but that we receive forgiveness of sin and become righteous before God by grace, for Christ's sake, through faith, when we believe that Christ suffered for us and that for his sake our sin is forgiven and righteousness and eternal life are given to us. For God will regard and reckon this faith as righteousness, as Paul says in Romans 3:21-26 and 4:5.

V. The Office of the Ministry

To obtain such faith God instituted the office of the ministry, that is, provided the Gospel and the sacraments. Through these, as through means, he gives the Holy Spirit, who works faith, when and where he pleases, in those who hear the Gospel. And the Gospel teaches that we have a gracious God, not by our own merits but by the merit of Christ, when we believe this.

Condemned are the Anabaptists and others who teach that the Holy Spirit comes to us through our own preparations, thoughts, and works without the external word of the Gospel.

VI. The New Obedience

It is also taught among us that such faith should produce good fruits and good works and that we must do all such good works as God has commanded, but we should do them for God's sake and not place our trust in them as if thereby to merit favor before God. For we receive forgiveness of sin and righteousness through faith in Christ, as Christ himself says, "So you also, when you have done all that is commanded you, say, 'We are unworthy servants'" (Luke 17:10). The Fathers also teach thus, for Ambrose says, "It is ordained of God that whoever believes in Christ shall be saved, and he shall have forgiveness of sins, not through works but through faith alone, without merit."

VII. The Church

It is also taught among us that one holy Christian church will be and remain forever. This is the assembly of all believers among whom the Gospel is preached in its purity and the holy sacraments are administered according to the Gospel. For it is sufficient for the true unity of the Christian church that the Gospel be preached in conformity with a pure understanding of it and that the sacraments be administered in accordance with the divine Word. It is not necessary for the true unity of the Christian church that ceremonies, instituted by men, should be observed uniformly in all places. It is as Paul says in Eph. 4:4,5, "There is one body and one Spirit, just as you were called to the one hope that belongs to your call, one Lord, one faith, one baptism."

VIII. What the Church Is

Again, although the Christian church, properly speaking, is nothing else than the assembly of all believers and saints, yet because in this life many false Christians, hypocrites, and even open sinners remain among the godly, the sacraments are efficacious even if the priests who administer them are wicked men, for as Christ himself indicated, "The Pharisees sit on Moses' seat" (Matt. 23:2).

Accordingly the Donatists and all others who hold contrary views are condemned.

IX. Baptism

It is taught among us that Baptism is necessary and that grace is offered through it. Children, too, should be baptized, for in Baptism they are committed to God and become acceptable to him.

On this account the Anabaptists who teach that infant Baptism is not right are rejected.

X. The Holy Supper of Our Lord

It is taught among us that the true body and blood of Christ are really present in the Supper of our Lord under the form of bread and wine and are there distributed and received. The contrary doctrine is therefore rejected.

XI. Confession

It is taught among us that private absolution should be retained and not allowed to fall into disuse. However, in confession it is not necessary to enumerate all trespasses and sins, for this is impossible. Ps. 19:12, "Who can discern his errors?"

XII. Repentance

It is taught among us that those who sin after Baptism receive forgiveness of sin whenever they come to repentance, and absolution should not be denied them by the church. Properly speaking, true repentance is nothing else than to have contrition and sorrow, or terror, on account of sin, and yet at the same time to believe the Gospel and absolution (namely, that sin has been forgiven and grace has been obtained through Christ), and this faith will comfort the heart and again set it at rest. Amendment of life and the forsaking of sin should then follow, for these must be the fruits of repentance, as John says, "Bear fruit that befits repentance" (Matt. 3:8).

Rejected here are those who teach that persons who have once become godly cannot fall again.

Condemned on the other hand are the Novatians who denied absolution to such as had sinned after Baptism.

Rejected also are those who teach that forgiveness of sin is not obtained through faith but through the satisfactions made by man.

XIII. The Use of the Sacraments

It is taught among us that the sacraments were instituted not only to be signs by which people might be identified outwardly as Christians, but that they are signs and testimonies of God's will toward us for the purpose of awakening and strengthening our faith. For this reason they require faith, and they are rightly used when they are received in faith and for the purpose of strengthening faith.

XIV. Order in the Church

It is taught among us that nobody should publicly teach or preach or administer the sacraments in the church without a regular call.

XV. Church Usages

With regard to church usages that have been established by men, it is taught among us that those usages are to be observed which may be observed without sin and which contribute to peace and good order in the church, among them being certain holy days, festivals, and the like. Yet we accompany these observances with instruction so that consciences may not be burdened by the notion that such things are necessary for salvation. Moreover it is taught that all ordinances and traditions instituted by men for the purpose of propitiating God and earning grace are contrary to the Gospel and the teaching about faith in Christ. Accordingly monastic vows and other traditions concerning distinctions of foods, days, etc., by which it is intended to earn grace and make satisfaction for sin, are useless and contrary to the Gospel.

XVI. Civil Government

It is taught among us that all government in the world and all established rule and laws were instituted and ordained by God for the sake of good order, and that Christians may without sin occupy civil offices or serve as princes and judges, render decisions and pass sentence according to imperial and other existing laws, punish evildoers with the sword, engage in just wars, serve as soldiers, buy and sell, take required oaths, possess property, be married, etc.

Condemned here are the Anabaptists who teach that none of the things indicated above is Christian.

Also condemned are those who teach that Christian perfection requires the forsaking of house and home, wife and child, and the renunciation of such activities as are mentioned above. Actually, true perfection consists alone of proper fear of God and real faith in God, for the Gospel does not teach an outward and temporal but an inward and eternal mode of existence and righteousness of the heart.

The Gospel does not overthrow civil authority, the state, and marriage but requires that all these be kept as true orders of God and that everyone, each according to his own calling, manifest Christian love and genuine good works in his station of life. Accordingly Christians are obliged to be subject to civil authority and obey its commands and laws in all that can be done without sin. But when commands of the civil authority cannot be obeyed without sin, we must obey God rather than men (Acts 5:29).

XVII. The Return of Christ to Judgment

It is also taught among us that our Lord Jesus Christ will return on the last day for judgment and will raise up all the dead, to give eternal life and everlasting joy to believers and the elect but to condemn ungodly men and the devil to hell and eternal punishment.

Rejected, therefore, are the Anabaptists who teach that the devil and condemned men will not suffer eternal pain and torment.

Rejected, too, are certain Jewish opinions which are even now making an appearance and which teach that, before the resurrection of the dead, saints and godly men will possess a worldly kingdom and annihilate all the godless.

XVIII. Freedom of the Will

It is also taught among us that man possesses some measure of freedom of the will which enables him to live an outwardly honorable life and to make choices among the things that reason comprehends. But without the grace, help, and activity of the Holy Spirit man is not capable of making himself acceptable to God, of fearing God and believing in God with his whole heart, or of expelling inborn evil lusts from his heart. This is accomplished by the Holy Spirit, who is given through the Word of God, for Paul says in I Cor. 2:14, "Natural man does not receive the gifts of the Spirit of God."

In order that it may be evident that this teaching is no novelty, the clear words of Augustine on free will are here quoted from the third book of his *Hypognosticon*: "We concede that all men have a free will, for all have a natural, innate understanding and reason. However, this does not enable them to act in matters pertaining to God (such as loving God with their whole heart or fearing him), for it is only in the outward acts of this life that they have freedom to choose good or evil. By good I mean what they are capable of by nature: whether or not to labor in the fields, whether or not to eat or drink or visit a friend, whether to dress or undress, whether to build a house, take a wife, engage in a trade, or do whatever else may be good and profitable. None of these is or exists without God, but all things are from him and through him. On the other hand, by his own choice man can also undertake evil, as when he wills to kneel before an idol, commit murder, etc."

XIX. The Cause of Sin

It is taught among us that although almighty God has created and still preserves nature, yet sin is caused in all wicked men and despisers of God by the perverted will. This is the will of the devil and of all ungodly men; as soon as God withdraws his support, the will turns away from God to evil. It is as Christ says in John 8:44, "When the devil lies, he speaks according to his own nature."

XX. Faith and Good Works

Our teachers have been falsely accused of forbidding good works. Their writings on the Ten Commandments, and other writings as well, show that they have given good and profitable accounts and instructions concerning true Christian estates and works. About these little was taught in former times, when for the most part sermons were concerned with childish and useless works like rosaries, the cult of saints, monasticism, pilgrimages, appointed fasts, holy days, brotherhoods, etc. Our opponents no longer praise these useless works so highly as they once did, and they have also learned to speak now of faith, about which they did not preach at all in former times. They do not teach now that we become righteous before God by our works alone, but they add faith in Christ and say that faith and works make us righteous before God. This teaching may offer a little more comfort than the teaching that we are to rely solely on our works.

Since the teaching about faith, which is the chief article in the Christian life, has been neglected so long (as all must admit) while nothing but works was preached everywhere, our people have been instructed as follows:

We begin by teaching that our works cannot reconcile us with God or obtain grace for us, for this happens only through faith, that is, when we believe that our sins are forgiven for Christ's sake, who alone is the mediator who reconciles the Father. Whoever imagines that he can accomplish this by works, or that he can merit grace, despises Christ and seeks his own way to God, contrary to the Gospel.

This teaching about faith is plainly and clearly treated by Paul in many passages, especially in Eph. 2:8,9, "For by grace you have been saved through faith; and this is not your own doing, it is the gift of God — not because of works, lest any man should boast," etc.

That no new interpretation is here introduced can be demonstrated from Augustine, who discusses this question thoroughly and teaches the same thing, namely, that we obtain grace and are justified before God through faith in Christ and not through works. His whole book, *De spiritu et litera*, proves this.

Although this teaching is held in great contempt among untried people, yet it is a matter of experience that weak and terrified consciences find it most comforting and salutary. The conscience cannot come to rest and peace through works, but only through faith, that is, when it is assured and knows that for Christ's sake it has a gracious God, as Paul says in Rom. 5:1, "Since we are justified by faith, we have peace with God."

In former times this comfort was not heard in preaching, but poor consciences were driven to rely on their own efforts, and all sorts of works were undertaken. Some were driven by their conscience into monasteries in the hope that there they might merit grace through monastic life. Others devised other works for the purpose of earning grace and making satisfaction for sins. Many of them discovered that they did not obtain peace by such means. It was therefore necessary to preach this doctrine about faith in Christ and diligently to apply it in order that men may know that the grace of God is appropriated without merits, through faith alone.

Instruction is also given among us to show that the faith here spoken of is not that possessed by the devil and the ungodly, who also believe the history of Christ's suffering and his resurrection from the dead, but we mean such true faith as believes that we receive grace and forgiveness of sin through Christ.

Whoever knows that in Christ he has a gracious God, truly knows God, calls upon him, and is not, like the heathen, without God. For the devil and the ungodly do not believe this article concerning the forgiveness of sin, and so they are at enmity with God, cannot call upon him, and have no hope of receiving good from him. Therefore, as has just been indicated, the Scriptures speak of faith but do not mean by it such knowledge as the devil and ungodly men possess. Heb. 11:1 teaches about faith in such a way as to make it clear that faith is not merely a knowledge of historical events but is a confidence in God and in the fulfillment of his promises. Augustine also reminds us that we should understand the word "faith" in the Scriptures to mean confidence in God, assurance that God is gracious to us, and not merely such a knowledge of historical events as the devil also possesses.

It is also taught among us that good works should and must be done, not that we are to rely on them to earn grace but that we may do God's will and glorify him. It is always faith alone that apprehends grace and forgiveness of sin. When through faith the Holy Spirit is given, the heart is moved to do good works. Before that, when it is without the Holy Spirit, the heart is too weak. Moreover, it is in the power of the devil, who drives poor human beings into many sins. We see this in the philosophers who undertook to lead honorable and blameless lives; they failed to accomplish this, and instead fell into many great and open sins. This is what happens when a man is without true faith and the Holy Spirit and governs himself by his own human strength alone.

Consequently this teaching concerning faith is not to be accused of forbidding good works but is rather to be praised for teaching that good works are to be done and for offering help as to how they may be done. For without faith and without Christ human nature and human strength are much too weak to do good works, call upon God, have patience in suffering, love one's neighbor, diligently engage in callings which are commanded, render obedience, avoid evil lusts, etc. Such great and genuine works cannot be done without the help of Christ, as he himself says in John 15:5, "Apart from me you can do nothing."

XXI. The Cult of Saints

It is also taught among us that saints should be kept in remembrance so that our faith may be strengthened when we see what grace they received and how they were sustained by faith. Moreover, their good works are to be an example for us, each of us in his own calling. So His Imperial Majesty may in salutary and godly fashion imitate the example of David in making war on the Turk, for both are incumbents of a royal office which demands the defense and protection of their subjects.

However, it cannot be proved from the Scriptures that we are to invoke saints or seek help from them. "For there is one mediator between God and men, Christ Jesus" (I Tim. 2:5), who is the only saviour, the only highpriest, advocate, and intercessor before God (Rom. 8:34). He alone has promised to hear our prayers. Moreover, according to the Scriptures, the highest form of divine service is sincerely to seek and call upon this same Jesus Christ in every time of need. "If anyone sins, we have an advocate with the Father, Jesus Christ the righteous" (I John 2:1).

This is just about a summary of the doctrines that are preached and taught in our churches for proper Christian instruction, the consolation of consciences, and the amendment of believers. Certainly we should not wish to put our own souls and consciences in grave peril before God by misusing his name or Word, nor should we wish to bequeath to our children and posterity any other teaching than that which agrees with the pure Word of God and Christian truth. Since this teaching is grounded clearly on the Holy Scriptures and is not contrary or opposed to that of the universal Christian church, or even of the Roman church (in so far as the latter's teaching is reflected in the writing of the Fathers), we think that our opponents cannot disagree with us in the articles set forth above. Therefore, those who presume to reject, avoid, and separate from our churches as if our teaching were heretical, act in an unkind and hasty fashion, contrary to all Christian unity and love, and do so without any solid basis of divine command or Scripture. The dispute and dissension are concerned chiefly with various traditions and abuses. Since, then, there is nothing unfounded or defective in the principal articles and since this our confession is seen to be godly and Christian, the bishops should in all fairness act more leniently, even if there were some defect among us in regard to traditions, although we hope to offer firm grounds and reasons why we have changed certain traditions and abuses.

3. ARTICLES OF RELIGION
From the 39 Articles of the Church of England, 1562

The Thirty-nine "Articles of Religion" remain to this day the official doctrinal statement of the Church of England. They are based on the Ten Articles of 1536, which was the first Anglican confession of faith, the Thirteen Articles of 1538, and the Forty-two Articles of 1552. They were made obligatory by Queen Elizabeth I in the year 1571.

Since 1975, ministers of the Church of England at their ordination declare their assent to the Thirty-nine Articles in the following words: "I, N., do so affirm, and accordingly declare my belief in the faith which is revealed in the Holy Scriptures and set forth in the catholic creeds and to which the historic formularies of the Church of England bear witness."[1]

Within the Anglican communion, the Thirty-nine Articles have been included in the doctrinal basis of the churches in Ireland, Nigeria, Tanzania, Uganda and Australia. In most Anglican provinces, they have the status of an important historical document though one which has no binding force.

The Articles can be grouped under the following headings:

I-V	*The triune God*
VI-VIII	*Holy scripture and the Creeds of the ancient church*
IX-XVIII	*Sin and justification*
XIX-XXIV	*The church*
XXV-XXXI	*The sacraments*
XXXII-XXXIX	*Church order and the state*

The Articles have been influenced by both Reformed and Lutheran traditions (the former, e.g. in the doctrine of the Lord's Supper and the latter, e.g. in the doctrine of the church). They combine both with a certain catholic broadmindedness and Anglo-Saxon pragmatism.

We reproduce here the first thirty-one Articles.

● Text in *The Book of Common Prayer, According to the Use of the Protestant Episcopal Church in the United States of America*, New York, 1976, pp.867-74.

---

[1] *The Declaration of Assent*, 1975.

I. Of Faith in the Holy Trinity

There is but one living and true God, everlasting, without body, parts, or passions; of infinite power, wisdom, and goodness; the Maker, and Preserver of all things both visible and invisible. And in unity of this Godhead there be three Persons, of one substance, power, and eternity; the Father, the Son, and the Holy Ghost.

II. Of the Word or Son of God, which was made very Man

The Son, which is the Word of the Father, begotten from everlasting of the Father, the very and eternal God, and of one substance with the Father, took Man's nature in the womb of the blessed Virgin, of her substance: so that two whole and perfect Natures, that is to say, the Godhead and Manhood, were joined together in one person, never to be divided, whereof is one Christ, very God, and very Man; who truly suffered, was crucified, dead, and buried, to reconcile his Father to us, and to be a sacrifice, not only for original guilt, but also for actual sins of men.

III. Of the going down of Christ into Hell

As Christ died for us, and was buried; so also is it to be believed, that he went down into Hell.

IV. Of the Resurrection of Christ

Christ did truly rise again from death, and took again his body, with flesh, bones, and all things appertaining to the perfection of Man's nature; wherewith he ascended into Heaven, and there sitteth, until he return to judge all Men at the last day.

V. Of the Holy Ghost

The Holy Ghost, proceeding from the Father and the Son, is of one substance, majesty, and glory, with the Father and the Son, very and eternal God.

VI. Of the Sufficiency of the Holy Scriptures for Salvation

Holy Scripture containeth all things necessary to salvation: so that whatsoever is not read therein, nor may be proved thereby, is not to be required of any man, that it should be believed as an article of the Faith, or be thought requisite or necessary to salvation. In the name of the Holy Scripture we do understand those canonical Books of the Old and New Testament, of whose authority was never any doubt in the Church.

(A list of the canonical books of the Old Testament follows.)

And the other Books (as Hierome saith) the Church doth read for example of life and instruction of manners; but yet doth it not apply them to establish any doctrine; such are these following:

(A list of the apocryphal writings of the Old Testament follows.)

All the Books of the New Testament, as they are commonly received, we do receive, and account them Canonical.

VII. Of the Old Testament

The Old Testament is not contrary to the New: for both in the Old and New Testament everlasting life is offered to Mankind by Christ, who is the only Mediator between God and Man, being both God and Man. Wherefore they are not to be heard, which feign that the old Fathers did look only for transitory promises. Although the

Law given from God by Moses, as touching Ceremonies and Rites, do not bind Christian men, nor the Civil precepts thereof ought of necessity to be received in any commonwealth; yet notwithstanding, no Christian man whatsoever is free from the obedience of the Commandments which are called Moral.

VIII. Of the Creeds

The Nicene Creed, and that which is commonly called the Apostles' Creed, ought thoroughly to be received and believed: for they may be proved by most certain warrants of Holy Scripture.

IX. Of Original or Birth-Sin

Original sin standeth not in the following of Adam, (as the Pelagians do vainly talk;) but it is the fault and corruption of the Nature of every man, that naturally is engendered of the offspring of Adam; whereby man is very far gone from original righteousness, and is of his own nature inclined to evil, so that the flesh lusteth always contrary to the Spirit; and therefore in every person born into this world, it deserveth God's wrath and damnation. And this infection of nature doth remain, yea in them that are regenerated; wherby the lust of the flesh, called in Greek, *fronema sarkos* (which some do expound the wisdom, some sensuality, some the affection, some the desire, of the flesh), is not subject to the Law of God. And although there is no condemnation for them that believe and are baptized; yet the Apostle doth confess, that concupiscence and lust hath of itself the nature of sin.

X. Of Free-Will

The condition of Man after the fall of Adam is such, that he cannot turn and prepare himself, by his own natural strength and good works, to faith, and calling upon God. Wherefore we have no power to do good works pleasant and acceptable to God, without the grace of God by Christ preventing us, that we may have a good will, and working with us, when we have that good will.

XI. Of the Justification of Man

We are accounted righteous before God, only for the merit of our Lord and Saviour Jesus Christ by Faith, and not for our own works or deservings. Wherefore, that we are justified by Faith only, is most wholesome Doctrine, and very full of comfort, as more largely is expressed in the Homily of Justification.

XII. Of Good Works

Albeit that Good Works, which are the fruits of Faith, and follow after Justification, cannot put away our sins, and endure the severity of God's judgment; yet are they pleasing and acceptable to God in Christ, and do spring out necessarily of a true and lively Faith; insomuch that by them a lively Faith may be as evidently known as a tree discerned by the fruit.

XIII. Of Works before Justification

Works done before the grace of Christ, and the Inspiration of his Spirit, are not pleasant to God, forasmuch as they spring not of faith in Jesus Christ; neither do they make men meet to receive grace, or (as the School-authors say) deserve grace of congruity; yea rather, for that they are not done as God hath willed and commanded them to be done, we doubt not but they have the nature of sin.

XIV. Of Works of Supererogation

Voluntary Works besides, over and above, God's Commandments, which they call Works of Supererogation, cannot be taught without arrogancy and impiety: for by them men do declare, that they do not only render unto God as much as they are bound to do, but that they do more for his sake, than of bounded duty is required: whereas Christ saith plainly, When ye have done all that are commanded to you say, We are unprofitable servants.

XV. Of Christ alone without Sin

Christ in the truth of our nature was made like unto us in all things, sin only except, from which he was clearly void, both in his flesh, and in his spirit. He came to be the Lamb without spot, who, by sacrifice of himself once made, should take away the sins of the world; and sin (as Saint John saith) was not in him. But all we the rest, although baptized, and born again in Christ, yet offend in many things; and if we say we have no sin, we deceive ourselves, and the truth is not in us.

XVI. Of Sin after Baptism

Not every deadly sin willingly committed after Baptism is sin against the Holy Ghost, and unpardonable. Wherefore the grant of repentance is not to be denied to such as fall into sin after Baptism. After we have received the Holy Ghost, we may depart from grace given, and fall into sin, and by grace of God we may arise again, and amend our lives. And therefore they are to be condemned, which say, they can no more sin as long as they live here, or deny the place of forgiveness to such as truly repent.

XVII. Of Predestination and Election

Predestination to Life is the everlasting purpose of God, whereby (before the foundations of the world were laid) he hath constantly decreed by his counsel secret to us, to deliver from curse and damnation those whom he hath chosen in Christ out of mankind, and to bring them by Christ to everlasting salvation, as vessels made to honour. Wherefore, they which be endued with so excellent a benefit of God, be called according to God's purpose by his Spirit working in due season: they through Grace obey the calling: they be justified freely: they be made sons of God by adoption: they be made like the image of his only-begotten Son Jesus Christ: they walk religiously in good works, and at length, by God's mercy, they attain to everlasting felicity.

As the godly consideration of Predestination, and our Election in Christ, is full of sweet, pleasant, and unspeakable comfort to godly persons, and such as feel in themselves the working of the Spirit of Christ, mortifying the works of the flesh, and their earthly members, and drawing up their mind to high and heavenly things, as well because it doth greatly establish and confirm their faith of eternal Salvation to be enjoyed through Christ, as well because it doth fervently kindle their love towards God: So, for curious and carnal persons, lacking the Spirit of Christ, to have continually before their eyes the sentence of God's Predestination, is a most dangerous downfall, whereby the Devil doth thrust them either into desperation, or into wretchlessness of most unclean living, no less perilous than desperation.

Furthermore, we must receive God's promises in such wise, as they be generally set forth to us in Holy Scripture: and, in our doings, that Will of God is to be followed, which we have expressly declared unto us in the Word of God.

XVIII. Of obtaining eternal Salvation only by the Name of Christ

They also are to be had accursed that presume to say, That every man shall be saved by the Law or Sect which he professeth, so that he be diligent to frame his life according to that Law, and the light of Nature. For Holy Scripture doth set out unto us only the Name of Jesus Christ, whereby men must be saved.

XIX. Of the Church

The visible Church of Christ is a congregation of faithful men, in which the pure Word of God is preached, and the Sacraments be duly ministered according to Christ's ordinance, in all those things that of necessity are requisite to the same.

As the Church of Jerusalem, Alexandria, and Antioch, have erred; so also the Church of Rome hath erred, not only in their living and manner of Ceremonies, but also in matters of Faith.

XX. Of the Authority of the Church

The Church hath power to decree Rites or Ceremonies, and authority in Controversies of Faith: and yet it is not lawful for the Church to ordain any thing that is contrary to God's Word written, neither may it so expound one place of Scripture, that it be repugnant to another. Wherefore, although the Church be a witness and a keeper of Holy Writ, yet, as it ought not to decree any thing against the same, so besides the same ought it not to enforce any thing to be believed for necessity of Salvation.

XXI. Of the Authority of General Councils

(The Twenty-first of the former Articles is omitted; because it is partly of a local and civil nature, and is provided for, as to the remaining parts of it, in other Articles.)

XXII. Of Purgatory

The Romish Doctrine concerning Purgatory, Pardons, Worshipping and Adoration, as well of Images as of Relics, and also Invocation of Saints, is a fond thing, vainly invented, and grounded upon no warranty of Scripture, but rather repugnant to the Word of God.

XXIII. Of Ministering in the Congregation

It is not lawful for any man to take upon him the office of public preaching, or ministering the sacraments in the Congregation, before he be lawfully called, and sent to execute the same. And those we ought to judge lawfully called and sent, which be chosen and called to this work by men who have public authority given unto them in the Congregation, to call and send Ministers into the Lord's vineyard.

XXIV. Of Speaking in the Congregation in such a Tongue as the people understandeth

It is a thing plainly repugnant to the Word of God, and the custom of the Primitive Church, to have public Prayer in the Church, or to minister the Sacraments, in a tongue not understood of the people.

XXV. Of the Sacraments

Sacraments ordained of Christ be not only badges or tokens of Christian men's profession, but rather they be certain sure witnesses, and effectual signs of grace, and God's good will towards us, by the which he doth work invisibly in us, and doth not only quicken, but also strengthen and confirm our Faith in him.

There are two Sacraments ordained of Christ our Lord in the Gospel, that is to say, Baptism, and the Supper of the Lord.

Those five commonly called Sacraments, that is to say, Confirmation, Penance, Orders, Matrimony, and Extreme Unction, are not to be counted for Sacraments of the Gospel, being such as have grown partly of the corrupt following of the Apostles, partly are states of life allowed in the Scriptures; but yet have not like nature of Sacraments with Baptism, and the Lord's Supper, for that they have not any visible sign or ceremony ordained of God.

The Sacraments were not ordained of Christ to be gazed upon, or to be carried about, but that we should duly use them. And in such only as worthily receive the same, they have a wholesome effect or operation: but they that receive them unworthily, purchase to themselves damnation, as Saint Paul saith.

XXVI. Of the Unworthiness of the Ministers, which hinders not the effect of the Sacraments

Although in the visible Church the evil be ever mingled with the good, and sometimes the evil have chief authority in the Ministration of the Word and Sacraments, yet forasmuch as they do not the same in their own name, but in Christ's, and do minister by his commission and authority, we may use their Ministry, both in hearing the Word of God, and in receiving the Sacraments. Neither is the effect of Christ's ordinance taken away by their wickedness, nor the grace of God's gifts diminished from such as by faith, and rightly, do receive the Sacraments ministered unto them; which be effectual, because of Christ's institution and promise, although they be ministered by evil men.

Nevertheless, it appertaineth to the discipline of the Church, that inquiry be made of evil Ministers, and that they be accused by those that have knowledge of their offences; and finally, being found guilty, by just judgment be deposed.

XXVII. Of Baptism

Baptism is not only a sign of profession, and mark of difference, whereby Christian men are discerned from others that be not christened, but it is also a sign of Regeneration or New-Birth, whereby, as by an instrument, they that receive Baptism rightly are grafted into the Church; the promises of the forgiveness of sin, and of our adoption to be the sons of God by the Holy Ghost, are visibly signed and sealed; Faith is confirmed, and Grace increased by virtue of prayer unto God.

The Baptism of young Children is in any wise to be retained in the Church, as most agreeable with the institution of Christ.

XXVIII. Of the Lord's Supper

The Supper of the Lord is not only a sign of the love that Christians ought to have among themselves one to another; but rather it is a Sacrament of our Redemption by Christ's death: insomuch that to such as rightly, worthily, and with faith, receive the same, the Bread which we break is a partaking of the Body of Christ; and likewise the Cup of Blessing is a partaking of the Blood of Christ.

Transubstantiation (or the change of the substance of Bread and Wine) in the Supper of the Lord, cannot be proved by Holy Writ; but is repugnant to the plain words of Scripture, overthroweth the nature of a Sacrament, and hath given occasion to many superstitions.

The Body of Christ is given, taken, and eaten, in the Supper, only after an heavenly and spiritual manner. And the mean whereby the Body of Christ is received and eaten in the Supper, is Faith.

The Sacrament of the Lord's Supper was not by Christ's ordinance reserved, carried about, lifted up, or worshipped.

XXIX. Of the Wicked, which eat not the Body of Christ in the use of the Lord's Supper

The Wicked, and such as be void of a lively faith, although they do carnally and visibly press with their teeth (as Saint Augustine saith) the Sacrament of the Body and Blood of Christ; yet in no wise are they partakers of Christ: but rather, to their condemnation, do eat and drink the sign or Sacrament of so great a thing.

XXX. Of both Kinds

The Cup of the Lord is not to be denied to the Lay-people: or both the parts of the Lord's Sacrament, by Christ's ordinance and commandment, ought to be ministered to all Christian men alike.

XXXI. Of the one Oblation of Christ finished upon the Cross

The Offering of Christ once made is that perfect redemption, propitiation, and satisfaction, for all the sins of the whole world, both original and actual; and there is none other satisfaction for sin, but that alone. Wherefore the sacrifices of Masses, in the which it was commonly said, that the Priest did offer Christ for the quick and the dead, to have remission of pain or guilt, were blasphemous fables, and dangerous deceits.

4. GOD, THE FATHER, THE SON AND THE HOLY GHOST
From Part II of the Heidelberg Catechism, 1563

The Heidelberg Catechism was drawn up at the instigation of the Elector Frederick III of the Palatinate, by a group of theologians under the directorship of Zacharias Ursinus, a pupil of Melanchthon. Its name comes from the endorsement of its fourth version by the Palatinate superintendents and consistory members in Heidelberg in 1563. It was subsequently included in the Palatinate Church Ordinances between the baptismal liturgy and the eucharistic liturgy, which contributed to its also being used in the worship and preaching of the Palatinate church. It used material from earlier catechisms and became, along with Luther's Small Catechism, *the most important of the catechisms of the Reformation period.*

The Heidelberg Catechism was soon accepted by other Reformed churches in Germany, Switzerland, Holland, Poland, Hungary, Bohemia, Siebenbürgen, North America and South Africa. It exists today in about forty different languages and constitutes a powerful ecumenical bond between Reformed churches throughout the world. It is not specifically referred to in the constitution of the World Alliance of Reformed Churches which speaks in an inclusive way of the "historic Reformed confessions" to which it affirms its commitment.

The Catechism falls into three parts:
I.   The misery of humanity (3-11)
II. The redemption of humanity (12-85)
III. Thankfulness (86-129).
Part II deals in detail with the role and work of Jesus Christ as Mediator (12-20), the trinitarian faith (21-64), and the sacraments (65-85).
The Catechism expounds the Apostles' Creed as follows:
God the Father (26-28)
God the Son (29-52)
God the Holy Spirit (53-64)
In the answer to question 48, the so-called "Extra Calvinisticum" is formulated: "Since the Godhead is incomprehensible and everywhere present, it must follow that it is indeed beyond the bounds of the Manhood which it has assumed and yet is none the less within it as well and remains personally united to it."

● Text in *The School of Faith: the Catechisms of the Reformed Church*, ed. T.F. Torrance, James Clarke & Co. Ltd., London, 1959, pp.73-80.

God the Father

Q.26. What do you believe when you say: I believe in God the Father Almighty, Maker of Heaven and Earth?

A. That the eternal Father of our Lord Jesus Christ, who created out of nothing the heaven and the earth, with all things in them, who also upholds and governs the same by His eternal counsel and providence, is for the sake of Christ His Son my God and my Father, in whom I so trust that I do not doubt that He will provide me with all things necessary for body and soul; and further, that whatever evil He sends upon me in this miserable life, He will turn to my good; for He is able to do it, as Almighty God, and He is willing to do it, as a faithful Father.

Q.27. What do you understand by the Providence of God?

A. The almighty and present power of God, whereby He still upholds, as it were by His hand, and governs heaven and earth, with all creatures, so that herbs and grass, rain and drought, fruitful and unfruitful year, meat and drink, health and sickness, riches and poverty, and all things, come upon us not by chance, but by His fatherly hand.

Q.28. What benefit do we derive from the knowledge of God's creation and providence?

A. That we ought to be patient in all adversity, thankful in prosperity, and for the future have great confidence in our faithful God and Father, assured that no creature shall separate us from His love, since all creatures are so in His hand that without His will they cannot even stir or move.

God the Son

Q.29. Why is the Son of God called Jesus, that is, Saviour?

A. Because He saves us from our sins, and because salvation is to be sought or found in no other.

Q.30. Do they, then, believe in the only Saviour Jesus who seek their blessing and salvation from saints, or themselves, or any other source?

A. No, for although they make boast of Him, yet in act they deny Jesus who alone brings blessing and salvation. For either Jesus is not a complete Saviour, or they who by true faith receive this Saviour must have in Him all that is necessary for their salvation.

Q.31. Why is He called Christ, that is, Anointed?

A. Because He is ordained of God the Father, and anointed with the Holy Spirit to be our chief Prophet and Teacher, who fully reveals to us the secret counsel and will of God concerning our redemption; to be our only High Priest, who by the one sacrifice of His body has redeemed us, and continually makes intercession for us with the Father; and to be our eternal King, who governs us by His Word and Spirit, and defends and maintains us in the redemption obtained for us.

Q.32. But why are you called a Christian?

A. Because by faith I am a member of Christ, and thus a partaker of His anointing, in order that I also may confess His name, may present myself a living sacrifice of thanksgiving to Him, and may with a free conscience fight against sin and the devil in this life, and hereafter, in eternity, rule with Him over all creatures.

Q.33. Why is He called God's only-begotten Son, since we also are God's Children?

A. Because Christ alone is the eternal natural Son of God, but we are adopted to be children of God through grace for His sake.

Q.34. Why do you call Him our Lord?

A. Because, not with gold or silver, but with His precious blood, He has redeemed and purchased us, body and soul, from sin and from all the power of the devil, to be His own.

Q.35. What is the meaning of Conceived by the Holy Ghost, born of the Virgin Mary?

A. That the eternal Son of God, who is and remains true and eternal God, took upon Him true human nature from the flesh and blood of the Virgin Mary, through the operation of the Holy Spirit, so that he also might be the true seed of David, like unto His brethren in all things, sin excepted.

Q.36. What benefit do you receive from the holy conception and birth of Christ?

A. That He is our Mediator, and with His innocence and perfect holiness He covers, before God's face, my sin wherein I was conceived.

Q.37. What do you understand by the word Suffered?

A. That all the time of His life on earth, but especially at the end of it, He bore, in body and soul, the wrath of God against the sin of the whole human race, in order that by His passion, as by the only atoning sacrifice, He might redeem our body and soul from everlasting damnation, and obtain for us God's grace, righteousness, and eternal life.

Q.38. Why did He suffer under Pontius Pilate, the judge?

A. That He, being innocent, might be condemned by the temporal judge, and thereby set us free from the severe judgement of God which ought to fall upon us.

Q.39. Is there anything more in His having been crucified than if He had died some other death?

A. Yes, for by this I am sure that He took on Himself the curse which lay upon me, because the death of the Cross was cursed by God.

Q.40. Why did Christ have to suffer death?

A. Because, on the ground of God's righeousness and truth, reparation for our sins could be made no other way than through the death of the Son of God.

Q.41. Why was He buried?

A. To show thereby that He was really dead.

Q.42. Since, then, Christ died for us, why must we also die?

A. Our death is not a reparation for our sin, but only a dying to sins and entering into eternal life.

Q.43. What further benefit do we receive from the sacrifice and death of Christ on the Cross?

A. That by his power our old man is with Him crucified, slain, and buried; so that the evil lusts of the flesh may no more reign in us, but that we may offer ourselves unto Him a sacrifice of thanksgiving.

Q.44. Why is it added: He descended into Hell?

A. That in the greatest assaults of evil upon me, I may be assured that Christ my Lord, by His unspeakable anguish, pains, and terrors which He suffered also in His soul on the Cross and before, has redeemed me from the anguish and torment of hell.

Q.45. What benefit do we receive from the resurrection of Christ?

A. First, by His resurrection He has overcome death, that He might make us partakers of the righteousness which He has obtained for us by His death. Secondly, we too are now by His power raised up to a new life. Thirdly, the resurrection of Christ is to us a sure pledge for our blessed resurrection.

Q.46. How do you understand the words, He ascended into Heaven?

A. That before the eyes of His disciples, Christ was taken up from the earth into heaven, and remains there for our good, until He comes again to judge the living and the dead.

Q.47. Is not Christ with us, unto the end of the world, as He has promised us?

A. Christ is true Man and true God. According to His human nature, He is now not on earth, but according to His Godhead, majesty, grace, and Spirit, He is never absent from us.

Q.48. But are not the two natures in Christ separated from one another in this way, if the Manhood is not wherever the Godhead is?

A. By no means. For since the Godhead is incomprehensible and everywhere present, it must follow that it is indeed beyond the bounds of the Manhood which it has assumed, and yet is none the less within it as well, and remains personally united to it.

Q.49. What benefit do we receive from Christ's ascension into Heaven?

A. First, that He is our advocate in Heaven before the face of His Father. Secondly, that we have our flesh in Heaven, as a sure pledge that He, as the Head, will also take us, His members, up to Himself. Thirdly, that He sends down to us His Spirit, as a counter-pledge by whose power we seek what is above, where Christ sits on the right hand of God, and not what is on earth.

Q.50. Why is it added, and sitteth at the right hand of God?

A. Because Christ ascended into Heaven for this end, that He might show Himself there as Head of His Christian Church, through whom the Father governs all things.

Q.51. What benefit do we receive from this glory of Christ, our Head?

A. First, that by His Holy Spirit He pours out heavenly gifts into us, His members; then, that by His power He protects and preserves us against all enemies.

Q.52. What comfort is it to you that Christ shall come again to judge the quick and the dead?

A. That in all afflictions and persecution, with uplifted head, I may wait for the Judge from Heaven who has already offered Himself to the judgement of God for me, and has taken away from me all curse; who will cast all His and my enemies into everlasting condemnation, but shall take me with all His chosen ones to Himself, into heavenly joy and glory.

God the Holy Ghost

Q.53. What do you believe concerning the Holy Ghost?

A. First, that He is co-eternal God with the Father and the Son. Secondly, that He is also given to me, makes me by a true faith partaker of Christ and all His benefits, comforts me, and shall abide with me forever.

Q.54. What do you believe concerning the Holy Catholic Church?

A. That out of the whole human race, from the beginning of the world to its end, the Son of God, by His Spirit and Word, gathers, protects, and preserves for Himself in the unity of the true faith and unto everlasting life, a chosen community; and that I am, and forever shall remain, a living member of the same.

Q.55. What do you understand by the communion of saints?

A. First, that believers, all and everyone, as His members have fellowship in the Lord Christ, and in all His treasures and gifts. Secondly, that each one must know that he is bound to use his gifts, readily and cheerfully, for the benefit and salvation of the other members.

Q.56. What do you believe concerning the forgiveness of sins?

A. That God, for the sake of Christ's satisfaction, will no more remember my sins, or the sinful nature with which I have to struggle all my life long, but graciously imparts to me the righteousness of Christ, that I may nevermore come into condemnation.

Q.57. What comfort do you derive from the resurrection of the body?

A. That not only shall my soul, after this life, be immediately taken up to Christ its Head, but also that this flesh of mine, raised by the power of Christ, shall again be united with my soul, and shall be made comfortable to the glorious body of Christ.

Q.58. What comfort do you have from the article on the life everlasting?

A. That, since I now feel in my heart the beginning of eternal joy, I shall possess after this life complete blessedness such as eye has not seen, nor ear heard, and which has not entered into the heart of man, therein to praise God for ever.

Q. 59. But what does it help you now that you believe all this?

A. That in Christ I am righteous before God, and an heir of eternal life.

Q.60. How are you righteous before God?

A. Only through true faith in Jesus Christ; wherefore although my conscience already accuses me that I have grievously sinned against all the commandments of God, and have not kept any one of them, and that I am still ever prone to all evil, yet God, without any merit of my own, out of sheer grace, grants and imputes to me the perfect satisfaction, righteousness, and holiness of Christ, as if I had never committed nor had a single sin, and had myself accomplished all the obedience which Christ has fulfilled for me, if only I receive such a benefit with a believing heart.

Q.61. Why do you say that you are righteous by faith alone?

A. Not because I please God on account of the worthiness of my faith; but because the satisfaction, righteousness, and holiness of Christ alone is my righteousness before God, and because I can receive it and make it my own in no other way than by faith alone.

Q.62. But why cannot our good works contribute in whole or part to our righteousness before God?

A. Because the righteousness which can stand before the judgement of God must be perfect throughout, and wholly comfortable to the Law, whereas even our best works in this life are all imperfect and defiled with sins.

Q.63. Do then our good works merit nothing, even when it is God's will to reward them in this and in the future life?

A. The reward derives not from merit, but from grace.

Q.64. But does not this teaching make people careless and profane?

A. No, for it is impossible that those who are ingrafted into Christ through true faith should not bring forth fruits of thankfulness.

5. TRIDENTINE PROFESSION OF FAITH
Professio Fidei Tridentinae, 1564

Pope Pius IV prescribed this doctrinal profession on 13 November 1564 in his bull Iniunctum nobis *as a response to the work of the Council of Trent (1545-1563). The* Professio Fidei Tridentinae *was thus not a confession of faith composed by the Council itself, but a summary of Roman Catholic faith as understood by the Council of Trent, formulated by Pope Pius IV under the influence of Peter Canisius. An addition was made to the Profession by the decree of 20 January 1877, concerning the primacy of the Pope and the infallible teaching office* (infallibile magisterium). *The Professio was placed at the forefront of the Codex Iuris Canonici (CIC), in force from 1917 to January 1983, which stipulated (can. 1406-1408) that it was to be required of every member of the clergy and renewed at every change of office. It was also used in the case of converts to the Roman Catholic Church.*

The Profession of Faith is in three parts:
I. The Nicene-Constantinopolitan Creed
II. The traditions of the Roman Catholic Church:
    1. Holy scripture
    2. The seven sacraments
    3. Original sin and justification
    4. The mass
    5. Purgatory and the saints
    6. Indulgences
    7. Roman Church and Roman Pope
    8. Canons and ecumenical councils
III. The true Catholic faith

The Tridentine Profession of Faith is a brief summary of the decisions reached at the Council of Trent in response to the Reformation. The summary and oppositional nature of this procedure makes the Professio the confession of faith of a confessional church. As its concluding part in particular makes quite clear, it has the character of a sworn declaration of obedience.

By a decision of the Vatican Congregatio Fidei *of 20 December 1967, Parts II and III of the* Professio Fidei Tridentinae *were replaced by the following formula:*

I also firmly acknowledge and embrace everything that has been proclaimed and declared by the Church in respect of doctrinal and moral teaching, whether it has been established by a solemn verdict or proclaimed and declared by the ordinary magisterium, wholly in the form in which the Church itself presents it; especially that which is related to the Mystery of Christ's Holy Church, its Sacraments, the Sacrifice of the Mass and the Primacy of the Roman Pope.[1]

● Text in *The Church Teaches: Documents of the Church in English Translation*, ed. J.F. Clarkson, J.H. Edwards, W.J. Kelly, J.J. Welch, St Louis, 1955, pp.7-9.

I, N., with firm faith believe and profess each and every article contained in the Symbol of faith which the holy Roman Church uses; namely: ... (text of the Nicene-Constantinopolitan Creed follows).

I resolutely accept and embrace the apostolic and ecclesiastical traditions and the other practices and regulations of that same Church. In like manner I accept Sacred Scripture according to the meaning which has been held by holy Mother Church and which she now holds. It is her prerogative to pass judgment on the true meaning and interpretation of Sacred Scripture. And I will never accept or interpret it in a manner different from the unanimous agreement of the Fathers.

I also acknowledge that there are truly and properly seven sacraments of the New Law, instituted by Jesus Christ our Lord, and that they are necessary for the salvation of the human race, although it is not necessary for each individual to receive them all. I acknowledge that the seven sacraments are: baptism, confirmation, Eucharist, penance, extreme unction, holy orders, and matrimony; and that they confer grace; and that of the seven, baptism, confirmation, and holy orders cannot be repeated without committing a sacrilege. I also accept and acknowledge the customary and approved rites of the Catholic Church in the solemn administration of these sacraments. I embrace and accept each and every article on original sin and justification declared and defined in the most holy Council of Trent.

I likewise profess that in the Mass a true, proper, and propitiatory sacrifice is offered to God on behalf of the living and the dead, and that the body and blood together with the soul and divinity of our Lord Jesus Christ is truly, really, and substantially present in the most holy sacrament of the Eucharist, and that there is a change of the whole substance of the bread into the body, and of the whole substance of the wine into blood; and this change the Catholic Church calls transubstantiation. I also profess that the whole and entire Christ and a true sacrament is received under each separate species.

I firmly hold that there is a purgatory, and that the souls detained there are helped by the prayers of the faithful. I likewise hold that the saints reigning together with Christ should be honored and invoked, that they offer prayers to God on our behalf, and that their relics should be venerated. I firmly assert that images of Christ, of the Mother of God ever Virgin, and of the other saints should be owned and kept, and that due honor and veneration should be given to them. I affirm that the power of indulgences was left in the keeping of the Church by Christ, and that the use of indulgences is very beneficial to Christians.

---

[1] Unofficial translation.

I acknowledge the holy, Catholic, and apostolic Roman Church as the mother and teacher of all churches; and I promise and swear true obedience to the Roman Pontiff, vicar of Christ and successor of Blessed Peter, Prince of the Apostles.

I unhesitatingly accept and profess all the doctrines (especially those concerning the primacy of the Roman Pontiff and his infallible teaching authority) handed down, defined, and explained by the sacred canons and ecumenical councils and especially those of this most holy Council of Trent (and by the ecumenical Vatican Council). And at the same time I condemn, reject, and anathematize everything that is contrary to those propositions, and all heresies without exception that have been condemned, rejected, and anathematized by the Church. I, N., promise, vow, and swear that, with God's help, I shall most constantly hold and profess this true Catholic faith, outside which no one can be saved and which I now freely profess and truly hold. With the help of God, I shall profess it whole and unblemished to my dying breath; and, to the best of my ability, I shall see to it that my subjects or those entrusted to me by virtue of my office hold it, teach it, and preach it. So help me God and his holy Gospel. *(The words in parentheses in this paragraph are now inserted into the Tridentine profession of faith by order of Pope Pius IX in a decree issued by the Holy Office, January 20, 1877.)*

6. THE CONFESSION OF DOSITHEUS
From the 18 Decrees of the Synod of Jerusalem, 1672

This confession is not, as its title might suggest, the private work of an Orthodox Patriarch but rather the fruit of the Synod of Jerusalem to which Dositheus, as host, had issued the invitations. The occasion which led to its formulation was furnished by Orthodox doctrinal statements from the years 1629 and 1633 which were attributed to Cyril Lucar, the Patriarch of Alexandria and Constantinople, and understood as a Calvinist distortion of the Orthodox faith. The purpose of the 18 Decrees of the Synod of Jerusalem was to define the Orthodox doctrine over against Protestantism. They complete a series of four Orthodox confessions of faith, all of which deal with the questions raised by the Reformation. The other three confessional documents are:

1. *The three responses of the Patriarch Jeremias II to the Lutheran theologians in Tübingen concerning the* Confessio Augustana *(1573-1581).*
2. *The doctrinal statement of Mitrofan Kritopoulos, which was composed at the request of Lutheran theologians from Helmstedt (1625).*
3. *The Orthodox confession of faith of Petru Movila, the Metropolitan of Kiev (1642), which became widespread in the Eastern church.*

The arrangement of the 18 Decrees of the Jerusalem Synod is as follows:

I-V	*The triune God: his word, his will, his providence*
VI-IX	*Sin and the redemption through Jesus Christ*
X-XII	*The Catholic Church and its direction by the Holy Spirit*
XIII-XIV	*Justification and renewal*
XV-XVII	*The seven sacraments*
XVIII	*The destiny of the departed*

Four questions on scripture, the veneration of ikons and the adoration of the saints are discussed in an appendix and the whole confession is rounded off with an epilogue. We reproduce here Decrees I-XIV with minor abbreviations.

● Text in *Creeds of the Churches: a Reader in Christian Doctrine from the Bible to the Present*, revised edition, ed. J.H. Leith, Atlanta, 1973, pp.486-98.

Dositheus, by the mercy of God, Patriarch of Jerusalem, to those that ask and inquire concerning the faith and worship of the Greeks, that is of the Eastern Church, how forsooth it thinketh concerning the Orthodox faith, in the common name of all Christians subject to our Apostolic Throne, and of the Orthodox worshippers that are sojourning in this holy and great city of Jerusalem (with whom the whole Catholic Church agreeth in all that concerneth the faith) publisheth this concise Confession, for a testimony both before God and before man, with a sincere conscience, and devoid of all dissimulation.

Decree I: The All-holy Trinity

We believe in one God, true, almighty, and infinite, the Father, the Son, and the Holy Spirit; the Father unbegotten; the Son begotten of the Father before the ages, and consubstantial with Him; and the Holy Spirit proceeding from the Father, and consubstantial with the Father and the Son. These three Persons in one essence we call the All-holy Trinity, — by all creation to be ever blessed, glorified, and adored.

Decree II: The Divine Scriptures

We believe the Divine and Sacred Scriptures to be God-taught; and, therefore, we ought to believe the same without doubting; yet not otherwise than as the Catholic Church hath interpreted and delivered the same. For every foul heresy receiveth, indeed, the Divine Scriptures, but perversely interpreteth the same, using metaphors, and homonymies, and sophistries of man's wisdom, confounding what ought to be distinguished, and trifling with what ought not to be trifled with. For if (we were to receive the same) otherwise, each man holding every day a different sense concerning the same, the Catholic Church would not (as she doth) by the grace of Christ continue to be the Church until this day, holding the same doctrine of faith, and always identically and steadfastly believing, but would be rent into innumerable parties, and subject to heresies; neither would the Church be holy, the pillar and ground of the truth, without spot or wrinkle; but would be the Church of the malignant; as it is manifest that of the heretics undoubtedly is, and especially that of Calvin, who are not ashamed to learn from the Church, and then to wickedly repudiate her. Wherefore, the witness also of the Catholic Church is, we believe, not of inferior authority to that of the Divine Scriptures. For one and the same Holy Spirit being the author of both, it is quite the same to be taught by the Scriptures and by the Catholic Church. Moreover, when any man speaketh from himself he is liable to err, and to deceive, and be deceived; but the Catholic Church, as never having spoken, or speaking from herself, but from the Spirit of God — who being her teacher, she is ever unfailingly rich — it is impossible for her to in any wise err, or to at all deceive, or be deceived; but like the Divine Scriptures, is infallible, and hath perpetual authority.

Decree III: The Divine Predestination

We believe the most good God to have from eternity predestinated unto glory those whom He hath chosen, and to have consigned unto condemnation those whom He hath rejected; but not so that He would justify the one, and consign and condemn the other without cause. For that were contrary to the nature of God, who is the common Father of all, and no respecter of persons, and would have all men to be saved, and to come to the knowledge of the truth; but since He foreknew the one would make a right use of their free-will, and the other a wrong, He predestinated the one, or condemned the other. And we understand the use of free-will thus, that the Divine and illuminating grace, and which we call preventing grace, being, as a light to those in darkness, by the Divine goodness imparted to all, to those that are willing to obey this — for it is of use only to the willing, not to the unwilling — and co-operate with it, in what it requireth as necessary to salvation, there is consequently granted particular grace; which, co-operating with us, and enabling us, and making us perseverant in the love of God, that is to say, in performing those good things that God would have us to do, and which His preventing grace admonisheth us that we should do, justifieth us, and maketh us predestinated. But those who will not obey, and co-operate with grace; and, therefore, will not observe things that God would have us perform, and that abuse in the service of Satan the free-will, which they have received of God to perform voluntarily what is good, are consigned to eternal condemnation.

But to say, as the most wicked heretics do — and as is contained in the chapter answering hereto — that God, in predestinating, or condemning, had in no wise regard to the works of those predestinated, or condemned, we know to be profane and impious. For thus Scripture would be opposed to itself, since it promiseth the believer salvation through works, yet supposeth God to be its sole author, by His sole illuminating grace, which He bestoweth without preceding works, to shew to man the truth of divine things, and to teach him how he may co-operate therewith, if he will, and do what is good and acceptable, and so obtain salvation. He taketh not away the power to will — to will to obey, or not obey him.

But than to affirm that the Divine Will is thus solely and without cause the author of their condemnation, what greater calumny can be fixed upon God? and what greater injury and blasphemy can be offered to the Most High? For that the Deity is not tempted with evils, and that He equally willeth the salvation of all, since there is no respect of persons with Him, we do know; and that for those who through their own wicked choice, and their impenitent heart, have become vessels of dishonour, there is, as is just, decreed condemnation, we do confess. But of eternal punishment, of cruelty, of pitilessness, and of inhumanity, we never, never say God is the author, who telleth us that there is joy in heaven over one sinner that repenteth. Far be it from us, while we have our senses, thus to believe, or to think; and we do subject to an eternal anathema those who say and think such things, and esteem them to be worse than any infidels.

Decree IV: The Maker of All Things

We believe the tri-personal God, the Father, the Son, and the Holy Spirit to be the maker of all things visible and invisible; and the invisible are the angelic Powers, rational souls, and demons — though God made not the demons what they afterwards became by their own choice, — but the visible are heaven and what is under heaven. And because the Maker is good by nature, He made all things very good whatsoever He hath made, nor can He ever be the maker of evil. But if there be aught evil, that is to say, sin, come about contrarily to the Divine Will, in man or in demon, — for that evil is simply in nature, we do not acknowledge, — it is either of man, or of the devil. For it is a true and infallible rule, that God is in no wise the author of evil, nor can it at all by just reasoning be attributed to God.

Decree V: The Divine Providence

We believe all things that are, whether visible or invisible, to be governed by the providence of God; but although God fore-knoweth evils, and permitteth them, yet in that they are evils, He is neither their contriver nor their author. But when such are come about, they may be over-ruled by the Supreme Goodness for something beneficial, not indeed as being their author, but as engrafting thereon something for the better. And we ought to adore, but not curiously pry into, Divine Providence in its ineffable and only partially revealed judgments. Albeit what is revealed to us in Divine Scripture concerning it as being conducive to eternal life, we ought honestly to search out, and then unhesitatingly to interpret the same agreeably to primary notions of God.

Decree VI: Human Sin

We believe the first man created by God to have fallen in Paradise, when, disregarding the Divine commandment, he yielded to the deceitful counsel of the serpent. And hence hereditary sin flowed to his posterity; so that none is born after the flesh who beareth not this burden, and experienceth not the fruits thereof in this present world. But by these fruits and this burden we do not understand (actual) sin, such as impiety, blasphemy, murder, sodomy, adultery, fornication, enmity, and whatsoever else is by our depraved choice committed contrarily to the Divine Will, not from nature; for many both of the Forefathers and of the Prophets, and vast numbers of others, as well of those under the shadow (of the Law), as under the truth (of the Gospel), such as the divine Precursor, and especially the Mother of God the Word, the ever-virgin Mary, experienced not these, or such like faults; but only what the Divine Justice inflicted upon man as a punishment for the (original) transgression, such as sweats in labour, afflictions, bodily sicknesses, pains in child-bearing, and in fine, while on our pilgrimage, to live a laborious life, and lastly, bodily death.

Decree VII: The Son of God

We believe the Son of God, Jesus Christ, to have emptied Himself, that is, to have taken into His own Person human flesh, being conceived of the Holy Spirit, in the womb of the ever-virgin Mary; and, becoming man, to have been born, without causing any pain or labour to His own Mother after the flesh, or injury to her virginity, to have suffered, to have been buried, to have risen again in glory on the third day, according to the Scriptures, to have ascended into the heavens, and to be seated at the right hand of God the Father. Whom also we look for to judge the living and the dead.

Decree VIII: Mediators for Human Beings

We believe our Lord Jesus Christ to be the only mediator, and that in giving Himself a ransom for all he hath through His own Blood made a reconciliation between God and man, and that Himself having a care for His own is advocate and propitiation for our sins. Albeit, in prayers and supplications unto Him, we say the Saints are intercessors, and, above all, the undefiled Mother of the very God the Word; the holy Angels too — whom we know to be set over us — the Apostles, Prophets, Martyrs, pure Ones, and all whom He hath glorified as having served Him faithfully. With whom we reckon also the Bishops and Priests, as standing about the Altar of God, and righteous men eminent for virtue. For that we should pray one for another, and that the prayer of the righteous availeth much, and that God heareth the Saints rather than those who are steeped in sins, we learn from the Sacred Oracles. And not only are the Saints while on their pilgrimage regarded as mediators and intercessors for us with God, but especially after their death, when all reflective vision being done away, they behold clearly the Holy Trinity; in whose infinite light they know what concerneth us. For as we doubt not but that the Prophets while they were in a body with the perceptions of the senses knew what was done in heaven, and thereby foretold what was future; so also that the Angels, and the Saints become as Angels, know in the infinite light of God what concerneth us, we doubt not, but rather unhesitatingly believe and confess.

Decree IX: Salvation by Faith

We believe no one to be saved without faith. And by faith we mean the right notion that is in us concerning God and divine things, which, working by love, that is to say, by (observing) the Divine commandments, justifieth us with Christ; and without this (faith) it is impossible to please God.

Decree X: The Catholic Church

We believe that what is called, or rather is, the Holy Catholic and Apostolic Church, and in which we have been taught to believe, containeth generally all the Faithful in Christ, who, that is to say, being still on their pilgrimage, have not yet reached their home in the Fatherland. But we do not in any wise confound this Church which is on its pilgrimage with that which is in the Fatherland, because it may be, as some of the heretics say, that the members of the two are sheep of God, the Chief Shepherd, and hallowed by the same Holy Spirit; for that is absurd and impossible, since the one is yet militant, and on its journey; and the other is triumphant, and settled in the Fatherland, and hath received the prize. Of which Catholic Church, since a mortal man cannot universally and perpetually be head, our Lord Jesus Christ Himself is head, and Himself holding the rudder is at the helm in the governing of the Church, through the Holy Fathers. And, therefore, over particular Churches, that are real Churches, and consist of real members (of the Catholic Church), the Holy Spirit hath appointed Bishops as leaders and shepherds, who being not at all by abuse, but properly, authorities and heads, look unto the Author and Finisher of our Salvation, and refer to Him what they do in their capacity of heads forsooth....

Decree XI: The Faithful as Members of the Catholic Church

We believe to be members of the Catholic Church all the Faithful, and only the Faithful; who, forsooth, having received the blameless Faith of the Saviour Christ, from Christ Himself, and the Apostles, and the Holy Œcumenical Synods, adhere to the same without wavering; although some of them may be guilty of all manner of sins. For unless the Faithful, even when living in sin, were members of the Church, they could not be judged by the Church. But now being judged by her, and called to repentance, and guided into the way of her salutary precepts, though they may be still defiled with sins, for this only, that they have not fallen into despair, and that they cleave to the Catholic and Orthodox faith, they are, and are regarded as, members of the Catholic Church.

Decree XII: The Teaching of the Holy Spirit

We believe the Catholic Church to be taught by the Holy Spirit. For he is the true Paraclete; whom Christ sendeth from the Father, to teach the truth, and to drive away darkness from the minds of the Faithful. The teaching of the Holy Spirit, however, doth not immediately, but through the holy Fathers and Leaders of the Catholic Church, illuminate the Church. For as all Scripture is, and is called, the word of the Holy Spirit; not that it was spoken immediately by Him, but that it was spoken by Him through the Apostles and Prophets; so also the Church is taught indeed by the Life-giving Spirit, but through the medium of the holy Fathers and Doctors (whose rule is acknowledged to be the Holy and Œcumenical Synods; for we shall not cease to say this ten thousand times); and, therefore, not only are we persuaded, but do profess as true and undoubtedly certain, that it is impossible for the Catholic Church to err, or at all be deceived, or ever to choose falsehood instead of truth. For the All-holy Spirit continually operating through the holy Fathers and Leaders faithfully ministering, delivereth the Church from error of every kind.

Decree XIII: Faith and Works
We believe a man to be not simply justified through faith alone, but through faith which worketh through love, that is to say, through faith and works. But (the notion) that faith fulfilling the function of a hand layeth hold on the righteousness which is in Christ, and applieth it unto us for salvation, we know to be far from all Orthodoxy. For faith so understood would be possible in all, and so none could miss salvation, which is obviously false. But on the contrary, we rather believe that it is not the correlative of faith, but the faith which is in us, justifieth through works, with Christ. But we regard works not as witnesses certifying our calling, but as being fruits in themselves, through which faith becometh efficacious, and as in themselves meriting, through the Divine promises, that each of the Faithful may receive what is done through his own body, whether it be good or bad, forsooth.

Decree XIV: The Free Will
We believe man in falling by the [original] transgression to have become comparable and like unto the beasts, that is, to have been utterly undone, and to have fallen from his perfection and impassibility, yet not to have lost the nature and power which he had received from the supremely good God. For otherwise he would not be rational, and consequently not man; but to have the same nature, in which he was created, and the same power of his nature, that is free-will, living and operating. So as to be by nature able to choose and do what is good, and to avoid and hate what is evil. For it is absurd to say that the nature which was created good by Him who is supremely good lacketh the power of doing good. For this would be to make that nature evil — than which what could be more impious? For the power of working dependeth upon nature, and nature upon its author, although in a different manner. And that a man is able by nature to do what is good, even our Lord Himself intimateth, saying, even the Gentiles love those that love them.

But this is taught most plainly by Paul also, in Romans chapter i. [ver.] 19, and elsewhere expressly, saying in so many words, "The Gentiles which have no law do by nature the things of the law." From which it is also manifest that the good which a man may do cannot forsooth be sin. For it is impossible that what is good can be evil. Albeit, being done by nature only, and tending to form the natural character of the doer, but not the spiritual, it contributeth not unto salvation thus alone without faith, nor yet indeed unto condemnation, for it is not possible that good, as such, can be the cause of evil. But in the regenerated, what is wrought by grace, and with grace, maketh the doer perfect, and rendereth him worthy of salvation.

A man, therefore, before he is regenerated, is able by nature to incline to what is good, and to choose and work moral good. But for the regenerated to do spiritual good — for the works of the believer being contributory to salvation and wrought by supernatural grace are properly called spiritual — it is necessary that he be guided and prevented by grace, as hath been said in treating of predestination; so that he is not able of himself to do any work worthy of a Christian life, although he hath it in his own power to will, or not to will, to co-operate with grace.

B.
THE ECUMENICAL MOVEMENT
OF THE TWENTIETH CENTURY

I.

Major Faith and Order
Conferences

1. LAUSANNE 1927

a) The Church's Message to the World — the Gospel
Report of Section II

*At its meeting in Berne (Switzerland) in the summer of 1926, the Continuation
Committee preparing for the Lausanne World Conference included this subject in the
agenda at the request of German theologians. The Subjects' Committee had produced
four theses as preparatory material for the members of the conference to consider and
use in complete freedom:*

*1. The message of the Church to all mankind is the Gospel, promised, prepared for, and
foreshadowed in the Old Testament, perfected in the New through the coming of Jesus
Christ, and proclaimed to the world through the preaching of His Apostles.*

*2. In the centre of the Gospel stands Jesus Christ Himself, Son of God and Son of man,
who through His life, His death and His resurrection, has redeemed mankind and brought
eternal life to light.*

*3. The Gospel conveys to men, through Jesus Christ and through His teaching, a
revelation of God Himself as our Father, and of our duties and hopes as children of God
and brothers in His family.*

*4. The Gospel offers to all mankind forgiveness of sins and eternal life in Jesus Christ our
Lord; it is "the power of God to salvation," for our deliverance from evil, and for the
transformation of all human life, individual and social, into the fullness of the glory of God.[1]*

*The report of the second section reproduced below was received by the full
conference* nemine contradicente *on 19 August 1927, after a series of discussions and
revisions. It was the first attempt in the new ecumenical movement to produce an
agreed account of the content of the Christian faith.*

*This "Lausanne Message" was widely disseminated and met with enthusiastic
response.*

● Text in *Faith and Order: Proceedings of the World Conference at Lausanne, 3-21 August 1927*, ed. H.N.
Bate, London, 1927, pp.461-63; and *A Documentary History of the Faith and Order Movement 1927-1963*,
ed. Lukas Vischer, Bethany Press, St Louis, Missouri, 1963, pp.29f.

[1] *Faith and Order Paper (First Series) No. 47*, Boston, 1927, p.12.

The message of the Church to the world is and must always remain the Gospel of Jesus Christ.

The Gospel is the joyful message of redemption, both here and hereafter, the gift of God to sinful man in Jesus Christ.

The world was prepared for the coming Christ through the activities of God's Spirit in all humanity, but especially in His revelation as given in the Old Testament; and in the fulness of time the eternal Word of God became incarnate, and was made man, Jesus Christ, the Son of God and the Son of Man, full of grace and truth.

Through His life and teaching, His call to repentance, His proclamation of the coming of the Kingdom of God and of judgment, His suffering and death, His resurrection and exaltation to the right hand of the Father, and by the mission of the Holy Spirit, He has brought to us forgiveness of sins, and has revealed the fulness of the living God, and His boundless love toward us. By the appeal of that love, shown in its completeness on the Cross, He summons us to the new life of faith, self-sacrifice, and devotion to His service and the service of men.

Jesus Christ, as the crucified and the living One, as Saviour and Lord, is also the centre of the world-wide Gospel of the Apostles and the Church. Because He Himself is the Gospel, the Gospel is the message of the Church to the world. It is more than a philosophical theory; more than a theological system; more than a programme for material betterment. The Gospel is rather the gift of a new world from God to this old world of sin and death; still more, it is the victory over sin and death, the revelation of eternal life in Him who has knit together the whole family in heaven and on earth in the communion of saints, united in the fellowship of service, of prayer, and of praise.

The Gospel is the prophetic call to sinful man to turn to God, the joyful tidings of justification and of sanctification to those who believe in Christ. It is the comfort of those who suffer; to those who are bound, it is the assurance of the glorious liberty of the sons of God. The Gospel brings peace and joy to the heart, and produces in men self-denial, readiness for brotherly service, and compassionate love. It offers the supreme goal for the aspirations of youth, strength to the toiler, rest to the weary, and the crown of life to the martyr.

The Gospel is the sure source of power for social regeneration. It proclaims the only way by which humanity can escape from those class and race hatreds which devastate society at present into the enjoyment of national well-being and international friendship and peace. It is also a gracious invitation to the non-Christian world, East and West, to enter into the joy of the living Lord.

Sympathising with the anguish of our generation, with its longing for intellectual sincerity, social justice and spiritual inspiration, the Church in the eternal Gospel meets the needs and fulfils the God-given aspirations of the modern world. Consequently, as in the past so also in the present, the Gospel is the only way of salvation. Thus, through His Church, the living Christ still says to men "Come unto me!... He that followeth me shall not walk in darkness, but shall have the light of life."

b) Concerning the Faith of the Reunited Church
Statement Prepared by the Subjects' Committee, 1923

Among the steps taken at the Preliminary Meeting in Geneva from 12-20 August 1920 was the appointment of a Subjects' Committee to take care of the theological preparations for the Lausanne World Conference. The committee's first step was to formulate four questions on the faith of the reunited church:

1. *What degree of unity in Faith will be necessary in a reunited church?*
2. *Is a statement of this one Faith in the form of a Creed necessary or desirable?*
3. *If so, what Creed should be used or what other formulary would be desirable?*
4. *What are the proper uses of a Creed and of a Confession of Faith?*[1]

These questions were translated into a number of languages and despatched to all parts of the world to be discussed by as many groups or small conferences as possible, with a request for written answers to be sent to the Subjects' Committee. Three years later, in September 1923, the committee met in Oxford to evaluate the few responses to these and other questions. On this occasion it summarized in a report the views expressed on the question of faith. This was printed together with other reports in 1926 and made available to members of the Lausanne conference as background material. The report has no official status. Its significance lies in the fact that it was the first summary of the questions in connection with the common faith arising in the new ecumenical movement. Its fifteen sections are mainly a summary of the various views concerning the origin, interpretation and use of such creeds as the Apostles' and Nicene Creeds. In section 14, the view is expressed "that it is not beyond the competence of the universal Church, when once more united, to frame another creed...."

● Text in "Statements by the Subjects Committee of the World Conference on Faith and Order", *Faith and Order Series No. 46*, Boston, 1926, pp.5-8.

It being acknowledged that the Church was founded by the Will of God expressed through His Son Jesus Christ, and is maintained by the same Will, it has to be determined what on the human side is necessary to the unity and the life of the Church.

1. It is agreed that it is necessary for every member of the Church to have a hearty belief or trust in God as He has revealed Himself to men in His Son Jesus Christ, and that this revelation must be brought home to their hearts by His Holy Spirit.

2. In the historical creeds the typical phrase "I believe in" means more than intellectual assent to a proposition or propositions; it means trust in and self-devotion to a Person Whose Nature is declared by the names, attributes and propositions which follow. For instance, "I believe in God the Father," does not only nor even primarily mean, "I believe that God is the Father," but "I utterly trust in, and completely devote

---

[1] Rouse and Neill, *A History of the Ecumenical Movement 1517-1948*, 2nd ed., London, SPCK, 1967, p.419.

myself to God, being, as He is, the Father." Thus those who use the historical creeds with understanding recognise in them, not compendious statements of intellectual positions, but means whereby individuals and bodies of men may make profession of that faith which is the heart's trust in a Person.

3. At the same time, "heart's trust" has intellectual implications. The need for setting out these implications varies with varying occasions and also with the capacities of those who make the professions.

4. Such statements of the heart's trust in God, with less or greater development of its intellectual implications, commonly take the form to which the name *creed* has been given. Creeds have been put to various uses, of which it is not necessary here to treat more than four, viz., (1) the profession of faith at baptism (baptismal or beginners' creeds), and, as connected with this, instruction before baptism or before admission to the full privileges of membership in the Church; (2) the protection of the Church against false doctrine (the creeds of the Councils or Teachers' Creeds); (3) confession of faith to God, especially in public worship; (4) confession of faith as witness before men (for this purpose longer statements such as the "Confessions" of the Reformation Age have also been used).

5. From the earliest times some verbal expression of this faith or "heart's trust" has been deemed to be necessary before admission to the Church. Hence arose the baptismal creeds. Attention may well be given to the experience gained from the instruction of adult converts from other religions as well as from the instruction of simple people who have been baptised in infancy. Both these forms of instruction witness to the advantage of the teaching about our Lord Jesus Christ by means of the facts of His life. This practical advantage coincides with doctrinal truth.

6. The present facts are that where a creed is used for the purposes mentioned in the preceding section, the Apostles' Creed is generally used, except by the Orthodox Church which uses the Nicene Creed, and that, where a creed is not used, instruction in the faith before, and profession of faith at the time of, baptism or admission to the full privileges of membership in the Church follow the general lines of the Apostles' Creed, though both that instruction and that profession may, and the instruction often does, go into greater detail.

7. It is suggested that agreement might be reached that the profession of faith at Baptism should be made either by means of the Apostles' Creed or the Nicene Creed or by acceptance of the substance of one of those creeds, according as any Church may determine.

8. Besides having a statement whereby beginners in Christ may profess their heart's trust in God, it is reasonable that the Church should also have more advanced and detailed statements for the guidance of its teachers and the avoidance of error. It will be agreed that the Holy Spirit gave the Church the best answer for each time to the actual questions of that time. These statements varied from relatively short creeds, which differed very little in length or contents from the baptismal creeds, to very long statements, sometimes called Confessions. While such statements of the belief of the Church as a teaching Church are necessary for the instruction and guidance of its teachers and for explanation of their commission to teach, the place of any one of them in relation to the whole Church depends on the relative importance of the problems with which it deals.

9. The Nicene Creed was in origin such a statement and in many parts of the Church holds at the present time a pre-eminent place, while most Churches define

more fully than is done in the Creed the standard of doctrine which their teachers are commissioned to teach. It will be for the United Church to consider how it will conserve in the teaching given on its behalf the unity of doctrine which exists in it. But in the meantime it is likely to be agreed that that teaching must include, as its centre, the substance of the Apostles' and the Nicene Creeds.

10. At the same time it will be regarded as reasonable that different parts of the United Church should from time to time adopt or draw up more detailed statements of doctrine for the guidance of their teachers, always provided that they be in accordance with the revelation of God contained in the Holy Scriptures; and whether they be so, or not, it will be for the United Church to decide.

11. It has been a custom in many parts of the Church to recite some form of creed in public worship. This for the individual worshipper is an act of renewal of his heart's trust in God and of thankfulness to God for the revelation of Himself which He has given. It is for the congregation a corporate act of reaffirmation of the dependence on God which makes their common worship acceptable to Him and binds them one to another. Some churches have chosen for this purpose the baptismal creed as that most generally intelligible; others one of the fuller creeds, which, when used in public worship, may be regarded as an expression of the mind of the whole Church or of the ideal to which the mind of the individual may attain.

Note: It should be remembered that while there is some early evidence of the use of the Creeds as "hymns," they were not primarily intended for recitation in public worship. However, similar dogmatic material is in free general use, for purposes of exultant or thankful corporate professions, in some of the great hymns of the Church: e.g., *Te Deum Laudamus, Adeste Fideles*, and Luther's hymn, *Wir glauben all' an einen Gott*.

12. This recitation of the creed in public worship is a godly practice, but is not essential to the unity and the life of the Church. It is suggested that any part of the Church should be free to use either the Nicene or the Apostles' Creed, or both, in public worship, or, if to its proper authorities it seem better, not to recite a creed in public worship.

13. In regard to the use of creeds for the purpose of bearing witness before men, we may advert to the custom in the earliest times of presenting the creed of a local Church to other Churches with a view to showing that the first-named Church held the truth and agreed with the rest of Christendom. We may also mention the object which was sought to be attained by various later Confessional statements framed "in order that the consent of the Churches might appear." The United Church will desire to bear witness to the decisive and fundamental truths which it professes and teaches, and the World Conference, as preparing for the United Church, will be concerned to give such witness, and in this connection will need to make some declaration of the common faith of Christendom whether by means of an ancient formula, or by means of a declaration couched in more modern terms.

14. It is suggested, further, that it is not beyond the competence of the universal Church, when once more united, to frame another creed either for one of the above-mentioned established purposes of a creed, or for some other purpose not hitherto contemplated, always provided that such new creed be in accordance with the revelations of God recorded in Holy Scripture, and that neither the framing of the new creed nor that creed when framed bring into question the validity of the two creeds

above mentioned, viz., the Nicene Creed and the Apostles' Creed, for the purposes for which and the times in which they were framed, and for use by all persons or Churches who desire to retain their use for the said purposes.

15. It is suggested, again, that it may be competent for any part of the universal Church when united to adopt with the consent of the whole Church a new form of creed for any of the purposes above mentioned or for some purpose not hitherto contemplated.

c) The Church's Common Confession of Faith
   Report of Section IV

The inclusion of this theme in the agenda of the Lausanne Conference had already been decided at the first Preparatory Conference in 1916. At that time, the formulation was: "The Catholic Creeds, as the safeguard of the Faith of the Church"; in 1925 it became: "The Church's Common Confession of Faith in God"; and then, in 1926, "The Church's Common Confession of Faith".[1]

In 1926, the Subjects' Committee had formulated three questions which were sent to the members of the Lausanne conference beforehand as an aid to discussion:

1. Is it requisite to Christian Unity that there should be general agreement in an explicit declaration of the Christian Faith?

2. Is it admitted that among the historic statements of that Faith the creeds commonly called the Apostles' and the Nicene Creed have such weight that with regard to these forms, at least, it is desirable that the Churches should attempt to reach an agreement?

3. Could a united Church agree

(a) To accept the Faith of Christ as taught in Holy Scripture, and handed down in the Apostles' and the Nicene Creeds?

(b) To leave the occasions for the use of these creeds to the decisions of local Churches?

(c) To recognise, while firmly adhering to the substance of these Creeds, that the Holy Spirit, leading the Church into all truth, may enable the Church to express the truths of revelation in other forms according to the needs of future times?[2]

The following report was the fruit of discussions on this theme in Section IV of the Lausanne conference. In the course of the discussions, Dr Headlam, the (Anglican) Bishop of Gloucester, proposed the following formulation: "We accept the faith of Christ as it has been taught us by the Holy Scriptures, and as it has been handed down to us in the Creed of the Catholic Church set forth at the Council of Chalcedon, and in the Apostles' Creed."

After a number of revisions, the final version of the Section IV report was received by the full conference nemine contradicente and without discussion on 19 August

---

[1] *Faith and Order Papers (First Series) No. 47*, Boston, 1927, p.15.
[2] *Ibid.*

1927. It emphasizes not only the common heritage of scripture and the creeds of the ancient church but also the continuing work of the Holy Spirit who can also enable the church "to express the truths of revelation in such other forms as new problems may from time to time demand".

● Text in *Faith and Order: Proceedings of the World Conference at Lausanne, 3-21 August 1927*, ed. H.N. Bate, London, 1927, p.202. And in *A Documentary History of the Faith and Order Movement 1927-1963*, ed. Lukas Vischer, Bethany Press, St Louis, Missouri, 1963, pp.33f.

We members of the Conference on Faith and Order, coming from all parts of the world in the interest of Christian unity, have with deep gratitude to God found ourselves united in common prayer, in God our heavenly Father and His Son Jesus Christ, our Saviour, in the fellowship of the Holy Spirit.

Notwithstanding the differences in doctrine among us, we are united in a common Christian Faith which is proclaimed in the Holy Scriptures and is witnessed to and safeguarded in the Ecumenical Creed, commonly called the Nicene, and in the Apostles' Creed, which Faith is continuously confirmed in the spiritual experience of the Church of Christ.

We believe that the Holy Spirit in leading the Church into all truth may enable it, while firmly adhering to the witness of these Creeds (our common heritage from the ancient Church), to express the truths of revelation in such other forms as new problems may from time to time demand.

Finally, we desire to leave on record our solemn and unanimous testimony that no external and written standards can suffice without an inward and personal experience of union with God in Christ.

Notes

1. It must be noted that the Orthodox Eastern Church can accept the Nicene Creed only in its uninterpolated form without the *filioque* clause; and that although the Apostles' Creed has no place in the formularies of this Church, it is in accordance with its teaching

2. It must be noted also that some of the Churches represented in this Conference conjoin tradition with the Scriptures, some are explicit in subordinating Creeds to the Scriptures, some attach a primary importance to their particular Confessions, and some make no use of Creeds.

3. It is understood that the use of these Creeds will be determined by the competent authority in each Church, and that the several Churches will continue to make use of such special Confessions as they possess.

2. EDINBURGH 1937
The Grace of Our Lord Jesus Christ
Report of Section I

The progress made in Edinburgh on "unity in faith" is evident from the following statement of Section VI on "Likeness in Faith or Confession as a Basis for Unity":[1]

We accept as the supreme standard of the faith the revelation of God contained in the Holy Scriptures of the Old and New Testaments and summed up in Jesus Christ.

We acknowledge the Apostles' Creed and the Creed commonly called the Nicene as witnessing to and safeguarding that faith which is continually verified in the spiritual experience of the Church and its members — remembering that these documents are sacred symbols and witnesses of the Christian faith rather than legalistic standards.

*We further affirm that the guidance of God's Holy Spirit did not cease with the closing of the canon of the Scripture, or with the formulation of the Creeds cited, but that there has been in the Church through the centuries, and still is, a divinely sustained consciousness of the presence of the living Christ. (*Note: *Known in the Orthodox Church as the Holy Tradition.)*

Finally, we are persuaded, in the classical words of one of the non-confessional communions, that "God has yet more light to break forth from His Holy Word" for a humble and waiting Church. We Christians of the present age should therefore seek the continued guidance of the Spirit of the living God as we confront our troubled time.[2]

The Continuation Committee had decided in 1930 that "the meaning of grace" should be one of the main subjects of the second world conference. The idea was to bring the main theme of the Reformation, the doctrine of justification, into the ecumenical debate. In 1931, the Theological Committee produced a preparatory report on "The Theology of Grace".[3]

Just prior to the Edinburgh conference, this report was supplemented by some notes on "The Grace of Our Lord Jesus Christ" by Leonard Hodgson, the theological secretary of the World Conference,[4] *in which he raised such questions as the following:*

---

[1] Vischer, *Documentary History*, p.64.
[2] *Ibid.*
[3] *Faith and Order Papers (First Series) No. 66*, Winchester, UK, and New York, 1931.
[4] *Faith and Order Papers (First Series) No. 88*, Winchester, UK, and New York, May 1937.

I. In what sense is this redeeming activity of God a fact?
II. What do we mean by calling God's redeeming activity in Jesus Christ necessary?
III. What do we mean by salvation?
IV. How is this redemption and salvation received?[5]

On 18 August 1937, the report of Section I was adopted nemine contradicente *by the full conference. It consisted of six sections:*
1. The meaning of grace
2. Justification and sanctification
3. The sovereignty of God and man's response
4. The church and grace
5. Grace, the word and the sacraments
6. Sola gratia
In their opening words, the authors declare: "With deep thankfulness... we agree on the following statement and recognize that there is in connection with this subject no ground for maintaining division between Churches."

● Text in *The Second World Conference on Faith and Order*, ed. L. Hodgson, London, 1938, pp.224-27; and *A Documentary History of the Faith and Order Movement 1927-1963*, ed. Lukas Vischer, Bethany Press, St Louis, Missouri, 1963, pp.40-43.

With deep thankfulness to God for the spirit of unity, which by His gracious blessing upon us has guided and controlled all our discussions on this subject, we agree on the following statement and recognise that there is in connection with this subject no ground for maintaining division between Churches.

1. The Meaning of Grace
When we speak of God's grace, we think of God Himself as revealed in His Son Jesus Christ. The meaning of divine grace is truly known only to those who know that God is Love, and that all that He does is done in love in fulfilment of His righteous purposes. His grace is manifested in our creation, preservation and all the blessings of this life, but above all in our redemption through the life, death and resurrection of Jesus Christ, in the sending of the holy and life-giving Spirit, in the fellowship of the Church and in the gift of the Word and Sacraments.

Man's salvation and welfare have their source in God alone, who is moved to His gracious activity towards man not by any merit on man's part, but solely by His free, outgoing love.

2. Justification and Sanctification
God in His free outgoing love justifies and sanctifies us through Christ, and His grace thus manifested is appropriated by faith, which itself is the gift of God.

Justification and Sanctification are two inseparable aspects of God's gracious action in dealing with sinful man.

---

[5] *Ibid.*, pp.5ff.

Justification is the act of God, whereby He forgives our sins and brings us into fellowship with Himself, who in Jesus Christ, and by His death upon the Cross, has condemned sin and manifested His love to sinners, reconciling the world to Himself.

Sanctification is the work of God, whereby through the Holy Spirit He continually renews us and the whole Church, delivering us from the power of sin, giving us increase in holiness, and transforming us into the likeness of His Son through participation in His death and in His risen life. This renewal, inspiring us to continual spiritual activity and conflict with evil, remains throughout the gift of God. Whatever our growth in holiness may be, our fellowship with God is always based upon God's forgiving grace.

Faith is more than intellectual acceptance of the revelation in Jesus Christ; it is whole-hearted trust in God and His promises, and committal of ourselves to Jesus Christ as Saviour and Lord.

3. The Sovereignty of God and Man's Response

In regard to the relation of God's grace and man's freedom, we all agree simply upon the basis of Holy Scripture and Christian experience that the sovereignty of God is supreme. By the sovereignty of God we mean His all-controlling, all-embracing will and purpose revealed in Jesus Christ for each man and for all mankind. And we wish further to insist that this eternal purpose is the expression of God's own loving and holy nature. Thus we men owe our whole salvation to His gracious will. But, on the other hand, it is the will of God that His grace should be actively appropriated by man's own will and that for such decision man should remain responsible.

Many theologians have made attempts on philosophical lines to reconcile the apparent antithesis of God's sovereignty and man's responsibility, but such theories are not part of the Christian Faith.

We are glad to report that in this difficult matter we have been able to speak with a united voice, so that we have found that here there ought to be no ground for maintaining any division between Churches.

4. The Church and Grace

We agree that the Church is the Body of Christ and the blessed company of all faithful people, whether in heaven or on earth, the communion of saints. It is at once the realisation of God's gracious purposes in creation and redemption, and the continuous organ of God's grace in Christ by the Holy Spirit, who is its pervading life, and who is constantly hallowing all its parts.

It is the function of the Church to glorify God in its life and worship, to proclaim the gospel to every creature, and to build up in the fellowship and life of the Spirit all believing people, of every race and nation. To this end God bestows His Grace in the Church on its members through His Word and Sacraments, and in abiding presence of the Holy Spirit.

5. Grace, the Word and the Sacraments

We agree that the Word and the Sacraments are gifts of God to the Church through Jesus Christ for the salvation of mankind. In both the grace of God in Christ is shown forth, given and through faith received; and this grace is one and indivisible.

The Word is the appointed means by which God's grace is made known to men, calling them to repentance, assuring them of forgiveness, drawing them to obedience and building them up in the fellowship of faith and love.

The Sacraments are not to be considered merely in themselves, but always as sacraments of the Church, which is the Body of Christ. They have their significance in the continual working of the Holy Spirit, who is the life of the Church. Through the sacraments God develops in all its members a life of perpetual communion lived within its fellowship, and thus enables them to embody His will in the life of the world; but the loving-kindness of God is not to be conceived as limited by His sacraments.

Among or within the Churches represented by us there is a certain difference of emphasis placed upon the Word and the Sacraments, but we agree that such a difference need not be a barrier to union.

6. Sola Gratia

Some Churches set great value on the expression *sola gratia*, while others avoid it. The phrase has been the subject of much controversy, but we can all join in the following statement: Our salvation is the gift of God and the fruit of His grace. It is not based on the merit of man, but has its root and foundation in the forgiveness which God in His grace grants to the sinner whom He receives to sanctify him. We do not, however, hold that the action of the divine grace overrides human freedom and responsibility; rather, it is only as response is made by faith to divine grace that true freedom is achieved. Resistance to the appeal of God's outgoing love spells, not freedom, but bondage, and perfect freedom is found only in complete conformity with the good and acceptable and perfect will of God.

3. LUND 1952
Christ and His Church
Report of Section I

On the question of "consensus in doctrine", Section III in Lund stated:

> *All accept the Holy Scriptures as either the sole authority for doctrine or the primary and decisive part of those authorities to which they would appeal. Most accept the Ecumenical Creeds as an interpretation of the truth of the Bible or as marking a distinctive stage in the working-out of the orthodox faith. Some assign a special importance to the credal documents of the early Ecumenical Councils. Some would say that to found unity on any creeds is to found it on something human, namely, our understanding of the Gospel and our theological work in formulating its meaning. Some judge in accordance with the Inner Light and the leadings of the Spirit and are therefore concerned to witness against the use of outward creeds when these are held to be necessary or sufficient.*
>
> *Many denominations possess confessional documents in which they express the Christian Faith as they read it in the Bible. It would generally be admitted, however, that these last documents would not be regarded as irreformable and they do not in fact occupy the same position in the Rule of Faith of all Churches which possess them.*[1]

The predominant theme at Lund was the question of the nature of the church. Contributions had been made to the study of this theme by theological commissions since 1939. The most important of these were published in the study volume The Nature of the Church *(1951).*[2] *This contains self-portraits of most of the confessions but no draft of a common doctrine of the church. The Section I report on "Christ and His Church" was the fruit of the work done at the conference itself and was received* nemine contradicente *on 27 August 1952. It consists of four parts:*

1. *Christ and his body*
2. *The unity of the church:*
   a) *The faith of the church in the Father, the Son and the Holy Spirit*
   b) *The nature and mission of the church*
   c) *The church between the first and the final coming of Christ*
3. *Consequences for the churches*
4. *Recommendation*

---

[1] *The Third World Conference on Faith and Order*, p.31; cf. also *Documentary History*, p.100.
[2] *The Nature of the Church*, ed. R.N. Flew, London, 1952.

The theological key to the document is to be found in the statement:

> *From the unity of Christ we seek to understand the unity of the Church on earth, and from the unity of Christ and His Body we seek a means of realizing that unity in the actual state of our divisions on earth.*[3]

● Text in *The Third World Conference on Faith and Order*, ed. O.S. Tomkins, London, 1953, pp.17-22.

We believe in Jesus Christ our Lord, who loved the Church and gave Himself for it, and has brought the Church into an abiding union with Himself. Because we believe in Jesus Christ we believe also in the Church as the Body of Christ.

I

We confess that without Christ we are lost, and without Him we are subject to the powers of sin and death, but that God has not abandoned us to the powers of destruction. He has given to us and all men His only begotten Son as Saviour and Redeemer. Through His life, His suffering, His death and His resurrection Jesus Christ as the mighty Victor has overcome sin and death, brought the ungodly powers to nought, and has given us freedom. When we believe in Jesus Christ these powers can no longer exercise Lordship over us. Thus we stand under a new Lord. It is Jesus Christ who is our Lord.

For He, in His incarnation, death and resurrection, has entered into oneness with man in his estrangement and in his existence under the judgment of God, and by making atonement for man's guilt has consecrated a new way in which man, reconciled with God, may live in union with Jesus Christ. Through Him God has given a lost humanity a new beginning, for in that Jesus Christ died and rose again, all who believe in Him die and rise again to a new life.

Jesus Christ is the King of the new People of God. He is "the chief cornerstone in which the whole building, fitly framed together, grows up into a holy temple in the Lord". He is the head of the Church which is His Body. Through His Spirit Jesus Christ Himself is present in His Church. Christ lives in His Church and the Church lives in Christ. Christ is never without His Church; the Church is never without Christ. Both belong inseparably together, the King and His people, the keystone and the temple, the Head and the Body. As members of His Body we are made one with Him in the fellowship of his life, death and resurrection, of His suffering and His glory. For what concerns Christ concerns His Body also. What has happened to Christ uniquely in His once-and-for-all death and resurrection on our behalf, happens also to the Church in its way as His Body. As the Church is made a partaker in the crucified Body of Christ, so also it is given to be partaker in the risen Body of the same Lord. This means that the Church is called to continue the mission of Jesus Christ to the world, so that the way of Christ is the way of His Church.

---

[3] Tomkins, *op. cit.*, p.18; cf. also Vischer, *Documentary History*, p.88.

II

On the ground of the apostolic witness to Jesus Christ, the Lord of the Church, and in obedience to Him, we seek to penetrate behind the divisions of the Church on earth to our common faith in the one Lord. From the unity of Christ we seek to understand the unity of the Church on earth, and from the unity of Christ and His Body we seek a means of realising that unity in the actual state of our divisions on earth.

We believe that many of our differences arise from a false antithesis between the Church's being in Christ and its mission in the world, and from a failure to understand the Church in the light of Jesus Christ as God and man, and in the light of His death and resurrection. In the following paragraphs we seek:

(1) to speak of the nature of the Church in terms of a double movement (its being called from the world and its being sent into the world) through which it is ever being built up into Jesus Christ its Head;

(2) to speak of the Church as the new creation, which, while it continues to live on earth as a community of forgiven sinners, expecting the redemption of the body, is already given to participate in the new life of the risen Christ.

The Faith of the Church in the Father, the Son and the Holy Spirit

In His eternal love the Father has sent His Son to redeem creation from sin and death. In Jesus Christ, God's Son became Man. By word and deed He proclaimed on earth the arrival of God's kingdom, bore away the sins of the world on the Cross, rose again from the dead, ascended into heaven, to the throne of His kingdom, at the right hand of God. At Pentecost God poured out His Spirit upon the Church, giving all who believe in Jesus Christ the power to become God's children. Through the indwelling of His Spirit Jesus Christ dwells in the midst of His Church. As Lord and King He will come again to judge the quick and the dead and to consummate the eternal kingdom of God in the whole creation.

The Nature and Mission of the Church

(a) The Lord Jesus Christ, through His Word and Spirit, calls His Church from the world. He forgives sins, delivers men from the Lordship of the powers of destruction and gathers out of this broken world the one People of God, the community of the justified and sanctified whose citizenship is in heaven and whose life is hid with Christ in God.

(b) Jesus Christ through His Word and Spirit sends His Church into the world to be the salt of the earth and the light of the world. That is, as Prophet, Priest and King He gives His Church to participate in His ministry of reconciliation, constraining it by His love to enter into His passion for the redemption of the world, and empowering it by His Spirit to proclaim the Gospel of salvation to all nations, calling them to obey the will of God in all the areas of political and social and cultural life and to live out in the divisions of the world the life of the one People of God, so that through its witness Jesus Christ is at work among men as Saviour, and brings all things in subjection under Himself as Lord and King of the world.

(c) By calling and sending His People, by granting them manifold spiritual gifts for the ministry, Jesus Christ builds up His Church as the living Temple of God. Thus the Church as the Body of Christ "grows up into him in all things who is the head, from whom the whole Body fitly joined together and compacted by that which every joint supplieth according to the effective working in the measure of every part, maketh increase of the Body unto the edifying of itself in love".

The Church between the First and the Final Coming of Christ

(a) At the same time the Church is a community of forgiven sinners eagerly expecting and patiently watching for the final consummation of its redemption. It continues to be a pilgrim people in a strange land, so that all its life and work on earth is incomplete. Ungodly powers and forces are still rampant in the whole creation in an alarming way, and they seek to confuse the Church and defeat its mission. But the Church continues to live and work by the power of Jesus Christ.

(b) At the end of its pilgrimage Jesus Christ, the Crucified and Risen, will come again to meet His Church in order to complete His work of redemption and judgment. Out of all peoples and ages He will gather His own who look for His appearing and for a new heaven and a new earth, and He will consummate the union between Christ and His Church in the eternal kingdom of God.

(c) Through the indwelling of the Holy Spirit the new age of the future is already present and through union with the risen Jesus Christ the Church on earth is already given to participate in the power of the resurrection. The Church of Jesus Christ in history is at once the congregation of sinners and the new creation, for although it continues to live and work within the brokenness and estrangement of this world and to share in its divisions, the Church belongs essentially to the new age and the new creation. As such the Church is summoned to perpetual renewal, to put off the old life, and by the renewal of its mind to be conformed to Christ, looking beyond its historical forms to the full unveiling of its new being in the coming Lord.

III

We have sought to declare in these brief paragraphs the inseparable relation between Christ and His Church. To these convictions about the Church we are led by our faith in Jesus Christ and by our shared acceptance of the authority of the Holy Scriptures. We cannot build the one Church by cleverly fitting together our divided inheritances. We can grow together towards fullness and unity in Christ only by being conformed to Him who is the Head of the Body and Lord of His people. And He manifests His fullness, however brokenly, in the gifts He has given to us even in our separations. Wherever two or three are gathered in His name, He is in the midst of them. Wherever men are met in obedience to Him, He is known. He may be found in the midst of those from whom we are separated and in the midst of those to whom we are sent.

When we place ourselves in our Churches under His judgment and in obedience to His calling and His sending, we shall know that we cannot manifest our unity and share in His fullness without being changed. Some of us who have been assured that we possess the true order and the true sacraments will find ourselves called to give its rightful place to the preaching of the Living Word. Some who have neglected the sacraments will be confronted by Him who humbled Himself in Baptism and broke bread and shared the cup to make us partakers of His passion and death. Those who have sought to show forth the glory of the Church as the Body and Bride of Christ must stand under the judgment of His simplicity and servanthood. Churches which have valued little His prayer that the oneness of His people be made manifest to men will be summoned to make His prayer their own. Churches complacent in the face of racial divisions in the Body will be brought to repentance by Him in whom bond and free, Jew and Gentile, Greek and barbarian, are one. Churches which have stressed one-sidedly that God in His Church gives Himself to men will be reminded that Christ in His humanity offered Himself to the Father. Those who are ever looking backward and have accumulated much precious ecclesiastical baggage, will perhaps be shown that pilgrims must travel light and that, if we are to share at last in the great Supper, we must let go much that we treasure. Churches settled and self-assured will have to hear again the Lord's heart-broken concern for the sheep without a shepherd and know that to be His Church is to share in His world-embracing mission. Churches too much at home in the world will hear themselves called out of the world. Churches too wrapped up in their own piety or their own survival will see again Him who identified Himself with the deprived and the oppressed.

We cannot know all that shall be disclosed to us when together we look to Him who is the Head of the Body. It is easy for us in our several Churches to think of what our separated brethren need to learn. Christ's love will make us more ready to learn what He can teach us through them. The truth we would hold fast is that because Christ is the Head and Lord of the Church, His way is the Church's way. He calls, He sends, He judges. The shape of His life is the shape of the Church's life. The mystery of His life is the mystery of the Church's life.

IV

Recommendation

In our work we have been led to the conviction that it is of decisive importance for the advance of ecumenical work that the doctrine of the Church be treated in close relation both to the doctrine of Christ and to the doctrine of the Holy Spirit. We believe that this must occupy a primary place in the future work of this movement, and we so recommend to the Faith and Order Commission, and to its Working Committee.

4. MONTREAL 1963
Scripture, Tradition and Traditions
From the Report of Section II

One of the decisions made at Lund was the establishment of a theological commission to study the relationship between the different church traditions and the one Tradition in Christ. This commission was divided into a North American and a European section, and the reports of their findings were published with the title "Tradition and Traditions" in 1963 in preparation for the Fourth World Conference on Faith and Order in Montreal.[1] The report of the North American section, "The Renewal of the Christian Tradition" concerned itself mainly with an inclusive ecumenical historiography which properly emphasizes the common Christian past. The report of the European section, "Tradition", sought a new interpretation of the Tradition from biblical and historical standpoints. It concluded with a summary of "Positions and Problems" by Jean-Louis Leuba:

  I. The points on which agreement seems possible
      1. The legitimacy of the subject
      2. Tradition as the work of the Holy Spirit
      3. The difference between Tradition and the traditions, and the need for a criterion to define the difference
      4. The two elements which enable us to find the criterion: Scripture and the Church
  II. The points on which it is not yet possible to reach agreement
      1. The relationship between Scripture and the Church
      2. The identity of the faith and the development of knowledge.[2]

Among the many preparatory papers for Montreal was a working paper produced by a small preparatory conference at Bossey, Geneva, to serve as starting point for the work of the Sections in Montreal.[3] The theme was discussed there in three subsections, each of which contributed its portion to the report of Section II:

Introduction
Part I: Scripture, Tradition and traditions

---

[1] *Faith and Order Findings: the Report to the Fourth World Conference on Faith and Order*, ed. Paul S. Minear, London, SCM Press Ltd., 1963, prints *all* the final reports of the Theological Commissions in a single volume. The report of the Theological Commission on "Tradition and Traditions" is *Faith and Order Paper No. 40*, Geneva, 1963.
[2] *Faith and Order Paper No. 40*, pp.56-63.
[3] Cf. David M. Paton, "Montreal Diary", in "The Fourth World Conference on Faith and Order, Montreal 1963", p.23f.

Part II: The unity of Tradition and the diversity of traditions
Part III: The Christian Tradition and cultural diversity
Appendix: The revision of catechisms in the light of the ecumenical movement
The introduction and Part I contain the basic statements and were fully endorsed by the Section, and we give below these two portions of the final report. The whole report was received nemine contradicente *by the full Conference on 26 July 1963. It concludes with the question, addressed to the church:*

> *What proportion of time is spent on teaching our common faith and our common history as Christians, and what proportion on teaching that history and doctrine which distinguishes your church from other churches?*[4]

● Text in "The Fourth World Conference on Faith and Order, Montreal 1963", ed. P.C. Rodger and L. Vischer, *Faith and Order Paper No. 42*, London, 1964, p.50-54.

Introduction

38. We find ourselves together in Montreal, delegates of churches with many different backgrounds and many different histories. And yet despite these differences we find that we are able to meet one another in faith and hope in the one Father, who by his Son Jesus Christ has sent the Holy Spirit to draw all men into unity with one another and with him. It is on the basis of this faith and hope, and in the context of a common prayer to the one God, Father, Son and Holy Spirit, that we have studied together anew the problem of the one Tradition and the many traditions, and despite the fact of our separations, have found that we can talk with one another and grow in mutual understanding. The Section warmly commends for study by the churches the report of the Theological Commission on "Tradition and Traditions" (*Faith and Order Findings,* Part IV, pp.3-63), which was the main documentary foundation of its work.

39. In our report we have distinguished between a number of different meanings of the word *tradition*. We speak of the *Tradition* (with a capital T), *tradition* (with a small t) and *traditions*. By *the Tradition* is meant the Gospel itself, transmitted from generation to generation in and by the Church, Christ himself present in the life of the Church. By *tradition* is meant the traditionary process. The term *traditions* is used in two senses, to indicate both the diversity of forms of expression and also what we call confessional traditions, for instance the Lutheran tradition or the Reformed tradition. In the latter part of our report the word appears in a further sense, when we speak of cultural traditions.

40. Our report contains the substance of the work of three sub-sections. The first considered the subject of the relation of Tradition to Scripture, regarded as the written prophetic and apostolic testimony to God's act in Christ, whose authority we all accept. The concern of the second was with the problem of the one Tradition and the many traditions of Christendom as they unfold in the course of the Church's history. The third discussed the urgent problems raised both in the life of the younger churches and in the churches of the West, concerning the translation of Christian Tradition into new cultures and languages.

---

[4] *Ibid.,* p.61.

41. Part I received a full discussion and the complete approval of the Section. Owing to the lack of time it was not possible to give the same detailed attention to Parts II and III. The Section in general recommends them for study.

I. Scripture, Tradition and traditions

42. As Christians we all acknowledge with thankfulness that God has revealed himself in the history of the people of God in the Old Testament and in Christ Jesus, his Son, the mediator between God and man. God's mercy and God's glory are the beginning and end of our own history. The testimony of prophets and apostles inaugurated the Tradition of his revelation. The once-for-all disclosure of God in Jesus Christ inspired the apostles and disciples to give witness to the revelation given in the person and work of Christ. No one could, and no one can, "say that Jesus is Lord, save by the Holy Spirit" (I Cor. 12.3). The oral and written tradition of the prophets and apostles under the guidance of the Holy Spirit led to the formation of Scriptures and to the canonization of the Old and New Testaments as the Bible of the Church. The very fact that Tradition precedes the Scriptures points to the significance of tradition, but also to the Bible as the treasure of the Word of God.

43. The Bible poses the problem of Tradition and Scripture in a more or less implicit manner; the history of Christian theology points to it explicitly. While in the Early Church the relation was not understood as problematical, ever since the Reformation "Scripture and Tradition" has been a matter of controversy in the dialogue between Roman Catholic and Protestant theology. On the Roman Catholic side, tradition has generally been understood as divine truth not expressed in Holy Scripture alone, but orally transmitted. The Protestant position has been an appeal to Holy Scripture alone, as the infallible and sufficient authority in all matters pertaining to salvation, to which all human traditions should be subjected. The voice of the Orthodox Church has hardly been heard in these Western discussions until quite recently.

44. For a variety of reasons, it has now become necessary to reconsider these positions. We are more aware of our living in various confessional traditions, e.g. that stated paradoxically in the saying "It has been the tradition of my church not to attribute any weight to tradition." Historical study and not least the encounter of the churches in the ecumenical movement have led us to realize that the proclamation of the Gospel is always inevitably historically conditioned. We are also aware that in Roman Catholic theology the concept of tradition is undergoing serious reconsideration.

45. In our present situation, we wish to reconsider the problem of Scripture and Tradition, or rather that of Tradition and Scripture. And therefore we wish to propose the following statement as a fruitful way of reformulating the question. Our starting-point is that we are all living in a tradition which goes back to our Lord and has its roots in the Old Testament, and are all indebted to that tradition inasmuch as we have received the revealed truth, the Gospel, through its being transmitted from one generation to another. Thus we can say that we exist as Christians by the Tradition of the Gospel (the *paradosis* of the *kerygma*) testified in Scripture, transmitted in and by the Church through the power of the Holy Spirit. Tradition taken in this sense is actualized in the preaching of the Word, in the administration of the Sacraments and worship, in Christian teaching and theology, and in mission and witness to Christ by the lives of the members of the Church.

46. What is transmitted in the process of tradition is the Christian faith, not only as a sum of tenets, but as a living reality transmitted through the operation of the Holy Spirit. We can speak of the Christian Tradition (with a capital T), whose content is God's revelation and self-giving in Christ, present in the life of the Church.

47. But this Tradition which is the work of the Holy Spirit is embodied in traditions (in the two senses of the word, both as referring to diversity in forms of expression, and in the sense of separate communions). The traditions in Christian history are distinct from, and yet connected with, the Tradition. They are the expressions and manifestations in diverse historical forms of the one truth and reality which is Christ.

48. This evaluation of the traditions poses serious problems. For some, questions such as these are raised. Is it possible to determine more precisely what the content of the one Tradition is, and by what means? Do all traditions which claim to be Christian contain the Tradition? How can we distinguish between traditions embodying the true Tradition and merely human traditions? Where do we find the genuine Tradition, and where impoverished tradition or even distortion of tradition? Tradition can be a faithful transmission of the Gospel, but also a distortion of it. In this ambiguity the seriousness of the problem of tradition is indicated.

49. These questions imply the search for a criterion. This has been a main concern for the Church since its beginning. In the New Testament we find warnings against false teaching and deviations from the truth of the Gospel. For the post-apostolic Church the appeal to the Tradition received from the apostles became the criterion. As this Tradition was embodied in the apostolic writings, it became natural to use those writings as an authority for determining where the true Tradition was to be found. In the midst of all tradition, these early records of divine revelation have a special basic value, because of their apostolic character. But the Gnostic crisis in the second century shows that the mere existence of apostolic writings did not solve the problem. The question of interpretation arose as soon as the appeal to written documents made its appearance. When the canon of the New Testament had been finally defined and recognized by the Church, it was still more natural to use this body of writings as an indispensable criterion.

50. The Tradition in its written form, as Holy Scripture (comprising both the Old and the New Testament), has to be interpreted by the Church in ever new situations. Such interpretation of the Tradition is to be found in the crystallization of tradition in the creeds, the liturgical forms of the sacraments and other forms of worship, and also in the preaching of the Word and in theological expositions of the Church's doctrine. A mere reiteration of the words of Holy Scripture would be a betrayal of the Gospel which has to be made understandable and has to convey a challenge to the world.

51. The necessity of interpretation raises again the question of the criterion for the genuine Tradition. Throughout the history of the Church the criterion has been sought in the Holy Scriptures rightly interpreted. But what is "right interpretation"?

52. The Scriptures as documents can be letter only. It is the Spirit who is the Lord and Giver of life. Accordingly we may say that the right interpretation (taking the words in the widest possible sense) is that interpretation which is guided by the Holy Spirit. But this does not solve the problem of criterion. We arrive at the quest for a hermeneutical principle.

53. This problem has been dealt with in different ways by the various churches. In some confessional traditions the accepted hermeneutical principle has been that any

portion of Scripture is to be interpreted in the light of Scripture as a whole. In others the key has been sought in what is considered to be the centre of Holy Scripture, and the emphasis has been primarily on the Incarnation, or on the Atonement and Redemption, or on justification by faith, or again on the message of the nearness of the Kingdom of God, or on the ethical teachings of Jesus. In yet others, all emphasis is laid upon what Scripture says to the individual conscience, under the guidance of the Holy Spirit. In the Orthodox Church the hermeneutical key is found in the mind of the Church, especially as expressed in the Fathers of the Church and in the Ecumenical Councils. In the Roman Catholic Church the key is found in the deposit of faith, of which the Church's *magisterium* is the guardian. In other traditions again the creeds, complemented by confessional documents or by the definitions of Ecumenical Councils and the witness of the Fathers, are considered to give the right key to the understanding of Scripture. In none of these cases where the principle of interpretation is found elsewhere than in Scripture is the authority thought to be alien to the central concept of Holy Scripture. On the contrary, it is considered as providing just a key to the understanding of what is said in Scripture.

54. Loyalty to our confessional understanding of Holy Scripture produces both convergence and divergence in the interpretation of Scripture. For example, an Anglican and a Baptist will certainly agree on many points when they interpret Holy Scripture (in the wide sense of interpretation), but they will disagree on others. As another example, there may be mentioned the divergent interpretations given to Matt. 16.18 in Roman Catholic theology on the one hand, and in Orthodox or Protestant theology on the other. How can we overcome the situation in which we all read Scripture in the light of our own traditions?

55. Modern biblical scholarship has already done much to bring the different churches together by conducting them towards the Tradition. It is along this line that the necessity for further thinking about the hermeneutical problem arises: i.e. how we can reach an adequate interpretation of the Scriptures, so that the Word of God addresses us and Scripture is safeguarded from subjective or arbitrary exegesis. Should not the very fact that God has blessed the Church with the Scriptures demand that we emphasize more than in the past a common study of Scripture whenever representatives of the various churches meet? Should we not study more the Fathers of all periods of the Church and their interpretations of the Scriptures in the light of our ecumenical task? Does not the ecumenical situation demand that we search for the Tradition by re-examining sincerely our own particular traditions?

5. BANGALORE 1978

a) A Common Account of Hope
Final Document

At its plenary meeting in Louvain, Belgium, in 1971, the Faith and Order Commission decided to launch a new study programme: "Giving Account of the Hope that is in Us". Its objective was to give an account of both the common basis of faith and common goal of faith. "To what extent and in what way can we express together what has been entrusted to us in the Gospel of Jesus Christ?"[1] From the outset a common "statement" was envisaged.

First of all, groups in all parts of the world were invited to study the theme and commit their findings to paper. The first responses were discussed at the next plenary Commission meeting in Accra, Ghana, in 1974 and summarized in a first "Affirmation of Hope in Christ".[2] In the succeeding years a surprisingly rich variety of contemporary testimonies of hope were available for publication[3] and these were evaluated at two consultations in 1977 and 1978. A selection of these testimonies was sent as preparatory material for those attending the full Commission meeting in Bangalore.[4] Discussions in Bangalore began with prepared "notes for discussion"[5] and then continued in ten smaller groups. The process was concluded on 30 August 1978 with the unanimous adoption of the "common account of hope".

The statement is divided into seven parts:
I.   Thanksgiving
II.   Voices of hope

---

[1] "Faith and Order, Louvain 1971: Study Reports and Documents", *Faith and Order Paper No. 59,* Geneva, WCC, 1971, p.239.
[2] "Uniting in Hope: Accra 1974", *Faith and Order Paper No. 72,* Geneva, WCC, 1975.
[3] In four booklets: (1) *Study Encounter* XI, 2, 1975; (2) *Study Encounter* XII, 1-2, 1976; (3) "Giving Account of the Hope Today", *Faith and Order Paper No. 81,* 1976; (4) "Giving Account of the Hope Together", *Faith and Order Paper No. 86,* 1978.
[4] "Sharing in One Hope: Bangalore 1978", *Faith and Order Paper No. 92,* Geneva, WCC, 1979, pp.51-145.
[5] *The Reasons for Our Hope* (notes for discussion), in "Giving Account of the Hope: Discussion Papers", FO/78:6, June 1978, pp.1-12.

III. Hopes encounter hopes
IV. Our hope in God
V. The church: a communion of hope
VI. Shared hopes in the face of the common future
VII. Hope as the invitation to risk
One of the key affirmations of the statement reads: "The Christian hope is a resistance movement against fatalism."

● Text in "Sharing in One Hope: Bangalore 1978", reports and documents from the meeting of the Faith and Order Commission, *Faith and Order Paper No. 92*, Geneva, WCC, 1979, pp.1-11.

I. Thanksgiving

Blessed be God! The Father and the Son and the Holy Spirit. Christ is our hope: the power of love stronger than the world. He lived on the earth: God's Yes for the world's salvation. He was crucified and is risen: the first fruit of the new humanity.

He is present in his Church; He is present in those who suffer;
— He is with us.
He will appear again in glory: our judgment and our hope,
— unveiling this Yes of salvation.
We have this gift from the living God.
— His spirit poured into our hearts.
Let us give thanks with rejoicing!

II. Voices of hope

In many places all over the world people are participating in this "yes". Even among the cries of despair we hear voices of hope.
A Latin American song:

Since He came into the world and into history;
broke down silence and suffering;
filled the world with his glory;
was the light in the coldness of our night;
was born in a dark manger;
in His life sowed love and light;
broke hardened hearts
but lifted up dejected souls;
So today we have hope;
today we persevere in our struggle;
today we face our future with confidence,
in this land which is ours.

Everywhere songs of hope and longing are being sung. We have been able to listen to many of them in the accounts of hope which we have studied. There is a bewildering variety: from those who hunger for bread, justice and peace; those who long for freedom from religious or political persecution; those who hope for deliverance from infirmities of body and mind; those seeking a new community of women and men; those who search for cultural authenticity; those who hope for a responsible use of science and technology; those who evangelize and work for the spread of the Gospel; those who labour for the visible unity of the churches. We have even become aware of intimations of hope from those who are silenced. In their silence itself is a word for those who can hear it.

III. Hopes encounter hopes

We have been listening to these voices because we ourselves are called to give an account of our hope (1 Pet.3:15). We are a group of 160 Christians gathered in India from many churches in every continent as the Faith and Order Commission of the World Council of Churches. Our mandate from the churches is to further the cause of visible unity. Central to that task is the growth of an ability among the churches to bear common witness to their faith.

As a preliminary step, the Commission has been working since 1971 to formulate a common account of hope. Today, we want to speak of our common future to church members everywhere and to any others who may be willing to listen. The problems have been formidable: confessional and cultural diversity, sharply divided political and social situations, the threat to relevance in a rapidly changing world, the need to draw upon new voices which have been marginal to the discussion of theology thus far. Yet, the common attempt itself has become a source of hope. We have discovered afresh the force of the Gospel to inspire common witness. We have been drawn together and new ways of communication have been established among those who hope.

The common account is based on the encounter among various accounts of hope. This encounter has proved significant. It has helped us distinguish between one level where specific things are hoped for, for example, to have enough to eat, and another level where the question emerges: "Why do you hope at all for what you cannot see?" (cf. Rom. 8:25).

The encounter has been *humbling* because of the provocation to become more self-critical. It is necessary to distinguish hopes from desires or wishes. Some of our expectations are little more than unexamined desires and wishes, or expressions of fears and anxieties. And these often contradict one another. A desire for an expanding economy in one country can cause poverty in another. A necessary struggle for power in one country may appear to contradict the responsible use of power in another. Some even say: "One's hopes become another's despair."

But we refuse to believe that the hopes of humankind are ultimately contradictory: God-given hopes are many-faceted and complementary. But human hearts are sinful, and their desires can be false. They need to be judged and purified. Christ is the judge of human hopes. He weighs our desires.

The encounter of human hopes is also *encouraging* to us, for in it we become aware of the power and direction of the Holy Spirit. Through that Spirit the hopes of others speak to us, often unintentionally, sometimes unexpectedly. The encounter of hopes points to a wider communion of hope with each other and with God's Spirit. Beyond that it can point to a wider communion between those who believe in Christ and those who do not. "One's hope becomes another's hope!"

IV. Our hope in God

The church is a fellowship of those who hope in God, and therefore a real encounter among our hopes is possible.

We are not the first to express such faith and hope. Many have gone before us. A cloud of witnesses surrounds us who gave their testimony even at the cost of their lives. The faithful witness of the human hope in God is Jesus Christ. And every time we celebrate the remembrance of him, we receive grace and power to give our testimony.

Jesus Christ is our hope. In his life he was completely obedient to God the Father. He identified himself with those who were despised by society. He preached a message of God's coming kingdom which sustains us with its vision of a tomorrow that cannot be denied. He was arrested, tortured and killed. In his cross and resurrection God dethroned the forces of sin, guilt, death and evil. God reconciled the world to himself. God defended his image in all — children, women and men — and opened to them a new dignity as the children of God. That is why we hope that everything which threatens human dignity, including death itself, will ultimately be destroyed: ultimately, for in this world those threatening forces, though overcome, are not yet destroyed; our present hope is anchored in God's actions in history and in the eternal life of the age to come. But we know that we are accepted by God as forgiven sinners, and therefore we are certain that we can here and now be co-workers with God in pointing to his rule. In Christ as in a mirror we see the will of God. Christ will come as the revelation of truth and righteousness. The ultimate judgment of the world is his, our assurance that the murderer will never ultimately triumph over the victim. This ultimate hope in the lordship of Christ and the coming kingdom of God cannot be divorced from, or identified with, our historical hopes for freedom, justice, equality and peace. Our struggles for human wellbeing are judged and transfigured in a life with God marked by the free gifts of forgiveness, new life and salvation. In anticipation we dare to hope that human longings and struggles are justified and that their ultimate outcome is in God's hands.

In giving his Son not to condemn the world but that the world might be saved through him (John 3:17), *God the Father* affirmed the world as his creation and manifested his faithfulness to it. We too will be faithful to the world. He loved the work of his hands and called it good. Therefore we hope for a society which does not violate the goodness of nature. In trust that He has willed the creative powers of the human creature as well, we have hope that human reason can be used responsibly in shaping the future. The Creator is righteous; his law and his justice will restore the right of those who are oppressed. Therefore we have hope in our striving for justice and human rights. This world is full of suffering and injustice, but as God's world it is the place of our obedience in the confidence that He will not let it fall out of his hand. When, following Christ, we fight against evil, we do so not only in the hope for more human happiness; we do it also in the hope that oppressors will repent and be oppressors no longer, and that all will turn to God in faith and together receive the blessing that He wills for them.

The living God becomes accessible to us by the *Holy Spirit* who confirms God's presence in our lives and makes us members of Christ's Body, the Church. By the Holy Spirit, we have hope that already our lives can show signs of the new creation. By the Spirit, God gives us his power and guidance. The Spirit sets us free from the powers of darkness, stirs up our spirits, rekindles our energies, gives us visions and dreams, presses us to work for real communion, overcoming the barriers which sin has erected. Through the Holy Spirit, God's love is poured into our hearts. There can be no real hope without love. Acting in hope is possible for all: for those who can work openly and visibly, and also for those whose love and action are expressed in suffering and prayer. Since God's promises concern the whole of humanity, we hope and pray that the Spirit will empower us to proclaim the good news of salvation and to strive for its realization in life. That is the one mission of the individual and of the Church as such.

V. The Church: a communion of hope

"The Lord is risen!" He is present and powerful in the midst of his people, making them members of one another and of his Body, the Church. He is the Master; they are the disciples. He is the vine; they are the branches. To those who put their faith in him, He gives a communion of hope, and He sends them as a sign of hope for all humanity.

They share his own divine life, the communion of the Father, Son and Holy Spirit, one God whose own being is mirrored in all creaturely love. In the Christian community of faith, sharing in the confession of the apostles, gathered around God's word and partaking of the sacraments, we are given the power to share with each other. We can rejoice with those who rejoice and weep with those who weep. We can bear one another's burdens. It is in this communion that we also learn to share one another's hopes. This encounter of hope in itself has been made by God to be a sign in every situation and place: Christ our hope, the power of love!

Because this is the spiritual reality of the Church, we are ashamed of how we in our churches actually look. The communion of hope is so obscured that it is almost unrecognizable. The common witness is wounded by divisions. Too often and too transparently, our churches reflect the sins of society, and are found on the side of the privileged and the powerful. Women are often denied their rightful places of leadership in church life. Members and ministers do not fully recognize each other. More scandalous still, our churches do not yet worship God together around the common table. Many of our contemporaries think it a travesty to call this people a sign of hope. Hope for the renewal and unity of our churches is often our most difficult spiritual task.

Nevertheless, we do hope for the Church of Christ to become more manifest in our churches. We hope for the recovery and fruitfulness of their mission. The communion, though obscured, is not lost; it is grounded not in its members, but in God. The Word has been given to it and the Word endures. The Spirit which has been at work throughout the ages is present in our times to re-establish a credible communion. Built on such foundations, this community will become a community of repentance!

Of this power among the churches we are witnesses. We do have hope for this communion. And we believe that this communion, incomplete as it is, can become a sign of hope for others. Communion in Christ provides the possibility of encounter across the human barriers. It re-establishes relations in mutual respect without sacrificing convictions. It can be a testing ground for the witness which each church bears. Without being pressed into conformity, churches can become accountable to each other. It is also a source of hope because as they live by God's forgiveness, they can extend forgiveness to other churches as well, and find in the witness and commitment of others an enrichment of their own. Finally, communion in Christ is a source of hope when it anticipates the reign of God and does not acquiesce in things as they are.

So the Church thanks God for a foretaste, here and now, of what it hopes for. Long since, it has anticipated its hope in its prayer: "Your kingdom come. Your will be done, on earth as in heaven. Give us our daily bread. Forgive us our sins. Deliver us from evil."

VI. Shared hopes in the face of the common future

"Christ is risen!" What does it mean to have common hope in a world where we face common threats? There are common Christian commitments; concerted action is possible, although the emphases are different in different parts of the world.

Our common hope is threatened by *increasing and already excessive concentrations of power with their threats of exploitation and poverty*. They are responsible for the ever-widening gap between rich and poor, not only between nations but within individual nations. Political exploitation and dependency, hunger and malnutrition are the price paid by the poor for the superabundance of goods and power enjoyed by the rich. Concentration of power also leads to the preservation of the existing and the formation of new class distinctions.

Nevertheless, we share a common hope; for we believe that God has taken sides in this struggle (Ps. 103:6).

Our common future is dominated by our *increasing capacity to shape the physical world*. Science and technology have bettered the human lot. Wisely used, they can help to feed the hungry, heal the sick, develop communication, strengthen community. The refusal to use these powers responsibly on the part of all people everywhere, and especially the ability of the affluent to appropriate these benefits for themselves, threatens us with environmental collapse, biological catastrophies and nuclear destruction. Nevertheless, we hope in the continual action of the Creator Spirit who will not abandon his creatures and who can prompt us to act responsibly as stewards of creation.

The most alarming concentration of power in our time is the *seemingly uncontrollable growth of armaments*. The present arsenal of nuclear warheads held by the superpowers numbers well above 10,000 — more than a million times the annihilating power which devastated Hiroshima. Even the so-called Third World has increased its commitment to armament from eight billion dollars in 1957 to forty billion in 1977. It is important not to overstate our hopes, but God's Spirit opens doors beyond human expectations. Evil is not necessary. The Spirit can plant the leaven of peace in unexpected surroundings, and create hope that it is possible to establish justice without resorting to war.

There are pressures and forces everywhere which threaten to disintegrate the human community. Races, classes, sexes, even religions are set against each other. In all places inherited patterns of society are dissolving and weakening the sense of belonging which community provides. At the same time new forms of community are emerging which in their newness can also create anxieties. Nevertheless, the Spirit works with a surprising freedom, preserving that which sustains life and bringing to birth something genuinely new. Therefore, we can have courage to experiment with new forms of association, new structures and institutions, new forms of human relationships.

Our common hope is threatened by *assaults on human dignity*. Statistics for programmes, stereotypes for discrimination, slaves, victims, or simply the forgotten. Human persons and human possibilities are everywhere threatened today. Individual human rights are violated by arbitrary arrest and "disappearances". We are appalled at the growing numbers of "prisoners of conscience" and at the increasingly systematic use of torture as an ordinary method of exercising power. But social human rights are likewise violated by denial of food, housing, jobs, education and health care, compounded by racism and sexism. There is no part of the world where some of these violations are not present. Those who dehumanize others thereby dehumanize themselves. Nevertheless, we have hope because God affirms the dignity of "the very last".

Commitment to the common future and life itself are eroded by *meaninglessness and absurdity*. In situations of affluence, this may result from "playing by the rules of the game" in a success-oriented culture. In situations of rapid cultural or social change, it may arise in the confusion of being called to fill previously undefined roles. In situations of exploitation, dependency and "marginalization" it may be imposed by the sense of impotence and frustration which comes from the inability to act for oneself or one's class. Nevertheless, we share a common hope, for the Son of God himself withstood the threat of meaninglessness and absurdity. God's healing word will come with different accents: to the affluent it is the challenge to renounce false gods; to the confused it offers the light of Jesus' life to clarify perplexity; to the dispossessed it comes as a challenge and empowerment to take up the struggle. To all it promises that life makes sense.

The problems seem overwhelming. The cry for realism is deep in each one of us, and it expresses a kind of ultimate question about Christian hope. But we believe that each rightful action counts because God blesses it. With the five loaves and two fishes which the young man brought to him, Jesus fed the multitude. Hope lives with special power in small actions.

Above all, we dare to hope in the face of *death*, the ultimate threat to our aspirations and actions. As sinners under the judgment of God we are bound to die. Therefore death is the "last enemy" of our hopes. It penetrates life with paralyzing power, especially where it takes away people before they have had a chance to live. Yet hope in Christ focuses precisely on this enemy. The triumph of God's grace is the resurrection — Christ's victory over death and sin with all their allies. The apostle says: "If in this life only we have hope in Christ, we are of all men most miserable" (1 Cor. 15:19). We rejoice that his crucial *if* is answered unequivocally: *not only* in this life. It is this "not only" that gives life its hopeful horizon. Fate is broken. There is a tomorrow for us today — and in the day of our death.

The Christian hope is a resistance movement against fatalism.

VII. Hope as the invitation to risk

"Christ is risen!" But the risen one is the crucified. This means that our life in hope is not a guarantee of safety, but an invitation to risk. To live in hope is never to have reached our goal, but always to be on a risk-laden journey.

To live in hope is to risk *struggle*. We are denied the privilege of being "neither hot nor cold", of adopting a pseudo-neutrality that covertly supports those in power. To struggle is to take sides openly, saying "yes" to some at the cost of saying "no" to others. If patient endurance is all that is possible, that too can be a form of protest. We can afford to fail, since God can use our failures in the fulfilment of his purposes. Hope embraces the risk of struggle.

To live in hope is to risk *the use of power*. Some have too much power to be trusted; most have too little to be effective. It is not right that a few should impose their decisions on the many. We must seek identification with the powerless and help them escape a life of dependency on others. But we must also minister to those in power, asking them to listen to "the wretched of the earth", to use power justly and share it with those who stand outside. Hope embraces the risk of the responsible use of power.

To live in hope is to risk *affirming the new and re-affirming the old*. To affirm the new is to acknowledge that Christ goes before us; to reaffirm the old is to acknowledge that He did not come to destroy, but to fulfil, for He is the same yesterday, today and forever. Hope sends us on untried ways and calls us to discover the new whether it is represented by the challenge of new cultural contexts, the call for new life-styles or previously unheeded cries for liberation. When we lock ourselves to the past we may become deaf to the groanings and pleadings of the Spirit. Yet, the Spirit will always reaffirm the truth of Christ. Therefore, hope embraces the risk both of new departures and of faithfulness to the past against the temptation of passing fashions.

To live in hope is to risk *self-criticism as the channel of renewal*. Within culture and within the Church, renewal comes through challenge to what is established, so that it can be revitalized or cast aside. But renewal in the true sense of the word is not within our power. It arises as we are judged by God and driven to repent and bear fruits worthy of repentance. This can also include, however, a certain light-heartedness, a willingness not to take ourselves too seriously. Only those who can smile at themselves can be ultimately serious about other selves. Hope embraces the risk of self-criticism as the way to renewal.

To live in hope is to risk *dialogue*. Genuine encounter with others can challenge us to vacate positions of special privilege and render ourselves vulnerable. To enter dialogue with people of other faiths and ideologies is to risk having one's own faith shaken and to discover that there are other ways to state the truth than we have yet learned ourselves. The dialogue with Jews holds special promise and difficulties; promise of enrichment, because with no other people are our common roots so deep; difficulties, because the theological and political questions which arise threaten to divide us from one another as well as from them. Because in dialogue we can receive a fuller understanding of our own faith and a deeper understanding of our neighbour, hope is not afraid of dialogue.

To live in hope is to risk *cooperation with those from whom we differ*. When we join with others in immediate human tasks we risk being used and absorbed. But when we find those who, not acknowledging the name of Christ, are serving humanity, we can side with them, both for the sake of all God's children and, if occasion permits, to give account of our own hope. Hope is willing to risk cooperation with those who are different.

To live in hope is to risk *new forms of community between women and men*. This calls for a grace and understanding that can take past structures, stereotypes and resentments and transmute them into new forms of living together, both inside and outside the Church. We are challenged to discover on the basis of scripture and tradition contemporary ways to express mutuality and equality, and especially to understand anew what it means to be created in the image of God.

To live in hope is to risk *scorn*. To most of our contemporaries our hope appears vain; it is at best irrelevant, at worst malevolent. To live in hope is nevertheless to continue to witness to the saving power of Jesus Christ, whether we are ignored or attacked. Because to spread the Gospel is not only our mission but also our privilege and joy, we can run the risk of ridicule.

To live in hope is to risk *death for the sake of that hope*. No Christian may decide that someone else should be a martyr. But each of us confronts the likelihood that faithful witness can be costly witness. The Christian hope is not that death can be avoided, but that death can be overcome. Those who truly live in hope have come to terms with death and can risk dying with Christ. For some that is rhetoric; for others it is the bedrock assurance from which they face each new day. To live in hope is to embrace the risk of death for the sake of that hope.

> "The saying is sure
>   if we have died with him, we shall also live with him;
>   if we suffer, we shall also reign with him;
>   if we deny him, he also will deny us;
>   if we are faithless, he remains faithful;
> for he cannot deny himself." (II Tim. 2:11-13)

b) A Common Statement of Our Faith
From the Report of Committee II

Work on the "Account of Hope" was thought of from the very start as a first attempt "to give account of our faith today".[1] At the end of this process in Bangalore in 1978, the Faith and Order Commission resolved to take up the theme of Lausanne 1927 and to start work on a "consensus in the apostolic faith".[2] The Bangalore report notes here:

> *Committee II reflected on the way in which the one Church is based on the confession of the one apostolic faith. Instead of proposing a set of general considerations about a possible confession of faith, the committee immediately tried to formulate a common statement of faith. Not surprisingly this attempt met with many problems. But the committee felt that the problems to be worked on in future could be brought out much more sharply by offering an actual statement.[3]*

The following statement, therefore, was drafted in Bangalore itself, with no prior drafts to work on. It consists of a preamble and two parts. Part I summarizes faith in Jesus Christ, God the Father and the Holy Spirit, as well as the "community of the faithful"; Part II develops the doxology found in Ephesians 1:3-15. The authors make the following comment on their statement:

> *We recommend to the Faith and Order Commission to receive this statement as a first attempt to state our faith, knowing full well that it represents nothing more than a proposal to be worked on.[4]*

● Text in "Sharing in One Hope: Bangalore 1978", *Faith and Order Paper No. 92*, Geneva, WCC, 1979, pp.244-46.

---

[1] Faith and Order, Louvain 1971, Study Reports and Documents, *Faith and Order Paper No. 59*, Geneva, 1971, p.239f.
[2] "Sharing in One Hope: Bangalore 1978", p.243.
[3] *Ibid.*, p.244.
[4] *Ibid.*, p.244.

Preamble

As we seek to give a common statement of our faith, we are mindful of the existing fellowship of churches which is marked by a common confession of "the Lord Jesus Christ as God and Saviour according to the Scriptures". Already we have joined hands seeking to fulfil together our "common calling to the glory of the one God, Father, Son and Holy Spirit".

Because we have travelled together on the road of faith, experiencing, in spite of our historical divisions, the unifying power of Jesus Christ and his salvation and growing together in his service, we desire to express more fully our common faith in the triune God who has called us to himself and wants us to share in his mission for the salvation of all humankind.

As we seek to confess our faith together, we want to be faithful to the apostolic faith according to the Scriptures, handed down to us through the centuries. At the same time we want to face the new situation and the challenge for mission today. Furthermore, we are aware that a common confession of faith should be the sign of our reconciliation.

Part I

As Christians we confess Jesus Christ, the only source of salvation for humankind and for each individual human person. He is the one Lord of his Church, the cornerstone of its unity. The Church is based on his ministry, remembers in her worship his incarnation, his suffering, crucifixion and death, proclaims with joy his resurrection and eagerly awaits his second coming. As our Saviour he is truly God and truly man. He has authority to grant us communion with God in the presence of his reign, which overcomes the power of death and sin in every misery, division and separation among us; but he also shares in our sufferings and temptations so that in spite of them we may have confidence in him and in the promise of his kingdom. He is the new Adam, in whom we recognize the destiny of human beings and into whose image our lives shall be transformed.

In Jesus' ministry we encounter the one God and creator of all things, whose eternal love is concerned for every single human person and thus constitutes the dignity of each human being. God, the Holy Spirit is the eternal link of love, between God the Father, and God the Son, and spreads abroad God's love to all his creatures to overcome their miseries and separations. In the ministry of the Spirit we receive life and are transfigured, inspired and liberated by the divine presence among his creatures and are sealed in hope. God, the Father, Son and Holy Spirit extends love and judgment to all creation to overcome its separations and calls the Church into the unity of one body, in order to be more fully the sign of a new humanity.

The one faith is confessed and lived in the community of the faithful who have been called through the preaching of the Gospel and gather around the Lord in the Spirit. We enter into this community through baptism which is our participation in the death and resurrection of Jesus Christ. We are incorporated into the eucharistic community in which the Word is proclaimed and the sacrament duly celebrated.

The one faith is the full responsibility of each member of the community, not, however, separately one from the other, but in communion. The presence of the Lord in the midst of his people expresses itself in a variety of charisms and services, which equip them for their mission among men. Such charisms and services are the instruments of the Holy Spirit in the building up of the Church, enabling its community to persevere in the apostolic teaching, in fraternal communion, in the breaking of bread, and in prayer (cf. Acts 2:42). The one(s) who presides over the community has the particular responsibility of being, in the Holy Spirit, the servant of the unity of the Church by the proclamation of the Word in the eucharistic community. His (their) service aims at reinforcing the communication in the community, with a vision of fuller communion.

The confession of the one faith is not a question of majority, but rather, it is a confession in one Spirit. Such a confession naturally implies a total commitment of life on the part of all members of the community.

The community experiences a communion in one Spirit which is not limited to one period in time or to one given place (*hic et nunc*); it is the communion with all witnesses to the apostolic faith in all places and at all times. It is a confession in the communion of saints.

Part II

Growing together in one faith, the divided Christian communities are prepared to share already now a doxology, taken from our common heritage, the Scriptures. One passage which condenses many aspects of our common confession is to be found in Ephesians 1:3-15.

Together with this doxology:

We confess God's involvement in the history of humankind, revealed through Israel, fulfilled in Jesus Christ, communicated to us by the Holy Spirit, into which fulfilment all humanity is called;

we confess the destiny and dignity of all *human beings*, rooted in God's initiative and design;

we confess our dependence upon *God's redeeming and liberating grace*, because we are caught up in the ambiguities of our history and because we live in sin;

we confess the reality of the *Event of Jesus Christ* — his life, his death, his resurrection — and the reality of our answer of faith, given to that Event, that brings us, through the Spirit, to the incorporation into Christ, which means our salvation;

we confess the reality of *the Church*, being the Body of Christ, called to be the nucleus and servant of the unity of humankind and of the universe. We confess our responsibility as Christians to have the mind of Christ and to live and act accordingly in the community of humankind; faith without work is dead;

we confess the presence and the working of *the Spirit*, the pledge and seal of the kingdom, into which we are confirmed.

II.
Assemblies of the
World Council of Churches

1. AMSTERDAM 1948

a) The Church's Witness to God's Design
From the Report of Section II

The message of the Amsterdam Assembly to all Christians opens with the words: "The World Council of Churches, meeting at Amsterdam, sends this message of greeting to all who are in Christ, and to all who are willing to hear... We are one in acknowledging Him as our God and Saviour." [1]

At the Assembly, which met from 22 August to 4 September, Sections I and II were mainly concerned with "God's Design" under the rubric: "The Church's Witness to God's Design". A few months earlier a study volume with the same title had appeared on this theme, with essays on various basic aspects, summarizing documents from a number of preparatory conferences, [2] *and sent as preparatory material to the members of section II. The section report had gone through four stages before being accepted by the full Assembly and recommended to the churches "for their serious consideration and appropriate action". The report is in five sections:*

I.   The purpose of God
II. The present situation
III. The church's task in the present day
IV. Missionary and evangelistic strategy
V.   "Now is the accepted time"

We reproduce here sections I to III.

● Text in *The First Assembly of the World Council of Churches*, ed. W.A. Visser 't Hooft, London, 1949, pp.64-68.

---

[1] *The First Assembly of the World Council of Churches*, p.9
[2] *The Church's Witness to God's Design*. Man's Disorder and God's Design II. Amsterdam Assembly Series, 1948.

I. The Purpose of God

The purpose of God is to reconcile all men to Himself and to one another in Jesus Christ his Son. That purpose was made manifest in Jesus Christ — His incarnation, His ministry of service, His death on the Cross, His resurrection and ascension. It continues in the gift of the Holy Spirit, in the command to make disciples of all nations, and in the abiding presence of Christ with His Church. It looks forward to its consummation in the gathering together of all things in Christ. Much in that purpose is still hidden from us. Three things are perfectly plain:

All that we need to know concerning God's purpose is already revealed in Christ.

It is God's will that the Gospel should be proclaimed to all men everywhere.

God is pleased to use human obedience in the fulfilment of His purpose.

To the Church, then, is given the privilege of so making Christ known to men that each is confronted with the necessity of a personal decision, Yes or No. The Gospel is the expression both of God's love to man, and of His claim to man's obedience. In this lies the solemnity of the decision. Those who obey are delivered from the power of the world in which sin reigns, and already, in the fellowship of the children of God, have the experience of eternal life. Those who reject the life of God remain under His judgment and are in danger of sharing in the impending doom of the world that is passing away.

II. The Present Situation

Two world wars have shaken the structure of the world. Social and political convulsions rage everywhere. The mood of many swings between despair, frustration and blind indifference. The millions of Asia and Africa, filled with new hope, are determined to seize now the opportunity of shaping their own destiny. Mankind, so clearly called even by its own interests to live at peace, seems still rent by a fanaticism of mutual destruction.

The word *faith* has acquired a new context. For most men it is now faith in the new society, now to be founded once for all, in which the "good life" will be realised. Even in the present-day confusion, there are still many who believe that man, by wise planning, can master his own situation. Such men are interested not in absolute truth, but in achievement. In face of many religions and philosophies, it is held that all truth is relative, and so the necessity of a costly personal decision is evaded.

A formidable obstacle to Christian faith is the conviction that it belongs definitely to a historical phase now past. To those who know little of it, it seems merely irrelevant. More thoughtful men, who hold that it enshrines some spiritual and cultural values, regard it as no longer honestly tenable as a system of belief. And yet there is an earnest desire for clearly formulated truth. The religions of Asia and Africa are being challenged and profoundly modified. In the period of transition, the minds of millions are more than usual open to the Gospel. But the tendency in these countries to press an ancient religion into service as one foundation for a politically homogeneous state already threatens the liberty of Christian action.

So the Church sees the world. What does the world see, or think it sees, when it looks at the Church?

It is a Church divided, and in its separated parts are often found hesitancy, complacency or the desire to domineer.

It is a Church that has largely lost touch with the dominant realities of modern life, and still tries to meet the modern world with a language and technique that may have been appropriate two hundred years ago.

It is a Church that, by its failure to speak effectively on the subject of war, has appeared impotent to deal with the realities of the human situation.

It is a Church accused by many of having been blind to the movement of God in history, of having sided with the vested interests of society and state, and of having failed to kindle the vision and to purify the will of men in a changing world.

It is a Church under suspicion in many quarters of having used its missionary enterprise to further the foreign policies of states and the imperialistic designs of the powers of the West.

Much in this indictment may be untrue; but the Church is called to deep shame and penitence for its failure to manifest Jesus Christ to men as He really is. Yet the Church is still the Church of God, in which, and in which alone He is pleased to reveal Himself and His redemptive purpose in Jesus Christ, in Whom and in Whom alone the renewal of man's life is possible.

It is a Church to which, through the upheavals of the modern world, God cries aloud and says, "Come let us reason together" (Isaiah i,18).

It is a Church that is, to millions of faithful people, the place where they receive the grace of Christ and are given strength to live by the power of His victory.

It is a Church awaking to its great opportunity to enter as the minister of the redemption wrought by Christ into that world with which God has confronted us.

It is a Church that to-day desires to treat evangelism as the common task of all the churches, and transcends the traditional distinction between the so-called Christian and so-called non-Christian lands.

The present day is the beginning of a new epoch of missionary enterprise, calling for the pioneering spirit, and for the dedication of many lives to the service of the Gospel of God.

III. The Church's Task in the Present Day

The duty of the Church at such a time can be expressed simply in one sentence — it is required to be faithful to the Gospel and to realise more fully its own nature as the Church. But fulfilment of this duty involves a revolution in thought and practice.

A. Worship and Witness

Worship and witness have sometimes been held in separation, but they belong inseparably together, as the fulfilment of the great command that men should love God and should love their neighbour as themselves.

When the ordinary man speaks of the Church, he thinks of a group of people worshipping in a building. By what that group is, the Church is judged. Effective witness becomes possible only as each worshipping group is so filled with the joy of the risen and living Lord that even the outsider becomes aware that, when the Church speaks, it speaks of real things.

But a worshipping group of individuals is not necessarily a community. It is essential that each group becomes a real fellowship, through acceptance by all of full Christian responsibility for mutual service, and by breaking down the barriers of race and class. It is intolerable that anyone should be excluded, because of his race or colour, from any Christian place of worship.

The world to-day is hungry for community. But to many it seems that the fellowship of the churches is much less satisfying than that which they find in their own secular or religious organisations and brotherhood. This cannot be put right until the churches more recognisably bear the marks of the Lord Jesus, and cease to hinder others, by the poverty of the fellowship they offer, from coming to Him.

B. A People of God in the World

The Church must find its way to the places where men really live. It must penetrate the alienated world from within, and make the minds of men familiar with the elementary realities of God, of sin and of purpose in life. This can be done partly through new ventures of self-identification by Christians with the life of that world, partly through Christians making the word of the Gospel heard in the places where decisions are made that affect the lives of men. It can be done fully only if, by the inspiration of the Holy Spirit, the Church recovers the spirit of prophecy to discern the signs of the times, to see the purpose of God working in the immense movements and revolutions of the present age, and again to speak to the nations the word of God with authority.

C. The Ecumenical Sense

Each Christian group must be conscious of the world-wide fellowship of which it is a part. Each Sunday as it comes is a reminder of the innumerable company throughout the world, who on that day are worshipping the same Lord Jesus Christ as God and Saviour. It can attain to fulness of Christian life only as it accepts its place in the great purpose of God that all men shall be saved, and takes up the responsibility for prayer, service and sacrificial missionary enterprise involved in that acceptance.

b) The Christian Approach to the Jews
From the Report of Committee IV

The task assigned to Committee IV in Amsterdam was to examine particular "concerns of the churches" raised at the Assembly by individual member churches. In all there were four subjects on its agenda:

1. The life and work of women in the church
2. The significance of the laity in the church
3. The Christian approach to the Jews
4. Christian reconstruction and interchurch aid

The report on Christian-Jewish relations sparked off a lively discussion in plenary, the views expressed ranging from unqualified endorsement to outright rejection. Finally, however, it was received by the Assembly as it stood. The outline of the report was as follows:

Introduction
1. The church's commission to preach the gospel to all men
2. The special meaning of the Jewish people for Christian faith
3. Barriers to be overcome
4. The Christian witness to the Jewish people
5. The emergence of Israel as a state
Recommendations
We reproduce here the text of the introduction and sections 1 to 3 and 5.

● Text in *The First Assembly of the World Council of Churches*, ed. W. A. Visser 't Hooft, London, 1949, pp.160-61.

The Report was received by the Assembly and commended to the churches for their serious consideration and appropriate action.

Introduction

A concern for the Christian approach to the Jewish people confronts us inescapably, as we meet together to look with open and penitent eyes on man's disorder and to rediscover together God's eternal purpose for His Church. This concern is ours because it is first a concern of God made known to us in Christ. No people in His one world have suffered more bitterly from the disorder of man than the Jewish people. We cannot forget that we meet in a land from which 110,000 Jews were taken to be murdered. Nor can we forget that we meet only five years after the extermination of 6 million Jews. To the Jews our God has bound us in a special solidarity linking our destinies together in His design. We call upon all our churches to make this concern their own as we share with them the results of our too brief wrestling with it.

1. The Church's commission to preach the Gospel to all men

All of our churches stand under the commission of our common Lord, "Go ye into all the world and preach the Gospel to every creature." The fulfilment of this commission requires that we include the Jewish people in our evangelistic task.

2. The special meaning of the Jewish people for Christian faith

In the design of God, Israel has a unique position. It was Israel with whom God made His covenant by the call of Abraham. It was Israel to whom God revealed His name and gave His law. It was to Israel that He sent His Prophets with their message of judgment and of grace. By the history of Israel God prepared the manger in which in the fulness of time He put the Redeemer of all mankind, Jesus Christ. The Church has received this spiritual heritage from Israel and is therefore in honour bound to render it back in the light of the Cross. We have, therefore, in humble conviction to proclaim to the Jews, "The Messiah for Whom you wait has come." The promise has been fulfilled by the coming of Jesus Christ.

For many the continued existence of a Jewish people which does not acknowledge Christ is a divine mystery which finds its only sufficient explanation in the purpose of God's unchanging faithfulness and mercy (Romans xi, 25-29).

3. Barriers to be overcome

Before our churches can hope to fulfil the commission laid upon us by our Lord there are high barriers to be overcome. We speak here particularly of the barriers which we have too often helped to build and which we alone can remove.

We must acknowledge in all humility that too often we have failed to manifest Christian love towards our Jewish neighbours, or even a resolute will for common social justice. We have failed to fight with all our strength the age-old disorder of man which anti-semitism represents. The churches in the past have helped to foster an image of the Jews as the sole enemies of Christ, which has contributed to anti-semitism in the secular world. In many lands virulent anti-semitism still threatens and in other lands the Jews are subjected to many indignities.

We call upon all the churches we represent to denounce anti-semitism, no matter what its origin, as absolutely irreconcilable with the profession and practice of the Christian faith. Anti-semitism is sin against God and man.

Only as we give convincing evidence to our Jewish neighbours that we seek for them the common rights and dignities which God wills for His children, can we come to such a meeting with them as would make it possible to share with them the best which God has given us in Christ. ...

5. The emergence of Israel as a state

The establishment of the state "Israel" adds a political dimension to the Christian approach to the Jews and threatens to complicate anti-semitism with political fears and enmities.

On the political aspects of the Palestine problem and the complex conflict of "rights" involved we do not undertake to express a judgment. Nevertheless, we appeal to the nations to deal with the problem not as one of expediency — political, strategic or economic — but as a moral and spiritual question that touches a nerve centre of the world's religious life.

Whatever position may be taken towards the establishment of a Jewish state and towards the "rights" and "wrongs" of Jews and Arabs, of Hebrew Christians and Arab Christians involved, the churches are in duty bound to pray and work for an order in Palestine as just as may be in the midst of our human disorder; to provide within their power for the relief of the victims of this warfare without discrimination; and to seek to influence the nations to provide a refuge for "Displaced Persons" far more generously than has yet been done.

2. EVANSTON 1954

a) Christ — the Hope of the World
A Message from the Second Assembly of the WCC

The main theme of the Second Assembly, held in Evanston, USA, from 15 to 31 August, was "Christ — the Hope of the World". This picked up the theme of the German Evangelical Kirchentag *held in Leipzig (GDR) in the summer of 1954: "Rejoice in hope!" At the very first plenary session of the Assembly a committee was appointed to draft a message to all Christians around the Assembly theme. Members of the Assembly were given an opportunity to comment at a "Hearing" on the first draft of the "Message". The revised version was adopted by the full Assembly on 31 August, after intensive debate.*

The Message is in two parts. In the first (paragraphs 1-5) "The Hope of God's People" is developed in the setting of the hopes and fears of the contemporary world. In the second part (paragraphs 6-11) questions are put to the churches concerning their ecumenical fellowship with one another and their responsibility for the world.

● Text in *The Evanston Report: the Second Assembly of the World Council of Churches 1954*, ed. W.A. Visser 't Hooft, London, 1955, pp.1-3.

To all our fellow Christians, and to our fellowmen everywhere, we send greetings in the name of Jesus Christ. We affirm our faith in Jesus Christ as the hope of the world, and desire to share that faith with all men. May God forgive us that by our sin we have often hidden this hope from the world.

In the ferment of our time there are both hopes and fears. It is indeed good to hope for freedom, justice and peace, and it is God's will that we should have these things. But He has made us for a higher end. He has made us for Himself, that we might know and love Him, worship and serve Him. Nothing other than God can ever satisfy the heart of man. Forgetting this, man becomes his own enemy. He seeks justice but creates oppression. He wants peace, but drifts towards war. His very mastery of nature threatens him with ruin. Whether he acknowledges it or not, he stands under the judgment of God and in the shadow of death.

Here where we stand, Jesus Christ stood with us. He came to us, true God and true Man, to seek and to save. Though we were the enemies of God, Christ died for us. We crucified Him, but God raised Him from the dead. He is risen. He has overcome the powers of sin and death. A new life has begun. And in His risen and ascended power, He has sent forth into the world a new community, bound together by His Spirit, sharing His divine life, and commissioned to make Him known throughout the world. He will come again as Judge and King to bring all things to their consummation. Then we shall see Him as He is and know as we are known. Together with the whole creation we wait for this with eager hope, knowing that God is faithful and that even now He holds all things in His hand.

This is the hope of God's people in every age, and we commend it afresh today to all who will listen. To accept it is to turn from our ways to God's way. It is to live as forgiven sinners, as children growing in His love. It is to have our citizenship in that Kingdom which all man's sin is impotent to destroy, that realm of love and joy and peace which lies about all men, though unseen. It is to enter with Christ into the suffering and despair of men, sharing with them the great secret of that Kingdom which they do not expect. It is to know that whatever men may do, Jesus reigns and shall reign.

With this assurance we can face the powers of evil and the threat of death with a good courage. Delivered from fear we are made free to love. For beyond the judgment of men and the judgment of history lies the judgment of the King who died for all men, and who will judge us according to what we have done to the least of His brethren. Thus our Christian hope directs us towards our neighbour. It constrains us to pray daily, "Thy will be done on earth as it is in heaven," and to act as we pray in every area of life. It begets a life of believing prayer and expectant action, looking to Jesus and pressing forward to the day of His return in glory.

Now we would speak through our member churches directly to each congregation. Six years ago our churches entered into a covenant to form this Council, and affirmed their intention to stay together. We thank God for His blessing on our work and fellowship during these six years. We enter now upon a second stage. To stay together is not enough. We must go forward. As we learn more of our unity in Christ, it becomes the more intolerable that we should be divided. We therefore ask you: Is your church seriously considering its relation to other churches in the light of our Lord's prayer that we may be sanctified in the truth and that we may all be one? Is your congregation, in fellowship with sister congregations around you, doing all it can do to ensure that your neighbours shall hear the voice of the one Shepherd calling all men into the one flock?

The forces that separate men from one another are strong. At our meeting here we have missed the presence of Chinese churches which were with us at Amsterdam. There are other lands and churches unrepresented in our Council, and we long ardently for their fellowship. But we are thankful that, separated as we are by the deepest political divisions of our time, here at Evanston we are united in Christ. And we rejoice also that, in the bond of prayer and a common hope, we maintain communion with our Christian brethren everywhere.

It is from within this communion that we have to speak about the fear and distrust which at present divide our world. Only at the Cross of Christ, where men know themselves as forgiven sinners, can they be made one. It is there that Christians must pray daily for their enemies. It is there that we must seek deliverance from self-righteousness, impatience and fear. And those who know that Christ is risen should have the courage to expect new power to break through every human barrier.

It is not enough that Christians should seek peace for themselves. They must seek justice for others. Great masses of people in many parts of the world are hungry for bread, and are compelled to live in conditions which mock their human worth. Does your church speak and act against such injustice? Millions of men and women are suffering segregation and discrimination on the ground of race. Is your church willing to declare, as this Assembly has declared, that this is contrary to the will of God and to act on that declaration? Do you pray regularly for those who suffer unjust discrimination on grounds of race, religion or political conviction?

The Church of Christ is today a world-wide fellowship, yet there are countless people to whom He is unknown. How much do you care about this? Does your congregation live for itself, or for the world around it and beyond it? Does its common life, and does the daily work of its members in the world, affirm the Lordship of Christ or deny it?

God does not leave any of us to stand alone. In every place He has gathered us together to be His family, in which His gifts and His forgiveness are received. Do you forgive one another as Christ forgave you? Is your congregation a true family of God, where every man can find a home and know that God loves him without limit?

We are not sufficient for these things. But Christ is sufficient. We do not know what is coming to us. But we know Who is coming. It is He who meets us every day and who will meet us at the end — Jesus Christ our Lord.

Therefore we say to you: Rejoice in hope.

b) Our Oneness in Christ and Our Disunity as Churches
From the Report of Section I on Faith and Order

As is clear from the sub-title, there was a direct causal nexus between this theme and the Third World Conference on Faith and Order in Lund (Sweden) in 1952 and in particular with the Lund statement on "Christ and His Church". The preparatory material for members of this section included a study entitled: "Our Oneness in Christ and Our Disunity as Churches".[1] The following report was produced on the basis of a working paper and adopted by the full Assembly on 30 August 1954 after thorough discussion. The document is in three sections:

Introduction
I.   Our oneness in Christ
II. Our disunity as churches
III. The action of faith
Appendix: The declaration of the Orthodox delegates concerning Faith and Order
We reproduce here the text of Parts I and III.

● Text in *The Evanston Report: the Second Assembly of the World Council of Churches*, ed. W.A. Visser 't Hooft, London, 1955, pp.83-87; 89-91.

[1] *Six Ecumenical Surveys: Preparatory Material for the Second Assembly of the World Council of Churches 1954*, New York, 1954, pp.1-55.

I. Our Oneness in Christ

A. Christ's Unifying Work

2. The New Testament conceives of the unity of the Church, not as sociological, but as having its essential reality in Christ Himself and in His indissoluble unity with His people (Acts 9:4ff.; I Cor. 12:12; Jn. 15:1f.). Hence we must still ask Paul's question about division in the Church: "Is Christ divided?" (I Cor. 1:13), and assert with the Apostle the indestructible unity that belongs to the Church in Christ. Christ is the *one* Lord who represents and gathers to Himself the *many* of redeemed humanity and it is therefore He alone who makes the many to be one in the Church (I Cor. 12:12; Eph. 1:10,22; cf. Jn. 14:20; 17:4ff.; I Cor. 6:16f.).

3. The New Testament speaks in many ways of the relationship of Christ and His people to describe their unity in Him. The Church is many members in one body (I Cor. 12:12); the several members are subject to the one Lord as Head of the body (Eph. 1:22; 4:15; 5:23; Col. 1:18; 2:19); the Church is His bride, to be united to Him, the bridegroom (Mk. 2:19; Rev. 19:7; cf. Mt. 22:2ff.; 25:10f.; Lk. 12:36; Eph. 1:22ff.); the faithful are His people (I Pet. 2:9f.; Col. 3:12; Rom. 11:2, 11f., 32); He is the new temple in whom true worship is offered (Jn. 2:19ff.; cf. 4:21ff.) or the one building of which the believers constitute living stones (I Pet. 2:5; Eph. 2:20; cf. I Cor. 3:9); He is the vine, of which we are the branches (Jn. 15:1ff.), or the shepherd whose flock we are (Jn. 10:1ff.).

4. The New Testament thinks of the one life of the Church as deriving from the whole Person and work of Jesus Christ as Saviour and Lord. The Church's unity is grounded in His taking of our nature upon Him; in His own words and works by which the power and life of His kingdom were manifested; in His calling of men into the fellowship of His kingdom, and in the appointing of the Twelve to share in His messianic ministry and work; in His passion and death, where sin was finally conquered and the power of divisiveness defeated; in His resurrection, where He manifested the new man unto whom we all grow (Eph. 4:11ff.), in whom all human divisions are done away (Gal. 3: 28); in His ascension and heavenly reign, by which all history is brought under His authority; in His outpouring of the Holy Spirit on the whole Church at Pentecost, which gives to each subsequent baptismal rite its deepest significance; and in His promise to come again as the triumphant and glorious king. Through the indwelling Spirit, the Comforter, who leads the Church into all truth, the unity of the Church even now is a foretaste of the fulness that is to be because it already is; therefore, the Church can work tirelessly and wait patiently and expectantly for the day when God shall sum up all things in Christ.

B. The Oneness of the Church in its Earthly Pilgrimage

5. From the beginning the Church has been given an indissoluble unity in Christ, by reason of His self-identification with His people. But the Church has never realized the fulness of that unity. From the beginning discord has marred the manifested unity of Christ's people (Lk. 22:24ff.; Mk. 10:35ff.). Thus we may speak of the oneness of the Church in its earthly pilgrimage as a growth from its unity, as given, to its unity, as fully manifested (Eph. 4:3,13). In this way we may think of the Church as we are able to think of the individual believer, who may be said at one and the same time to be both a justified man and a sinner (*simul justus et peccator*). In each Christian there is

both the "new man" who has been created and yet must be put on daily (2 Cor. 5:17) and also the "old man" who has been crucified with Christ and yet must be daily mortified (Col. 3:1-5). So the Church is already one in Christ, by virtue of His identification of Himself with it (Jn. 14:20; 15:1-5) and must become one in Christ, so as to manifest its true unity (Eph. 4:11-16) in the mortification of its divisions.

6. Christ of His love and grace has given His Church such gifts as it needs for its growth from unity to unity. The gifts are severally and together none other than Christ Himself, but each has its place and its function in the life of the Church as it strives to give obedience to its Lord. Christ has given His Spirit, which is the bond of peace and love, and the guide to all truth. He has given apostles, prophets, evangelists, pastors and teachers, that the unity of the body may be continually built up. He has given Scriptures, the preaching of the Word, Baptism and Eucharist by which the Church proclaims the forgiveness of sins and by which, in the power of the Holy Spirit, faith is quickened and nourished. He has given the Church the gift and power of prayer, by which the Church can plead both for its own unity and for the reconciliation of men to God and to one another. He has given it faith and hope and love, that in its own life a new divine unity shall be manifested in deeds, and that its service to the world shall be both a manifestation of unity and a summons to it.

7. The New Testament, therefore, testifies to us that the Church shares in the life both of this world and of that which is to come. Indeed the Church's life is encompassed by a "great cloud of witnesses" (Heb. 12:2) — and the Church must never forget that its citizenship is really there, in the heavenly places (Eph. 2:6). Its responsibilities must be discharged in this present world, but it must never become conformed to the world.

8. Thus the fellowship (*koinonia*) that the members of the Church have is not simply human fellowship; it is fellowship with the Father and with His Son Jesus Christ through the Holy Spirit and fellowship with the saints, in the Church triumphant. In all the Church's life there is being manifested not simply the activity of mortal men, but the life of the whole Church, militant on earth, triumphant in heaven, as it has its unity in the one Lord of the Church, who is its life.

9. But all this cannot be asserted without understanding that the unity given to the Church in Christ, and gifts given to the Church to help and enable it to manifest its given unity, are not for the sake of the Church as an historical society, but for the sake of the world. The Church has its being and its unity in the "Son of Man, who came not to be ministered unto, but to minister and to give his life a ransom for many." The being and unity of the Church belong to Christ and therefore to His mission, to His enduring the Cross for the joy that was set before Him. Christ wrought "one new man" for us all by His death, and it is by entering into His passion for the redemption of a sinful and divided world that the Church finds its unity in its crucified and risen Lord.

C. The Oneness of the Church Partially Realized

10. Jesus Christ has given to His Church the gift of Himself and thereby the means of corporate life. These gifts were given not solely to the Church of New Testament days, nor are they reserved for the Church in some ideal state which ought to exist but unhappily does not. We acknowledge these gifts as being in a real sense present possessions.

11. It would be ungrateful to a merciful God if we did not speak now of those gifts which assure us that the undivided Christ is present amongst us, pouring His life into us all, in spite of our divisions.

12. We all wait upon the Father, through the one Holy Spirit, praying that we may be ready to hear and obey when he takes of the things of Christ and shows them to us. We all read the Holy Scriptures and proclaim the gospel from them in the faith that the Word speaking through them draws us to Himself and into the apostolic faith. We all receive His gift of Baptism whereby, in faith, we are engrafted in Him even while we have not yet allowed it fully to unite us with each other. We all hear His command to "do this" and His word "This is my body... this is my blood" in the Sacrament of the Eucharist, even whilst our celebration of the Lord's Supper is not yet at one Table. We all receive a ministry of the Word and Sacraments, even whilst our ministries are not yet recognized by all and not understood in the same sense. We all are called to be imitators of Christ and to follow Him in moral obedience as we confess Him before men even though we are still unprofitable servants.

13. As we have come to know each other better in the World Council of Churches, we have come to appreciate the immense range of common practice and intention which we share. The *fact* of our common (though diverse) use of these gifts is a powerful evidence of our unity in Christ and a powerful aid to reminding us that unity lies in His work and not in our own achievements. We have also discovered that the old confessional divisions are being criss-crossed by new lines of agreement and disagreement.

14. We give thanks to our Father for these evidences that our unity in Christ is a present reality, both in the World Council of Churches and in relation to other Christians whose fellowship we do not as yet fully enjoy. But the very fact that, in every case, our benefit from these mercies is marred by our separation from each other, compels us now to examine seriously how it is that our disunity as churches contradicts our unity in Christ....

III. The Action of Faith

20. Christ has made us one by breaking down walls of partition. We are nevertheless disunited as churches. How are we to act in the obedience of faith and hope in our one Lord?

21. At least we all ought to be united in thinking of our divisions with repentance: not the repentance we may expect of others, but that which *we* undertake ourselves — cost what it may — even when others are unwilling to follow. True repentance is the acknowledgment before God that we have sinned so as to be caught in the net of inexplicable evil and rendered unable to heal our divisions by ourselves. But we cannot in sincerity and truth repent of our various understandings of God's will for His Church, unless the Spirit Himself reveals that our understandings have been in error. Penitence cannot be hypocrisy. Neither can it truly be expressed without desire for forgiveness and amendment of life.

22. All of us as members of churches believe that we have been entrusted by God with certain elements of the one Church of Christ which we cannot forfeit. But at least we in the World Council of Churches are committed to a fellowship in which we are ready to bring our convictions under scrutiny in the presence of our fellow Christians and in the presence of the living Christ. In common we seek to know the judgment of

the Word of God upon these convictions as to any error which may be involved in them.

23. Together we suggest the following ways in which, being both united and divided, we all must seek to be obedient:

(i) In thanking God joyfully for the actual oneness He has given us in the World Council of Churches, we must try to understand the theological implications of this ecumenical fact and to implement it in the concrete relations of neighbour churches. With the Lund Conference on Faith and Order, we ask the churches "whether they should not act together in all matters except those in which deep differences of conviction compel them to act separately". We do not minimize the deep differences separating some churches. Nor do we ignore the numerous attempts to unite churches and the achievements of such reunion. In the World Council of Churches we still "intend to stay together." But beyond that, as the Holy Spirit may guide us, we intend to unite. "The World Council of Churches is not... a Super-Church."[1] Hence we do not ask the World Council of Churches to initiate plans for union, but to keep providing occasions for honest encounter between divided Christians.

24. (ii) We must all listen together in the midst of our disunity to our one Lord speaking to us through Holy Scripture. This is a hard thing to do. We still struggle to comprehend the meaning and authority of Holy Scripture. Yet whenever we are prepared to undertake together the study of the Word of God and are resolved to be obedient to what we are told, we are on the way toward realizing the oneness of the Church in Christ in the actual state of our dividedness on earth. In this connection we need also to study together the significance of Christian tradition and our various traditions, as reflected in liturgy, preaching and teaching.

25. (iii) We must consider frankly the influence of social and cultural differences upon the matters of faith and order which cause divisions, and also perceive how the events and developments of current history make disunity a most urgent question.

26. (iv) We must speak the truth in love with one another and practise that love towards those with whom we disagree (Eph. 4: 15,25). Sometimes this involves us in judgments which fellow Christians cannot recognize as being made in love. At other times, we are so conscious of both the sin and the cultural conditioning with which all our judgments are infected that we are tempted to be more tolerant than truth allows.

27. (v) We must learn afresh the implications of the one Baptism for our sharing in the one Eucharist. For some, but not for all, it follows that the churches can only be conformed to the dying and rising again in Christ, which both Sacraments set forth, if they renounce their eucharistic separateness. We must explore the deeper meaning of these two sacramental gifts of the Lord to His Church as they are rooted in His own redeeming work.

28. (vi) We must seek to acknowledge beyond the bounds of our own church each ministry that preaches the gospel of reconciliation as a means whereby Christ performs His saving deeds. Especially need we to discover the meaning of the ministry of the laity for Christian unity.

29. (vii) We must bear witness together to the gospel of Him who has already overcome our sins and divisions and who graciously uses sinners as His servants. Our

---

[1] See "The Church, the Churches, and the World Council of Churches," WCC Central Committee, Toronto, 1950.

divided witness is a necessarily effective witness, and indeed a scandal in the face of the non-Christian world. We have scarcely begun to work out the essential connection between "mission" and "unity." Our Lord's own prayer (Jn. 17:21f.) must become our own, not only on our lips but in our lives.

30. (viii) The measure of our concern for unity is the degree to which we pray for it. We cannot expect God to give us unity unless we prepare ourselves to receive His gift by costly and purifying prayer. To pray *together* is to be drawn together. We urge, wherever possible, the observance of the Week of Prayer for Christian Unity, January 18-25 (or some other period suited to local conditions) as a public testimony to prayer as the road to unity.

31. We cannot discern all that will be disclosed to us when we look to Him who is the Head of the body and affirm our oneness in Him. We know that we shall be changed, but wherein we shall be changed we cannot know until, in the act of faith and self-denial, we are given to discern, through crucifixion and resurrection, the lineaments of the one true Body of Christ which our sinful dividedness obscures from ourselves and from the world. Rejoicing in the grace which has been bestowed upon us in His various gifts even in our sin and separateness, we here set our hope on our one Lord Jesus Christ, who comes to take control over our divided and broken estate and to heal it by His grace and power. At Amsterdam we said that we intend to stay together. He has kept us together. He has shown Himself again as our Hope. Emboldened by this Hope, we dedicate ourselves to God anew, that He may enable us to grow together.

3. NEW DELHI 1961
Jesus Christ: the Saviour of the World
From the Report of Section I on Witness

The New Delhi declaration on unity[1] speaks of the confession of "the one apostolic faith" as one of the marks of a "fully committed" ecumenical fellowship. Elsewhere the report on "unity" states that "the one apostolic faith... is, first and last, faith in Christ as Lord and Saviour to the glory of God the Father". It goes on to say that "an obvious practical corollary of this understanding is the recommendation that a next step towards unity, at the denominational level, would be a fresh consideration of our various doctrinal bases, in the light of the primacy of Scripture and its safeguarding in the Church by the Holy Spirit".[2]

The following declaration, "Jesus Christ: the Saviour of the World" seeks to set forth the content of this apostolic faith in "Jesus Christ as Lord and Saviour". It was produced in the section on "witness" on the basis of an "annotated agenda" in which were outlined the most important themes and questions which had crystallized in the course of the two years preparatory period.[3] The pattern of the "witness" report as a whole is as follows:

Introduction
A. Jesus Christ: the Saviour of the world
B. Communicating the gospel
C. Reshaping the witnessing community

The statement "Jesus Christ: the Saviour of the World" consists of three parts with a trinitarian pattern: the first part speaks of God's action in the history of Israel, in Jesus Christ, and in the church; the second part deals with reconciliation in Christ and its consequences for the "realisation of our true humanity"; the third part focuses on the work of the Holy Spirit within the church and outside it.

● Text in *The New Delhi Report: the Third Assembly of the World Council of Churches 1961*, ed. W.A. Visser 't Hooft, London, 1962, pp.78-82.

---

[1] The Assembly was held from 18 November to 6 December 1961.
[2] *The New Delhi Report*, p.126f.
[3] *Ibid.*, p.330.

6. Jesus of Nazareth, the Christ, is the universal Lord and Saviour. This is our common faith, and it has been confirmed in us by our worship and study together in the Third Assembly of the World Council of Churches. As we have reflected on his Lordship we have realized afresh that the whole world is the continuing concern of the Father's love. It was for the sake of all men that the Son of God became man. The mighty acts of his ministry, death and resurrection and ascension were the out-working of a single purpose, the redemption of the world.

7. We say these words about Christ, not about ourselves. We are not the world's saviour. We are called to witness to him as the Saviour and Lord of all. We cannot bear his name, without coming under the searching light of his judgment on all men, beginning with us. This means asking some practical questions in our churches: whether we love men enough to be able to witness to them; whether we are sensitive to the ceaseless work of the Holy Spirit among men; whether we think and act as though Christ died for all men and not just for us. But we acknowledge our blindness and faithlessness and accepting our forgiveness we can testify that Christ never has forsaken his Church; by his spirit its life is sustained and many are brought by him into its faith and fellowship.

I

8. God is his own witness; that is to say, God has been and is at work authenticating his own message to men. When we speak of witness we mean testimony to the whole activity of God in the creation and preservation of the world, but especially in his mighty acts in Israel's history and in the redemption of the world by Jesus Christ. To this testimony the Holy Spirit in the Church bears witness.

9. God continues to bear witness to the Son, as the only Lord and Saviour of all men. In the apostolic witness, coming to us in Scripture in the Spirit-filled Church, God gives us the foundation of all subsequent witness. In the sacraments of baptism and the eucharist, God down the ages of the Church has drawn near to men in Jesus Christ and born witness to his own faithfulness. In the faithful preaching of his Word, God himself bears testimony to the truth. In the very existence of the Church, there is a constant witness — in silence as it were — to the reality of God's dealing with men in Jesus Christ.

10. We stand today in this long tradition of the Church's witness, having its origin in God himself, repeating itself constantly in the life of the Church. Therefore, we have confidence and enter with joy into the task of witness which has been laid upon us. We can speak as those who know in our own lives that "he who believes in the Son of God has this testimony in his own heart". We are convinced that Jesus is the risen, living Lord, victorious over sin and death. Of him and of the restored fellowship with God which he has worked for us and for all men, we would speak to our brothers for whom Christ died.

11. Today men fear death, not so much as formerly because of the sanctions of judgment and hell, as because it brings a total end to their enjoyment of this world, apart from which they know of no other life. The Church in preaching Christ's death proclaims victory over the power of death itself and the reality of a fuller and richer life than this world knows. Baptism signifies passing through the waters of death and entering here and now upon the life of the age to come.

II

12. In Jesus Christ, God has shown man his true nature and destiny. Through faith in Christ men receive power to become the sons of God. Christ has taken our manhood into God and "our real life is hid with Christ in God". So we look forward with eager longing to the glorious consummation of all things, when we shall share the fullness of the life of God. Nothing less than this can be the measure of what it means to be human, the fullness of the stature of Christ.

13. Because God in Christ has reconciled the world to himself, we may no longer judge our brother man by ordinarily accepted standards. God has not condemned us: we may not condemn any man. Only the rebellious will of man stands between us men and the realization of our true humanity and our eternal destiny. Joyfully we affirm our solidarity with all men, for our Lord has joined himself to us all by becoming man. Solidarity with all men of every nation, class, colour and faith without distinction in our common manhood is a starting point of the renewal of the life and witness of our churches by the Holy Spirit.

14. In Christ, the promise of God that man should have dominion over the created world is confirmed and demonstrated. The witness of Christ is that the full responsibility for ordering life in this world is with men, and that grace and truth for this task are available to them in him. He sets men free to know that the uncreated God alone is Lord over men, and that all created things are made to serve man in him. The new knowledge and enhanced power of modern man call aloud for a majestic witness to Christ in the fullness of his Lordship over nature and history, so that man may be able to accept the forgiveness of sins and find peace, wisdom and courage to handle the events of our time.

III

15. The gathering of the Church by Jesus Christ in every age demonstrates the loving purpose of God to draw men out of isolation and sinful separation into a community of brothers with a common Father, God himself. In Christ there is no place for pride in race, language, authority or sex. All are made equal with the humblest that all may share the glory of the Son. By the Spirit the Church is moved to the service of neighbour without distinction or discrimination. Through his Church God witnesses to his purpose to gather all nations, peoples and tongues, all sorts and conditions of men into his city. The story of God's dealing with Israel is the clue for our understanding of God's will for all nations and his present work among them.

16. In a time of rapid social change men find liberation from the constriction of old forms of community, but are demoralized because they do not find true community in their new surroundings. God calls the churches to witness in a life of humble interdependence and mutual service so that the will and imagination of men may be made strong to work for new and just relationships between nations, races and classes, and between the generations and the sexes.

17. Above all else, the Spirit stirs up the Church to proclaim Christ as Lord and Saviour to all the nations and in all spheres of life. The Church is sent, knowing that God has not left himself without witness even among men who do not yet know Christ, and knowing also that the reconciliation wrought through Christ embraces all creation

and the whole of mankind. We are aware that this great truth has deep implications when we go out to meet men of other faiths. But there are differences of opinion amongst us when we attempt to define the relation and response of such men to the activity of God amongst them. We are glad to note that the study of this question will be a main concern in the continuing study on "The Word of God and the Living Faiths of Men". We would stress the urgency of this study. In the churches, we have but little understanding of the wisdom, love and power which God has given to men of other faiths and of no faith, or of the changes wrought in other faiths by their long encounter with Christianity. We must take up the conversations about Christ with them, knowing that Christ addresses them through us and us through them.

4. UPPSALA 1968
The Holy Spirit and the Catholicity of the Church
Report of Section I

At Amsterdam, theology had been at the forefront; at Evanston and New Delhi, Christology; at Uppsala from 4 to 20 July, it was the turn of pneumatology. It was impossible here to miss the affinities of the report of Section I with the Second Vatican Council of the Roman Catholic Church, both in the formulation and in the detailed development of the theme, especially with the dogmatic constitution on the church, Lumen Gentium, with which the present report has much common ground.

In January 1968 a "section draft" had been published on this as on the other Assembly themes,[1] to serve as basis for discussions in the section. The final text was adopted on 18 July with the concluding note: "The above document is presented as a basis and instrument for further discussion. It represents an agreed summary of matters considered in the section. A variety of theological positions was expressed in honest and vigorous interchange, and the convergence of thought convinces us that further substantial progress can be made in the future."[2]

The document is in two main parts. Part one, in which the theological foundations are laid, is concerned with the work of the Holy Spirit as this finds expression in the catholicity of the church — in its root sense as gift and task. The text refers to the Holy Spirit as "Lord and Giver of Life", as well as to the other marks of the church — its oneness, holiness and apostolicity — and, in both cases, to the Third Article of the Constantinopolitan Creed. Part two discusses four specific aspects of catholicity:

The quest for diversity
The quest for continuity
The quest for the unity of the whole church
The quest for the unity of mankind

The report urges "a genuinely universal council... for all Christians" and claims for a truly "catholic" church that is "bold in speaking of itself as the sign of the coming unity of mankind".

● Text in *The Uppsala Report 1968*, official report of the Fourth Assembly of the World Council of Churches, ed. Norman Goodall, Geneva, 1968, pp.8-16.

---

[1] *Drafts for Sections*, Uppsala 1968, pp.7-27.
[2] *The Uppsala Report*, p.19.

1. We give thanks to God the Holy Spirit that at this very time he is leading us into a fresh and exhilarating understanding of the Body of Christ, to the glory of God the Father. He is transforming the relationships between separated Christian communities, so that we now speak to each other with greater mutual trust and with more hope of reconciliation than ever before.

2. We recall many recent events which fill us with deep gratitude and humility: advances towards the union of separated churches; the formation of ecumenical groups in thousands of different places, small as well as large; the discovery of a new togetherness in prayer and praise, in mission and social action; the mutual contributions of Eastern and Western churches, and of older and younger churches; the powerful signs of renewal within the Roman Catholic Church.

3. Yet at the very time when we can see that the Holy Spirit is producing such promising fruit, we are confronted with the fact that the basis of our endeavour for unity is being widely questioned. It seems to many, inside and outside the Church, that the struggle for Christian unity in it present form is irrelevant to the immediate crisis of our times. The Church, they say, should seek its unity through solidarity with those forces in modern life, such as the struggle for racial equality, which are drawing men more closely together, and should give up its concern with patching up its own internal disputes. To this challenge we must listen and make our response.

4. The same Spirit who is bringing us together in the Church does, in fact, make us more aware of the needs of the world and of our solidarity with a creation which is "groaning in travail together" (Romans 8:22 RSV). We cannot be isolated from the shocks and turmoils of our time, as conflicts between races and nations tear apart the fabric of our common life, as developed and developing countries become more and more alienated from each other, and ideologies and crusades clash in deadly struggle for survival. The miseries of men multiply. In such a time it is the Holy Spirit who calls us to share Christ's unlimited love, to accept his condemnation of our fears and treasons, and for his sake to endure shame, oppression, and apparent defeat. In the agonising arena of contemporary history — and very often among the members of the Churches — we see the work of demonic forces that battle against the rights and liberties of man, but we can also see the activity of the life-giving Spirit of God. We have come to view this world of men as the place where God is already at work to make all things new, and where he summons us to work with him.

5. Engagement in such work enables us to see fresh implications in the oneness, the holiness, the catholicity and the apostolicity which in close interdependence have always characterized the authentic life of the Church. Each of these basic qualities is God's gift; each is also our quest. Oneness in the same Body through the same Spirit is manifested in the proclamation of the Gospel, in Baptism and in the celebration of the Eucharist, but this very oneness is defaced by our sinful divisions. The holiness of the Church is imparted by God alone and has been made manifest by the Holy Spirit in creating a community which shows its holiness by living for God and for others; but it is constantly counteracted by our preoccupation with ourselves. The apostolicity of the Church is derived from the Lord's own sending of his apostles to preach the Gospel to all men, yet the Church which in the Christ-given authority of the apostles enters into their mission has not fully achieved her embassy of reconciliation on the world's battle-fronts.

6. Yet it is within this very world that God makes catholicity available to men through the ministry of Christ in his Church. The purpose of Christ is to bring people of all times, of all races, of all places, of all conditions, into an organic and living unity in Christ by the Holy Spirit under the universal fatherhood of God. This unity is not solely external; it has a deeper, internal dimension, which is also expressed by the term "catholicity". Catholicity reaches its completion when what God has already begun in history is finally disclosed and fulfilled.

7. Since Christ lived, died and rose again from all mankind, catholicity is the opposite of all kinds of egoism and particularism. It is the quality by which the Church expresses the fullness, the integrity and the totality of life in Christ. The Church is catholic, and should be catholic, in all her elements and in all aspects of her life, and especially in her worship. Members of the Church should reflect the integrity and wholeness which is the essential character of the Church. One measure of her internal unity is that it is said of believers that they have but one heart and one soul (Acts 4:32; Phil. 2:1-12). There are then two factors in it: the unifying grace of the Spirit and the humble efforts of believers, who do not seek their own, but are united in faith, in adoration, and in love and service of Christ for the sake of the world. Catholicity is a gift of the Spirit, but it is also a task, a call and an engagement.

8. The Church gladly confesses the Holy Spirit as "the Lord, and giver of life". This is the eternal life which God the Father shares with all those who are in fellowship with his Son (I John 1:1-4). It is an inheritance of the kingdom of that Son, a kingdom which, though fully real, is yet to be fully realized in his coming. In giving this life the Holy Spirit

— brings sinful men through repentance and Baptism into the universal fellowship of the forgiven;

— bears witness through the Church to the truth of the Gospel, and makes it credible to men;

— builds up the Church in each place through the proclamation of the Word and the celebration of the Eucharist;

— stirs the conscience of the Church by the voice of prophets to keep her in the mercy and judgment of God;

— maintains the Church in communion and continuity with the people of God in all ages and places;

— equips the Church to accept and make use of the great variety of God's gifts bestowed upon its members for the enrichment of human life;

— empowers the Church in her unity to be a ferment in society, for the renewal and unity of mankind;

— sends men into the world equipped to prepare the way for God's rule on earth by proclaiming freedom to the captives and sight to the blind;

— awakens Christians to watch for the Lord's coming, when he will judge the living and the dead, and open the gates of his city to all his people.

9. God's gift of catholicity is received in faith and obedience. The Church must express this catholicity in its worship by providing a home for all sorts and conditions of men and women; and in its witness and service by working for the realization of genuine humanity. The Church hinders the manifestation of its given catholicity when it breaks down at any of these points.

10. God offers this gift to men in their freedom. The activity of the Spirit never forces men, but opens before them the doors of God's love and gives them the power to cooperate in God's creative and redeeming action. Such power is needed to overcome individual and collective egoism, to reconcile enemies, and to free slaves of habit from their chains. But men misuse this freedom, refusing the gift of catholicity both individually and corporately. This happens whenever Christians confuse the unity and catholicity of the Church with other solidarities and communities. Examples of this confusion occur wherever Christian communities

— allow the Gospel to be obscured by prejudices which prevent them from seeking unity;
— allow their membership to be determined by discrimination based on race, wealth, social class or education;
— do not exhibit in all the variety of their life together the essential oneness in Christ of men and women;
— allow cultural, ethnic or political allegiances to prevent the organic union of churches which confess the same faith within the same region;
— prescribe their own customary practices as binding on other Christians as the condition for cooperation and unity;
— permit loyalty to their own nation to hinder or to destroy their desire for mutual fellowship with Christians of another nation;
— allow themselves to be forced into a unity by the State for nationalistic ends, or break their unity for political reasons.

By recognizing these confusions and by seeking to eliminate them, our churches may find themselves on the way to overcoming the forces which still keep us apart from each other.

11. We have described the denials of catholicity in quite general terms. That leaves it easy to suppose that it is others, individuals or communities, who are culpable. But where do we really stand? We shall turn to examine four areas where the gift and calling of catholicity are coming to us, hoping that by thanksgiving and repentance we may be renewed to receive and actualize that catholicity which is God's gift to his people.

The Quest for Diversity

12. The quest for catholicity faces us with the question whether we betray God's gift by ignoring the diversities of the Spirit's working. Diversity may be a perversion of catholicity but often it is a genuine expression of the apostolic vocation of the Church. This is illustrated by the New Testament, where through a wide range of doctrinal and liturgical forms relevant to differing situations, the one unchanging apostolic heritage finds expression. Behind the variety of apostolic activities we discern a double movement: the Church is always "being called out of the world and being sent into the world" (Lund 1952). This double movement is basic to a dynamic catholicity. Each of the two movements requires different words and actions in different situations, but always the two movements belong together. The constitutive centre of this double movement is corporate worship in which Christ himself is the one who both calls and sends.

13. Here we also discern a basis for evaluating the Spirit's gift. A diversity which frustrates the calling and the sending is demonic; the diversities which encourage and

advance the double movement, and therefore enhance catholicity, are of different kinds. There are now as in the New Testament rich varieties of charismatic gifts, such as are described in I Cor. 12-14; there are diverse ways of proclaiming the Gospel and setting forth its mysteries; there are manifold ways of presenting doctrinal truths and of celebrating sacramental and liturgical events; churches in different areas adopt different patterns of organization. By such diversities, intrinsic to the double movement, the Spirit leads us forward on the way to a fully catholic mission and ministry.

The Quest for Continuity

14. We give thanks that down the ages the continuing life of the people of God can be discerned. For the Holy Spirit, who created this people in time, has continued with it through the centuries, preserving its worship and enabling it to bring God's good news to the world. The Church is revealed as the one body of Christ, the one people of God in every age, and so its continuity is made actual
— in the "faith once given to the saints", embodied in the Scriptures, confessed in the Church and proclaimed to the world;
— in the liturgical life of the Church, its worship and sacraments;
— in the continuous succession of the apostolic ministry of Word and Sacrament;
— in constantly preparing the people of God to go into the world and meet human needs;
— in the unbroken witness of the lives of prophets, martyrs and saints.

15. The Holy Spirit has not only preserved the Church in continuity with her past; He is also continuously present in the Church, effecting her inward renewal and re-creation. The Church in heaven is indeed one with the Church on earth, yet the Church on earth does not stand outside the historical process. As the pilgrim people of God she finds herself at every point of time implicated in the varying hopes, problems and fears of men and women, and in the changing patterns of human history. The Church is faced by the twin demands, of continuity in the one Holy Spirit, and of renewal in response to the call of the Spirit amid the changes of human history.

16. The Church is apostolic in the sense that all that makes the Church the Church is derived from Christ through the apostles. Apostolicity also means the continuous transmission of the Gospel to all men and nations through acts of worship, witness and human service in the world. The Church is therefore apostolic because she remains true to the faith and mission of the apostles. We are now called afresh to repentance and humility in the search for one ministry recognized by the whole Church, and for an understanding of ministry more adequate to the New Testament, to the Church and to the needs of our own times. We seek to present the apostolic faith unimpaired: we must beware among ourselves of a perversion of catholicity into a justification for a blind defence of political and religious establishments, as well as being watchful against distortions of the apostolic faith by those who confuse the novel with the new.

The Quest for the Unity of the Whole Church

17. The New Delhi Assembly emphasized with good effect the need to manifest the unity of "all Christians in each place". Even so, much still needs to be done in drawing separated congregations to recognize each other and to share in such activities as common worship, Bible study, ecumenical offerings and joint response to human needs. We must continue to seek the unity of all Christians in a common profession of

the faith in the observance of Baptism and the Eucharist, and in recognition of a ministry for the whole Church.

18. So to the emphasis on "all in each place" we would now add a fresh understanding of the unity of all Christians in all places. This calls the churches in all places to realize that they belong together and are called to act together. In a time when human interdependence is so evident, it is the more imperative to make visible the bonds which unite Christians in universal fellowship.

19. But there are hindrances. No church can properly avoid responsibility for the life of its own nation and culture. Yet if that should militate against fellowship with churches and Christians of other lands, then distortion has entered the Church's life at a vital point. But the clearest obstacle to manifestation of the churches' universality is their inability to understand the measure in which they already belong together in one body. Some real experience of universality is provided by establishing regional and international confessional fellowships. But such experiences of universality are inevitably partial. The ecumenical movement helps to enlarge this experience of universality, and its regional councils and its World Council may be regarded as a transitional opportunity for eventually actualizing a truly universal ecumenical concil-iar form of common life and witness. The members of the World Council of Churches, committed to each other, should work for the time when a genuinely universal council may once more speak for all Christians, and lead the way into the future.

The Quest for the Unity of Mankind

20. The Church is bold in speaking of itself as the sign of the coming unity of mankind. However well founded the claim, the world hears it sceptically, and points to "secular catholicities" of its own. For secular society has produced instruments of conciliation and unification which often seem more effective than the Church itself. To the outsider, the churches often seem remote and irrelevant, and busy to the point of tediousness with their own concerns. The churches need a new openness to the world in its aspirations, its achievements, its restlessness and its despair.

21. This is the more evident at a time when technology is drawing men into a single secular culture, a fact which underlines the essential truth of human nature as of one blood, in equal right and dignity through every diversity of race and kind. This unity of man is grounded for the Christian not only in his creation by the one God in his own image, but in Jesus Christ who "for us men" became man, was crucified, and who constitutes the Church which is his body as a new community of new creatures. The catholicity of the Church means this given reality of grace in which the purpose of creation is restored and sinful men are reconciled in the one divine sonship of which Christ is both author and finisher.

22. It is by this truth of man made new in Christ that we must judge and repudiate the tragic distortions of humanity in the life of mankind, some found even in the Christian community. The churches have declaimed against racism of every kind; but racial segregations are found in them, so that even when they gather in Christ's name some are excluded on account of their colour. Such a denial of catholicity demands the speediest and most passionate rejection. How long, O Lord, how long? Renewal must begin in the local community, by detecting and dethroning all exclusiveness of race and class and by fighting all economic, political and social degradation and exploita-tion of men.

23. Catholicity is also a constant possession and pursuit of the mystery of faith, the sacramental experience of that incorporation into Christ and involvement with mankind of which the Church is the form and the Eucharist the substantial focus. In its deepest sense liturgy is the hallowing of all we are for the sake of all that is, that God may be all in all. And finally, catholicity is expectant. The Church lives in the world for her Lord and therefore for those not yet in her fellowship. The Church's mission to the world will bring an enrichment from the world into the Church. Only in the fulness of redeemed humanity shall we experience the fulness of the Spirit's gifts.

24. When we consider the vision of unity granted to this generation and the resources of God's bounty available for the enrichment of mankind, we become newly aware of the tragic character of the divisions that separate us, including the divisions among us at this Assembly. We confess how empty and deceptive our talk of catholicity may sound, and how far we lag behind the summons of the Spirit. We have been reminded that by nature we are united with that world which was judged on Golgotha, and will be judged on the Last Day; and in Christ through the Spirit we are united with that community renewed at Pentecost and which will be renewed in the Year of the Lord. With a single voice all members of the Assembly pray "Come, creator Spirit", knowing that any answer to this prayer should open our eyes to God's future, which is already breaking in upon us.

5. NAIROBI 1975
Confessing Christ Today
Report and Recommendations of Section I

Together with other important ecumenical conferences, the Nairobi Assembly, from 23 November to 10 December, constitutes part of a single complex pattern: there was the World Missionary Conference in Bangkok in 1973 on "Salvation Today", the Faith and Order Commission meeting in Accra in 1974 on "Giving Account of the Hope that is within Us", the Lausanne Congress of 1974 on "The Evangelization of the World", and the Bishop's Synod of the Roman Catholic Church in Rome in 1974 on "Evangelism in the Modern World". Each of these left its mark on the report of Section I in Nairobi, which gave special emphasis to cultural diversity and Christian identity (cf. Bangkok 1973), to the confessing community (cf. Lausanne 1974), and to the wholeness of the confession of Christ (cf. Accra 1974). Members of the Section had before them a provisional draft in the shape of "Notes for Sections".[1] The report "Confessing Christ Today" had the following outline:
  Introduction
  Confessing Christ as an act of conversion
  Many cultures, one Christ
  The confessing community
  Confessing Christ in worship and life
  A call to confess and proclaim
  Recommendations
Nairobi's "Call to Confess and Proclaim" embraces "the whole Gospel", "the whole person", "the whole world", and "the whole Church". Recommendation 16 calls on the churches to recognize "Christ confessed by Christians from other parts of the world, particularly those churches which have traditionally sent missionaries to other countries but have never received missionaries".

● Text in *Breaking Barriers: Nairobi 1975*, the official report of the Fifth Assembly of the World Council of Churches, ed. D.M. Paton, London, 1976, pp.43-57.

---

[1] Notes for Sections, "Section I: Confessing Christ Today", Fifth Assembly of the WCC, Geneva, 1975, pp.5-70.

Introduction

1. Today's world offers many political lords as well as secular and religious saviours. Nevertheless, as representatives of churches gathered together in the World Council of Churches, we boldly confess Christ alone as Saviour and Lord. We confidently trust in the power of the gospel to free and unite all children of God throughout the world.

2. Amid today's cries of anguish and shouts of oppression, we have been led by the Holy Spirit to confess Jesus Christ as our Divine Confessor. Confident in the Word of God of the holy Scriptures, we confess both our human weakness and our divine strength: "Since then we have a great high priest who has passed through the heavens, Jesus, the Son of God, let us hold fast to our confession" (Heb. 4.14).

3. As our high priest, Christ mediates God's new covenant through both salvation and service. Through the power of the cross, Christ promises God's righteousness and commands true justice. As the royal priesthood, Christians are therefore called to engage in both evangelism and social action. We are commissioned to proclaim the gospel of Christ to the ends of the earth. Simultaneously, we are commanded to struggle to realize God's will for peace, justice, and freedom throughout society.

4. In the same high priestly prayer which bids "that they may be one", Jesus also discloses the distinctive life-style of those who have been set apart to serve in the Church's universal priesthood. While we are "not of" the world, even as he was not of the world, so we are also sent "into" the world, just as he was sent into the world (John 17.16,18).

5. Christians witness in word and deed to the inbreaking reign of God. We experience the power of the Holy Spirit to confess Christ in a life marked by both suffering and joy. Christ's decisive battle has been won at Easter, and we are baptized into his death that we might walk in newness of life (Rom. 6.4). Yet we must still battle daily against those already dethroned, but not yet destroyed, "principalities and powers" of this rebellious age. The Holy Spirit leads us into all truth, engrafting persons into the Body of Christ in which all things are being restored by God.

6. Our life together is thereby committed to the costly discipleship of the Church's Divine Confessor. His name is above every name: "that at the name of Jesus every knee should bow, in heaven and on earth and under the earth, and every tongue confess that Jesus Christ is Lord, to the glory of God the Father" (Phil. 2.10-11).

Confessing Christ as an Act of Conversion

The Christ of God

7. Jesus asks: "Who do you say that I am?" At the same time he calls us into his discipleship: "If anyone would come after me, let him deny himself and take up his cross and follow me" (Matt. 16.15,24). We confess Jesus as the Christ of God, the hope of the world, and commit ourselves to his will. Before we confess him, he confesses us, and in all our ways, he precedes us. We therefore confess with great joy:

8. Jesus Christ is the *one witness of God*, to whom we listen and witness as the incarnate Son of God in life and death (John 14.8). "You are my witnesses.... I am the first and the last. There is no God except me" was said to Israel (Isa. 43.8-11). So we are the witnesses of Christ and his Kingdom to all people until the end of the world.

9. Jesus Christ is the *true witness of God* (Rev. 3.14). Into the world of lies,

ambiguity, and idolatry, he brings "the truth that liberates" (John 8.32). And as God has sent him, so he sends us.

10. Jesus Christ is the *faithful witness to God* (Rev. 1.5). In his self-offering on the Cross he redeems us from sin and godless powers and reconciles creation with God. Therefore, we shall live for God and shall be saved in God. "There is no condemnation for those who are in Christ Jesus, who walk not after the flesh, but after the Spirit" (Rom. 8.1ff).

11. We believe with certainty in the *presence and guidance of the Holy Spirit*, who proceeds from the Father and bears witness to Christ (John 15.26). Our witness to Christ is made strong in the Holy Spirit and is alive in the confessing community of the Church.

Our Discipleship, His Lordship

12. In our confessing Christ today and in our continuing conversion to the way of Christ, we encourage and support one another.

13. *Confessing Christ and being converted to his discipleship belong inseparably together*. Those who confess Jesus Christ deny themselves, their selfishness and slavery to the godless "principalities and powers", take up their crosses and follow him. Without clear confession of Christ our discipleship cannot be recognized; without costly discipleship people will hesitate to believe our confession. The costs of discipleship — e.g. becoming a stranger among one's own people, being despised because of the gospel, persecuted because of resistance to oppressive powers, and imprisoned because of love for the poor and lost — are bearable in face of the costly love of God, revealed in the passion of Jesus.

14. We *deplore* cheap conversions, without consequences. We *deplore* a superficial gospel-preaching, an empty gospel without a call into personal and communal discipleship. We *confess* our own fear of suffering with Jesus. We are afraid of persecutions, fear, and death. Yet, the more we look upon the crucified Christ alone and trust the power of the Holy Spirit, the more our anxiety is overcome. "When we suffer with him, we shall also be glorified with him" (Rom. 8.17). We revere the martyrs of all ages and of our time, and look to their example for courage.

15. We *deplore* conversions without witness to Christ. There are millions who have never heard the good news. We *confess* that we are often ashamed of the gospel. We find it more comfortable to remain in our own Christian circles than to witness in the world. The more we look upon our risen Lord, the more our indolence is overcome and we are enabled to confess: "Woe to me if I do not preach the gospel" (1 Cor. 9.16).

16. We *deplore* also that our confessing Christ today is hindered by the different denominations, which split the confessing community of the Church. We understand the confessions of faith of our different traditions as guidelines, not as substitutes, for our actual confessing in the face of today's challenges. Because being converted to Christ necessarily includes membership in the confessing body of Christ, we *long and strive* for a world-wide community.

17. *In confessing Christ and in being converted to his Lordship, we experience the freedom of the Holy Spirit and express the ultimate hope for the world*. Through his true and faithful witness Jesus Christ has set us free from the slavery of sin to the glorious freedom of the Spirit. Within the vicious circles of sin, death, and the devil are the vicious circles of hunger, oppression, and violence. Likewise, liberation to

justice, better community, and human dignity on earth is within the great freedom of the Spirit, who is nothing less than the power of the new creation.

18. We regret all divisions in thinking and practice between the personal and the corporate dimensions. "The whole gospel for the whole person and the whole world" means that we cannot leave any area of human life and suffering without the witness of hope.

19. We regret that some reduce liberation from sin and evil to social and political dimensions, just as we regret that others limit liberation to the private and eternal dimensions.

20. In the witness of our whole life and our confessing community we *work* with passionate love for the total liberation of the people and *anticipate* God's Kingdom to come. We *pray* in the freedom of the Spirit and *groan* with our suffering fellow human beings and the whole groaning creation until the glory of the Triune God is revealed and will be all in all. Come, Lord Jesus, come to us, come to the world!

Many Cultures, One Christ

Search for Cultural Identity

21. In all societies today there is a search for cultural identity; Christians around the world find themselves caught up in this quest. The Bangkok Conference on Salvation Today (1973) asked: "Culture shapes the human voice that answers the voice of Christ.... How can we responsibly answer the voice of Christ instead of copying foreign models of conversion... imposed, not truly accepted?"

22. In our sharing with one another we have discovered that the Christ who meets us in our own cultural contexts is revealed to us in a new way as we confess him. Further, since Christ shares in a special way with all who are exploited and oppressed, we find when we meet with them that our understanding of him is enlarged and enriched.

23. We affirm the necessity of confessing Christ as specifically as possible with regard to our own cultural settings. We have heard him confessed in that way at this Assembly by Christians from all parts of the world. In partial answer to the question raised by the Bangkok Conference, we can say that Jesus Christ does not make copies; he makes originals. We have found this confession of Christ out of our various cultural contexts to be not only a mutually inspiring, but also a mutually corrective exchange. Without this sharing our individual affirmations would gradually become poorer and narrower. We need each other to regain the lost dimensions of confessing Christ and even to discover dimensions unknown to us before. Sharing in this way we are all changed and our cultures are transformed.

24. There is great diversity in our confessions of Christ. Nevertheless, through the illumination of the Holy Spirit, we have been able to recognize him in the proclamation of Christians in cultural situations different from our own. This is possible because we confess Christ as God and Saviour *according to the Scriptures*. And although our reading and interpretation of the Scriptures is to a certain extent itself culturally conditioned, we believe that it is part of the mystery of Christ that even as we confess him in different ways it is he who draws us together.

25. We believe that in addition to listening to one another, we need to know what people of other faiths and no faith are saying about Jesus Christ and his followers.

While we cannot agree on whether or how Christ is present in other religions, we do believe that God has not left himself without witness in any generation or any society. Nor can we exclude the possibility that God speaks to Christians from outside the Church. While we oppose any form of syncretism, we affirm the necessity for dialogue with men and women of other faiths and ideologies as a means of mutual understanding and practical co-operation.

Structures That Obscure the Confession of Christ

26. We recognize that there are power structures and social factors that obscure the Christ we seek to confess. It is difficult for a black Christian, for example, to believe that the Christ whom he or she confesses is the same Christ whom white Christians confess. The structures of racist oppression have obscured the image of Christ. It is difficult for a woman to confess a Christ who frees and unites when she has been taught subordination to men — in church and society — in the name of this same Christ. The structures of sexism also obscure the image of Christ. Religious expression is severely restricted both in states that pretend to be Christian and others which do not. In both kinds of societies there may be political structures that can and do obscure the confession of Christ. In such societies Christians are called to be as committed in their confession of Christ as are those who may seek to oppose or undermine their confession.

27. Economic structures may also obscure the confession of Christ. In consumer economies, whether capitalistic or socialistic, there are different forms of stress upon productivity, competition, and materialistic values. This increases the gap between the industrialized nations and the Third World and further decreases the quality of life in the industrialized societies. Thus while we confess a Christ who frees and unites, the economic structures in which we live tend to enslave to wealth and divide.

28. How do we meet this materialism which obstructs the confession of Christ and leads to uncaring societies? We find hope where churches, whatever the cultural context, confess Christ by standing for that which is truly human, where Christians "bear the marks of Christ" among suffering humankind, where churches address public issues in the name of Christ, and where communities of Christians are radically changing their life style as a sign of their discipleship.

29. In our discussions with one another we were also sensitized to the fact that a kind of nationalism can develop which is a distortion of the legitimate search for cultural identity and can obscure our confession of Jesus Christ the Unifier. We want to testify that in this Assembly we have found it possible to meet others of different national and cultural traditions and yet remain ourselves because we all belong to him.

30. We also know that it is not only societal power structures that can obscure the confession of Christ. Sometimes the institutional structures of the churches themselves are oppressive and dehumanizing; often they uncritically reflect the values of their own culture. Where churches are identified with wealth and privilege both the preaching and the hearing of the gospel are hindered and Christ is obscured. Unless we who belong to the Church have met him in our own lives and been changed by him, we shall not be able to name his name with power and authenticity. In this connection the issue of a "moratorium" in mission funding has been raised and is receiving serious consideration in other sections of this Assembly.

31. Despite all of our cultural differences, despite the structures in society and in the Church that obscure our confession of Christ, and despite our own sinfulness, we affirm and confess Christ together, for we have found that he is not alien to any culture and that he redeems and judges in all our societies. Our common confession is Jesus Christ frees and unites.

The Confessing Community

Community in the Spirit

32. Confessing Christ is not only intensely personal; it is also essentially communal.

33. Those who take part in the life of Christ and confess him as Lord and Saviour, Liberator and Unifier, are gathered in a community of which the author and sustainer is the Holy Spirit. This communion of the Spirit finds its primary aim and ultimate purpose in the eucharistic celebration and the glorification of the Triune God. The doxology is the supreme confession which transcends all our divisions.

34. Through word, sacrament, and mutual care he transforms us, makes us grow, and leads us to the integration of worship and action. This power fills our weakness.

35. Confessing Christ *today* means that the Spirit makes us struggle with all the issues this Assembly has talked about: sin and forgiveness, power and powerlessness, exploitation and misery, the universal search for identity, the widespread loss of Christian motivation, and the spiritual longings of those who have not heard Christ's name.

36. It means that we are in communion with the prophets who announced God's will and promise for humankind and society, with the martyrs who sealed their confession with suffering and death, and also with the doubtful who can only whisper their confession of the Name. The confession of Christ holds in one communion our divided churches and the many communities, new and old, within and around them.

37. When the Holy Spirit empowers us to confess Christ today, we are called to speak and act with concern and solidarity for the whole of God's creation. Concretely: when the powerful confess Christ, the suffering must be enabled to concur; when the exploited confess Christ, the rich should be enabled to hear in such confession their own freedom announced.

38. Within the communion of the Church, we witness in our time the emergence of many new communities: missionary orders, ecumenical experiments, communes and action groups, which are trying out age-old or spontaneous and new forms of worship and action. All these groups represent attempts to find answers to the fragmentation of our societies and to the loneliness which results from the disintegration of traditional community life. They also express the lasting strength of the call of the gospel to communion and mutual care, which the Spirit instills in everybody who is touched. Despite the problems these groups often give to the institutional churches, we recognize a creative challenge in them. We urge the churches to be sensitive towards such groups, to respect the search for authenticity which they represent, and not to reject them, lest such groups turn away from the larger communion and lose the opportunity to share their discoveries and spiritual fruits with all the others.

39. Again: all Christian community life is a creation of the Spirit of Christ, nourished by his word and sacrament, held together by love, and pushed forward by

hope. Worship is its anchor and the source of its energy. So, through informed intercessions, naming people far away and close by, they live in solidarity with the whole community of grace and also, irresistibly, with all those who suffer and yearn for dignity. Through these prayers and through old and new forms of direct *diakonia*, they forge links which embrace the earth, breaking through man-made divisions of race and class, power and exploitation.

Prayer and Suffering

40. Worship, especially the Eucharist, is the instrument through which all these communities open themselves up to God and his creation; thus it breaks down walls of divisions and stimulates creative forms of solidarity. In worship we are constantly reminded of the age to come and made to live in anticipation of the messianic kingdom; thus confidence and urgency are wedded in one common life. It is our lasting shame and pain that we have not overcome our divisions at the Lord's table, where we experience God's salvation for and on behalf of all humanity. In many of our churches growing numbers of people disregard the theological and juridical barriers which make common celebration of the Eucharist impossible. Here we are not in agreement in our reaction to such developments, but we find a strong common bond in the recognition of the urgency of the call of our Lord for full unity.

41. Confessing Christ in communion means confessing the suffering and the risen Lord. We should not refuse his Cross. He will not refuse us his life.

42. We know that the acceptance of the suffering Christ is the only way to overcome our feelings of powerlessness over against evil. We also know that this acceptance would make us once again credible in the eyes of the world. We therefore pray that our churches will again and again return to the reality and the promise of the Cross, so that together we may find ourselves the stewards of the new life in Christ.

Confessing Christ in Worship and Life

Facing Reality

43. "Confessing Christ" or "Christian Witness" describes, above all, that continuous act by which a Christian or Christian community proclaims God's acts in history and seeks to manifest Christ as "the Word that was made flesh and dwelt among us (John 1.14). Our confessing Christ today would deny God's incarnation if it would be limited to only some areas of life. It concerns the wholeness of human life: our words and acts; our personal and communal existence; our worship and responsible service; our particular and ecumenical context.

44. All this is done under the guidance of the Holy Spirit in order that all may be reconciled and be gathered into Christ's one and only Body (Col. 1.18; Eph. 1.22-23) and attain life everlasting — to know and love the true God and him whom he has sent (John 17.3).

45. Confessing Christ is an act of gratitude for God's faithfulness and his liberating presence in our life. His is the power and the glory. At the same time, Christian witness has to do with Christians struggling against the power of evil within themselves, within the churches, and in society. This power expresses itself in many ways — in temptation of various kinds, in prejudices nurtured in us by birth, sex, class, race, religion, or nationality; in dehumanizing political and socio-economic

forces; in hostility which disrupts human relationships; in selfish ambition which thrives on the misery and sufferings of others; in sicknesses which have no cure. In the midst of such reality each of us is called in our baptism to confess Christ according to the special gift (*charisma*) which one has received from God.

46. Liturgical worship, an action of the Church centred around the Eucharist, in itself thankfully proclaims the death and resurrection of the Lord "until he comes again" and incorporates people into mystical union with God, because in the act of baptism they have been identified with that death and resurrection. Confessions of faith and creeds are expressions of the communion of the Christian life both of yesterday and today. Our witness is rooted and nourished in that communion. Yesterday flows into today, the present engages the past, in continual dialogue. We approach our biblical and confessional heritage with questions that arise from contemporary involvement. At the same time, we gratefully receive from that heritage both criticism and encouragement for concrete service and fellowship.

Christian Authenticity

47. Though it seems flat and even naive on paper, we insist on repeating that the key to authentic confession is the Christian who indeed is a Christian within the community of the faith. Authentic Christians live the death and resurrection of Christ by living the forgiven life in selfless service to others, and believe in the Spirit by whose power alone we are able to live our life of discipleship (1 Cor. 12.3). Especially in a secularized environment or in situations where religious commitments are scorned or even attacked, the primary confessors are precisely these non-publicized unsensa-tional people who gather together in small, caring communities. They remain free to proclaim Christ even out of their self-acknowledged condition of weakness and sin. Their individual and communal life-style provokes the questions: "What is the meaning of your life, and why do you live as you do?" One must name the Name. Yet shared experiences reveal how often today Christ is confessed not in loud and frequent words or in massive programmes of varied activities, but in the very silence of a prison cell or of a restricted but still serving, waiting, praying Church. Today, as always in the Church, we are blessed by confessors, martyrs "even unto death".

48. Indeed, in those milieux which seem so hardened to any religious confession or in areas which for centuries have seen so little "success", confessing Christ may rest in the very hope that flows from our incorporation through the Spirit into the mission, death, and life of Jesus Christ. Only that hope holds us, only that hope never abandons us.

49. The call to confess Christ is a vocation also to that *common* witness in each place which the churches, even while separated, bear together. By sharing resources and experiences in mission, they witness to whatever divine gifts of truth and life they already share in common. Such witness should proclaim together the content of Christian faith, as fully as possible. Furthermore, such ecumenical faithfulness of the churches in each place includes fidelity to the needs of the local churches which elsewhere are also striving to give common witness.

50. For many Christians in very diverse situations, confessing Christ amounts almost to the same thing as involvement in struggles for justice and freedom. In many instances, Christian faith has become a dynamic force, awakening the conscience of the people and bringing new hope to hopeless situations. In this way, confessing Christ

is liberated from mere verbalism which renders the life and ministry of the Church stagnant, introverted, and contentious.

51. What are our hesitations about explicitly confessing our faith before others?

(a) A loss of confidence in the God we proclaim and in the power of the gospel so that we lack confidence in our mission as Christians?

(b) By not experiencing deeply enough the joyful, healing love of God so that we are unable *honestly* to give an account of the hope within us?

(c) An unreadiness to be different before those to whom the good news is heard as bad news?

(d) By misunderstanding our belief in the uniqueness and finality of Jesus Christ as "arrogant doctrinal superiority", and not understanding it as the humble and obedient stewardship of the Church which knows it has been "put in trust with the gospel"?

52. We confess Christ in the perspective of the coming Kingdom. His Spirit is the Spirit of the New Age. This vision makes us both sober and hopeful. None of the achievements as individuals, churches, societies will in themselves inaugurate the messianic era. Never can women and men be justified by works. Yet the promise of the Kingdom is valid and encourages Christians to respond in prayer and action. Confessing Christ shall not be in vain.

A Call to Confess and Proclaim

53. We do not have the option of keeping the good news to ourselves. The uncommunicated gospel is a patent contradiction.

54. We are called to preach Christ crucified, the power of God and the wisdom of God (1 Cor. 1.23,24).

55. Evangelism, therefore, is rooted in gratitude for God's self-sacrificing love, in obedience to the risen Lord.

56. Evangelism is like a beggar telling another beggar where they both can find bread.

The Whole Gospel

57. The gospel is good news from God, our Creator and Redeemer. On its way from Jerusalem to Galilee and to the ends of the earth, the Spirit discloses ever new aspects and dimensions of God's decisive revelation in Jesus Christ. The gospel always includes: the announcement of God's Kingdom and love through Jesus Christ, the offer of grace and forgiveness of sins, the invitation to repentance and faith in him, the summons to fellowship in God's Church, the command to witness to God's saving words and deeds, the responsibility to participate in the struggle for justice and human dignity, the obligation to denounce all that hinders human wholeness, and a commitment to risk life itself. In our time, to the oppressed the gospel may be new as a message of courage to persevere in the struggle for liberation in this world as a sign of hope for God's inbreaking Kingdom. To women the gospel may bring news of a Christ who empowered women to be bold in the midst of cultural expectations of submissiveness. To children the gospel may be a call of love for the "little ones" and to the rich and powerful it may reveal the responsibility to share the poverty of the poor.

58. While we rejoice hearing the gospel speak to our particular situations and while we must try to communicate the gospel to particular contexts, we must remain faithful

to the historical apostolic witness as we find it in the holy Scriptures and tradition as it is centred in Jesus Christ — lest we accommodate them to our own desires and interests.

The Whole Person

59. The gospel, through the power of the Holy Spirit, speaks to all human needs, transforms our lives. In bringing forgiveness, it reconciles us to our Creator, sparks within us the true joy of knowing God, and promises eternal life. In uniting us as God's people, it answers our need for community and fellowship. In revealing God's love for all persons, it makes us responsible, critical and creative members of the societies in which we live. The good news of Jesus' resurrection assures us that God's righteous purpose in history will be fulfilled and frees us to work for that fulfilment with hope and courage.

The Whole World

60. The world is not only God's creation; it is also the arena of God's mission. Because God loved the whole world, the Church cannot neglect any part of it — neither those who have heard the saving Name nor the vast majority who have not yet heard it. Our obedience to God and our solidarity with the human family demand that we obey Christ's command to proclaim and demonstrate God's love to every person, of every class and race, on every continent, in every culture, in every setting and historical context.

The Whole Church

61. Evangelism cannot be delegated to either gifted individuals or specialized agencies. It is entrusted to the "whole Church", the body of Christ, in which the particular gifts and functions of all members are but expressions of the life of the whole body.

62. This wholeness must take expression in every particular cultural, social, and political context. Therefore, the evangelization of the world starts at the level of the congregation, in the local and ecumenical dimensions of its life: worship, sacrament, preaching, teaching and healing, fellowship and service, witnessing in life and death.

63. Too often we as churches and congregations stand in the way of the gospel — because of our lack of missionary zeal and missionary structures, because of our divisions, our self-complacency, our lack of catholicity and ecumenical spirit.

64. The call to evangelism, therefore, implies a call to repentance, renewal, and commitment for visible unity. We also deplore proselytism of any sort which further divides the Church.

65. Yet, even imperfect and broken, we are called to put ourselves humbly and gladly at the service of the unfinished mission. We are commissioned to carry the gospel to the whole world and to allow it to permeate all realms of human life. We recognize the signs that the Holy Spirit is in these days calling the Church to a new commitment to evangelism, as evidenced by his voice to the Bangkok conference on "Salvation Today" (1973), the Accra conference on "Giving Account of the Hope that is Within Us" (1974), the Lausanne congress on "The Evangelization of the World" (1974), and the Synod of Bishops of the Roman Catholic Church on "Evangelization in the Modern World" (1974). Clearly this is a common mandate which deserves common support.

On Methodology

66. In our times many churches, Christian individuals, and groups find themselves under pressures and challenges which demand a clear choice between confessing or denying Christ. Others, however, face ambiguous situations in which the question arises: When is the appropriate time to confess and how should we do it? This leads to the question of education for mission. Programmes of lay training ought to be encouraged in order to equip lay workers for communicating the gospel at their particular place in everyday life, including those who, for professional reasons, cross cultural frontiers.

67. Never before has the Church universal had at its disposal such a comprehensive set of means of communication as we have today — literature, audiovisuals, electronic media. While we need to improve our use of such media, nothing can replace the living witness in words and deeds of Christian persons, groups, and congregations who participate in the sufferings and joys, in the struggles and celebrations, in the frustrations and hopes of the people with whom they want to share the gospel. Whatever "methodologies" of communication may seem to be appropriate in different situations, they should be directed by a humble spirit of sensitivity and participation.

68. Careful listening is an essential part of our witness. Only as we are sensitive to the needs and aspirations of others will we know what Christ is saying through our dialogue. What we should like to call "holistic methodology" or "methodology in wholeness" transcends mere techniques or tactics. It is rooted in God's own "strategy of love" which liberates us to respond freely to his call to union with him and our fellow human beings.

A Sense of Urgency

69. We need to recover the sense of urgency. Questions about theological definitions there may be. Problems of precise implementation will arise. But neither theoretical nor practical differences must be allowed to dampen the fires of evangelism.

70. Confessing Christ must be done *today*. "Behold, now is the acceptable time; behold, now is the day of salvation" (2 Cor. 6.2). It cannot wait for a time that is comfortable for us. We must be prepared to proclaim the gospel when human beings need to hear it. But in our zeal to spread the good news, we must guard against fanaticism which disrupts the hearing of the gospel and breaks the community of God. The world requires, and God demands, that we recognize the urgency to proclaim the saving word of God — today. God's acceptable time demands that we respond in all haste. "And how terrible it would be for me if I did not preach the gospel!" (1 Cor. 9.16).

Recommendations

71. We, the delegates of the Fifth Assembly of the World Council of Churches, meeting in Nairobi, have shared a moment of time in a great ecumenical experience to confess and to proclaim Jesus Christ as Lord and Saviour under the theme "Jesus Christ frees and unites".

72. We invite all our brothers and sisters around the world to consider some of the concerns voiced at Nairobi, and to join us as we continue in this ongoing process. We urge all people committed to Christ's discipleship to share with us in confessing him in this ecumenical movement initiated by the Holy Spirit.

73. In this spirit of ecumenical discipleship to which we are committed we invite our fellow-Christians to share with us the following concerns, which *we recommend to the WCC member churches:*

73.1. That the churches utilize for study within the local congregations the report of Assembly Section I on Confessing Christ Today, translating the report into the language spoken within their country or region;

73.2. That the churches and local congregations find ways to relate the content of the report on Confessing Christ Today to their own ecclesiastical, cultural, social, political, economic structures so that the whole gospel may be proclaimed to all persons in every situation;

73.3. That the churches encourage and support the study of intercultural communication and the processes of communication applicable to matters of faith and the interpretation of Scriptures, and that they give special attention to the question as to how their own interpretation of the Bible is culturally conditioned;

73.4. That regional or local clusters of churches engage in reflections based on Bible study and common experience, on the common content of their faith, in order to produce educational materials related to their particular situation;

73.5. That the churches use the best talents inside and outside the church to write hymns, prayers, and other liturgical texts which relate to vital contemporary concerns and issues, and to share such texts widely within the ecumenical movement;

73.6. That the churches develop ways in which those suffering in the name of Christ are included by name in the intercessions of all congregations and that the faithful are informed about the situations of people thus mentioned. No one — imprisoned, tortured, harassed, or persecuted — should escape the vigilance of the praying Church;

73.7. That the churches increase their efforts to overcome the barriers which hinder common celebration of the Eucharist;

73.8. That the churches encourage and promote broader participation on all church levels in ecumenical studies pertaining to confessing Christ, such as the study on "Giving account of the hope that is in us";

73.9. That the churches share with each other and with national/regional ecumenical councils to which they belong statements of faith and theological reflection on actual concerns so that they can help each other assure that in such statements the interests of the poor and the discriminated can be heard, and the powerful and rich may hear their liberation announced. In so doing, churches may be helped in their own attempts to confess Christ;

73.10. That the churches study and practise continuous efforts at developing fresh and communicable methods of expressing their confession of Christ today, learning especially from the universally understood methods of modern art in theatre, film, and other artistic expressions;

73.11. That theological training programmes should include studies in mission and evangelism as a normal part of their curriculum;

73.12. That the churches examine the relationship between Christian and national identity in their particular contexts so that members may gain the courage to give priority to their Christian identity;

73.13. That churches within "consumer societies" encourage and even establish "counter-cultural communities" where persons are accepted without being "productive" or "successful", and in this way help the members to change their consumer-oriented life styles;

73.14. That the churches encourage all Christians to witness to Christ by a holy life and by their daily participation and struggle along with others for a just order in Church and society as means of broadening the scope of the Church's ministry with all people;

73.15. That the churches assist groups and communities of Christian concern, inside and outside the ecclesiastical structure, to relate to each other and to the churches, to meet, exchange, and develop common planning and action;

73.16. That the churches recognize the need to hear and see Christ confessed by Christians from other parts of the world, particularly those churches which have traditionally sent missionaries to other countries, but have never received missionaries; we need to encourage a cross-cultural mission in six continents and to share our gifts and our best models for evangelism;

73.17. That the churches examine the extent to which their missionary structures obscure the confession of Christ, and study the reasons for and the different aspects of the call for a moratorium which has been extended by some churches in their concern for greater effectiveness of mission;

73.18. That the churches provide means of exchange and mutual feedback between church leaders and congregational members (i.e. hearings or consultations on crucial issues for the laity) to enrich the common confession of Christ;

73.19. That churches recognize, stimulate, and make use of evangelistic gifts in individuals and voluntary groups for the benefit of the whole local church and community;

73.20. That churches with different cultural backgrounds within multi-cultural societies not only speak to one another about confessing Christ, but proclaim Christ together;

73.21. That churches in a local situation co-operate in:

(a) studying their given situation and the challenge in it to the Church, especially with regard to realms of life and social levels neglected so far in their witness and service;

(b) serving the needs of the community in ways that lead towards self-help and wholeness;

(c) suffering in solidarity with those whose plight they cannot change (e.g. the bereaved) or whose plight they are struggling to change (e.g. victims of discrimination).

6. VANCOUVER 1983

Witnessing in a Divided World

Report and Recommendations of Issue Group I

At the Sixth Assembly in Vancouver from 24 July to 10 August, the worship services, and especially the celebration of the eucharist using the "Lima liturgy", were an outstanding feature. Under the heading "Eucharistic vision", the report of Issue Group 2 had this to say concerning it: "Our eucharistic vision thus encompasses the whole reality of Christian worship, life and witness, and tends — when truly discovered — to shed new light on Christian unity in its full richness of diversity. It also sharpens the pain of our present division at the table of the Lord; but in bringing forth the organic unity of Christian commitment and of its unique source in the incarnate self-sacrifice of Christ, the eucharistic vision provides us with a new and inspiring guidance on our journey towards a full and credible realization of our given unity."[1]

The report of Issue Group I is an attempt to articulate this "whole reality of Christian worship, life and witness". As preparatory material, members of this Issue Group had before them a discussion paper on the issue of "Witnessing in a Divided World".[2] Issue Group I was under severe pressure of time in drafting its report, which was accepted only by the Central Committee at its meeting immediately after the Assembly. The following is its outline:

Introduction

Culture: the context for our witnessing

Worship: the perspective and the power with which we witness

Special areas of concern: witnessing among children

Special areas of concern: witnessing among the poor

Special areas of concern: witnessing among people of living faiths

Recommendations to member churches.

The report emphasizes especially "witnessing among the poor": "A more simple lifestyle and even a life of poverty is laid on the Church and Christians as a witness to the poverty of Christ... As the Church ministers to those who are affluent it must call them to repentance and declare to them the good news of liberation from enslavement

---

[1] *Gathered for Life*, p.45.

[2] *Issues*, discussion papers on issues arising out of the life and work of the WCC in preparation for its Sixth Assembly in Vancouver, Canada, 24 July to 10 August. Issue Paper I, Witnessing in a Divided World.

to worldly possessions... All Christians and churches have the duty... to denounce... the adherence to the values of high consumption and the investment in death represented by the arms race."

● Text in *Gathered for Life*, official report of the Sixth Assembly of the World Council of Churches, ed. D. Gill, Geneva, 1983, pp.31-42.

Introduction

1. The starting point for our thinking is Jesus Christ. He taught and prayed, proclaimed and healed, lived for God and neighbour; he accepted people, forgave and renewed, and brought change into the lives of those who were open to hear him.

2. To be a witness means to live the life of Christ in the place where we are; it means listening and seeking to understand the faith and perspectives of our neighbours, it means speaking about Jesus the Christ as the Life of the World.

3. Christians are called to witness to Christ in all ages; in each generation we are called to examine the nature of our witness. In discussing this theme we have dealt with five areas in which the World Council of Churches has been engaged during the period since Nairobi. The following is our report.

Culture: the context for our witnessing

4. The question of the nature of the relationship between the Gospel and culture has been with us for some time, but the issue of culture has arisen in a fresh way because we are coming (a) to a deeper understanding of the meaning and function of culture and of its plurality, (b) to a better understanding of the ways in which the Gospel has interacted with cultures, and (c) to a clearer realization of the problems that have been caused by ignoring or denigrating the receptor cultures during the Western missionary era that often went hand in hand with Western colonial expansion.

5. Culture is what holds a community together, giving a common framework of meaning. It is preserved in language, thought patterns, ways of life, attitudes, symbols and presuppositions, and is celebrated in art, music, drama, literature and the like. It constitutes the collective memory of the people and the collective heritage which will be handed down to generations still to come.

6. While we affirm and celebrate cultures as expressing the plural wonder of God's creation, we recognize that not all aspects of every culture are necessarily good. There are aspects within each culture which deny life and oppress people. Also emerging in our time are certain forms of religious culture and sub-cultures which are demonic because they manipulate people and project a world-view and values which are life-denying rather than life-affirming.

7. Given on the one hand the richness and variety of cultures, and on the other the conflict between life-affirming and life-denying aspects within each culture, we need to look again at the whole issue of Christ and culture in the present historical situation.

8. In making this suggestion, we have, amongst others, two particular historical instances of the encounter of the Gospel with culture that we will draw upon.

9. Christ transcends all cultural settings. In confronting and being confronted by the world, into which the Gospel came, Christianity shed some of its Jewish-Hellenistic characteristics, while acquiring characteristics from its receptor cultures. In so doing it sometimes accepted certain elements as they were, at other times transforming them, and at yet other times rejecting elements that were considered to be inimical to the Gospel. This process continued as the Christian message spread throughout Europe and into parts of the Eastern world.

10. The later missionary enterprise which carried the Christian message to the Americas, Africa, Asia and the Pacific, raised a new problem in understanding the relationship between the Gospel and culture. This missionary movement brought the Gospel to all parts of the world. There have always been people who like Paul became a Jew to the Jews and a Greek to the Greeks. Confronted by cultures whose world-view, thought-forms and artistic expressions were strange, "Western" missionaries however by and large denigrated these cultures as pagan and heathen and as inimical to the Gospel. As they did this, many missionaries did not realize that the Gospel they preached was already influenced by centuries-old interaction with many and different cultures and that they were at this point imposing a culturally-bound Christian proclamation on other people. Neither did they realize that they were in fact inhibiting the Gospel from taking root in the cultural soil into which it had come.

11. However, we now have indigenous or local expressions of the Christian faith in many parts of the world, which present more manifestations of diverse forms of Christianity. The Gospel message becomes a transforming power within the life of a community when it is expressed in the cultural forms in which the community understands itself.

12. Therefore, in the search for a theological understanding of culture we are working towards a new ecumenical agenda in which various cultural expressions of the Christian faith may be in conversation with each other. In this encounter the theology, missionary perspectives and historical experiences of many churches, from the most diverse traditions (for example Orthodox and Roman Catholic churches) offer fresh possibilities. So too do the contributions made by women and young people in this search for a new ecumenical agenda.

13. With this background in mind we need to take specific steps:

a) In the search for a theological understanding of culture, we can do the following: share a rich diversity of manifestations of the Christian faith; discover the unity that binds these together; and affirm together the Christological centre and Trinitarian source of our faith in all of its varied expressions.

b) We need to be aware of the possibility of our witness to the Gospel becoming captive to any culture, recognizing the fact that all cultures are judged by the Gospel.

c) In contemporary societies there is an evolution of a new culture due in part to modernization and technology. There is a search for a culture that will preserve human values and build community. We need to reassess the role played by, in particular, secular and religious ideologies in the formation of culture, and the relationship between this process and the demands of the Gospel and our witness to it.

d) While we recognize the emergence of Christian communities within minority groups that affirm their cultural identity, we should pay special attention to the fact that many of these are in danger of being destroyed because they are seen as a threat to a dominant culture.

e) We need to look again at the whole matter of witnessing to the Gospel across cultural boundaries, realizing that listening to and learning from the receptor culture is an essential part of the proclamation of the Christian message.

Worship: the perspective and the power with which we witness

14. Gathered in this Assembly as members of churches from different confessions, continents and cultures, we were reminded again that we are receivers first. As receivers of God's love we are expected to share in witnessing to our neighbours in everyday life, what we receive in the worshipping community. If we do not we shall not go on receiving. Our witness to Jesus Christ as the life of the world is our response to the liberating and uniting work of God's Spirit that we experience despite the divisions of our world.

15. During the various meetings at this Assembly we expressed the urgent need for justice, equality, and solidarity with the poor. But do we really share, or do we in the end prefer ourselves?

16. The basic question is, who can free us from this captivity to ourselves? According to the apostolic experience, only a living fellowship with Christ — as received in prayer and worship — can free us from our personal interests and concerns and renew the spirit of sacrifice and courage so that we may fight for justice even when situations appear hopeless.

17. We have appreciated the central role daily worship has played in this Assembly. It renewed the fellowship of the Spirit and gave us spiritual strength to cope with the different challenges and even frustrations with which we were confronted.

18. Worship is the central act of the life and mission, witness and service of the Church. It is a way in which women and men, rich and poor, able and disabled, share in God's grace and seek forgiveness. It is a liturgical, sacramental and public realization of the unique act of Jesus Christ for the life of the world. The evangelistic, redeeming power of worship lies in the very fact of the "announcement of the death of the Lord until he comes" (1 Cor. 11:26).

19. Worship should be the central act of the life of the Church; however, we heard about a widespread tiredness towards Sunday worship. Where this is true, worship does not have the public witnessing character it should.

20. What are the reasons behind this? Besides a general lack of spiritual enthusiasm in our congregations, people may find worship boring because:
a) there is a language barrier which makes meaningful participation impossible for many;
b) it is formal and does not provide scope for meaningful and spontaneous participation by the congregation;
c) there is often a lack of real fellowship;
d) worship does not bring the anxieties of the people before God; rather it seems to be irrelevant for the daily life of believers and the surrounding human community.

21. How can we overcome this dilemma? We heard about encouraging examples of a cross-fertilization between different liturgical traditions arising out of mutual visits to worship with members of another confession. Some churches are experienc-

ing liturgical renewal. Old liturgies are being reintroduced into the liturgical life of some churches and new forms of worship are being created. The dimension of witness in worship is often emphasized in services for young people, and for parents and children. Worshipping together as families is commended as a fruitful way of sharing the Christian faith. Active participation from all members of the worshipping community is to be encouraged. We also need to pray for each other.

22. Confessing the apostolic creed in our worship we affirm our belief in the community of saints. Thus we are reminded that we live together with the martyrs of all times. Christians who give their lives for the sake of the kingdom are martyrs. We remember them in our worship as encouraging examples. They are symbols of the total Church. They give us inspiration as to how "worship and work must be one". We have learned that the unity between worship and daily Christian life needs urgently to be recovered.

23. For the sake of the witnessing vocation of the Church we need to find a true rhythm of Christian involvement in the world. The Church is gathered for worship and scattered for everyday life. Whilst in some situations in the witnessing dimension of worship there must be a "liturgy after the liturgy", service to the world as praise to God, in other contexts it must be stressed that there is no Christian service to the world unless it is rooted in the service of worship.

Special areas of concern: witnessing among children

24. The child is a living parable of the way the kingdom is to be received and appreciated. The Bible speaks of God's special concern for "little ones":

> Let the children come to me, and do not hinder them; for to such belongs the kingdom of heaven (Matt. 19:14, RSV).

On another occasion Jesus and the disciples were discussing the question: "Who is the greatest in the kingdom of heaven?" — when Jesus called to him a child and said:

> Truly I say to you unless you turn and become like children, you will never enter the kingdom of heaven. Whoever humbles himself or herself like this child, that person is the greatest in the kingdom of heaven (Matt. 18:3-4, RSV).

25. The population of the world is growing rapidly. In some places children constitute the majority of the population, and they raise questions for the adults. In Jesus' encounter with children we see the Gospel at work. Forgiveness and love are given and received with a freedom or openness adults quickly lose. Children, because they are powerless and vulnerable, respond to God's love in warm, accepting ways. However, children are not idealized by the Bible. They stand in need of the grace and love of God. And yet Jesus proclaimed, "theirs is the kingdom". Their very vulnerability and powerlessness demand that we so speak for them and stand with them, that we use their needs and situations as a yardstick for our churches' thinking, programmes and priorities.

26. Stories about children can help focus the global issues we face and place question marks against our priorities and attitudes. Through them we can begin to understand the Gospel in a new way. Tonight and every night, thousands of children will sleep on the streets of our cities and in the open. Thousands of malnourished children will eventually become mentally retarded adults unable to participate as fully in their society as they may have done if they had been given adequate food.

Thousands of children are left homeless, orphaned and mutilated by war. Young teenagers throw rocks and carry weapons, caught up in the cruelty and hatred of war created by an adult world.

27. Our environment is polluted and threatened. "Jelly babies" and deformed children are born in the Pacific Islands because of nuclear testing. A child refuses to think of the future and loses dreams of hope because of a belief that the world will be destroyed by nuclear war before school is finished. Thousands of children die unnecessarily each day from curable and preventable diseases.

28. The attitudes and priorities of our adult society are questioned by what happens to children in our world.

29. The baptism or dedication of a child in a parish is a time of celebration and rejoicing. However, children are often not included in worship, sometimes not able to participate in the eucharist. A child at 14 joins an occult sect asserting that she has found meaning and value in that group and not in the Church. The parents and the Church are deeply disappointed and puzzled by her action. Some children feel they do not belong to the Church and that they have no real place in it. Many children will never hear the Gospel as their parents are indifferent to the Christian faith or have no faith at all.

30. These stories raise important issues for the churches in relation to our witness in a real and divided world.

31. "Do not hinder the children," says Jesus. Everything we do in the name of Jesus Christ needs to be seen in the light of this demand. There is, therefore, an urgent need for the churches through the WCC to take up the challenge that our children pose for us.

Special areas of concern: witnessing among the poor

32. The Church is called to witness to the good news of the life, death and resurrection of Jesus Christ, to a world where there is a frightening and growing gap between rich and poor nations and between rich and poor within nations. Poverty exists on an unprecedented global scale. In a world which is today torn by conflicting ideologies, the poor are most apt to be ignored and forgotten. An increasing number of people find themselves marginalized, second-class citizens unable to control their own destiny and resigned to being and remaining poor. Children, the disabled, and women are among those who suffer most seriously the cruelty and despair of poverty. Racism, exploitation, militarization, and the resources expended in the arms race are different ways in which poverty is promoted and increased. Poverty is treated as a problem, rather than as a scandal calling for radical action to attack its causes and roots in human sinfulness and an unwillingness to share.

33. The Christian Gospel of salvation is good news to all people, but especially to the poor (cf. Luke 7:22). To them, as to all, is addressed the offer of God's forgiveness, the call to repentance, and the vision of a new heaven and a new earth. The message of the prophets is that God in no way assumes a neutral position between the rich and the poor. God is on the side of the poor and champions their cause for justice and fullness of life. They are blessed not because they are poor but because in their poverty Christ has come to offer them the gift of the kingdom. The poor have possibilities of a new awareness of the riches that are in Christ and therefore have much to give.

34. In not sharing the good news of the Gospel there has been a double injustice: the poor are victims of social, economic and political oppression and often have been deprived of the knowledge of God's special love for them and the energizing liberation which such knowledge brings. In the parable of the last judgment (Matt. 25:30ff.) Jesus identifies himself with the hungry, the homeless, the naked, the sick and prisoners. This demands of us as Christians a corresponding allegiance. If we are to follow Christ then we must care for the poor and seek to reverse their situation.

35. The Church's call to witness in the life of the poor is therefore a call for the people of God to rethink its priorities in its missions and its programmes, and it is a challenge to its lifestyle on both a corporate and an individual level. A more simple lifestyle and even a life of poverty is laid on the Church and Christians as a witness to the poverty of Christ "who though he was rich for our sake became poor" (2 Cor. 8:9). Christians and churches, of course, find themselves in very different circumstances, some rich and others poor. To all, the call to share the good news with the poor comes as a priority and a specific challenge. The Gospel must be proclaimed in both word and deed; word without service is empty and service without the word is without power. The churches today are learning afresh, through the call to witness to the poor, to overcome the old dichotomy between evangelism and social action. In Jesus' announcement of the kingdom the spiritual and material Gospel belong together.

36. As the Church witnesses to the Gospel it needs to reflect faithfully the totality and universality of God's mission in a world divided into rich and poor, different ideological camps, male and female, young and old, slave and free, able and disabled. In its witness to the poor and the oppressed it can and must be the voice of those who are often rendered voiceless. God's own upholding of the right of the poor, the outcast, the widows and the orphan is a rebuke to complacent Christians and churches, and a summons to repentance and a new commitment to the cause of justice. To claim to witness to the poor and to side with them without working to change the conditions which make for poverty is hypocritical. The churches must struggle to put in place a new international order for a more just world and be willing to change their own structures in response. It must call on those who have power to use their power to make human life more human.

37. As the church ministers to those who are affluent, it must call them to repentance and declare to them the good news of liberation from enslavement to worldly possessions. There is a poverty in the human condition which riches cannot mask and the Church has a ministry of testifying to the Christ who can liberate people from all their need. We must help our church members understand that affluence has a way of sometimes impoverishing, separating and blinding the rich so that they do not see the poor (Luke 16:19-31). Those who concentrate on riches, such as the rich farmer in Jesus' parable, are in danger of losing their souls. Thus the New Testament writers warn against the dangers of wealth, particularly the apostle James who delivers the stern warnings to the rich (5:1-3) and censures them for exploiting the poor (5:4-6).

38. All Christians and churches have the duty, as part of their prophetic mission, to denounce the concentration of goods in the hands of a few, the adherence to the values of high consumption and the investment in death represented by the arms race which is one of the principle causes for the growing gap between the rich and the poor and the consequent failure to invest for the alleviation of poverty. Churches which have are called to share with churches which have not, and within the churches there must be a

sharing so that the apostolic standard "there was not a needy person among them" (Acts 4:34) may be realized.

39. We rejoice that the churches are growing today among the poor of the earth and that new insights and perspectives on the Gospel are coming to the whole Church from communities of the poor. They are discovering and making known dimensions of the Gospel which have long been neglected and forgotten by the Church. The richness and freshness of their experience is an inspiration, blessing and challenge to the established churches. The centres of missionary expansion are moving from the North to the South as the poor have become not just the subjects but also the bearers of the good news; when people discover Christ they discover for themselves a liberating initiative and a new ethos towards the fullness of life. In the words of the Melbourne affirmation: "God is working through the poor of the earth to awaken the consciousness of humanity to his call for repentance, for justice and for love."

Special areas of concern: witnessing among people of living faiths

40. We live as people and as Christians in a religiously and ideologically pluralistic world. Christians from all parts of the oikumene raise questions about living alongside of, and witnessing to, neighbours of other faiths and diverse ideological commitments who have their own specific testimonies to offer. In such situations witness is not a one-way process: "from us to them". There is also a witness from "them to us", except in certain cases of martyrdom, the witness up to death, which could be understood as an extreme example of one-way testimony. However, in most normal circumstances, we, as human beings, are caught up in a search for reality and fulfilment, seeking to be understood and to understand and thus discover meaning for living. Of all the things we do as Christians, witnessing among peoples of living faiths and ideologies causes the most difficulty and confusion. In this task we are hesitant learners, and need to acquire sensitivity not only to the peoples of other faiths and ideologies, but also to Christians caught up in situations of witness and dialogue in different parts of the world.

41. In our discussions and reflections on the question of witnessing to Christ among people of other faiths we have heard encouraging reports of many examples of dialogue in local situations. But we have also become aware of some matters which remain to be explored in the years that lie ahead. We note amongst other things the following:

a) We wish to place on record our appreciation to our friends from other faiths who have been present with us in this Sixth Assembly. We value their contribution, and their presence has raised for us questions about the special nature of the witness Christians bring to the world community.

b) While affirming the uniqueness of the birth, life, death and resurrection of Jesus, to which we bear witness, we recognize God's creative work in the seeking for religious truth among people of other faiths.

c) We acknowledge the experience of common action and cooperation between Christians and persons of other faiths and the urgency of working together, especially in areas concerning the poor, basic human dignity, justice and peace, economic reconstruction, and the eradication of hunger and disease.

42. We see, however, the need to distinguish between witness and dialogue, whilst at the same time affirming their inter-relatedness.

43. Witness may be described as those acts and words by which a Christian or community gives testimony to Christ and invites others to make their response to him. In witness we expect to share the good news of Jesus and be challenged in relation to our understanding of, and our obedience to that good news.

44. Dialogue may be described as that encounter where people holding different claims about ultimate reality can meet and explore these claims in a context of mutual respect. From dialogue we expect to discern more about how God is active in our world, and to appreciate for their own sake the insights and experiences people of other faiths have of ultimate reality.

45. Dialogue is not a device for nor a denial of Christians witness. It is rather a mutual venture to bear witness to each other and the world, in relation to different perceptions of ultimate reality.

46. While distinctions can be made between dialogue, cooperation and mutual witness in the real experience of living in a religiously and ideologically pluralistic situation they in practice intermingle and are closely inter-related.

47. All these must be seen in the context of shared responsibility for a common future, based on mutual respect, equal rights, and equal obligations.

48. There are still many questions remaining for further studies:

a) When witnessing among people of living faiths, an account must be taken of the influence of the dominant ideologies on religious belief and practices present and active in the particular cultural context.

b) An important concern is the degree to which Christians of different confessions can work towards sharing a common understanding of what it means to be human, an understanding of what it means to be the Church, and how these concerns relate to the witness of the Christian community and the involvement of Christians in dialogue with people of living faiths and ideologies.

c) Meeting in Vancouver and hearing about the religious life of the Native peoples has focused attention on the need to give a higher profile to dialogue with people from traditional religions.

d) The question of shared worship or prayer with people from other faiths needs to be explored.

e) Another of the religious phenomena of our day is the influence of various kinds of new religious movements. We need to discover more about these.

In all these explorations of faith it is important to involve women and young people. Their self-understanding of their role in the faith community will deepen and widen the theological quest.

49. We are encouraged by the insights and experience which have been gradually built up through various meetings between Christians and people of other living faiths. We look forward to the fruits of further encounters. In the next seven years we anticipate theological reflection on the nature of witness and dialogue which will encourage the life of the Christian community in many different parts of the world.

50. *Recommendations to member churches:*

a) That member churches be encouraged to engage actively in their calling to witness to their faith: towards that end they are encouraged to translate and distribute widely the document *Mission and Evangelism: an Ecumenical Affirmation.*

b) That member churches be encouraged to visit each other at local parish level in order to share in each other's worship and build up partner relationships with different liturgical traditions.

c) That member churches be asked to study the report of the Melbourne conference, especially the section on the poor, and to continue or to initiate programmes of action based on this.

d) That member churches be encouraged to translate, distribute and study the *Guidelines on Dialogue*.

e) That member churches be encouraged to share with one another their experiences of witness and dialogue among peoples of living faiths, and among people of no religion, through the World Council of Churches.

f) That member churches initiate studies on Gospel and culture in cooperation with regional councils of churches and the World Council of Churches.

III.
Various Documents

1. BARMEN THEOLOGICAL DECLARATION
Theological Declaration on the Present Situation of the German Evangelical Church, 1934

The Barmen Declaration is the most important document of the church struggle between the "Confessing Church" and the "German Christian" movement during the National Socialist period in Germany. It was the work of a three-man preparatory theological committee composed of the two Lutheran theologians, Hans Asmussen and Thomas Breit, and the Reformed theologian Karl Barth, meeting in Frankfurt-am-Main on 15 and 16 May 1934, on the basis of an initial draft by Karl Barth ("Frankfurt concord"). After thorough discussion and revision in the interconfessional committee, the Declaration reproduced below was unanimously endorsed by the 138 delegates to the First Confessional Synod of the German Evangelical Church on 31 May 1934 in Wuppertal-Barmen (now in the Federal Republic of Germany). The Barmen Declaration is the first confessional document within German Protestantism since the time of the Reformation. Its purpose was to give theological guidance in the controversy with the "false doctrine" of the "German Christian" movement. Theses 1 and 2 define the Christological basis, Theses 3 to 6 deal with the nature of the church, its task and its ministries. Thesis 5, on the relation of church and state, is especially important, containing as it does approaches to a political ethic so urgently needed today.

The Barmen Declaration affirms its continuity with the Nicene-Constantinopolitan Creed of 381; it explicitly appeals in its introduction to "the confession of the One Lord of the One, Holy, Catholic and Apostolic Church". With respect to its implications for future relations between Lutheran, Reformed and United churches, it declares in its introduction: "We commit to God what this may mean for the relationships of the Confessional Churches with each other."

Most of the German churches, and some non-German churches (as e.g. the Netherlands Reformed Church), have included the Barmen Declaration in one form or another in their basic constitutional articles. In some countries of Latin America, South Africa and Asia today, the Barmen Declaration serves as a model in the struggle for a credible Christian community.

● Text in *The German Phoenix: Men and Movements in the Church in Germany,* ed. F.H. Littel, New York, 1960, pp.184-88. Also in Wilhelm Niesel, *Reformed Symbolics: a Comparison of Catholicism, Orthodoxy and Protestantism,* tr. David Lewis, Oliver & Boyd, Edinburgh and London, 1962, pp.357ff.

According to the introductory words of its constitution of 11 July 1933, the German Evangelical Church is a federal union of confessional churches which grew out of the Reformation, of equal rights and parallel existence. The theological premise of the association of these churches is given in Article 1 and Article 2, paragraph 1 of the constitution of the German Evangelical Church, recognized by the national government on 14 July 1933:

Article 1: The impregnable foundation of the German Evangelical Church is the Gospel of Jesus Christ, as it is revealed in Holy Scripture and came again to the light in the creeds of the Reformation. In this way the authorities, which the church needs for her mission, are defined and limited.

Article 2, paragraph 1: The German Evangelical Church consists of churches (territorial churches).

We, assembled representatives of Lutheran, Reformed and United churches, independent synods, *Kirchentage* and local church groups, hereby declare that we stand together on the foundation of the German Evangelical Church as a federal union of German confessional churches. We are held together by confession of the one Lord of the one, holy, universal and apostolic church.

We declare, before the public view of all the Evangelical Churches of Germany, that the unity of this confession and thereby also the unity of the German Evangelical Church is severely threatened. In this year of the existence of the German Evangelical Church it is endangered by the more and more clearly evident style of teaching and action of the ruling ecclesiastical party of the German Christians and the church government which they run. This threat comes from the fact that the theological premise in which the German Evangelical Church is united is constantly and basically contradicted and rendered invalid, both by the leaders and spokesmen of the German Christians and also by the church government, by means of strange propositions. If they obtain, the church — according to all the creeds which are authoritative among us — ceases to be the church. If they obtain, moreover, the German Evangelical Church will become impossible as a federal union of confessional churches.

Together we may and must, as members of Lutheran, Reformed and United churches, speak today to this situation. Precisely because we want to be and remain true to our various confessions of faith, we may not keep silent, for we believe that in a time of common need and trial (*Anfechtung*) a common word has been placed in our mouth. We commit to God what this may mean for the relationship of the confessional churches with each other.

In view of the destructive errors of the German Christians and the present national church government, we pledge ourselves to the following evangelical truths:

1. "I am the way and the truth and the life: no man cometh unto the Father, but by me" (John 14:6).

"Verily, verily, I say unto you, he that entereth not by the door into the sheepfold, but climbeth up some other way, the same is a thief and a robber... I am the door: by me if any man enter in, he shall be saved" (John 10:1,9).

Jesus Christ, as he is testified to us in the Holy Scripture, is the one Word of God, whom we are to hear, whom we are to trust and obey in life and in death.

We repudiate the false teaching that the church can and must recognize yet other happenings and powers, images and truths as divine revelation alongside this one Word of God, as a source of her preaching.

2. "But of him are ye in Christ Jesus, who of God is made unto us wisdom, and righteousness, and sanctification, and redemption" (1 Cor. 1:30).

Just as Jesus Christ is the pledge of the forgiveness of all our sins, just so — and with the same earnestness — is he also God's mighty claim on our whole life; in him we encounter a joyous liberation from the godless claims of this world to free and thankful service of his creatures.

We repudiate the false teaching that there are areas of our life in which we belong not to Jesus Christ but another lord, areas in which we do not need justification and sanctification through him.

3. "But speaking the truth in love, may grow up into him in all things, which is the head, even Christ: from whom the whole body (is) fitly joined together and compacted..." (Eph. 4:15-16).

The Christian church is the community of brethren, in which Jesus Christ presently works in the word and sacraments through the Holy Spirit. With her faith as well as her obedience, with her message as well as her ordinances, she has to witness in the midst of the world of sin as the church of forgiven sinners that she is his alone, that she lives and wishes to live only by his comfort and his counsel in expectation of his appearance.

We repudiate the false teaching that the church can turn over the form of her message and ordinances at will or according to some dominant ideological and political convictions.

4. "Ye know that the princes of the Gentiles exercise dominion over them, and they that are great exercise authority upon them. But it shall not be so among you: but whosoever will be great among you, let him be your minister" (Matt. 20:25-26).

The various offices in the church establish no rule of one over the other but the exercise of the service entrusted and commanded to the whole congregation.

We repudiate the false teaching that the church can and may, apart from this ministry, set up special leaders (*Führer*) equipped with powers to rule.

5. "Fear God, honor the king!" (1 Pet. 2:17).

The Bible tells us that according to divine arrangement the state has the responsibility to provide for justice and peace in the yet unredeemed world, in which the church also stands, according to the measure of human insight and human possibility, by the threat and use of force.

The church recognizes with thanks and reverence toward God the benevolence of this, his provision. She reminds men of God's Kingdom, God's commandment and righteousness, and thereby the responsibility of rulers and ruled. She trusts and obeys the power of the word, through which God maintains all things.

We repudiate the false teaching that the state can and should expand beyond its special responsibility to become the single and total order of human life, and also thereby fulfill the commission of the church.

We repudiate the false teaching that the church can and should expand beyond its special responsibility to take on the characteristics, functions and dignities of the state, and thereby become itself an organ of the state.

6. "Lo, I am with you alway, even unto the end of the world" (Matt. 28:20). "The word of God is not bound" (2 Tim. 2:9).

The commission of the church, in which her freedom is founded, consists in this: in place of Christ and thus in the service of his own word and work, to extend through word and sacrament the message of the free grace of God to all people.

We repudiate the false teaching that the church, in human self-esteem, can put the word and work of the Lord in the service of some wishes, purposes and plans or other, chosen according to desire.

The confessing synod of the German Evangelical Church declares that she sees in the acknowledgment of these truths and in the repudiation of these errors the not-to-be-circumvented theological foundation of the German Evangelical Church as a federal union of confessional churches. [The synod] calls upon all who can join in its declaration to be aware of these theological lessons in their ecclesiastical decisions. It begs all concerned to turn again in the unity of faith, of love, and of hope.

Verbum Dei manet in aeternum.

2. THE BASIS OF UNION
Theological Guidelines
of the Church of South India, 1941

As early as 1919, efforts were being made to achieve union in South India between the United Church (of Presbyterians and Congregationalists) and the Anglican and Methodist churches. After decades of negotiation, the following theological "Basis of Union" and a draft constitution were agreed. Together they constitute the foundation of the united "Church of South India" which came into being on 27 September 1947. The original source of the "Basis of Union" was the Lambeth quadrilateral of 1888. A first draft was already published in 1929; the seventh version, that of 1941, became the official one. In the main it was taken into the constitution of the Church of South India as Chapter II on "The Governing Principles of the Church". It is one of the oldest theological documents relative to church union. It is historically significant, and it can furnish a model for churches engaged in union negotiations.

The Basis of Union consists of 18 sections dealing with fundamental questions of faith and order:

1   The purpose and nature of the union
2-3   Foundations of faith
4-5   Sacraments and ministries
6-9   Congregational, presbyterial and episcopal elements
10-13 Structure and autonomy
14-18 Relationships with other churches
We give below the text of sections 1-7 and 13.

● Text in *The Constitution of the Church of South India*, Madras, 1963, pp.81-86, 90-91.

The Purpose and Nature of the Union

1. The uniting Churches affirm that the purpose of the union into which they hope to enter is the carrying out of God's will as this is expressed in our Lord's prayer — "That they all may be one... that the world may believe that Thou didst send me." They believe that by this union the Church in South India will become a more effective instrument for God's work, and that the result of union will be greater peace, closer fellowship, and fuller life within the Church, and also renewed eagerness and power for the proclamation of the Gospel of Christ. It is their hope that the Church thus united

may be a true leaven of unity in the life of India, and that through it there may be a greater release of divine power for the fulfilment of God's purpose for His world.

The uniting Churches believe that the unity of His Church for which Christ prayed is a unity in Him and in the Father through the Holy Spirit, and is therefore fundamentally a reality of the spiritual realm. They seek the unity of the Spirit in the bond of peace. But this unity of the Spirit must find expression in the faith and order of the Church, in its worship, in its organization and in its whole life, so that, as the Body of Christ, it may be a fit instrument for carrying out His gracious purposes in the world.

It is the will of Christ that His Church should be one, and the manifold gifts of His grace were promised to the Church which is His Body. It is also His will that there should be a ministry accepted and fully effective throughout the world-wide Church. In the present divided state of Christendom there is no ministry which in this respect fully corresponds with the purpose of God, and the ministry can recover fulness only by the union of all the parts of the one Body. The uniting Churches recognize, however, that God has bestowed His grace with undistinguishing regard through all their ministers, in His use of them for His work of enlightening the world, converting sinners and perfecting saints. They acknowledge each other's ministries to be real ministries of the Word and Sacraments, and thankfully recognize the spiritual efficacy of sacraments and other ministrations which God has so clearly blessed. They confidently expect that these ministries hitherto separate will, when united, be used for a yet fuller manifestation of God's power and glory. Each Church, in separation, has borne special witness to certain elements of the truth; therefore for the perfecting of the whole body the heritage of each is needed. Each, maintaining the continuity of its own life, will be enriched by the gifts and graces of the others.

Wherever union takes place, it comes into being only by the working of the spirit of Christ, Who is both truth and love. In His spirit of love, all the ministers of the uniting Churches will from the inauguration of the union be recognized as equally ministers of the united Church without distinction or difference. The united Church will be formed by a combination of different elements, each bringing its contribution to the whole, and not by the absorption of any one by any other. It will, therefore, also be a comprehensive Church; and its members, firmly holding the fundamentals of the faith and order of the Church Universal, will be allowed wide freedom of opinion in all other matters, and wide freedom of action in such differences of practice as are consistent with the general framework of the Church as one organized body.

The uniting Churches are agreed that, in every effort to bring together divided members of Christ's body into one organization, the final aim must be the union in the Universal Church of all who acknowledge the name of Christ, and that the test of all local schemes of union is that they should express locally the principle of the great catholic unity of the Body of Christ. They trust, therefore, that the united Church, conserving all that is of spiritual value in its Indian heritage, will express under Indian conditions and in Indian forms the spirit, the thought and the life of the Church Universal.

It is the intention and hope of the uniting Churches that all the actions of the united Church will be regulated by the principles that it should maintain fellowship with all those branches of the Church of Christ with which the uniting Churches now severally enjoy such fellowship, and that it should continually seek to widen and strengthen this fellowship and to work towards the goal of the full union in one body of all parts of the Church of Christ.

They pray that this scheme of union may under God's providence be a contribution towards the uniting of His Church and the ordering of its life in freedom and truth, and they trust that the united Church in South India will never so use the provisions of the Constitution under which it will begin its life that they will become barriers against the fuller truth and richer life to be attained in a wider fellowship, but that it will always be ready to correct and amend them as God's will becomes more clearly known through the growing together of the several parts of the now divided Church into a common mind and spirit under the guidance of the one Holy Spirit.

The Church and its Membership

2. The uniting Churches acknowledge that the Church is the Body of Christ and its members are the members of His Body: and that those are members according to the will and purpose of God who have been baptized into the name of the Father and of the Son and of the Holy Spirit, and, receiving the calling and grace of God with faith, continue steadfast therein, maintaining by the same faith, through the various means of grace which He has provided in His Church, their vital union with the Head of the Body, and through Him their fellowship one with another.

The Faith of the Church

3. The uniting Churches accept the Holy Scriptures of the Old and New Testaments as containing all things necessary to salvation and as the supreme and decisive standard of faith; and acknowledge that the Church must always be ready to correct and reform itself in accordance with the teaching of those Scriptures as the Holy Spirit shall reveal it.

They also accept the Apostles' Creed and the Creed commonly called the Nicene, as witnessing to and safe-guarding that faith; and they thankfully acknowledge that same faith to be continuously confirmed by the Holy Spirit in the experience of the Church of Christ.

Thus they believe in God, the Father, the Creator of all things, by whose love we are preserved;

They believe in Jesus Christ, the incarnate Son of God and Redeemer of the world, in whom alone we are saved by grace, being justified from our sins by faith in Him;

They believe in the Holy Spirit, by whom we are sanctified and built up in Christ and in the fellowship of His Body;

And in this faith they worship the Father, Son and Holy Spirit, one God in Trinity and Trinity in Unity.

Notes

(i) The uniting Churches accept the fundamental truths embodied in the Creeds named above as providing a sufficient basis of Union; but do not intend thereby to demand the assent of individuals to every word and phrase in them, or to exclude reasonable liberty of interpretation, or to assert that those Creeds are a complete expression of the Christian faith.

(ii) It is understood that it will be competent to the united Church to issue supplementary statements concerning the faith for the guidance of its teachers and the edification of the faithful, provided that such statements are not contrary to the truths of our religion revealed in the Holy Scriptures.

(iii) The act of union will not debar any teacher of the united Church from using for the instruction of the faithful any confession of faith which had been employed in any of the uniting Churches before the union, and which is not inconsistent with the doctrinal standards officially set forth by the united Church.

The Sacraments in the Church

4. The uniting Churches believe that the Sacraments of Baptism and the Supper of the Lord are means of grace through which God works in us, and that while the mercy of God to all mankind cannot be limited, there is in the teaching of Christ the plain command that men should follow His appointed way of salvation by a definite act of reception into the family of God and by continued acts of fellowship with Him in that family, and that this teaching is made explicit in the two Sacraments which He has given us. In every Communion the true Celebrant is Christ alone, who continues in the Church today that which He began in the upper room. In the visible Church, the celebration of the Lord's Supper is an act of the Church, the company of believers redeemed by Christ, who act as the local manifestation of the whole Church of Christ in heaven and on earth. It has in experience been found best that one minister should lead the worship of the church, and pronounce the words of consecration in the service of Holy Communion. From very early times it has been the custom of the Church that those only should exercise this function who have received full and solemn commission from the Church to do so; this commission has ordinarily been given by the laying on of hands in ordination.

The only indispensable conditions for the ministration of the grace of God in the Church are the unchangeable promise of God Himself and the gathering together of God's elect people in the power of the Holy Ghost. God is a God of order; it has been His good pleasure to use visible Church and its regularly constituted ministries as the normal means of the operation of His Spirit. But it is not open to any to limit the operation of the grace of God to any particular channel, or to deny the reality of His grace when it is visibly manifest in the lives of Churches and individuals.

In the united Church the Sacraments will be observed with unfailing use of Christ's words of institution and of the elements ordained by Him.

The Ministry in the Church

5. The uniting Churches believe that the ministry is a gift of God through Christ to His Church, which He has given for the perfecting of the life and service of all its members. All members of the Church have equally access to God. All, according to their measure, share in the heavenly High Priesthood of the risen and ascended Christ, from which alone the Church derives its character as a royal priesthood. All alike are called to continue upon earth the priestly work of Christ by showing forth in life and word the glory of the redeeming power of God in Him. No individual and no one order in the Church can claim exclusive possession of this heavenly priesthood.

But in the Church there has at all times been a special ministry, to which men have been called by God and set apart in the Church. Those who are ordained to the ministry of the Word and Sacraments can exercise their offices only in and for the Church, through the power of Christ the one High Priest.

The vocation of the ordained ministry is to bring sinners to repentance, and to lead God's people in worship, prayer, and praise, and through pastoral ministrations, the preaching of the Gospel and the administration of the Sacraments (all these being made effective through faith) to assist men to receive the saving and sanctifying benefits of Christ and to fit them for service. The uniting Churches believe that in ordination God, in answer to the prayers of His Church, bestows on and assures to those whom He has called and His Church as accepted for any particular form of the ministry, a commission for it and the grace appropriate to it.

Necessary Elements in the Life of the United Church

6. The uniting Churches recognize that episcopal, presbyteral and congregational elements must all have their place in the order of life of the united Church, and that the episcopate, the presbyterate, and the congregation of the faithful should all in their several spheres have responsibility and exercise authority in the life and work of the Church, in its governance and administration, in its evangelistic and pastoral work, in its discipline, and in its worship.

The Congregation in the United Church

7. The uniting Churches believe that as the Church of a whole region, being in fellowship with other regional Churches, is ideally the embodiment of the Church Universal in that region, and as similarly the Church of a diocese as a living part of a regional Church is the Church Universal expressing its one life in the diocese, so also in the purpose of God every local group of the faithful organised for Christian life and worship as a congregation or pastorate within the fellowship of the diocese, represents in that place the same one, holy, catholic and apostolic Church.

Subject therefore to such general regulations as may be issued by the Synod of the united Church or by a Diocesan Council, every congregation of the united Church will, with its pastor, be responsible for watching over its members, for keeping its life and doctrine pure, for ordering its worship, and for the proclaiming of the Gospel to those outside the Church; and every pastorate will have general administrative authority within its area, will have certain responsibilities in Church discipline, and will have an opportunity of expressing its judgment both as to the appointment of its pastor and the selection of candidates for ordination from that pastorate....

The Autonomy of the United Church

13. The uniting Churches agree that the united Church should of right be free in all spiritual matters from the direction or interposition of any civil government.

They further agree that the united Church must be an autonomous Church and free from any control, legal or otherwise, of any Church or Society external to itself. At the same time they remember that the united Church, on account of its origin and history, must have special relations with the Churches in the West through which it has come into existence, and they are confident that it will so regulate its acts as to maintain fellowship both with those Churches and with other branches of the Catholic Church with which the uniting Churches are now in communion.

They also recognize that the united Church, as a part of the Church Universal, must give full weight to the pronouncements of bodies representative of the whole Church, and, in particular, would desire to take part in the deliberations and decisions of an Ecumenical Council, if such should in the mercy of God be some day called together.

3. DOGMATIC CONSTITUTION ON DIVINE REVELATION
Dei Verbum, 1965

Along with the dogmatic Constitution on the Church (Lumen Gentium)*, this Dogmatic Constitution on Divine Revelation constitutes the most important of the declarations of the Second Vatican Council. "Dogmatic constitutions" are pronouncements of the supreme teaching authority of the Roman Catholic Church.*

In 1962 the Preparatory Theological Commission first presented a schema, De fontibus revelationis *("On the sources of revelation"). In the course of vigorous debates it was clear that no consensus would be achieved on this schema, and Pope John XXIII appointed a new commission under the joint presidency of Cardinals Bea and Ottaviani to produce a fresh draft, this time "on the divine revelation". Conciliar discussions on this schema lasted over two and a half years before the fourth version of the new text was accepted by an overwhelming majority (2,344 in favour and only 6 against!) on 18 November and promulgated on the same day. The structure of the Constitution is as follows:*

Prologue
I. Divine revelation itself
II. The transmission of divine revelation
III. Sacred scripture: its divine inspiration and its interpretation
IV. The Old Testament
V. The New Testament
VI. Sacred scripture in the life of the church

It was the first time in the history of the Roman Catholic Church that a Council had pronounced in such a full and detailed way on the word of God and holy scripture. This document threw the doors wide open for ecumenical dialogue on God's revelation as well as on the relationship between scripture and tradition. To an astonishing degree this Constitution coincides in content with the Montreal Statement of the Faith and Order Commission in 1963 on "Scripture, Tradition and Traditions". It closes with the statement: "Just as from constant attendance at the eucharistic mystery the life of the Church draws increase, so a new impulse of spiritual life may be expected from increased veneration of the Word of God which 'stands forever'."

● Text in *Documents of Vatican II*, ed. Austin P. Flannery, Eerdmans Publishing Company, Grand Rapids, USA, 1975, pp.750-65.

Prologue

1. Hearing the Word of God with reverence, and proclaiming it with faith, the sacred Synod assents to the words of St. John, who says: "We proclaim to you the eternal life which was with the Father and was made manifest to us — that which we have seen and heard we proclaim also to you, so that you may have fellowship with us; and our fellowship is with the Father and with his Son Jesus Christ." (1 Jn. 1:2-3). Following, then, in the steps of the Councils of Trent and Vatican I, this Synod wishes to set forth the true doctrine on divine Revelation and its transmission. For it wants the whole world to hear the summons to salvation, so that through hearing it may believe, through belief it may hope, through hope it may come to love.

Chapter I: Divine Revelation Itself

2. It pleased God, in his goodness and wisdom, to reveal himself and to make known the mystery of his will (cf. Eph. 1:9). His will was that men should have access to the Father, through Christ, the Word made flesh, in the Holy Spirit, and thus become sharers in the divine nature (cf. Eph. 2:18; 2 Pet. 1:4). By this revelation, then, the invisible God (cf. Col. 1:15; 1 Tim. 1:17), from the fullness of his love, addresses men as his friends (cf. Ex. 33:11; Jn. 15:14-15), and moves among them (cf. Bar. 3:38), in order to invite and receive them into his own company. This economy of Revelation is realized by deeds and words, which are intrinsically bound up with each other. As a result, the works performed by God in the history of salvation show forth and bear out the doctrine and realities signified by the words; the words, for their part, proclaim the works, and bring to light the mystery they contain. The most intimate truth which this revelation gives us about God and the salvation of man shines forth in Christ, who is himself both the mediator and the sum total of Revelation.

3. God, who creates and conserves all things by his Word (cf. Jn. 1:3), provides men with constant evidence of himself in created realities (cf. Rom. 1:19-20). And furthermore, wishing to open up the way to heavenly salvation, he manifested himself to our first parents from the very beginning. After the fall, he buoyed them up with the hope of salvation, by promising redemption (cf. Gen. 3:15); and he has never ceased to take care of the human race. For he wishes to give eternal life to all those who seek salvation by patience in well-doing (cf. Rom. 2:6-7). In his own time God called Abraham, and made him into a great nation (cf. Gen. 12:2). After the era of the patriarchs, he taught this nation, by Moses and the prophets, to recognize him as the only living and true God, as a provident Father and just judge. He taught them, too, to look for the promised Saviour. And so, throughout the ages, he prepared the way for the Gospel.

4. After God had spoken many times and in various ways through the prophets, "in these last days he has spoken to us by a Son" (Heb. 1:1-2). For he sent his Son, the eternal Word who enlightens all men, to dwell among men and to tell them about the inner life of God. Hence, Jesus Christ, sent as "a man among men," "speaks the words of God" (Jn. 3:34), and accomplishes the saving work which the Father gave him to do (cf. Jn. 5:36; 17:4). As a result, he himself — to see whom is to see the Father (cf. Jn. 14:9) — completed and perfected Revelation and confirmed it with divine guarantees. He did this by the total fact of his presence and self-manifestation — by words and works, signs and miracles, but above all by his death and glorious resurrection from the dead, and finally by sending the Spirit of truth. He revealed that God was with us, to deliver us from the darkness of sin and death, and to raise us up to eternal life.

The Christian economy, therefore, since it is the new and definitive covenant, will never pass away; and no new public revelation is to be expected before the glorious manifestation of our Lord, Jesus Christ (cf. 1 Tim. 6:14 and Tit. 2:13).

5. "The obedience of faith" (Rom. 16:26; cf. Rom. 1:5; 2 Cor. 10:5-6) must be given to God as he reveals himself. By faith man freely commits his entire self to God, making "the full submission of his intellect and will to God who reveals," and willingly assenting to the Revelation given by him. Before this faith can be exercised, man must have the grace of God to move and assist him; he must have the interior helps of the Holy Spirit, who moves the heart and converts it to God, who opens the eyes of the mind and "makes it easy for all to accept and believe the truth." The same Holy Spirit constantly perfects faith by his gifts, so that Revelation may be more and more profoundly understood.

6. By divine Revelation God wished to manifest and communicate both himself and the eternal decrees of his will concerning the salvation of mankind. He wished, in other words, "to share with us divine benefits which entirely surpass the powers of the human mind to understand."

The sacred Synod professes that "God, the first principle and last end of all things, can be known with certainty from the created world, by the natural light of human reason" (cf. Rom. 1:20). It teaches that it is to his Revelation that we must attribute the fact "that those things, which in themselves are not beyond the grasp of human reason, can, in the present condition of the human race, be known by all men with ease, with firm certainty, and without the contamination of error."

Chapter II: The Transmission of Divine Revelation

7. God graciously arranged that the things he had once revealed for the salvation of all peoples should remain in their entirety, throughout the ages, and be transmitted to all generations. Therefore, Christ the Lord, in whom the entire Revelation of the most high God is summed up (cf. 2 Cor. 1:20; 3:16-4:6) commanded the apostles to preach the Gospel, which had been promised beforehand by the prophets, and which he fulfilled in his own person and promulgated with his own lips. In preaching the Gospel they were to communicate the gifts of God to all men. This Gospel was to be the source of all saving truth and moral discipline. This was faithfully done: it was done by the apostles who handed on, by the spoken word of their preaching, by the example they gave, by the institutions they established, what they themselves had received — whether from the lips of Christ, from his way of life and his works, or whether they had learned it at the prompting of the Holy Spirit; it was done by those apostles and other men associated with the apostles who, under the inspiration of the same Holy Spirit, committed the message of salvation to writing.

In order that the full and living Gospel might always be preserved in the Church the apostles left bishops as their successors. They gave them "their own position of teaching authority." This sacred Tradition, then, and the sacred Scripture of both Testaments, are like a mirror, in which the Church, during its pilgrim journey here on earth, contemplates God, from whom she receives everything, until such time as she is brought to see him face to face as he really is (cf. Jn.3:2).

8. Thus, the apostolic preaching, which is expressed in a special way in the inspired books, was to be preserved in a continuous line of succession until the end of time. Hence the apostles, in handing on what they themselves had received, warn the

faithful to maintain the traditions which they had learned either by word of mouth or by letter (cf. 2 Th. 2:15); and they warn them to fight hard for the faith that had been handed on to them once and for all (cf. Jude 3). What was handed on by the apostles comprises everything that serves to make the People of God live their lives in holiness and increase their faith. In this way the Church, in her doctrine, life and worship, perpetuates and transmits to every generation all that she herself is, all that she believes.

The Tradition that comes from the apostles makes progress in the Church, with the help of the Holy Spirit. There is a growth in insight into the realities and words that are being passed on. This comes about in various ways. It comes through the contemplation and study of believers who ponder these things in their hearts (cf. Lk. 2:19 and 51). It comes from the intimate sense of spiritual realities which they experience. And it comes from the preaching of those who have received, along with their right of succession in the episcopate, the sure charism of truth. Thus, as the centuries go by, the Church is always advancing towards the plenitude of divine truth, until eventually the words of God are fulfilled in her.

The sayings of the Holy Fathers are a witness to the life-giving presence of this Tradition, showing how its riches are poured out in the practice and life of the Church, in her belief and her prayer. By means of the same Tradition the full canon of the sacred books is known to the Church and the holy Scriptures themselves are more thoroughly understood and constantly actualized in the Church. Thus God, who spoke in the past, continues to converse with the spouse of his beloved Son. And the Holy Spirit, through whom the living voice of the Gospel rings out in the Church — and through her in the world — leads believers to the full truth, and makes the Word of Christ dwell in them in all its richness (cf. Col. 3:16).

9. Sacred Tradition and sacred Scripture, then, are bound closely together, and communicate one with the other. For both of them, flowing out from the same divine well-spring, come together in some fashion to form one thing, and move towards the same goal. Sacred Scripture is the speech of God as it is put down in writing under the breath of the Holy Spirit. And Tradition transmits in its entirety the Word of God which has been entrusted to the apostles by Christ the Lord and the Holy Spirit. It transmits it to the successors of the apostles so that, enlightened by the Spirit of truth, they may faithfully preserve, expound and spread it abroad by their preaching. Thus it comes about that the Church does not draw her certainty about all revealed truths from the holy Scriptures alone. Hence, both Scripture and Tradition must be accepted and honored with equal feelings of devotion and reverence.

10. Sacred Tradition and sacred Scripture make up a single sacred deposit of the Word of God, which is entrusted to the Church. By adhering to it the entire holy people, united to its pastors, remains always faithful to the teaching of the apostles, to the brotherhood, to the breaking of bread and the prayers (cf. Acts 2:42 Greek). So, in maintaining, practicing and professing the faith that has been handed on there should be a remarkable harmony between the bishops and the faithful.

But the task of giving an authentic interpretation of the Word of God, whether in its written form or in the form of Tradition, has been entrusted to the living teaching office of the Church alone. Its authority in this matter is exercised in the name of Jesus Christ. Yet this Magisterium is not superior to the Word of God, but is its servant. It teaches only what has been handed on to it. At the divine command and with the help of the Holy Spirit, it listens to this devotedly, guards it with dedication and expounds it faithfully. All that it proposes for belief as being divinely revealed is drawn from this single deposit of faith.

It is clear, therefore, that, in the supremely wise arrangement of God, sacred Tradition, sacred Scripture and the Magisterium of the Church are so connected and associated that one of them cannot stand without the others. Working together, each in its own way under the action of the one Holy Spirit, they all contribute effectively to the salvation of souls.

Chapter III: Sacred Scripture: Its Divine Inspiration and Its Interpretation

11. The divinely revealed realities, which are contained and presented in the text of sacred Scripture, have been written down under the inspiration of the Holy Spirit. For Holy Mother Church relying on the faith of the apostolic age, accepts as sacred and canonical the books of the Old and the New Testaments, whole and entire, with all their parts, on the grounds that, written under the inspiration of the Holy Spirit (cf. Jn. 20:31; 2 Tim. 3:16; 2 Pet. 1:19-21; 3:15-16), they have God as their author, and have been handed on as such to the Church herself. To compose the sacred books, God chose certain men who, all the while he employed them in this task, made full use of their powers and faculties so that, though he acted in them and by them, it was as true authors that they consigned to writing whatever he wanted written, and no more.

Since, therefore, all that the inspired authors, or sacred writers, affirm should be regarded as affirmed by the Holy Spirit, we must acknowledge that the books of Scripture, firmly, faithfully and without error, teach that truth which God, for the sake of our salvation, wished to see confided to the sacred Scriptures. Thus "all Scripture is inspired by God, and profitable for teaching, for reproof, for correction and for training in righteousness, so that the man of God may be complete, equipped for every good work" (2 Tim. 3:16-17, Gk. text).

12. Seeing that, in sacred Scripture, God speaks through men in human fashion, it follows that the interpreter of sacred Scriptures, if he is to ascertain what God has wished to communicate to us, should carefully search out the meaning which the sacred writers really had in mind, that meaning which God had thought well to manifest through the medium of their words.

In determining the intention of the sacred writers, attention must be paid, *inter alia*, to "literary forms for the fact is that truth is differently presented and expressed in the various types of historical writing, in prophetical and poetical texts," and in other forms of literary expression. Hence the exegete must look for that meaning which the sacred writer, in a determined situation and given the circumstances of his time and culture, intended to express and did in fact express, through the medium of a contemporary literary form. Rightly to understand what the sacred author wanted to affirm in his work, due attention must be paid both to the customary and characteristic patterns of perception, speech and narrative which prevailed at the age of the sacred writer, and to the conventions which the people of his time followed in their dealings with one another.

But since sacred Scripture must be read and interpreted with its divine authorship in mind, no less attention must be devoted to the content and unity of the whole of Scripture, taking into account the Tradition of the entire Church and the analogy of faith, if we are to derive their true meaning from the sacred texts. It is the task of exegetes to work, according to these rules, towards a better understanding and explanation of the meaning of sacred Scripture in order that their research may help the Church to form a firmer judgment. For, of course, all that has been said about the manner of interpreting Scripture is ultimately subject to the judgment of the Church which exercises the divinely conferred commission and ministry of watching over and interpreting the Word of God.

13. Hence, in sacred Scripture, without prejudice to God's truth and holiness, the marvellous "condescension" of eternal wisdom is plain to be seen "that we may come to know the ineffable loving-kindness of God and see for ourselves how far he has gone in adapting his language with thoughtful concern for our nature." Indeed the words of human language, just as the Word of the eternal Father, when he took on himself the flesh of human weakness, became like men.

Chapter IV: The Old Testament

14. God, with loving concern contemplating, and making preparation for, the salvation of the whole human race, in a singular undertaking chose for himself a people to whom he would entrust his promises. By his covenant with Abraham (cf. Gen. 15:18) and, through Moses, with the race of Israel (cf. Ex. 24:8), he did acquire a people for himself, and to them he revealed himself in words and deeds as the one, true, living God, so that Israel might experience the ways of God with men. Moreover, by listening to the voice of God speaking to them through the prophets, they had daily to understand his ways more fully and more clearly, and make them more widely known among the nations (cf. Ps. 21:28-29; 95:1-3; Is. 2:1-4; Jer. 3:17). Now the economy of salvation, foretold, recounted and explained by the sacred authors, appears as the true Word of God in the books of the Old Testament, that is why these books, divinely inspired, preserve a lasting value: "For whatever was written in former days was written for our instruction, that by steadfastness and the encouragement of the Scriptures we might have hope" (Rom. 15:4).

15. The economy of the Old Testament was deliberately so orientated that it should prepare for and declare in prophecy the coming of Christ, redeemer of all men, and of the messianic kingdom (cf. Lk. 24:44; Jn. 5:39; 1 Pet. 1:10), and should indicate it by means of different types (cf. 1 Cor. 10:11). For in the context of the human situation before the era of salvation established by Christ, the books of the Old Testament provide an understanding of God and man and make clear to all men how a just and merciful God deals with mankind. These books, even though they contain matters imperfect and provisional, nevertheless show us authentic divine teaching. Christians should accept with veneration these writings which give expression to a lively sense of God, which are a storehouse of sublime teaching on God and of sound wisdom on human life, as well as a wonderful treasury of prayers; in them, too, the mystery of our salvation is present in a hidden way.

16. God, the inspirer and author of the books of both Testaments, in his wisdom has so brought it about that the New should be hidden in the Old and that the Old should be made manifest in the New. For, although Christ founded the New Covenant in his blood (cf. Lk. 22:20; 1 Cor. 11:25), still the books of the Old Testament, all of them caught up into the Gospel message, attain and show forth their full meaning in the New Testament (cf. Mt. 5:17; Lk. 24:27; Rom. 16:25-26; 2 Cor. 3:14-16) and, in their turn, shed light on it and explain it.

Chapter V: The New Testament

17. The Word of God, which is the power of God for salvation to everyone who has faith (cf. Rom. 1:16), is set forth and displays its power in a most wonderful way in the writings of the New Testament. For when the time had fully come (cf. Gal. 4:4), the Word became flesh and dwelt among us full of grace and truth (cf. Jn. 1:14). Christ established on earth the kingdom of God, revealed his Father and himself by deeds and words; and by his death, resurrection and glorious ascension, as well as by sending the Holy Spirit, completed his work. Lifted up from the earth he draws all men to himself (cf. Jn 10:32, Gk. text), for he alone has the words of eternal life (cf. Jn. 6:68). This mystery was not made known to other generations as it has now been revealed to his holy apostles and prophets by the Holy Spirit (cf. Eph. 3:4-6, Gk. text), that they might preach the Gospel, stir up faith in Jesus Christ and the Lord, and bring together the Church. The writings of the New Testament stand as a perpetual and divine witness to these realities.

18. It is common knowledge that among all the inspired writings, even among those of the New Testament, the Gospels have a special place, and rightly so, because they are our principal source for the life and teaching of the Incarnate Word, our Saviour.

The Church has always and everywhere maintained, and continues to maintain, the apostolic origin of the four Gospels. The apostles preached, as Christ had charged them to do, and then, under the inspiration of the Holy Spirit, they and others of the apostolic age handed on to us in writing the same message they had preached, the foundation of our faith: the fourfold Gospel, according to Matthew, Mark, Luke and John.

19. Holy Mother Church has firmly and with absolute constancy maintained and continues to maintain, that the four Gospels just named, whose historicity she unhesitatingly affirms, faithfully hand on what Jesus, the Son of God, while he lived among men, really did and taught for their eternal salvation, until the day when he was taken up (cf. Acts 1:1-2). For, after the ascension of the Lord, the apostles handed on to their hearers what he had said and done, but with that fuller understanding which they, instructed by the glorious events of Christ and enlightened by the Spirit of truth, now enjoyed. The sacred authors, in writing the four Gospels, selected certain of the many elements which had been handed on, either orally or already in written form, others they synthesized or explained with an eye to the situation of the churches, the while sustaining the form of preaching, but always in such a fashion that they have told us the honest truth about Jesus. Whether they relied on their own memory and recollections or on the testimony of those who "from the beginning were eyewitnesses and ministers of the Word," their purpose in writing was that we might know the "truth" concerning the things of which we have been informed (cf. Lk. 1:2-4).

20. Besides the four Gospels, the New Testament also contains the Epistles of St. Paul and other apostolic writings composed under the inspiration of the Holy Spirit. In accordance with the wide design of God these writings firmly establish those matters which concern Christ the Lord, formulate more and more precisely his authentic teaching, preach the saving power of Christ's divine work and foretell its glorious consummation.

For the Lord Jesus was with his apostles as he had promised (cf. Mt. 28:20) and he had sent to them the Spirit, the Counsellor, who would guide them into all the truth (cf. Jn. 16:13).

Chapter VI: Sacred Scripture in the Life of the Church

21. The Church has always venerated the divine Scriptures as she venerated the Body of the Lord, in so far as she never ceases, particularly in the sacred liturgy, to partake of the bread of life and to offer it to the faithful from the one table of the Word of God and the Body of Christ. She has always regarded, and continues to regard the Scriptures, taken together with sacred Tradition, as the supreme rule of her faith. For, since they are inspired by God and committed to writing once and for all time, they present God's own Word in an unalterable form, and they make the voice of the Holy Spirit sound again and again in the words of the prophets and apostles. It follows that all the preaching of the Church, as indeed the entire Christian religion, should be nourished and ruled by sacred Scripture. In the sacred books the Father who is in heaven comes lovingly to meet his children, and talks with them. And such is the force and power of the Word of God that it can serve the Church as her support and vigor, and the children of the Church as strength for their faith, food for the soul, and a pure and lasting fount of spiritual life. Scripture verifies in the most perfect way the words: "The Word of God is living and active" (Heb. 4:12), and "is able to build you up and to give you the inheritance among all those who are sanctified" (Acts 20:32; cf. 1 Th. 2:13).

22. Access to sacred Scripture ought to be open wide to the Christian faithful. For this reason the Church, from the very beginning, made her own the ancient translation of the Old Testament called the Septuagint; she honors also the other Eastern translations, and the Latin translations, especially that which is called the Vulgate. But since the Word of God must be readily available at all times, the Church, with motherly concern, sees to it that suitable and correct translations are made into various languages, especially from the original texts of the sacred books. If it should happen that, when the opportunity presents itself and the authorities of the Church agree, these translations are made in a joint effort with the separated brethren, they may be used by all Christians.

23. The spouse of the incarnate Word, which is the Church, is taught by the Holy Spirit. She strives to reach day by day a more profound understanding of the sacred Scriptures, in order to provide her children with food from the divine words. For this reason also she duly fosters the study of the Fathers, both Eastern and Western, and of the sacred liturgies. Catholic exegetes and other workers in the field of sacred theology should zealously combine their efforts. Under the watchful eye of the sacred Magisterium, and using appropriate techniques they should together set about examining and explaining the sacred texts in such a way that as many as possible of those who are ministers of the divine Word may be able to distribute fruitfully the nourishment of the Scriptures of the People of God. This nourishment enlightens the mind, strengthens the will and fires the hearts of men with the love of God. The sacred Synod encourages those sons of the Church who are engaged in biblical studies constantly to renew their efforts, in order to carry on the work they have so happily begun, with complete dedication and in accordance with the mind of the Church.

24. Sacred theology relies on the written Word of God, taken together with sacred Tradition, as on a permanent foundation. By this Word it is most firmly strengthened and constantly rejuvenated, as it searches out, under the light of faith, the full truth stored up in the mystery of Christ. Therefore, the "study of the sacred page" should be the very soul of sacred theology. The ministry of the Word, too — pastoral preaching,

catechetics and all forms of Christian instruction, among which the liturgical homily should hold pride of place — is healthily nourished and thrives in holiness through the Word of Scripture.

25. Therefore, all clerics, particularly priests of Christ and others who, as deacons or catechists, are officially engaged in the ministry of the Word, should immerse themselves in the Scriptures by constant sacred reading and diligent study. For it must not happen that anyone becomes "an empty preacher of the Word of God to others, not being a hearer of the Word in his own heart," when he ought to be sharing the boundless riches of the divine Word with the faithful committed to his care, especially in the sacred liturgy. Likewise, the sacred Synod forcefully and specifically exhorts all the Christian faithful, especially those who live the religious life, to learn "the surpassing knowledge of Jesus Christ" (Phil. 3:8) by frequent reading of the divine Scriptures. "Ignorance of the Scriptures is ignorance of Christ." Therefore, let them go gladly to the sacred text itself, whether in the sacred liturgy, which is full of the divine words, or in devout reading, or in such suitable exercises and various other helps which, with the approval and guidance of the pastors of the Church, are happily spreading everywhere in our day. Let them remember, however, that prayer should accompany the reading of sacred Scripture, so that a dialogue takes place between God and man. For, "we speak to him when we pray; we listen to him when we read the divine oracles."

It is for the bishops, "with whom the apostolic doctrine resides" suitably to instruct the faithful entrusted to them in the correct use of the divine books, especially of the New Testament, and in particular of the Gospels. They do this by giving them translations of the sacred texts which are equipped with necessary and really adequate explanations. Thus the children of the Church can familiarize themselves safely and profitably with the sacred Scriptures, and become steeped in their spirit.

Moreover, editions of sacred Scripture, provided with suitable notes, should be prepared for the use of even non-Christians, and adapted to their circumstances. These should be prudently circulated, either by pastors of souls, or by Christians of any rank.

26. So may it come that, by the reading and study of the sacred books "the Word of God may speed on and triumph" (2 Th. 3:1) and the treasure of Revelation entrusted to the Church may more and more fill the hearts of men. Just as from constant attendance at the eucharistic mystery the life of the Church draws increase, so a new impulse of spiritual life may be expected from increased veneration of the Word of God, which "stands forever" (Is. 40:8; cf. 1 Pet. 1:23-25).

4. AGREED STATEMENT

Second Unofficial Consultation between
Theologians of the Non-Chalcedonian
and the Chalcedonian Orthodox Churches, 1967

For over fifteen centuries, i.e. since the Fourth Ecumenical Council in Chalcedon in 451 A.D., differences of view concerning the relation between the human and the divine natures in Christ have existed between the Eastern and the Oriental Orthodox churches, making impossible full church fellowship between them. To the Eastern Orthodox tradition belong the four ancient church patriarchates of Constantinople, Alexandria, Antioch and Jerusalem, the "modern" partriarchates of Russia, Romania, Serbia and Bulgaria, as well as such autocephalous churches as those of Cyprus, Greece and Poland. All these churches accept the Seven Ecumenical Councils. To the Oriental Orthodox tradition belong the five ancient churches of Egypt (the Coptic Church), Armenia, Ethiopia, India and Syria, which accept only the first three Ecumenical Councils of Nicea (325), Constantinople (381) and Ephesus (431).

In connection with meetings of the Faith and Order Commission, a series of four unofficial conversations took place between Eastern and Oriental Orthodox theologians from 1964 to 1971: in Aarhus, Denmark, in 1964; in Bristol, England, in 1967; in Geneva, Switzerland, in 1970; and in Addis Ababa, Ethiopia, in 1971. In the agreed statement of the first of these conferences in Aarhus, the participants had declared: "We recognize in each other the one orthodox faith of the Church. Fifteen centuries of alienation have not led us astray from the faith of our Fathers.... On the essence of the Christological dogma we found ourselves in full agreement. Through the different terminologies used by each side, we saw the same truth expressed.[1]

As Metropolitan Paulos Mar Gregorios (Syrian Orthodox Church) and Prof. Nikos Nissiotis (Orthodox Church of Greece), the initiators of the discussion (both erstwhile members of the staff of the World Council of Churches) state, these informal theological conversations were seen as preparation for official steps by the churches themselves: "In the light of our experience and discussions, we would respectfully urge our respective Church authorities to explore the ways and means for continuing the work which so hopefully started with these four unofficial consultations."[2]

We reproduce below the statement of the second conversation of 29 July 1967 in Bristol, in which the theological agreements are stressed. Part I formulates the

---

[1] *Does Chalcedon Divide or Unite?* p.3.
[2] *Ibid.*, p.xii.

*common understanding of "our Lord Jesus Christ" (paragraphs 2-6); Part II spells
out certain suitable measures "to restore the full communion between our Churches"
(paragraphs 7-10).*

● Text in *Does Chalcedon Divide or Unite? Towards Convergence in Orthodox Christology*, eds P.
Gregorios, W.H. Lazareth, N.A. Nissiotis, Geneva, WCC, 1981, pp.5-7.

1. We give thanks to God that we have been able to come together for the second
time as a study group, with the blessing of the authorities of our respective Churches. In
Aarhus we discovered much common ground for seeking closer ties among our Churches. In Bristol we have found several new areas of agreement. Many questions still
remain to be studied and settled. But we wish to make a few common affirmations.

I

2. God's infinite love for mankind, by which He has both created and saved us, is
our starting point for apprehending the mystery of the union of perfect Godhead and
perfect manhood in our Lord Jesus Christ. It is for our salvation that God the Word
became one of us. Thus He who is consubstantial with the Father became by the
Incarnation consubstantial also with us. By His infinite grace God has called us to
attain to His uncreated glory. God became by nature man that man may become by
grace God. The manhood of Christ thus reveals and realizes the true vocation of man.
God draws us into fulness of Communion with Himself in the Body of Christ, that we
may be transfigured from glory to glory. It is in this soteriological perspective that we
have approached the Christological question.

3. We are reminded again of our common Fathers in the universal Church — St
Ignatius and St Ireneus, St Anthony and St Anthanasius, St Basil and St Gregory of
Nyssa, and St John Chrysostom, St Ephrem Syrus and St Cyril of Alexandria and
many others of venerable memory. Based on their teaching, we see the integral
relation between Christology and soteriology and also the close relation of both to the
doctrine of God and to the doctrine of man, to ecclesiology and to spirituality, and to
the whole liturgical life of the Church.

4. Ever since the fifth century, we have used different formulae to confess our
common faith in the One Lord Jesus Christ, perfect God and perfect Man. Some of us
affirm two natures, wills and energies hypostatically united in the One Lord Jesus
Christ. Some of us affirm one united divine-human nature, will and energy in the same
Christ. But both sides speak of a union without confusion, without change, without
division, without separation. The four adverbs belong to our common tradition. Both
affirm the dynamic permanence of the God-head and Manhood, with all their natural
properties and faculties, in the One Christ. Those who speak in terms of "two" do not
thereby divide or separate. Those who speak in terms of "one" do not thereby
commingle or confuse. The "without division, without separation" of those who say
"two" and the "without change, without confusion" of those who say "one" need to be
specially underlined, in order that we may understand each other.

5. In this spirit, we have discussed also the continuity of doctrine in the Councils of the Church, and especially the monenergistic and monothelete controversies of the seventh century. All of us agree that the human will is neither absorbed nor suppressed by the divine will in the Incarnate Logos, nor are they contrary one to the other. The uncreated and created natures, with the fulness of their natural properties and faculties, were united without confusion or separation, and continue to operate in the one Christ, our Saviour. The position of those who wish to speak of one divine-human will and energy united without confusion or separation does not appear therefore to be incompatible with the decision of the Council of Constantinople (680-81), which affirms two natural wills and two natural energies in Him existing indivisibly, inconvertibly, inseparably, inconfusedly.

6. We have sought to formulate several questions which need further study before the full communion between our Churches can be restored. But we are encouraged by the common mind we have on some fundamental issues to pursue our task of common study in the hope that despite the difficulties we have encountered the Holy Spirit will lead us on into full agreement.

II

7. Our mutual contacts in the recent past have convinced us that it is a first priority for our Churches to explore with a great sense of urgency adequate steps to restore the full communion between our Churches, which has been sadly interrupted for centuries now. Our conversations at Aarhus in 1964 and at Bristol in 1967 have shown us that, in order to achieve this end by the grace of God, our Churches need to pursue certain preliminary actions.

8. The remarkable measure of agreement so far reached among the theologians on the Christological teaching of our Churches should soon lead to the formulation of a joint declaration in which we express together in the same formula our common faith in the One Lord Jesus Christ whom we all acknowledge to be perfect God and perfect Man. This formula, which will not have the status of a confession of faith or of a creed, should be drawn up by a group of theologians officially commissioned by the Churches, and submitted to the Churches for formal and authoritative approval, or for suggestions for modifications which will have to be considered by the Commission before a final text is approved by the Churches.

9. In addition to proposing a formula of agreement on the basic Christological faith in relation to the nature, will and energy of our One Lord Jesus Christ, the joint theological commission will also have to examine the canonical, liturgical and jurisdictional problems involved, e.g. anathemas and liturgical deprecations by some Churches or theologians regarded by others as doctors and saints of the Church, the acceptance and non-acceptance of some Councils, and the jurisdictional assurances and agreements necessary before formal restoration of communion.

10. We submit this agreed statement to the authorities and peoples of our Churches with great humility and deep respect. We see our task as a study group only in terms of exploring together common possibilities which will facilitate action by the Churches. Much work still needs to be done, both by us and by the Churches, in order that the unity for which our Lord prayed may become real in the life of the Churches.

5. LEUENBERG AGREEMENT
Agreement of Reformation Churches in Europe, 1973

The "Leuenberg Conversations" on church fellowship among the Reformation churches in Europe took place at the Swiss Conference Centre in Leuenberg near Basle from 1969 to 1970. There it was agreed that an "Agreement" (Concord) should be produced, to form a basis for the church fellowship sought. The first preparatory conference, held in Leuenberg from 19 to 24 September 1971, approved a first draft of such an agreement and sent it to the participating churches for study and comment. On the basis of 63 responses, the continuation committee revised the text and the result was adopted at the end of the second preparatory conference on 16 March 1973 in Leuenberg. This "Leuenberg Agreement" was finally sent to Reformation churches with a request that they should approve in writing this form of the theological agreement. Roughly 70, i.e. almost all the churches concerned, have so far made this declaration; and even a few non-European churches (e.g. the Evangelical Church of the River Plate in Argentina) have associated themselves with the Agreement. Some of them have included the Leuenberg Agreement in the fundamental articles of their constitutions. The pattern of the Leuenberg Agreement is as follows:

I.   The road to fellowship

II. The common understanding of the gospel

III. Accord in respect of the doctrinal condemnations of the Reformation era

IV. The declaration and realization of church fellowship

The signatory churches "accord each other fellowship in word and sacrament and strive for the fullest possible cooperation in witness and service to the world".

This church fellowship has been in force since 1 October 1974; its goal is "to promote the ecumenical fellowship of all Christian Churches". This is likewise the purpose of further doctrinal discussions which have been held since 1973. A Continuation Committee coordinates the various European work groups; two continuation conferences have been held in Sigtuna, Sweden, in 1976, and in Driebergen, Holland, in 1981; the next is planned for 1987.

● Text in *The Ecumenical Review*, Vol. 25, No. 3, July 1973, pp.355ff; and *The Lutheran World*, 20, 1973, pp.349-53.

1. On the basis of their doctrinal discussions, the churches assenting to this Agreement — namely, Lutheran and Reformed churches in Europe along with the Union churches which grew out of them, and the related pre-Reformation churches, the Waldensian Church and the Church of the Czech Brethren — affirm together the common understanding of the gospel elaborated below. This common understanding of the gospel enables them to declare and to realize church fellowship. Thankful that they have been led closer together, they confess at the same time that guilt and suffering have also accompanied and still accompany the struggle for truth and unity in the church.

2. The church is founded upon Jesus Christ alone. It is he who gathers the church and sends it forth, by the bestowal of his salvation in preaching and the sacraments. In the view of the Reformation, it follows that agreement in the right teaching of the gospel, and in the right administration of the sacraments, is the necessary and sufficient prerequisite for the true unity of the church. It is from these Reformation criteria that the participating churches derive their view of church fellowship as set out below.

I. The Road to Fellowship

3. Faced with real differences in style of theological thinking and church practice, the fathers of the Reformation, despite much that they had in common, did not see themselves in a position, on grounds of faith and conscience, to avoid divisions. In this Agreement the participating churches acknowledge that their relationship to one another has changed since the time of the Reformation.

1. Common Aspects at the Outset of the Reformation

4. With the advantage of historical distance, it is easier today to discern the common elements in the witness of the churches of the Reformation, in spite of the differences between them: their starting point was a new experience of the power of the gospel to liberate and assure. In standing up for the truth which they saw, the Reformers found themselves drawn together in opposition to the church traditions of that time. They were, therefore, at one in confessing that the church's life and doctrine are to be gauged by the original and pure testimony to the gospel in Scripture. They were at one in bearing witness to God's free and unconditional grace in the life, death, and resurrection of Jesus Christ for all those who believe this promise. They were at one in confessing that the practice and form of the church should be determined only by the commission to deliver this testimony to the world, and that the word of God remains sovereign over every human ordering of the Christian community. In so doing, they were at one with the whole of Christendom in receiving and renewing the confession of the triune God and the God-manhood of Jesus Christ as expressed in the ancient creeds of the church.

2. Changed Elements in the Contemporary Situation

5. In the course of 400 years of history, the churches of the Reformation have been led to new and similar ways of thinking and living: by theological wrestling with the questions of modern times, by advances in biblical research, by the movements of church renewal, and by the rediscovery of the ecumenical horizon. These developments certainly have also brought with them new differences cutting right across the

confessions. But, time and again, there has also been an experience of brotherly fellowship, particularly in times of common suffering. The result of all these factors was a new concern on the part of the churches, especially since the revival movements, to achieve a contemporary expression both of biblical witness and of the Reformation confessions of faith and their historically-conditioned thought forms. Because these confessions of faith bear witness to the gospel as the living word of God in Jesus Christ, far from barring the way to continued responsible testimony to the Word, they open up this way with a summons to follow it in the freedom of faith.

II. The Common Understanding of the Gospel

6. In what follows, the participating churches describe their common understanding of the gospel insofar as this is required for establishing church fellowship between them.

1. The Message of Justification as the Message of the Free Grace of God

7. The gospel is the message of Jesus Christ, the salvation of the world, in fulfilment of the promise given to the people of the Old Covenant.

8. (a) The true understanding of the gospel was expressed by the fathers of the Reformation in the doctrine of justification.

9. (b) In this message, Jesus Christ is acknowledged as the one in whom God became man and bound himself to man; as the crucified and risen one who took God's judgment upon himself and, in so doing, demonstrated God's love to sinners; and as the coming one who, as Judge and Saviour, leads the world to its consummation.

10. (c) Through his word, God by his Holy Spirit calls all men to repent and believe, and assures the believing sinner of his righteousness in Jesus Christ. Whoever puts his trust in the gospel is justified in God's sight for the sake of Jesus Christ, and set free from the accusation of the law. In daily repentance and renewal, he lives within the fellowship in praise of God and in service to others, in the assurance that God will bring his kingdom in all its fulness. In this way, God creates new life, and plants in the midst of the world the seed of a new humanity.

11. (d) This message sets Christians free for responsible service in the world and makes them ready to suffer in this service. They know that God's will, as demand and succour, embraces the whole world. They stand up for temporal justice and peace between individuals and nations. To do this they have to join with others in seeking rational and appropriate criteria, and play their part in applying these criteria. They do so in the confidence that God sustains the world and as those who are accountable to him.

12. (e) In this understanding of the gospel, we take our stand on the basis of the ancient creeds of the church, and reaffirm the common conviction of the Reformation confessions that the unique mediation of Jesus Christ in salvation is the heart of the Scriptures, and that the message of justification as the message of God's free grace is the measure of all the church's preaching.

2. Preaching, Baptism, and the Lord's Supper

13. The fundamental witness to the gospel is the testimony of the apostles and prophets in the Holy Scriptures of the Old and New Testaments. It is the task of the church to spread this gospel by the spoken word in preaching, by individual counselling, and by baptism and the Lord's Supper. In preaching, baptism, and the

Lord's Supper, Jesus Christ is present through the Holy Spirit. Justification in Christ is thus imparted to men, and in this way the Lord gathers his people. In doing so he employs various forms of ministry and service, as well as the witness of all those belonging to his people.

a) Baptism

14. Baptism is administered in the name of the Father and of the Son and of the Holy Spirit with water. In baptism, Jesus Christ irrevocably receives man, fallen prey to sin and death, into his fellowship of salvation so that he may become a new creature. In the power of his Holy Spirit, he calls him into his community and to a new life of faith, to daily repentance, and to discipleship.

b) The Lord's Supper

15. In the Lord's Supper the risen Christ imparts himself in his body and blood, given up for all, through his word of promise with bread and wine. He thereby grants us forgiveness of sins, and sets us free for a new life of faith. He enables us to experience anew that we are members of his body. He strengthens us for service to all men.

16. When we celebrate the Lord's Supper we proclaim the death of Christ through which God has reconciled the world with himself. We proclaim the presence of the risen Lord in our midst. Rejoicing that the Lord has come to us, we await his future coming in glory.

III. Accord in Respect of the Doctrinal Condemnations of the Reformation Era

17. The differences which from the time of the Reformation onwards have made church fellowship between the Lutheran and Reformed churches impossible, and have led them to pronounce mutual condemnation, relate to the doctrine of the Lord's Supper, christology, and the doctrine of predestination. We take the decisions of the Reformation fathers seriously, but are today able to agree on the following statements in respect of these condemnations:

1. The Lord's Supper

18. In the Lord's Supper the risen Jesus Christ imparts himself in his body and blood, given up for all, through his word of promise with bread and wine. He thus gives himself unreservedly to all who receive the bread and wine; faith receives the Lord's Supper for salvation, unfaith for judgment.

19. We cannot separate communion with Jesus Christ in his body and blood from the act of eating and drinking. To be concerned about the manner of Christ's presence in the Lord's Supper in abstraction from this act is to run the risk of obscuring the meaning of the Lord's Supper.

20. Where such a consensus exists between the churches, the condemnations pronounced by the Reformation confessions are inapplicable to the doctrinal position of these churches.

2. Christology

21. In the true man Jesus Christ, the eternal Son, and so God himself, has bestowed himself upon lost mankind for its salvation. In the word of the promise and

in the sacraments, the Holy Spirit, and so God himself, makes the crucified and risen Jesus present to us.

22. Believing in this self-bestowal of God in his Son, the task facing us, in view of the historically-conditioned character of traditional thought forms, is to give renewed and effective expression to the special insights of the Reformed tradition, with its concern to maintain unimpaired the divinity and humanity of Jesus, and to those of the Lutheran tradition, with its concern to maintain the unity of Jesus as a person.

23. In these circumstances, it is impossible for us to reaffirm the former condemnations today.

3. Predestination

24. In the gospel we have the promise of God's unconditional acceptance of sinful man. Whoever puts his trust in the gospel can know that he is saved, and praise God for his election. For this reason we can speak of election only with respect to the call to salvation in Christ.

25. Faith knows by experience that the message of salvation is not accepted by all; yet it respects the mystery of God's dealings with men. It bears witness to the seriousness of human decisions, and at the same time to the reality of God's universal purpose of salvation. The witness of the Scriptures to Christ forbids us to suppose that God has uttered an eternal decree for the final condemnation of specific individuals or of a particular people.

26. When such a consensus exists between churches, the condemnations pronounced by the Reformation confessions of faith are inapplicable to the doctrinal position of these churches.

4. Conclusions

27. Wherever these statements are accepted, the condemnations of the Reformation confessions in respect of the Lord's Supper, christology, and predestination are inapplicable to the doctrinal position. This does not mean that the condemnations pronounced by the Reformation fathers are irrelevant; but they are no longer an obstacle to church fellowship.

28. There remain considerable differences between our churches in forms of worship, types of spirituality, and church order. These differences are often more deeply felt in the congregations than the traditional doctrinal differences. Nevertheless, in fidelity to the New Testament and Reformation criteria for church fellowship, we cannot discern in these differences any factors which should divide the church.

IV. The Declaration and Realization of Church Fellowship

29. In the sense intended in this agreement, church fellowship means that, on the basis of the consensus they have reached in their understanding of the gospel, churches with different confessional positions accord each other fellowship in word and sacrament, and strive to the fullest possible cooperation in witness and service to the world.

1. Declaration of Church Fellowship

30. In assenting to this agreement the churches, in loyalty to the confessions of faith which bind them, or with due respect for their traditions, declare:

31. (a) that they are one in understanding the gospel as set out in Parts II and III;

32. (b) that, in accordance with what is said in Part III, the doctrinal condemnations expressed in the confessional documents no longer apply to the contemporary doctrinal position of the assenting churches;

33. (c) that they accord each other table and pulpit fellowship; this includes the mutual recognition of ordination and the freedom to provide for intercelebration.

34. With these statements, church fellowship is declared. The divisions which have barred the way to this fellowship since the 16th century are removed. The participating churches are convinced that they have part together in the one church of Jesus Christ, and that the Lord liberates them for, and lays upon them the obligation of, common service.

2. Realizing Church Fellowship

35. It is in the life of the churches and congregations that church fellowship becomes a reality. Believing in the unifying power of the Holy Spirit, they bear their witness and perform their service together, and strive to deepen and strengthen the fellowship they have found together.

a) Witness and Service

36. The preaching of the churches gains credibility in the world when they are at one in their witness to the gospel. The gospel liberates and binds together the churches to render common service. Being the service of love, it turns to man in his distress and seeks to remove the causes of that distress. The struggle for justice and peace in the world increasingly demands of the churches the acceptance of a common responsibility.

b) The Continuing Theological Task

37. The Agreement leaves intact the binding force of the confessions within the participating churches. It is not to be regarded as a new confession of faith. It sets forth a consensus reached about central matters; one which makes church fellowship possible between churches of different confessional positions. In accordance with this consensus, the participating churches will seek to establish a common witness and service, and pledge themselves to their common doctrinal discussions.

38. The common understanding of the gospel on which church fellowship is based must be further deepened, tested in the light of the witness of Holy Scripture, and continually made relevant in the contemporary scene.

39. The churches have the task of studying further these differences of doctrine which, while they do not have divisive force, still persist within and between the participating churches. These include: hermeneutical questions concerning the understanding of Scripture, confession of faith, and church; the relation between law and gospel; baptismal practice; ministry and ordination; the "two kingdom" doctrine, and the doctrine of the sovereignty of Christ; and church and society. At the same time newly emerging problems relating to witness and service, order and practice, have to be considered.

40. On the basis of their common heritage, the churches of the Reformation must determine their attitude to trends towards theological polarization increasingly in evidence today. To some extent the problems here go beyond the doctrinal differences which were once at the basis of the Lutheran-Reformed controversy.

41. It will be the task of common theological study to testify to the truth of the gospel and to distinguish it from all distortions.

c) Organizational Consequences

42. This declaration of church fellowship does not anticipate provisions of church law on particular matters of interchurch relations, or within the churches. The churches will, however, take the Agreement into account in considering such provisions.

43. As a general rule, the affirmation of pulpit and table fellowship and the mutual recognition of ordination do not affect the rules in force in the participating churches for induction to a pastoral charge, the exercise of the pastoral ministry, or the ordering of congregational life.

44. The question of organic union between particular participating churches can only be decided in the situation in which these churches live. In examining this question the following points should be kept in mind:

45. Any union detrimental to the lively plurality in styles of preaching, ways of worship, church order, and in diaconal and social action, would contradict the very nature of the church fellowship inaugurated by this declaration. On the other hand, in certain situations, because of the intimate connection between witness and order, the church's service may call for formal legal unification. Where organizational consequences are drawn from this declaration, it should not be at the expense of freedom of decision in minority churches.

d) Ecumenical Aspects

46. In establishing and realizing church fellowship among themselves, the participating churches do so as part of their responsibility to promote the ecumenical fellowship of all Christian churches.

47. They regard such a fellowship of churches in the European area as a contribution to this end. They hope that the ending of their previous separation will influence churches in Europe and elsewhere who are related to them confessionally. They are ready to examine with them the possibilities of wider church fellowship.

48. This hope applies equally to the relationship between the Lutheran World Federation and the World Alliance of Reformed Churches.

49. They also hope that the achievement of church fellowship with each other will provide a fresh stimulus to conference and cooperation with churches of other confessions. They affirm their readiness to set their doctrinal discussions within this wider context.

6. THE ECUMENICAL NATURE OF THE ORTHODOX WITNESS
Report of a Consultation of Orthodox Theologians, 1977

Among the emphases which emerged from the WCC's Fifth Assembly were the following: "the unity of the church", "confessing Christ today", and "the church's responsibility in the world". To define more exactly the contribution which the Orthodox churches could make in these three areas, an Orthodox consultation was held in New Valamo, Finland, from 24 to 30 September 1977.

The three parts of the report indicate the three themes on which the consultation concentrated:

1. The local church

2. The proclamation and articulation of our faith

3. The church's responsibility in the world today

The report is to be understood not as an official Orthodox theological statement but as a "working paper" receptive to comments, improvements and criticisms. It is nevertheless a considerable clarification of the task of the Orthodox churches in the ecumenical movement and can also help the non-Orthodox churches to gain a deeper appreciation of the Orthodox heritage.

● Text in *The New Valamo Consultation: the Ecumenical Nature of Orthodox Witness*, ed. WCC Orthodox Task Force, Geneva, 1977, pp.17-21; and *Orthodox Thought: Reports of Orthodox Consultations Organized by the WCC*, ed. G. Tsetsis, Geneva, 1983, pp.23-27.

A Consultation of Orthodox Theologians on the "ecumenical nature of Orthodox witness", organized by the Orthodox Task Force of the World Council of Churches, was held at the New Valamo Monastery from 24 to 30 September 1977, at the invitation of the Orthodox Church of Finland.

The purpose of the Consultation was to respond to certain ecumenical priorities which have emerged since the Fifth Assembly of the WCC in Nairobi, and to bring some Orthodox insights to bear on issues and programmes as these affect the life and activities both of the WCC and of the Churches themselves.

The Consultation dealt with three specific items on today's ecumenical agenda, namely "The Local Church", "The Proclamation and Articulation of our Faith", and "The Churches' Responsibility in the World Today".

The contents of the present report reflect a variety of opinions expressed throughout the meeting and they should be regarded as points calling for further reflection both within the various sub-units of the WCC and in the Orthodox Churches. In considering the main theme of the Consultation we felt it necessary to examine the ecclesiological basis of our ecumenical commitment, namely our eucharistic understanding of the Church.

I

The Orthodox understand the Church in the light of the Eucharist. The whole life of the Church, the word and the sacraments, stem from and find their fulfilment in the Holy Eucharist. Thus the Eucharist is not just a "sacrament", but the great mystery of our participation in the life of the Holy Trinity, the recapitulation of the entire history of salvation in Christ and the foretaste of the Kingdom to come. In the Eucharist, therefore, the Church is placed in the very centre of history, sanctifying and transforming the world, by being a new creation, creating a new mode of life. At the same time she is placed at the end of history as a sign of the Kingdom, judging the world (I Cor. 5-6) in the light of the eschatological realities of which the Eucharist is a manifestation (cf. *Didache* 10).

The Church which has this eucharistic character is not an abstract or speculative idea, but a concrete reality. Whenever the people of God are gathered together in a certain place (*epi to auto*, see I Cor. 11,20) in order to form the eucharistic body of Christ, the Church becomes a reality. The Church, therefore, is primarily identified with the local eucharistic community in each place. It is by being incorporated into this concrete local community that we are saved and proclaim the salvation of the world in Christ "until He comes".

In order to be such a saving community the local Church must overcome and transcend the divisions which sin and death create in the world. The local community is a true and authentic manifestation of the Church of God only if it is catholic in its composition and structure. It cannot be based on divisions and discriminations either of a natural kind, such as race, nation, language, age, sex, physical handicap, etc., or of a social type, such as class, profession, etc.

Even the divisions created by time and space have to be overcome in this community. For this reason the eucharistic community includes in itself also the departed members of the Church, and although it is in fact a *local* community it offers the Eucharist on behalf of the entire "oikoumene", thus acquiring truly *ecumenical* dimensions in which the divisions of space are also overcome.

This catholic nature of the Church which is revealed in the Eucharist is safeguarded through the office of the bishop. The specific ministry of the bishop is to transcend in his person all the divisions that may exist within a particular area and also to relate a local Church to the rest of the local Churches both in space and in time. This link is sacramentally expressed in the synodal consecration of bishops. Because of the character of episcopacy it is essential that there should exist only one bishop in a given area and that all eucharistic communities should acquire their ecclesial authenticity through his ministry. The local Church, therefore, is not necessarily present in every eucharistic assembly but in the episcopal diocese through which each eucharistic gathering acquires its catholic nature.

This understanding of the local Church has always been essential to the Orthodox tradition. In the course of history circumstances often necessitated the creation of larger ecclesial units, such as the metropolis, the patriarchate, the autocephalous church, etc. However, in the function of these units, natural, social or cultural and racial divisions should not distort the original eucharistic understanding of the Church. The canonical structure of the Orthodox Church, as it was formed in the early centuries, has helped and can still help to protect Orthodoxy from succumbing to such dangers.

II

The community of the Church is united in confessing one faith. This faith is essentially identical with the apostolic teaching and with the "faith once delivered to the Saints". It found its articulation in the entire living tradition of the Church, especially in creeds accepted by the ecumenical Church and in the decisions of the Ecumenical Councils. The Orthodox Church regards the decisions of the Ecumenical Councils as faithful expressions of the one apostolic faith and therefore binding on all the members of the Church.

This faithfulness to past Councils, however, must always be understood as a living continuity. This includes two essential aspects: fidelity and renewal, both of which are integral parts of Orthodox life and Orthodox witness. Fidelity is never merely a formal repetition of the things once given, but basically faithfulness to the original apostolic truth, in the spirit of creative obedience. Renewal thus comes to mean, in the first place, responding to new, changing situations on the basis of the truth once given. It may also be said, therefore, that renewal in this sense means the application of the apostolic tradition to contemporary questions and needs. This principle implies, first, that fidelity does not become a sterile, static attitude, without relation to the prevailing human and historical realities and, second, that renewal is not an end in itself nor something which can take just any direction whatsoever, but is always based on the original truth of the apostolic tradition.

This process of applying the apostolic faith to new historical situations explains the idea of the "reception" of a Council. Reception does not mean a "formal approval" of the Council. The faith which is pronounced by a Council establishes itself as Truth, by being received and re-received by the community of the Church in the Holy Spirit. Every form of confession of faith is shown to be in the end a matter of participation in the local eucharistic community. Faith becomes salvation only when it is life in the community of the Church.

This raises the issue of confessionalism. The Orthodox Church possesses its own "confessions" of faith in the forms of creeds and the decisions of the ancient Councils, especially the Ecumenical Councils. This makes it appear as a "confessional body" or "family" and it is often treated as such by the non-Orthodox. And yet such an understanding of Orthodoxy, sometimes encouraged by the Orthodox themselves, would contradict the fundamental character of its ecclesiology.

The Orthodox, if they are faithful to their ecclesiology, will have to deny the identification of the Church with a particular confession. A Church which is ultimately identified by its "confessions" is a confessional body but not *the* Church.

The Orthodox are actively involved in the ecumenical movement and have been members of the World Council of Churches since its foundation. How can their ecclesiology, as it was described above, fit into the context of this movement and in programmes and activities undertaken by the WCC?

In the first place it must be stressed that the participation of the Orthodox in the ecumenical movement of today is not, in principle, a revolution in the history of Orthodoxy, but it is a natural consequence of the constant prayer of the Church "for the union of all". It constitutes another attempt, like those made in the Patristic period, to apply the apostolic faith to new historical situations and existential demands. What is in a sense new today is the fact that this attempt is being made together with other Christian bodies with whom there is no full unity. It is here that the difficulties arise, but it is precisely here that there also are many signs of real hope for growing fellowship, understanding and cooperation.

The World Council of Churches is made up mostly of Churches whose identity is basically confessional, in the sense in which we have just defined the word "confessional". As a result, they normally see no reason why eucharistic communion should not be practised among the member churches.

The refusal of the Orthodox to practise "intercommunion" is thus seen as arrogance on their part precisely because it is assumed that they are another confessional body which regards itself as superior compared with the rest. In this situation it becomes difficult for the Orthodox to point to an ecclesiology so radically different from that assumed by the other members of the WCC. It is difficult to show in this context that to belong to a confessional body is not the ultimate thing in the Church and that the Orthodox Church regards itself as *the* Church not on the confessional basis but on the basis of the fact that it identifies itself with the eucharistic community in what it regards as its proper and saving form. Only when this is made clear can the frustration stemming from the issue of "intercommunion" be removed. It will then be understood why it is more natural for the Orthodox to speak of "communion" rather than of "intercommunion" or "shared eucharist".

But this would lead to further consequences with regard to the Orthodox participation in the ecumenical movement. It will imply a re-orientation of the ecumenical problematic as a whole. This means basically that the unity which we seek in the ecumenical movement cannot be the product of theological agreements, such as a common signing of a *confessio fidei*. Theological work is certainly needed and should be of a serious kind and high quality. But its aim should be directed towards the understanding of the existential significance of the community of the Church, particularly of her visible structure which provides man with the possibility of entering into new and saving relationships with God and the world.

The dynamics of the liturgical reality (eucharistic community) as expounded here is rooted in the experience of the Trinitarian life in Christ which continuously saves and illuminates man and history. The members of the Church living, practising and witnessing this eucharistic experience create a new life-style. This life-style was realized in the life of the Apostles, martyrs and all the saints who throughout history refused to change the "heavenly" for the "earthly". This mortal life is manifested today in the sins of our times, especially in a culture of individualism, rationalism, consumerism, racism, militarism, deprivation and exploitation in all forms. In each culture the eucharistic dynamics leads into a "liturgy after the liturgy", i.e. a liturgical use of the material world, a transformation of human association in society into *Koinonia*, of consumerism into an ascetic attitude towards the creation and the restoration of human dignity.

III

The dynamics of the concept of "liturgy after the liturgy" is to be found in several programmes and activities of the WCC which have emerged since Nairobi and to which the Orthodox Churches have given their support based on their ecumenical solidarity. The emphasis on helping "the poorest of the poor", on establishing peace and justice between nations and states, on eradicating hunger, destitution and sickness, on promoting human rights, on diminishing tensions, on searching for a just and responsible society and on directing science and technology along creative lines, on the peaceful and safe use of atomic and other sources of energy, should be given due attention by our Churches as the above issues are part of their Christian concern and an integral element in their social witness.

The reality of salvation is not a narrow religious experience, but it includes the dynamic which — through the synergy (cooperation) of God and man — transforms human individuals into persons according to that image of God which is revealed in the Incarnation, and societies into Koinonia, through history, into the image of Trinitarian life.

Thus the eucharistic communion is the Church with all its implications. As the Saints have said: "Save yourself and you will save those around you".

The Nairobi Assembly has defined that the WCC is constituted "... to call the churches to the goal of visible unity in one faith and in one eucharistic fellowship expressed in worship and in common life in Christ, and to advance towards that unity in order that the world may believe". The Consultation expressed its appreciation that the WCC has already launched the debate on the local Church and it expressed its hope that the WCC will do more to direct the attention of its members to the importance of the eucharistic understanding of the local Church and the eucharistic community within the continuity of the apostolic faith as the basis of the unity we seek and to disentangle its constitution from some elements and possibly some structures which make it so difficult for the Churches to find their way to unity. This would make it easier for the Orthodox to take a full and creative part in the ecumenical movement. In that respect the Consultation expressed its appreciation of the fact that the decision of the First Preconciliar Pan-Orthodox Conference to ask for a fuller and integrated participation of the Orthodox in the WCC has been taken into account by the WCC and that negotiations have been initiated in order to implement that decision.

7. TOWARDS A CONFESSION OF THE COMMON FAITH
A Plan of Work of the Joint Working Group
of the Roman Catholic Church and the
World Council of Churches, 1980

"Preface

"*Communion in faith is at the very heart of the communion the churches are seeking to recover. How is such communion to be attained? The text published here is an attempt by theologians of different traditions to give a joint answer to this question.*

"*In its Fourth Official Report (1975), the Joint Working Group between the Roman Catholic Church and the World Council of Churches gave pride of place to the study on the unity of the Church. In the following year it decided to begin a joint reflection on 'The Unity of the Church: the Goal and the Way' with a view to making further progress in the search for visible unity in one and the same faith and one and the same eucharistic community. The Joint Working Group entrusted the organization of this study to the Commission on Faith and Order, on the understanding that its results would be submitted to the Joint Working Group.*

"*This first theme to be examined was that of unity in faith. When we talk of unity we speak of the necessity of professing the same apostolic faith; but we do not all understand this reference in the same way. A colloquium on this subject was held at Venice (12-16 June 1978) and its report was presented to the Joint Working Group when it met at Louverain (Neuchâtel, Switzerland) in February 1979. The Group asked that this text should be submitted to a number of theologians on both sides and then revised in the light of their remarks and suggestions.*

"*The text presented... is the outcome of this process. Every effort has been made to incorporate the criticisms of fifty theologians who sent comments on the draft text. The report is now being published in the hope that it will give rise to a fruitful debate on this central theme in the quest for unity.*

"*Clearly, in view of the agreement for which we are striving, the discussion has still to be pursued at a deeper level. The present document is a working paper which reflects the present state of this discussion. It has been drawn up by the theologians of different churches who set out to indicate the crucial points around which the debate now needs to be continued.*

"*The meeting of the Faith and Order Commission at Bangalore (1978) recognized*

180

the urgency of this theme and decided to promote deeper discussion of it in the years ahead."

Pierre Duprey
Vatican Secretariat for
Promoting Christian Unity

Lukas Vischer
WCC Commission
on Faith and Order

Outline
1. *Unity in the faith*
2. *The apostolic faith*
3. *The content of the apostolic faith*
4. *The form of a profession of faith today*
5. *Unity of faith and communion of churches*
Conclusion

● Text in "Towards a Confession of the Common Faith", *Faith and Order Paper No. 100*, Geneva, WCC, 1980, pp.1-14; and *The Ecumenical Review*, Vol. 32, No. 3, July 1980, pp.309ff.

1. Unity in the Faith

The last decade could be judged a stage of capital importance in the common search for the unity willed by Christ. Important strides have been made in essential areas: growth in mutual understanding, respect for different traditions, common commitment to the service of the world in the name of the Gospel, concerted efforts with a view to evangelization. More important still, despite still unresolved difficulties, consensus documents regarding essential points are being worked out not only as the outcome of bilateral dialogues but even at the level of the Christian churches and communions as a whole. A case in point is the agreement prepared by the Faith and Order Commission on baptism, eucharist and ministry, of which a revised text is being prepared.

This gives ground for hope. In our present divided state, in fact, visible unity cannot be restored unless, turning towards Christ, each Church takes the decision to repent in so far as it is a community of sinful Christians. Its repentance will be genuine only to the extent to which it implies a resolve to what the complete re-establishment of communion demands of it: conversion through a constant return to the source which is Christ, a persevering effort of purification, a desire for authentic change. Such repentance will be truly constructive of unity only if it leads.it to offer to others its own characteristic goods and to receive from others what it lacks itself.

Now, at the heart of such repentance is the need to reach agreement on a common profession of faith which, after centuries of mutual exclusion, will permit the churches to recognize each other as true brothers, to live in communion, and to commit themselves together to mission without any reservations. For faith is expressed in different ways: the principal ones are liturgical life, catechetical instruction, explicit proclamation of the Word, witness before the world. For to believe really implies a life lived in fidelity to Christ, the submission to his authority of one's whole existence and one's every action. This is why it is that wherever Christians, in the name of the faith, take certain attitudes or stand together for values commended by the Gospel, such common action itself represents a confession in practice of their faith. But they must also know who it is they believe in, who is the God to whom He bears witness, what is the content of the salvation He brings. The different practical expressions of faith in Christ are all linked to and in a way governed by doctrinal expressions that translate the essential of the Christian mystery and constitute, beyond words, what is called the *regula fidei*. This represents, as it were, the understanding of the Gospel by the Church. Full ecclesial communion, then, requires that one comes to confess the faith in common prayer, action and witness, but also in doctrinal formulas. It is with these above all that we are concerned here. Nevertheless, we shall try not to isolate them from the whole dynamic of the common search for unity. Just as a theology "in act" normally precedes the enunciation of doctrines, so communion in common commitment in the name of the faith leads to the profession of common faith. It is in doing the truth that we come to the light.

2. The Apostolic Faith

The essential elements of the Christian mystery are known to us through the witness of the apostolic community, transmitted in the Scriptures. These are the fruit of the Gospel and of the action of the Spirit in the primitive Church. On the one hand, they bear witness of the apostolic Church's understanding of the mystery of Christ. On the other hand, however, the truth they transmit could be fully grasped only in the context of the life of that early community faithful to the teaching of the apostles, to the fellowship of the brethren, to the breaking of bread and to prayer (cf. Acts 2:42). And so we can say that we exist as Christians through the apostolic tradition (the *paradosis* of the *kerygma*), attested in Scripture and transmitted in and through the Church by the power of the Holy Spirit. Tradition thus understood is made a present reality in the preaching of the Word, the administration of the sacraments, worship, Christian instruction, theology, mission, the witness given to Christ by the life of Christians (cf. Montreal 1963, Section II, 45-46).

After the, normative, apostolic period the Church, bearer of the Spirit but engaged in history, saw itself led to make more explicit the faith it had received from the apostles. What it lived in its liturgy and bore witness to, sometimes to the point of martyrdom, it had to express in terms which would allow it to safeguard its unity and give an account of its hope. At that time it was immersed in a particular culture, permeated with the concepts of a Greek philosophy, and subject to various political situations. However, this effort to find in this new cultural and historical context an adequate expression of its faith was an essential contribution to the course of its history. In formulating the faith it enriched the Christian heritage. In fact the Spirit then led the Church to make explicit the elements necessary for its communion with the apostolic faith.

This building-period is that of the Fathers, of the creeds, of the birth of the great liturgies, of the great Councils. The conciliar definitions about God-in-Trinity and the person of Christ Jesus, particularly, gave the Church a steady vision of the points that are at the very heart of its understanding of the Christian mystery. Certainly, in every age the Church lives and grows in the Holy Spirit and thus builds itself up in charity and faith. Moreover, since their divisions the churches have each given for themselves either conciliar decrees or confessions to which they attach a real authority. But this authority remains always subject not only to the authority of Scripture but also to that of those universally received documents which concern the centre of faith and which the Church holds from this period which was qualified to be its building-period.

3. The Content of the Apostolic Faith

The New Testament itself bears witness to the way in which, in different contexts and situations, the apostolic Church understood the essentials of the faith necessary for salvation. Some very short affirmations — such as "Jesus is Lord" — were made more explicit in fuller professions of faith. Thus two verses of the Epistle to the Romans put the emphasis on the event of the death and resurrection as the heart of the faith: "If you confess with your lips that Jesus is Lord and believe in your heart that God raised him from the dead, you will be saved" (10:8-9). A text like John 3:16 insists above all on the source and purpose of the mystery of faith, that is, the love of the Father and eternal life: "God so loved the world that he gave his only Son, that whoever believes in him should not perish but should have eternal life." In another context, probably liturgical (Eph. 1:3-23), expression of the faith takes on such breadth as to include a synthetic reminder of the history of salvation, contain the roots of a trinitarian confession, and conclude in a vision of the Church, the Body of Christ, looking forward to its fullness.

In that apostolic period and in the subsequent building-period, cultural contexts and historical situations explain the diversity of ways in which the mystery is grasped and of the forms then taken by profession of the one faith. The profession of ecclesial faith is made in reliance on Jesus' own promise to save those who will acknowledge him before the world (Luke 12:8-9). Its purpose is always to make entry into salvation possible for every Christian. But to this is added the need for a liturgical proclamation of the faith by the community gathered for worship. From this will derive the baptismal professions which will be, so to speak, the liturgical seal on the process of catechesis, summarizing its essential axial points. Very soon the denial of central points of faith within the community provokes, as early as the New Testament period, declarations like that in 1 John 4:2-3 in face of gnostic infiltrations: "Every spirit which confesses that Jesus Christ has come in the flesh is of God, and every spirit which does not confess Jesus is not of God." Peter's preaching on the day of Pentecost is itself conditioned by the Jewish context. The classical creeds, in their turn, differ according to the circumstances in which they appeared: the apostles' creed somes from the baptismal liturgy, while that of Nicaea (Constantinople) was composed to act as a barrier against deviations from the traditional faith. But all insist on the person and the work of Jesus. Salvation — through the remission of sins and the coming of the new world which the resurrection inaugurates — is, they say, the purpose of God's coming in flesh. Inserted into the baptismal and then into the eucharistic liturgy, these creeds will be important for the course of tradition. They will, in fact, become the sign and the test of fidelity to the content of the apostolic faith.

The rise of heresies and the need to express the Gospel in relation to new cultures will soon oblige the churches to expound the meaning of the profession of faith in Jesus as Lord and Saviour. He will be affirmed to be true God and true man, two natures united in one person. This will be the work of the great Councils. They will say of the God of faith that He is one God in three persons. The Church will further assert that from Pentecost to the parousia it has the mission of being the Spirit's instrument to liberate humanity through the forgiveness of sins and the inauguration of the new life, above all through the preaching of the Word and the celebration of the sacraments of the Lord.

Yet the faith thus translated in the creeds and conciliar definitions is also that which is expressed, nourished and deepened in the life of the community. Formulas of faith find their meaning only as closely linked to the whole of the Christian experience. This is, moreover, why, in what we have called the building-period, there was unanimous recognition that the fidelity which seals adherence to dogmatic affirmations is professed par excellence in the eucharistic memorial, the sacrament of communion in the Body of Christ. As custodian of the good deposit of faith, the apostolic ministry has the function of guaranteeing the bond between the eucharistic celebration of each community — and so also of its faith — and that of other communities, and also of the bond between all and the apostolic community.

Ceaselessly threatened by schism, the Christian community has known tension and even divisions from its very beginning. Later on, several of these even led to fundamental divergences on how the Church sees itself as Church and how it understands its own nature. The churches continue not to agree on what constitutes the full manifestation of God's plan through them. Some, in fact, attribute essential importance to visible elements, in particular to the sacraments, while others hold that the invisible reality of grace is the sole essential even in the time between Easter and the definitive coming of the reign of God. These divergences are, moreover, closely tied to different views of justification. Even so it must be recognized that this has not prevented the churches calling themselves bearers of the Spirit, commissioned to bring salvation to the world. Despite divisions, Christ has not withdrawn his grace, and baptism celebrated in fidelity to the apostolic tradition inserts all believers into his ecclesial Body. But the fact remains that the scandal of our division is a grave wound to God's will for his people and is one of the chief obstacles to the credibility of our witness.

4. The Form of a Profession of Faith Today

The ancient professions of faith and the great conciliar definitions were very often in response either to the challenges posed by tensions between the adequate expression of the faith and the new cultures, or to the internal problems of the Christian community. It was necessary to remain faithful both to the catholicity of an evangelical message destined to humanity as a whole at all times and in all environments, and to its authentic content, above all in what concerns the person of Jesus, revelation of God's saving grace. Thus the formulas of faith shed light on Christian existence by recalling to it its deepest source and meaning. At the same time they permitted each community to remain united in itself and in communion with the sole sum of Christian communities, despite temptations to division, even to schism.

Today the Church finds itself faced with analogous difficulties. They come both from the churches' new realization of a close relationship with the cultures in which they have taken root, and also from the situation of division which is ours today. So the Church needs to discover how to live the faith in such a way that it will meet the aspirations on which peoples and persons set their hopes today, and how to proclaim this faith unanimously by overcoming its divisions. In fact, these two tasks are complementary. The Church is required to proclaim the traditional faith in new ways, in response to the new conditions of humanity; but it cannot do this in a credible way unless it relies on the witness of its unity in confessing Christ. Moreover, to get out of the impasse into which confessional divisions have led it, it has need of an expression of its faith, which, at this fundamental level, will re-establish mutual confidence between the churches and clear away suspicions or reservations. For the state of disunity, reinforced by a long history of polemics, means that we are not always sure of being unanimous even on essential points, fearing lest a difference in interpretation may conceal a more profound disagreement that touches on the faith itself.

In our world the apostolic faith is challenged from all sides. This questioning touches first of all on beliefs in a Creator God who is leading the world to its fulfilment. Without the sense of a divine mystery, transcendant and yet present at the heart of the world with the power to reconcile it and renew it while bringing it to perfection, the Christian faith would lose its foundation. For it is this mystery of the transcendant God that makes itself present to the world through Jesus Christ in his Church. Now this truth is contested today — as much as and more than by theoretical atheism — by the very widespread practical attitude which sees the visible and finite world as the only sure reality with which humanity has to reckon. The churches therefore have to speak once again the word of faith, handed down ever since the apostolic community, which will bring light in this situation. But they must express it in a new way which will save our contemporaries from the illusion that they are emancipated from all dependence (even on God) and from the dream of attaining fulfilment through human powers alone. For the faith, which knows that a person is perfectly free only within his relationship to God, that illusion leads to the loss of true liberty. And because the Church knows that human beings are fully human only under the grace of God, it also holds that humanity's community vocation is not fully satisfied in the social and political community (with the necessary transformations) but in the Kingdom of God. Awaited in relationship to the resurrection of the dead, this is already mysteriously present under the signs of the sacramental life. Occasionally, moreover, elements from the Christian tradition, even the faith itself, are appropriated by political powers or movements of the left or of the right for goals which are radically incompatible with the spirit of the Gospel. So it is important to draw out all there is in the faith that is opposed to such cases. But simple protests or vague accusations are not enough in such cases. There is need for firm and precise expression of evangelical conviction and of what it rests on.

Other needs of the contemporary world could lead the churches to give new emphasis to aspects of the apostolic texts which in the past were not included in the explicit object of professions of faith. Confessing Christ implies today a special insistence on the connection between Christian salvation and the realization in our world of a state of justice and peace, abolishing discriminations, and thus announcing the reign of God inaugurated in Jesus. This can become a priority when there is question of defending the dignity of the person in regions or circumstances where it is threatened. It is clear, however, that this verbal profession will be authentic only if what it expresses in words finds its practical expression in the activity of ecclesial communities to second the efforts being made everywhere in the world for the establishment of this justice and of respect for these human rights. For this is a matter of confessing the same apostolic faith, but now in its "existential" aspect without which the profession of the creeds of the past would be seriously weakened. The confession of Christ through action is, in fact, the logical outcome of adherence to the fundamental articles of faith in God the Creator and in the Incarnation "for us men and for our salvation".

It is, then, for each church not, of course, to rewrite the traditional creed, but to translate the confession of apostolic faith with a view to its own cultural context or its own historical situation. Clearly it must be careful not to push into the background that personal communion with God to which faith opens the way by reason of the mystery of Christ. For the act of faith does not stop at formulas giving intelligible expression to the mystery of God or laying down an evangelical mode of behaviour. Its goal is the very person of God, beyond any image or idea which, through revelation, we form for ourselves but always in a limited way. The apostolic texts present the faith to us as a vital dynamism by which the whole person (spirit, heart, will), recognizing in Jesus Christ his God and his Saviour, welcomes him through the Holy Spirit and in doing so yields himself to him in all that his mystery admits of and promises. For in giving himself to us He enables us, always in the Holy Spirit, to give ourselves to him also. Conversion and docility to the Spirit find their source here. And this explains the coming together of the churches in efforts to enable the new creation of which the Risen Christ is the Lord to shine forth even now.

5. Unity of Faith and Communion of Churches

Since the Nairobi Assembly Faith and Order has been concentrating mainly on the "conciliar community" as final result of the ecumenical quest, since this would bind the churches in an authentic communion. To bring this about there has even been talk of all the churches committing themselves in advance to preparation for a council. However, if the aim is that this should really have the ecumenical character of the first Council it is necessary that the churches taking part should first mutually recognize each other in the same faith, the same baptism and the same eucharist while admitting the equivalence of their respective ministries. For this purpose an assembly of reconciliation could be envisaged as the conclusion of the preparation on which we are already implicitly engaged. The consensus on baptism, eucharist and ministry, once it has been completed and accepted by all the churches, would be a promising step along this path.

But such a reconciliation also requires that the churches should have successfully completed their search for an authentic consensus concerning the faith with a view to the time when they will come to the point of proclaiming that faith "with one heart and one voice to the glory of God, the Father of the Lord Jesus Christ" (Rom. 15:6). In our present context, to have some impact and to serve as a firm basis for witness, the profession of faith must, in fact, be ecumenical. Certainly, to the extent to which it does not stop short at propositions to which the believing intelligence assents but attains to the transcendant reality which the words seek to express, the act of faith transcends divisions or confessional quarrels. But this does not suppress their object, nor their importance, nor the need to try to overcome them if the churches mean to respond fully to God's plan as Jesus proclaimed it: "That all may be one so that the world may believe that thou has sent me."

At the basis of this search should be the will to understand other churches and no longer to anathematize them, without, however, giving up the task of discovering the objective reasons that show that this or that position held on principle by a church is opposed to the truth of the faith. The translation of the apostolic faith by a church in view of its particular situation should not, certainly not, lead to destruction of the profession of ecclesial faith. Where this translation maintains what the Church in its building-period saw as essential to its faith, the churches of other regions — especially those which have contributed to the appearance of new Christianities elsewhere than in the western world — should be ready to accept it. This recognition of the true faith under forms which are, perhaps, no longer those bequeathed to them, forms part of their conversion to the practical requirements of unity in the circumstances which will be ours henceforth. Such recognition also represents a communion in the mystery of the One who "was rich and became poor" so that the Father's plan might be fulfilled.

There must also be readiness not to demand more than is required for a true communion that bears on what may be called the essential core of the Christian faith. By this is meant one which contains, at least implicitly, all that without which the mystery of Jesus Christ would be irremediably falsified or so impoverished that the master-conviction of the apostolic community would lose its meaning. Churches for which the content of the faith is expressed in a fuller form must not *a priori* consider other churches, whose doctrinal traditions are less explicit, as willingly or through ill-will betraying the wholeness of the Christian heritage. They must put trust in what is implicit and in the way of life it permits. In their turn, clearly, churches which are more restrained in their doctrinal affirmations and in their sacramental life must be on their guard against considering *a priori* that other churches, with richer formulas of faith and rites, are polluting the purity of faith with adventitious or parasitical additions. They should not deny, but should leave the question open. The churches have then to state precisely what in their corpus of doctrine they judge to be either a point on which they must require an explicit affirmation from other churches so that the unity God himself wishes to give to his Church may become a reality at the level of faith, or, on the contrary, to be an aspect which can remain implicit without thereby radically compromising unity of faith. Once reconciled, they will grow together towards the fullness of truth.

Diversity of doctrinal expressions is not necessarily a sign of rupture of faith. Only what is contradictory to or denies the apostolic faith should be seen as an obstacle to ecclesial communion. Moreover, unity in faith is not merely not opposed to allowing a diversity of traditions, doctrinal emphases and theological syntheses; very often it requires them. In this way are shown both the transcendance and the inexhaustible richness of the object of faith.

Conclusion

This paper has stressed the importance of the common commitment of Christians to the evangelization of the world and to efforts to make it "the world which God wants". Here they are often already living the mystery of a communion of faith which they have not yet come to express adequately in wholly satisfactory doctrinal agreements. Already engaged as they are in a movement towards the "conciliar community", the churches can already join in doxological proclamation of their faith, that which we find in the hymn which opens the Epistle to the Ephesians (Eph. 1:3-23) even while they continue their search for doctrinal agreement. If faith is directed towards God, doxological language expresses it just as much as do the words of dogmatic creeds. This inspired text, which belongs to our common heritage and takes up the truth of faith while being free of doctrinal controversies, could become the opening blessing of our ecumenical meetings and the common profession of that faith whose demands we are trying to discern more clearly.

8. COMMON WITNESS

A Study Document of the Joint Working Group
of the Roman Catholic Church
and the World Council of Churches, 1982

Forms of common witness which are possible for the different churches even before they have achieved complete agreement on the understanding of the faith were sought by the Joint Working Group almost immediately after it was established in 1965. It published a first statement on this in 1970: "Common Witness and Proselytism".[1] One of the purposes of this study was to end the competitive struggle between the churches, and by a common witness to enhance the credibility of Christian mission in particular. Supported in this endeavour both by the Roman Catholic Synod of Bishops in 1974 and the Nairobi Assembly of the World Council of Churches in 1975, the JWG returned once more to the theme in the latter half of the seventies. It was guided by first-hand reports of common witness in various regions. The findings of this more recent study, which spanned several years, were published in 1982 under the title "Common Witness". A selection from the first-hand reports of common Christian witness throughout the world is provided in an appendix. In an introductory word "to our readers", it is pointed out: "It will take discernment to see this underlayer of experience, this hidden structure in the document." The document is not intended as a final word on the subject but rather as a "progress report on the common witness in the years just past". It is a call to continuing witness within the emerging tradition of common witness in the years ahead, so that "the world might believe".

   Outline
   To our readers
   I.   The fact of common witness
   II.   Christian witness — common witness
   III. Realizations of common witness
   IV. Struggle and hope
   V.   Appendix: Common witness in practice
We reprint here parts I to IV.

● Text in *Common Witness: a Study Document of the Joint Working Group of the Roman Catholic Church and the World Council of Churches*, WCC Commission on World Mission and Evangelism, Mission Series No. 1, 1982, pp.7-28.

---

[1] *The Ecumenical Review*, Vol. 23, No. 1, January 1971, pp.9-43.

I. The Fact of Common Witness

A) NEW INITIATIVES

1. All over the world Christians and churches have been increasingly able to give common witness. Formal theological dialogue about unity and the ways to overcome the existing divisions can record notable progress. At the same time the differences of many centuries are not quickly overcome and a good deal remains to be done before Christians reach the point where they are able to make a common confession of faith. Still it is already possible to point to many kinds of experience which have a positive potential for common witness in spite of ambiguities, difficulties, obstacles.

The impulse to a common witness comes not from any strategy but from the personal and community experience of Jesus Christ. Awareness of the communion with Christ and with each other generates the dynamism that impels Christians to give a visible witness together.

2. It is now quite normal that Christians of different confessions should come together in common celebrations to mark the week of prayer for unity, for some of the great Christian festivals and for many other occasions often of local significance. The liturgical texts and songs, new or old, which are used on these occasions become part of a new common heritage and serve to create a kind of basis for unity which continues long after the actual ecumenical ceremonies and which give even to those who were not present signs by which to identify the Christian mystery.

3. On many occasions Christians from all backgrounds meet to read and study the Bible which thus becomes an integral part of their Christian life. *These kinds of gatherings are a powerful ecumenical bond and also an occasion of missionary encounter* both because of the wide public interest in the Bible and because of the opportunities they offer of an encounter with secular appreciations of the Bible whether traditional or contemporary.

4. A common witness is given by a growing cooperation in theological work in all its various aspects. *Scripture research makes ecumenical editions of the Bible possible.* Theological teaching and research as well as the theological formation of the faithful for witness are sometimes being undertaken in common or with collaboration at various levels. Theological and religious publications, as well as the relation of religious literature and art, are a field of growing cooperation at the various stages of production and editing and this too is a contribution to evangelization.

5. In a number of places, through their official representatives, the churches have been able to approach the civil authorities together to make known to them the Christian witness in political matters where human rights and dignity as well as spiritual and moral values are at stake. Such official interventions of the churches have become so frequent that in some cases specialized joint bodies have been set up, sometimes also in collaboration with communities of other faiths, with secular associations, or with public bodies at the national or international level.

6. Several common programmes of direct evangelization have been carried out or are under way in the six continents and under various political regimes. In every case local agreements have been made to define the degree of participation of each church and to fix the ground of the pastoral approach to be undertaken by those to be involved in the new proclamation of the Gospel.

7. Many ecumenical groups have been set up on an informal basis. Some have arisen from spontaneous initiatives while others have grown out of centralized or organized movements. All aim at giving a more specific common witness in the different fields of Christian life and conduct. Sometimes this is being done in places or territories newly settled or occupied only temporarily, in situations for example where migration takes place. Other times it is among sections of the population discovering a new social and cultural identity which old confessional traditions have not taken sufficiently into account.

8. A number of ecumenical organizations have come into being in order to enable joint action and other forms of cooperation, thereby promoting common witness as well as expressing the real if imperfect communion between churches. Many of them in which the Roman Catholic Church participates are referred to in the document of the Secretariat for Promoting Christian Unity, "Ecumenical Collaboration at the Regional, National and Local Levels" (1975). The range and diversity of such organizations speak clearly of the extent to which Christians have become conscious of the need to be and act together in their daily efforts to be faithful to the witness and work of their common Lord. The kind of organization is normally determined by the needs of the place and situation. Hence it runs from joint working groups, to service councils and committees, and to study and action groups of every kind, and further forms may be expected to appear as renewed faithfulness in mission impels Christians towards unity.

Of special interest are councils of churches at various levels which in their own situations make possible significant initiatives of common witness. The Roman Catholic Church has joined in a considerable number of places and even where this has not happened, it has a close working relation with many of them often by means of a joint working group and by participating in some of their programmes.

B) NEW CONSCIOUSNESS OF COMMON WITNESS

9. *The Holy Spirit, in calling Christians to act together in these unprecedented ways to respond to new situations, has also awakened a consciousness of the urgency of common witness.* Churches and church leaders have begun to identify and authenticate these experiences of collaboration and common action, urging that they be continued and intensified.

10. Following the thought of the Second Vatican Council the Joint Working Group between the World Council of Churches and the Roman Catholic Church in the study *Common Witness and Proselytism* (1970) reflected on the spiritual gifts shared by Christians (cf. *Unitatis Redintegratio* 4). The study spoke of the privilege and obligation of the churches to give witness to the truth and new life which is theirs in Jesus Christ. For this reason Christians cannot remain divided in their witness. (See par. 11 and 13).

11. The 5th Assembly of the WCC, meeting at Nairobi in 1975, reflected on significant discussions about evangelization in several meetings which had immediately preceded it. The Assembly said, "The confession of Christ holds in one communion our divided churches and the many communities, new and old, within and around them" (*Confessing Christ Today*: 36). *There are striking and clear convergences on evangelization in the reports of the Bangkok Assembly on "Salvation Today" (1973); the International Evangelical Congress on World Evangelization at Lausanne (1974); and the papal document, issued after the 1974 Synod in Rome on*

evangelization in the modern world, Evangelii Nuntiandi. The latter called for a greater common witness to Christ before the world in the work of evangelization (Par. 77).

12. In 1979 Pope John Paul II appealed strongly and urgently to all who follow Christ to meet and unite around the one Lord. He acknowledged the need for getting to know each other and removing the obstacles blocking the way to perfect unity, but emphasized that "we can and must immediately reach and display to the world our unity in proclaiming the mystery of Christ; in revealing the divine dimension and also the human dimension of the redemption, and struggling with unwearying perseverance for the dignity that human beings have reached and can continually reach in Christ". "In this unity in mission, which is decided principally by Christ himself, all Christians must find what already unites them, even before their full communion is achieved" (*Redemptor Hominis*, 11, 12).

C) RENEWAL FOR WITNESS

13. The Holy Spirit constantly renews Christians and their communities in their relation to Christ. *This renewal centres in Christ and calls forth a new obedience and a new way of life which is itself a witnessing communion*. The Spirit invites each Christian community to conversion so that it may participate responsibly in the plan of salvation. It is a continuing conversion which renews the commitment of the individual and the community to Christ (vid *Evangelii Nuntiandi* n. 15 & 36). A common renewal requires openness to the Spirit who works in us teaching us in an evolving world to seek clear ways of expressing our faith, ways marked by our mutual love for each other (John 15:17).

14. The urging of the Holy Spirit to unity and mission through common renewal can open the ears of Christians to hear what God is saying to them through churches and communities other than their own. *It is an awakening to active appreciation of the gifts of grace, truth and witness found in those communities*. "The gifts which the churches have received and share in Christ have demanded and made urgent a common witness to the world" (*Common Witness and Proselytism*, 14). By opening Christians to the world and its needs, the Holy Spirit gives witness to them, impelling them to bring the living communion of Christ in his Church to those people and places where it has not yet come. This will bring into being new communities facing new cultural social and theological situations and challenges.

II. Christian Witness — Common Witness

A) THE COMMON GROUND

15. The command of Jesus Christ and the power of his grace lead the Church to proclaim the Good News he has brought us; finally this Good News is Christ Himself. *This Gospel message gives Christian communities the common ground for their proclamation*. They accept the content of the biblical witness and the Creeds of the early Church. Today they desire to reach beyond what separates them by stressing the essential and returning to the foundation of their faith, Jesus Christ (I Cor.3:11), (cf. *Common Witness and Proselytism*, 2). They recognize that baptism, as the effective sign of their unity, brings them into communion with Christ's followers and empowers them to confess him as Lord and Saviour. Therefore the Lord's gift of unity already

exists among Christians and, although it is not yet realized perfectly, it is real and operative. This unmerited gift requires that witness be borne in common as an act of gratitude and the witness in turn is a means of expressing and deepening unity.

B) THE SOURCE OF WITNESS

16. i) The Father

Christian witness has its source in the Father who testified to Christ his beloved Son, sent visibly into the world. He bore witness to him on the cross and by raising him from the dead through the Holy Spirit. So Christ received the fulness of the Holy Spirit to be in the world, himself the divine fulness for the human family (Col. 2:9-10).

"When God raised up his servant, he sent him to bless you" (Acts 3:26; 26:23). Jesus could say: "I am going away and I shall come back to you" (John 14:28). He who "has become for us wisdom and justification, sanctification and liberation" (I Cor. 1:30) has been sent into the world that those who receive him in faith may find in him that sanctification and liberation. God now sends him into the world in the Church which he has made his body in spite of the sin of its members. The disciple can say: "Christ lives in me" (Gal. 2:20; cf. II Cor. 4:10-12) and "Christ speaks in me" (II Cor. 13:3). *Christian witness is an epiphany of Christ who took the form of a servant, and became obedient unto death* (Phil. 2:6).

17. ii) Jesus Christ

Jesus Christ is the one witness of God, true and faithful (Rev. 3:14; 1:5; vid. *Confessing Christ Today*: 8,9,10). The witness he gave to the Father through his life was sealed by the martyrdom of the cross. His death evidenced total dedication to the witness he bore; it was the testimony he gave to himself as "the truth that liberates" (John 8:32). The cause of the Father had consumed his life to the point of martyrdom. *In his death and resurrection his entire existence disclosed the meaning of the message.* Through those events he breathed forth his Spirit to animate his followers, drawing them together in the community of witness, his mystical body which is the Church. It would pay a similar price for the witness which he would give through it (I Pet. 5:9). From the beginning the followers of Jesus as confessors and martyrs became the vehicle of the Spirit in their suffering unto death, inseparably linked with the inspired words they uttered in the power of the same Spirit.

18. iii) The Holy Spirit

The Spirit plays such an important role in Christian witness that he too can be said to be the witness of Christ in the world: "The Spirit of truth himself who comes from the Father will bear witness to me" (John 15:26). For it is in the Spirit that God raises Christ (Rom. 8:11); it is in the Spirit that he glorifies him (John 16:14-15); it is the Spirit who convicts the world in the trial which brings it into contradiction with Jesus (John 16:8). The Spirit bears this witness by means of the Church. He makes the Church the body (I Cor. 12:13) and thus the manifestation of Christ in this world. *The Spirit is communion* (II Cor. 13:13) *so he unites us to Christ; and in the same movement, brings about communion among men and women.*

19. The Spirit comes upon the faithful and makes them also witnesses of Christ (Acts 1:8). In him the word and action of Christians becomes a "demonstration of

Spirit and power" (I Cor. 2:4). We must encounter Christ to be his witnesses, to be able to say what we know about him (cf. I John 1:3-4; 4:14). *It is the Holy Spirit who enables the faithful to meet Christ to experience him. Believers are led to witness to their faith before humankind, because the Spirit witnesses to Jesus in their hearts* (John 15:16-17; Rom. 8:16; Gal. 4:6). In the debate between Jesus and the world, he takes the part of Jesus in strengthening believers in their faith (John 16:8; cf. I John 5:6) but he also deepens the faith of believers by leading them to the whole truth (John 16:13). He is thus the master of Christian witness enabling us to say "Jesus is Lord" (I Cor. 12:3), he is the inspiration and teacher of the Church (John 16:13).

C) THE CHURCH

20. The Church received its commission from the Lord Jesus Christ himself, "You shall be my witnesses" (Acts 1:8). It takes upon itself the witness which the Father bore to his Son (cf. John 5:32) when, in front of those who put him to death, he raised him and made him Christ and Lord for the salvation of all (Acts 2:23,24,36). *The Christian witness receives its incarnation and force out of the calling of the People of God to be a pilgrim people giving witness to Christ our Lord in communion with the cloud of witnesses* (Heb. 12:1).

21. Following the apostles (Acts 2:32) the Church today testifies to these saving acts of God in front of the world and proclaims that Jesus Christ is Saviour and Lord of all mankind and of all creation. Such is the object of the Christian witness. Through proclamation and bearing witness, Christians are making known the saving Lordship of Christ, so that the one in whom God wills to achieve this salvation may be "believed in the world" (I Tim. 3:16), so that people may confess "that Jesus Christ is Lord to the glory of God the Father" (Phil. 2:11).

The Church as a whole is the primary subject of Christian witness. *As the Church is one body of many members, Christian witness is by its nature communitarian.* When one of the faithful acts in individual witness this is related to the witness of the whole Christian community. Even when the witness is given by Christians in separated churches it should be witness to the same Christ and necessarily has a communitarian aspect.

D) CHARACTERISTICS OF CHRISTIAN WITNESS

22. Witness was a distinctive mark of the Church in the time of the apostles. In giving its witness today the Church continues to be faithful to this apostolic commission. Through the same Holy Spirit it shares their motivation and power. *As the body of Christ the Church manifests him in the world. Its nature is to give witness.*

23. Witness is what we are before God. It consists in the first place in being. It ought to be rooted in contemplation. *The Church is already giving witness then when it deepens its spiritual life and when it devises new styles of life which commend the Gospel in today's world.* In many parts of the world Christians are discovering this afresh by their experiences in small communities, but the need of renewal extends to all manifestations of the life of the Body.

Aware of the failings of those who belong to it, the Church seeks in its worship to be transformed into the likeness of Christ. He must be shown to the world in its members. For this the Church needs the nourishment it draws from prayer, the Word and the Sacraments. It depends on the continual renewal they provide for the authenticity and effectiveness of its witness.

24. Authentic witness is a channel of the divine love to all people. *That love expresses itself in discerning the ways in which witness can be given most tellingly in each circumstance of contact.* In some sense readiness for martyrdom is the norm of witness since it testifies to the orientation of a life which is itself a sign of a person's conviction and devotion to a cause, even to the point of dying for one's belief. *It is conviction incarnated in life which must make proclamation credible. The authenticity of witness is finally to be judged not by the listener's response but before God.* From this point of view there is a gratuitousness about witness that is to be associated with the gratuitousness of God's grace in his dealings with humankind. It is in the life of the witness that the message of the Gospel has to be made present. The life of the witness is the valid exposition of the message. It is from this point that the necessary effort to make the Christian message speak to people and situations has to begin and no ready-made formula can be a substitute. There must always be a dialogue established between situations and people and the Church, for there is a necessary listening process in discovering effective means of witness. Since the medium through which the sign comes to others and communicates its meaning to them is important, the sign has to be given expression in terms of each society and culture.

25. *Witness seeks a response, but there is always an element of mystery and miracle about the way in which the witness the Spirit gives to Jesus comes home to the heart of a person. It is always something fresh, often totally surprising and unexpected.*

26. The witness of Christ has to be given and shaped by the community which lives in Christ and is animated by a spirit of love and freedom, confidence and joy. *Words alone cannot stress sufficiently that the love of God has come to us through Christ, that it has overcome sin and death, and that it lives on among us. It demands a comprehensive witness, credible and full of love, given both by the Christian and the Church in every part of life.* Without love such witness is only "a sounding gong or clanging cymbal" (I Cor.13:1). The liberating action of Christ must mean that witness is given in freedom and with respect for the freedom of those to whom it is addressed.

27. Christian witness also must be given in humility. Its source is in the Father who, by the Spirit, raised Christ from the dead and sends him visibly to humankind by means of those who are his witnesses. *It is therefore a commission from God, not something one takes upon oneself.* It requires the witness to listen before proclaiming the Good News and to cooperate with the unpredictable leading of the Spirit. It does not provide a blueprint that will guarantee success in all situations. Rather it is the task of a co-worker with God in the service of all peoples.

E) EFFECTS OF WITNESS

28. Witness moves from one unity to another — from that of the members of the Body of Christ in the one Spirit to the greater unity in which all things in heaven and earth will come together under the one Head who is Christ (Eph.1:10). Essentially it is a work of reconciliation, of people with God and with one another. To take part in Christian witness also deepens the unity that already exists among Christians. *Witness tends always to extend the fellowship of the Spirit, creating new community.* At the same time it is an essential help for Christians themselves. It promotes among them the conversion and renewal which they always need. It can strengthen their faith and open

up new aspects of the truth of Christ. As such it is a fundamental part of the life of the community that is fully committed to Christ.

29. When witness is being given in a context of unbelief it often calls forth opposition. The Church has to be ready to pay the price of misunderstanding, frustration and suffering, even, on occasion, of martyrdom. From the beginning the reality of the Cross has been the inevitable context of Christian witness (II Cor. 4:8-12). That witness has to be made also before the principalities and powers of this age (Eph. 6:12; cf. Rom. 8:38-39). The experience of Christians in exile, prison and the arena in other times is often repeated today. *The Church has to bring its message of love and reconciliation to even the most difficult situations so it is not surprised when its witness has to be given even at the cost of life itself.*

F) COMMON WITNESS

30. When he prayed that all be one so the world might believe (John 17:21), Jesus made a clear connection between the unity of the Church and the acceptance of the Gospel. Unhappily Christians are still divided in their churches and the testimony they give to the Gospel is thus weakened. There are, however, even now many signs of the initial unity that already exists among all followers of Christ and indications that it is developing in important ways. *What we have in common, and the hope that is in us, enable us to be bold in proclaiming the Gospel and trustful that the world will receive it.* Common witness is the essential calling of the Church and in an especial way it responds to the spirit of this ecumenical age in the Church's life. It expresses our actual unity and increases our service to God's Word, strengthening the churches both in proclaiming the Gospel and in seeking for the fulness of unity.

31. *Yet the tragedy of our divisions remains with us at the focal point of our testimony to Jesus: the Holy Eucharist.* It is urgent that all Christians intensify their prayer for the full realization of this unity and witness.

"This fellowship in prayer, nevertheless, sharpens the pain of the churches' division at the point of eucharistic fellowship which should be the most manifest witness of the one sacrifice of Christ for the whole world" (*Common Witness and Proselytism*, 16).

G) SITUATIONS OF COMMON WITNESS

32. Common witness is called for in a great many different situations. The variety of groups and individuals taking part in some act of common witness should make it possible to have a more realistic awareness of the situation, to adapt to it in solidarity and to orient the witness concretely to it.

33. This does not at all mean diluting the truth of the Gospel to fit every situation. Rather those who hand it on and those who receive it must undergo change. Thus common witness should bring about the creative transformation of a given situation.

34. *Witness does not mean debating possibilities but brings people to face reality.* It calls forth reflection, discussion, decision. In every thing those who witness should show they have Good News to proclaim. The Kingdom of God whose coming they have to proclaim in word and deed consists in "justice, peace and joy in the Holy Spirit" (Rom. 14:17).

H) IN THE WORLD

35. In bearing this witness Christians are committing themselves to the service of others, for it is the Good News of God they are bringing (Acts 13:32,33). *Through proclaiming the cross and resurrection of Christ they affirm that God wills the salvation of his people in all dimensions of their being, both eternal and earthly.*

36. The whole of creation groans and is in travail as it seeks adoption and redemption (Rom. 8:22). Salvation in Jesus Christ has cosmic dimensions. Christian witness is given not only to fulfil a missionary vocation but also to respond to the aspirations of the universe. Human needs and the challenge of a broken and unbelieving world compel the churches to cooperate with God in using his gifts for the reconciliation of all peoples and things in Christ.

The contemporary thirst for meaning, for a spiritual base, for God, is also an occasion for common witness by the full manifestation of Jesus Christ in prayer, worship and in daily life.

37. The search for Gospel values such as human dignity, justice, peace and fraternity invites participation by a common witness, which always points to Jesus Christ as Lord and Saviour of all. *This means Christian involvement in matters of social justice in the name of the poor and the oppressed. We must relearn the patristic lesson that the Church is the mouth and the voice of the oppressed in the presence of the powers that be.* Thus Christian witness will mean participation in the struggle for human rights, at all levels, in economic sharing and in liberation from social and political oppression. All are parts of the task required by obedience to the truth of God and its consequences.

38. In fact in the last decade there has been a most positive advance in a variety of common witness at all these levels of Christian life. A growing sensitivity to the manipulative attitudes and behaviour often fostered by contemporary cultures is forcing Christian churches and communities to a drastic reappraisal of their relation to the world in mission, and is bringing them together to witness to the gifts of truth and life bestowed in Christ, which are the source of their life and which provide access to salvation (cf. *Common Witness and Proselytism*, 11).

III. Realizations of Common Witness

A) OCCASIONS AND POSSIBILITIES

39. *Christ's commission to his Church* (Matt. 28:18-20) *and the gift of the Spirit to enable this task to be fulfilled impose a missionary obligation upon Christians in every circumstance. It causes them to cross social and geographical boundaries: yet it is present also in their everyday surroundings. It demands obedience even in situations where explicit preaching is impossible and witness has usually to be silent.*

40. The inspired phrase from the Faith and Order meeting in Lund 1952 invited the churches to do all things together except where fidelity to conscience would forbid. Yet so many years later we are not yet putting this into practice. It is a principle which if applied would multiply enormously the occasions of common witness, putting it in the daily agenda of each church. Its intent was expressed in *Common Witness and Proselytism*, 13: "Christians cannot remain divided in their witness. Any situation

where contact and cooperation between churches are refused must be regarded as abnormal."

41. By coming together in witness it becomes possible to know and recognize the manifold gifts that God has granted to his Church. The peculiar history, tradition and experience which each brings enriches the quality of the common witness. Instead of each losing identity, it is seen in the wider context of the one Church willed by Christ in which all are to grow to the fulness of Christ in whom is their final destiny. Specific gifts are not eliminated but rather increase their potential for witness, and the value of other traditions is discovered and enhanced.

42. Thus common witness influences the whole of our witness to Jesus Christ.

It does not eliminate distinctive witness but enriches it and it centres the emphasis in the common treasure of the Gospel — Jesus Christ is Lord and Saviour. *The invitation to join the family of the Church will always be made with due respect to the integrity of the Gospel message, to the catholicity of the Church and the fulness of unity which is sought.* The respective witness of various confessions could often respond to geographical, linguistic and cultural situations. As Christians and churches grow together in unity, the witness given in separation will become progressively a dimension and complementary part of the total witness given by all Christians to Jesus Christ.

43. Common initiatives defending and promoting human dignity are by their nature a privileged field of common witness. The group engaged in them often have a deep experience of Christian community especially when they draw their strength from common prayer and Bible work and to the extent that the members are rooted in their own liturgies. Such communities of service are a sign of the kingdom.

44. Evangelization by direct proclamation which is organized together, retreats, Bible courses, study and action groups, religious education undertaken jointly or in collaboration are an expression of growing acceptance of the primacy of the saving truth and essential kerygma which announces Jesus as Lord and Saviour, present and acting now in his Spirit. Therefore, joint or coordinated pastoral and missionary actions are instances of common witness or at least prepare the ground and the preliminary structures to enable it.

45. Intrinsic clarity of meaning is a test which must be applied to witness. Do people really experience it as a good gift coming from above? Is it transparent to those of good will?

46. Common witness is also given through reciprocal support. The hope is to see Christians of all confessions side by side as they share by word and deed in testifying to the saving will of God. For various reasons of language, history, ideology, this is not always possible. In such a case the witness given by one church or group of Christians can however be supported by the prayers, gifts, visits and sympathy of others. Thus the witness given by Orthodox, Catholics, Anglicans or Protestants becomes in a sense the vicarious means of presenting the witness of other Christians too. *So the faithful witness given by one church in a particular place can be part of the rich and diverse witness of the whole Church. The Church cannot shut its eyes to the sufferings, injustices and violence taking place within a large proportion of humankind but, when she is not able to express openly the cries and appeals of all those who suffer, she should seek to make possible a silent witness of solidarity and intercession.*

B) PROBLEMS AND TENSIONS

47. We recognize that for "conscience sake" our churches sometimes feel obliged not only to a separate witness, but even to a contradictory one. While we pray and work for the fulness of church unity we recognize the existence of divisions as a reality to be taken into account. The honesty of our common witness is demonstrated by the open and public nature of our disagreement. We believe that the expression of different solutions for ethical issues will highlight the importance and credibility of our common witness. A divided witness can become a counter witness. The reality of our divisions will therefore always be a call to common prayer, study and research, in the hope that we will grow in unity and love.

48. In its witness the Church addresses the Gospel to a specific situation or context. Common witness also in order to be effective must be concrete. The challenge and condition for common witness may be very different from one situation to another. Cultural, historical, and socio-political factors will contribute to the shaping of it.

This can however lead to tensions and even new divisions within one church or between churches. What is a powerful common witness in one place may be perceived as a source of division in another. The more honestly this problem is being recognized the more creative the tension may become.

49. The activities entailed in giving witness can bring tensions. Some of these are healthy; others create or exacerbate tension between or within churches. It may be for example that some Christians who are active in local communities feel the pace of ecumenical advance should be more rapid. In their own informal experiences of living, working, and praying together they may have discovered a communion which they claim is so developed as to call for expressions that go beyond what official teaching or discipline permit. In such cases it can be very difficult to work out a solution that respects the values at stake and the integrity of those concerned. Hence the need to keep alive dialogue and communication. The occurrence and difficulty of such situations seems to indicate there should be some study of them as an ecumenical problem that calls for attention.

50. Christians of all churches agree that membership in the Church is an essential part of the Christian message. *The Gospel invitation to accept Christ as Lord and Saviour is an invitation also to be a member of His Body, a member of a local church in communion with all the churches, which together live the word of God in faith, sacrament and witness.*

51. When churches are still divided and not yet at one in understanding the Gospel of Christ, this necessary connection of witness and community, of proclamation and church-membership raises the question of those kinds of witness which are distorted by certain motives, attitudes, behaviour and methods. These are called proselytism and must be evaluated as an unworthy kind of witness. The problem has been stated and treated in the 1970 study *Common Witness and Proselytism*, 25-28. Much of the material is still useful for situations where the problem is actual.

52. In the first place proselytism includes whatever violates the right of the human person, Christian or non-Christian, to be free from every type of physical coercion, moral restraint or psychological pressure which could deprive a person or a community of freedom of judgement and responsible choice. The truth and love of God must always be offered and accepted in freedom.

53. Proselytism also means anything in the proclamation of the Gospel which replaces selfless love by personal or group egoism, substitutes the primary trust in the surprises of the Spirit with an over-confidence in one's own predetermined methods and programmes, fears the truth by misrepresenting the beliefs and practices of other religious communities in the hope of winning adherents.

C) LEVELS AND STRUCTURES

54. Common witness happens and is needed at all levels of church life. Each has its own importance. Local churches and communities have evident occasions for common witness. They share the same cultural milieu and are challenged to give a clear testimony to Jesus Christ. Even small changes in attitudes at local level are a beginning for the renewal of the whole Church. There should be always an interplay between witness on the local level and that on regional, national and world levels. It is important that the work for common witness takes place at all levels simultaneously.

55. Ecumenical groups with a specific vocation give common witness at a special level. These groups are often of a charismatic or monastic type. In dialogue with the churches they are free to search for new ways to express Christian life and common witness. They should be given support and account be taken of their findings where these have value. Church leaders could then recommend the new forms of common witness that have been tested by such groups and found to be of value.

56. The renewal or rediscovery of the life of monastic and religious communities in a number of churches has a special significance for common witness. In the first place it gives a new impetus to witness as such. The monastic aim springs from the desire to seek God, to bring enthusiasm for Jesus Christ into the daily routine, and to enable confession of him to dominate and colour a particular form of human existence. It embodies in a special way the keen desire that others, hearing his word and the message it contains, should also come to follow Christ. It does this especially through the witness of Christian existence of a very deep and intense kind. Thus it makes the faith-inspired motivation which enlivens all the People of God stand out in bold relief.

57. As the communities of religious life in the different churches are discovering each other and their various traditions of life and witness across confessional separations, they have the potential for a major contribution to common witness. Their singleness of purpose along with their freedom to adapt to special tasks have already enabled them to contribute substantially to the ecumenical movement, but, so far, this is only a beginning in terms of the considerable spiritual resources which accrue to the vocation to the religious life.

58. Religious communities have a key role to play in spiritual ecumenism and in the prayer for unity. Their regular pattern of intercession gives them abundant opportunity of supporting spiritually the common witness of Christians and churches. Here those communities devoted to the liturgical and contemplative life can make a special contribution.

59. All groups, at local, regional or national level, have the responsibility of encouraging and inspiring each other so that they can provide examples of common witness to be used and promoted at the world level. It is highly desirable that the churches seek means of giving expression to common witness at a world level. Here the Joint Working Group between the Roman Catholic Church and the World Council of Churches may be able to give ideas and explore possibilities.

60. Ecumenical structures, at different levels, prove a normal occasion to discover, plan, and promote common witness. The specific purpose of such ecumenical structures is to encourage the churches in common witness and service.

61. These structures are of very diverse nature and range from national councils of churches through a whole variety of structures for ecumenical cooperation, to informal meetings of persons responsible for different aspects of the church's life. All can help to provide the consultation necessary to discover the situations that demand common witness.

62. These structures have a varied scope:
a) to encourage manifestations of common witness at local level;
b) to support those manifestations with the worldwide experience of Christians engaged in common witness and working to promote unity;
c) to introduce the ecumenical dimension into communities or groups which are already engaged in Christian witness in specific areas;
d) to organize national and regional events of a witnessing character.

IV. Struggle and hope

63. *Common witness is deeply rooted in our faith and is a demand of the very Gospel we proclaim.* Its urgency is underlined when we realize the seriousness of the human predicament and the tremendous task waiting for the churches at present. *Common witness is not an abstract theological concept. It is very much more than friendly ecumenical relations. It is a responsible way of relating to the human problems of today: the growing traffic in human life through prostitution or in drugs, the corruption in international economic practice, the armaments race, the growing power of the mass media in shaping people's minds. We discover that those challenges touch each and all of the churches when we look beyond our own and see the millions of people who do not know the Gospel of Jesus Christ.* There is a pressing need to join forces to proclaim the Gospel of the kingdom to all peoples. A common effort is required that will multiply our capacity to give a clear and powerful witness. Faced with the challenge of the world, the churches in joining forces to witness to Jesus Christ will find new spiritual strength, new relevance for the human predicament.

64. Often it is socially and politically more difficult to witness together since the powers of this world promote division. In such situations common witness is particularly precious and Christ-like. *Witness that dares to be common is a powerful sign of unity coming directly and visibly from Christ and a glimpse of his kingdom.*

65. In a world where there is confusion, where many people seem uncertain, the search for unity and a common witness is an act and sign of hope. Unity is required to face the challenge, and as the churches respond they will in turn be led into the fuller unity which the Lord wills and by the means he wills. It is an integral part of the hope that all humankind will be confronted with the full presence of God in judgement and grace. Waiting for the eschatological test of their witness, already rejoicing in the risen life of Christ through the gifts of the Holy Spirit, Christians are required to give courageous account of the hope that is in them.

9. OUR CREDO — SOURCE OF HOPE
Declaration by Participants
of the Third European Ecumenical Encounter, 1984

The Conference of European Churches (CEC), which is the association of the majority of Orthodox and Reformation churches in Europe, and the Council of European Bishops' Conferences (CCEE), which is the representative organ of the Roman Catholic Bishops' Conferences in Europe, decided at their second European Ecumenical Encounter in Løgumkloster, Denmark, in 1981, to work at an agreed interpretation of the Christian faith on the basis of the Nicene-Constantinopolitan Creed of 381. A small theological working group was established for this purpose, consisting of Orthodox (Prof. D. Popescu, Romania and Geneva), Protestant (Dr H. Goltz, Halle, German Democratic Republic) and Roman Catholic (Prof. W. Löser, Frankfurt, Federal Republic of Germany) representatives. In the course of two years, this working group produced eight different versions of a document. At the Third European Ecumenical Encounter in Riva del Garda (Italy) from 3 to 8 October 1984, on the theme "Confessing the Faith Together — a Source of Hope", the following document was adopted.

The statement is not, however, officially recognized by the two associations involved but one for which the participants themselves accept responsibility personally. It was transmitted to the European churches in the hope that they would study and receive it and find inspiration in the common heritage of faith. The Declaration has no pretensions to be a new credal statement; it sees itself rather as a historical and theological commentary on the Nicene-Constantinopolitan Creed in the face of the contemporary situation in Europe. It stresses the contemporary relevance of the Creed of 381 for "a common expression of the apostolic faith today".

The Declaration is in three parts:
1. Third Ecumenical Encounter between the CCEE and the CEC
2. European context
3. The common creed

● Text in *Report of the Third European Ecumenical Encounter*, Geneva, 1985.

1. Third Ecumenical Encounter between the Council of European Bishops' Conferences and the Conference of European Churches

(1) The Third Ecumenical Encounter between representatives of the Council of European Bishops' Conferences (CCEE) and of the Conference of European Churches (CEC) has gathered us, from 3 to 8 October 1984, in Riva del Garda and Trent, in order to confess our faith together in the words of the Creed of Constantinople. The theme of our first meeting (Chantilly, 1978) was "To be one that the world may believe"; that of our second conference (Løgumkloster, 1981) "Called to one hope — ecumenical fellowship in prayer, witness and service". We are now concerned with the question of what we can do together in order that the "confession of our hope" (Heb. 10:23) be better expressed than it has been until now in prayer, witness and service. We are convinced that this is of decisive importance for Europe and for the world. Together, we therefore want to pass on what we have perceived in our meeting. What we acknowledged in the solemn worship service in Trent cathedral should bear fruit in the witness daily given by us and the churches to which we belong. We do this on our personal responsibility; and we hope that our churches will take up our common declaration on the Creed of Constantinople and make it their own, as far as seems possible to them, even at local congregational level. We recognize that in all this we are closely united with the work of the Commission on Faith and Order of the World Council of Churches, "Towards the Common Expression of the Apostolic Faith Today".

(2) The name Trent calls to mind the council held in this city by the Roman Catholic Church in the sixteenth century. That council brought longed-for renewal to that church in various important fields. It also led, however, to a hardening against the ideas of the reformers, and it showed up in sharp contrast the divisions which had arisen between Christians. Our present meeting in Trent is an expression of our mutual concern for reconciliation and is understood by us to be a step on the way towards a genuinely universal council.

(3) Trent also reminds us of three martyrs who are honoured here: Sisinnius, Martyrius and Alexander. These three came from Cappadocia towards the end of the fourth century to persuade people to believe the gospel. On 29 May 397 they gave their lives as martyrs. Thus they attest — as messengers of the Eastern Church to the West — the faith of still-divided Christendom and — as martyrs for the sake of the gospel — the hope of the life promised us by the Risen Christ.

2. European context

(4) We come from a wide variety of European countries. We are keenly aware of the situation of our continent today. The character of Europe has been shaped by the Christian faith. Europe is heir to an immeasurably rich cultural and religious heritage. It is true, of course, that many people in the countries from which we come are no longer convinced of the values contained in that heritage or of the opportunities and resources for life it affords. They often view them with considerable reserve and even with indifference. They substitute for them other values and resources. Many place their hope for the future in the advance of technological civilization, only to find that, the more this advance is achieved, the more they create problems for themselves which are difficult to solve or even — as many fear — no longer soluble at all. Our natural, cultural and moral environment has been thrown off balance and in many places is

sick. Europe today is no longer a "Christian society". This new situation, which causes the churches considerable difficulties, presents us also, however, with a new opportunity: Christians can no longer rely on worldly power and are being challenged to bear a personal and sincere witness.

(5) The situation in Europe and in the world gives many causes for anxiety. For a long time Europe has no longer been a self-contained entity. Modern means of communication have enabled us to realize vividly that while Europe is an important part of the world it is nevertheless only a small part of it. Its responsibility vis-à-vis the people of other continents has acquired new dimensions and made European privileges questionable. At the religious, social, cultural and political levels, we Europeans are faced with questions and challenges of unprecedented range and importance because of this encounter with people of other continents. In the countries of Europe a massive movement and intermingling of population has taken place in recent decades. Millions of people from other countries live and work alongside us with their own languages, customs and religious convictions. We do not find it easy to treat them with the respect which is their due as human beings.

(6) Our continent is split into east and west. The countries of the east and of the west live under the shadow of the great powers with their mutual distrust. Europe is a continent in which immense quantities of weapons of all sorts stand in readiness and it fears for its future. Because the power blocs have until now proved unable to achieve effective disarmament, the longing for a lasting peace is in danger of turning into resignation. Reverence for life has suffered a setback. The right to life and the right to freedom of many individuals and even of entire peoples are being violated. Countless infants are being killed even before they are born. In many places infants who are born find themselves in an environment which rejects them. Old, sick and disabled people are often regarded as a burden and pushed to the margin of society. Millions are unemployed. In some cases, this experience of hopelessness leads to violence; in other cases escape is sought in drugs or sex or in unrestrained consumerism. On the other hand, these developments have led many to begin once more to seek the meaning of human life and to be ready to commit themselves in a responsible way.

(7) Many problems confronting contemporary Europe are rooted ultimately in our failure as human beings to live our lives in gratitude to God our Maker, but, on the contrary, we deny our origin in God and our dependence upon him. So we turn to false gods and no longer glorify God our only Maker and sovereign Lord (Rom. 1:21f.). Accordingly we become unjust or self-righteous and our works correspondingly the works of sin. We Christians, too, are entangled in such sinful conduct. We acknowledge our own share in the guilt for developments which have produced our present problems. In this situation, however, it is also our privilege, indeed our duty, to declare plainly that "when the time had fully come, God sent forth his Son... to redeem those who were under the law, so that we might receive adoption as sons (and daughters)" (Gal. 4:4-5). The gospel brings us news of this and, if we accept it in faith and by baptism become members of Christ's body, the church, opens to us the life of the new creation. This faith stirs up in us hope and makes this hope enduring, indeed, makes it grow, even if the situation in which this hope is to be displayed seems hopeless. *Our faith in the triune God revealed in Jesus Christ enables us to view even the continent of Europe with hope.*

(8) Our common confession of this faith offers no direct answer to the questions posed, and no direct solution to the tasks set us, by the situation of Europe. It is, however, a heartening reminder that God in his loving compassion for his creation has already met its deepest need and that we have been justified by God's grace and in faith, hope and love are able, despite all resistance, to continue along the way which leads to reconciliation and peace in Europe.

3. The Common Creed

(9) We are able to make common confession of our faith in the triune God. Our risen Lord empowers us to do so in his commission: "Go... and make disciples of all nations, baptizing them in the name of the Father and of the Son and of the Holy Spirit..." (Matt. 28:19). The Creed of Constantinople, in which we confess our faith in the triune God, itself goes back to the baptismal liturgy of the early church. It was accepted by the whole church in the year 451 at the ecumenical synod of Chalcedon, and it is still in liturgical use today, if with varying frequency, in all the Orthodox churches, in the Roman Catholic Church, in the Anglican communion and in the churches of the Reformation. In this creed we confess our faith in God. We are seeking a common understanding of this creed. It is a bond uniting the divided churches. These churches, which all confess the gospel to which the New Testament bears witness, are also able to recite the Creed of Constantinople together. Their enduring conviction that they are able to do this places upon them the forceful obligation to overcome those differences in their understanding of it which separates the churches. These differences continue to the present day and are among the reasons for the continuing division between the churches.

(10) Despite understandable hesitations, the very antiquity of the Creed represents a unique opportunity. To abandon this tradition of the whole church in an attempt to reformulate the Christian Creed could threaten the basic and indispensable unity and coherence of the Christian faith at all times and in all places. Only a council in which all the churches would once again take part would have the right to undertake a reformulation of the universal Creed on the basis of the apostolic faith. The Creed of Constantinople is an exhortation to us to establish the unity of the churches. From ancient times it has been intimately connected with the sources of Christian unity, with baptism and with the eucharistic community. The reconciliation of the separated Christian churches is an important contribution required of us on the road to a human family living at peace. Calls for the reconciliation and solidarity of the human race remain mere words if we in the churches fail to take steps in this direction. By the common confession and witness of our faith, we acknowledge our duty to pave the way for and, by God's grace, to take such steps.

> We believe in one God, the Father, the Almighty,
> Maker of Heaven and Earth, of all that is, seen and unseen.

4. (11) "We believe..." — so the Creed begins. This "we" originally meant the bishops met together in the Council. Since they confessed this faith on behalf of the churches they represented, and therefore as the representatives of the universal church, this "we" embraces all Christians. Christians still today take up the strain "we believe". This common confession of faith does not relieve the individual Christian of the need also to utter his or her own personal and irreplaceable "I believe". This "I

believe", however, at once points beyond itself. It is just one voice in that vast chorus of voices of those who at all times and in all places confess their common faith in the triune God. It is the community, indeed the one church, of Jesus Christ, which speaks in this "we believe". This faith has its origin in acceptance of the gospel of the resurrection of the crucified Jesus. "Because, if you confess with your lips that Jesus is Lord and believe in your heart that God raised him from the dead, you will be saved" (Rom. 10:9). This gospel sums up in all its fullness the faith which we find in a binding developed form in the Creed of Constantinople. Despite the division of our churches in Europe and in the world, this "we believe" is affirmed by them all together. It seeks to lead, and it can lead, not only the divided churches but also the whole of humanity, scarred by so many divisions and tensions, into that communion with the triune God which gives life and peace. Many people in Europe fail to find any access to God. This makes us realize that faith is a gift of grace which we can only receive in the power of the Holy Spirit.

5. (12) We believe in the *one God*. He is the one God because he alone claims our hearts and our life completely. "We know that 'an idol has no real existence' and that 'there is no God but one'. For although there may be so-called gods in heaven or on earth — as indeed there are many 'gods' and many 'lords' — yet for us there is one God, the Father..." (1 Cor. 8:4f.).

(13) This one God has revealed himself already to Israel and given them as his first commandment: "You shall have no other gods before me" (Ex. 20:3; Deut. 5:7). When as Christians we confess our faith in the one God, we are echoing the Creed repeatedly recited by our Jewish brothers and sisters: "Hear, O Israel! The Lord our God is one Lord, and you shall love the Lord your God with all your heart, and with all your soul, and with all your might" (Deut. 6:4). However different the church of Jesus Christ may be from the synagogue, the confession of faith in the God of Abraham, Isaac and Jacob binds both together. Our determination as European Christians to remain aware of this deep solidarity with the Jews, in accordance with the will and purpose of God, is reinforced by the recollection that it was on the soil of our continent that immense suffering and injustice has been inflicted, even by Christians, on the Jews.

(14) "No God but God" — this is also the religious conviction of Islam. In many of our countries we find Muslims. They live in our midst. Strange though the forms of their religious observance may be to us and painful though the tensions may often be today between Muslims and Christians, we may not forget that they, too, along with the Jews and with us Christians, believe in the one God.

(15) Christ has revealed to us the mystery: the one God is the triune God of love, the communion of Father, Son and Holy Spirit. It is this one God who turns his face towards us, who calls us to himself and who forbids us to seek our life from the strange gods that again and again rise up before us. We declare our faith in the *one* God by acknowledging God as the Father. For he is, indeed, from everlasting to everlasting, the unoriginated origin of the one Son, coeternal with him, and of the Spirit, coeternal with him.

6. (16) By his word in the power of the Holy Spirit, the Father creates heaven and earth. From his hand all things come forth. He is and remains, therefore, the Lord of all created things, the Pantocrator. He is thus the source of all unity and of all diversity. God is our Father because he is our *Creator*. "Have we not all one father? Has not one God created us?" (Mal. 2:10; cf. also Eph. 4:6). God the Creator, the

Father, does not leave us outside his caring love. "As a father pities his children, so the Lord pities those who fear him" (Ps. 103:13). He also assumes, therefore, the features of a mother: "As one whom his mother comforts, so I will comfort you" (Isa. 66:13).

(17) God is the creator of heaven and earth; we are the work of his hands. We are therefore his "image" (Gen. 1:26f.). Badly as the glory of this "image of God" in us has been obscured by sin, God does not repent of his work and thus enables us to seek his grace and find it in Jesus Christ. In our world and in Europe, too, human beings — who are in the "image of God" — often find their rights obstructed and dignity violated. Governed by our faith in God, the Father and Creator of all human beings, we intend, as much as we possibly can, today and in the future to champion the cause of human beings, wherever and no matter how their faces are disfigured. We are determined to obtain a hearing for all who can make their presence felt only little or even not at all. Behind many of the injustices suffered by human beings often lie ideologies which misrepresent humanity in individualistic or collectivistic terms. They obscure and endanger the true nature of humanity as in "God's image". Communion with the triune God delivers us from our self-absorption and makes us aware of and open to our neighbour and our society. The all-embracing view of humanity inaugurated for us by Christian faith is an alternative to ideology in all its forms: human beings are seen as persons and, at the same time, as members of the community.

(18) God has also created *heaven*, the invisible world. In unison with the choir of angels and saints we are able to render all glory and honour through Christ in the Holy Spirit to the Almighty Father.

(19) The *earth*, together with the vegetable and animal worlds, has been entrusted to us human beings with a view to our making it fruitful for us as "good stewards" and ensuring that it remains a habitable home, but not in order that we should do violence to it and make it uninhabitable. Humanity and nature live and suffer together. In the created world, too, there is a "hoping" and "groaning" for it to be set free "from its bondage to decay and obtain the glorious liberty of the children of God" (Rom. 8:21f.). The inner structure of the cosmos is rooted in God's word as Creator, in the Logos. Science, technology and art explore and make use of this inner structure. We affirm these human activities and wish to contribute to a responsible solidarity so that all may be done in obedience to God the Creator and in the service of humankind and for its healing. We are commanded by our faith in God, the Creator and Father of all things visible and invisible, to bend all our energies to putting a halt to the exploitation and destruction of the environment. We must work to ensure that the world in which we live is preserved for coming generations, too, as the Creator's work and praise.

7. (20) To confess our faith in God the Father means also, and above all, confessing him as "the God and Father of our Lord Jesus Christ" (Eph. 1:3). From him, the eternal word is conceived and born. Jesus Christ, the incarnate word, is sent from him to bring us life in all its fullness. It was in his love that the Father abandoned Jesus to death on the cross and in his love that he raised him from the dead. At the end of time, the Son will lay everything at his feet, that it may in this way find its fulfilment. In trust and confidence, Jesus prayed to his Father. Even in the hour of dereliction from the Father, Jesus cried out to him: "Abba, Father" (Mark 14:36). With Jesus, we too have in God our Father a Thou who hears and answers our prayers. Having attained through Jesus the status of God's children, "God has sent the Spirit of his Son into our hearts, crying 'Abba, Father!' (Gal. 4:6; Rom. 8:15). As individuals

or in communion with our brothers and sisters, therefore, we ceaselessly dare to offer to the Father, with Jesus, in the power of the Holy Spirit, all honour and glory. Trusting in his power and goodness, we also make our requests known to him in prayer. By prayer, our selves and our world are opened up to the ground and goal of all things. It is often hard for us to avoid a hectic activism and the inevitable burden this imposes on our spirits. Through prayer, God is able to give us concentration and direction in our work.

> We believe in one Lord, Jesus Christ, the only Son of God,
> Eternally begotten of the Father, Light from Light,
> True God from true God, begotten, not made, of one being
> With the Father; through him all things were made.
> For us and for our salvation he came down from heaven;
> By the power of the Holy Spirit he became incarnate
> from the Virgin Mary and was made man.
> For our sake he was crucified under Pontius Pilate;
> He suffered death and was buried; on the third day
> he rose again in accordance with the scriptures;
> he ascended into heaven.
> He is seated at the right of the Father.
> He will come again in glory to judge the living
> and the dead, and his kingdom will have no end.

8. (21) Jesus of Nazareth, the crucified and risen Lord, revealed the Father's love. He, "the only Son, who is in the bosom of the Father, has made God known" (John 1:18). Jesus prayed to the Father, "…that they may all be one; even as thou, Father, art in me, and I in thee, that they also may be in us…" (John 17:21). His prayer shows his eternal relation to the Father. Faced with the theological controversies of the fourth century over the person of Christ, the church found itself compelled to declare solemnly and bindingly at the Council of Nicea (325) that Jesus is the Son of the Father from all eternity. He is "of one substance" with the Father. He is not a creature, for he belongs indeed to the Father from everlasting to everlasting. He is "God from God", "Light from Light", "… the doctrine of God the Trinity, comprehending out of light (the Father), light (the Son), in light (the Spirit)" (Gregory Nazianzus, fifth theological address).

(22) The Father acknowledges the Son as the one different from him and causes the Holy Spirit to proceed from himself for communion with the Son. In and through the Son, the Father, through the Spirit, created the world and us human beings for communion with himself. With the Son, therefore, we are privileged to know ourselves also willed and acknowledged by the Father in our difference from him. According to God's will, it is good that there is this finite world and us as human beings within it. What does that signify? Whereas many philosophies and religions counsel us to seek eagerly the dissolution of ourselves and the world in the absolute ground of the universe, Christians are able, on the basis of faith in the triune God, to accept the world and themselves in all their finitude and difference from God. For centuries, the Christian church helped to shape our European continent. In our own time an intensive dialogue has begun with the religious traditions of other continents, especially of Asia. In this dialogue we have many things to learn from our partners, but we have also something of our own to attest and impart. The most important thing

here is that, on the basis of faith in the God who himself creates and affirms the world and ourselves as human beings, in the Son, it is possible to affirm the world and its history. Christian spirituality, therefore, is also a turning towards the world whereby we share in the process of its affirmation by God. Taking the form of discipleship of the crucified Lord, this spirituality does not exclude sacrifice and renunciation.

9. (23) God did not cancel his affirmation of the world or of us human beings when *sin* came on the scene and increased its power. "For God so loved the world that he gave his only Son, that whoever believes in him should not perish but have eternal life" (John 3:16). Jesus issued from his people. He was born of the Virgin Mary, the "daughter of Zion" and the "remnant of Israel" in person. Yet he also came "from heaven". He is more than a product of human history. He was sent from the Father and, by the Holy Spirit, assumed human flesh in Mary. He is both true God and truly human. "Though he was in the form of God, he did not count equality with God a thing to be grasped, but emptied himself, taking the form of a servant, being born in human likeness" (Phil. 2:6f.). In Jesus, the triune God once and for all took his place alongside us human beings, in order to redeem us from sin and to accompany us on all our ways. He remains alongside us, indeed, takes our place, even when we believe ourselves to be lost and abandoned by God. So the crucified Jesus demonstrates that he, and in him the triune God, accepts and upholds us right to the very end.

(24) To us the "word of the cross" (1 Cor. 1:18) is "the power of God". We would encourage especially all those whose faith is assailed to hear this word afresh. Perhaps they imagine that God is impotent, unworthy therefore of trust, and point to the immeasurable suffering in the world as proof of this. In contrast to that, however, the "word of the cross" affirms that in the cross of Jesus Christ God is no stranger to death and weakness; there precisely is he the living and mighty God. In the cross of Jesus, he overcomes sin and justifies us. Here the "new creation" (2 Cor. 5:17f.) dawns. The death of Jesus on the cross "for us", therefore, is the source of the new life, breaking through fully and sanctifying us in the raising of the crucified Jesus from the dead.

(25) The Father raised the crucified Jesus from the dead and exalted him to his right hand. In doing so, God justified him (1 Tim. 3:16), authenticating him in face of the rejection purposed by his opponents in putting him to death on the cross. Now he lives, the foundation of complete salvation, as the *kyrios* in the glory of the Father. On the basis of the resurrection and in the light of the cross we confess Jesus as "the way, the truth and the life" (John 14:6). The Risen Lord makes us partakers of his glory, by giving us his peace (John 20:19-21) and his joy. "Christ is risen from all death's pains! In this should all rejoice. Our comfort is Christ's choice" (ancient Easter carol).

10. (26) The exalted Lord is already present: in the *church* "where two or three are gathered in his name" and where the gospel is preached and the sacraments celebrated. At the end of time, however, he will be revealed in all his glory. In hope we travel towards this meeting with the returning Lord. This meeting includes the final judgment on our life and death. We are confident that this judgment brings us salvation and life. For the Judge is indeed our Deliverer, Jesus, who has already shown in his cross and resurrection that what he desires is our life and not our death. This is why Paul could write to the church in Corinth: "Do not pronounce judgment before the time, before the Lord comes, who will bring to light the things now hidden in darkness and will disclose the purposes of the heart. Then every one of us will receive his or her commendation from God" (1 Cor. 4:5). Hope in the Lord's return places us in a new

relationship to the world and its history. It delivers us from the notion that world history is itself the final judgment. When world history claims to be the final court of appeal, it turns into a merciless judgment, for its criterion is success. We confess, on the contrary, that the final judgment is the prerogative of the returning Lord. The meaning of history cannot be unlocked, therefore, from within history itself. The returning Christ's word of judgment is a message of joy, for the one who pronounces judgment here is no mere embodiment of the "logic of history" but rather the friend and brother of those who, brought before the bar of the court which world history claims to be, present a most unimpressive appearance, not having any outstanding successes to their credit; the poor, children, all of us indeed who are sinners. Hope in the returning Lord thus touches a sensitive nerve, that of our attitude to history.

> We believe in the Holy Spirit,
> the Lord, the Giver of Life,
> who proceeds from the Father;
> with the Father and the Son
> he is worshipped and glorified;
> he has spoken through the prophets.
> We believe in one, holy, catholic and apostolic church.
> We acknowledge one baptism for the forgiveness of sins.
> We look for the resurrection of the dead,
> and the life of the world to come.

11. (27) As we confess together in the Creed, the *Holy Spirit* is, like the Father and the Son, himself divine person. He proceeds from the Father and with the Father and the Son together is worshipped and glorified.

(28) The filioque is a customary addition to the Creed of Constantinople in the western churches. Some western churches are currently considering the use of the original, conciliar form of the Creed.

(29) The Holy Spirit is the divine love shown by the Father to the Son and by the Son to the Father. In the Holy Spirit there is living communion between the Father and the Son. It is through the Spirit that the divine love of Father and Son is manifest in the world. The Spirit, therefore, is the source of life, the "life-giver". The Holy Spirit is the giver of all life, and life, therefore, is God's gift.

(30) The saving deeds of God, Father and Son, are done in the power of the Holy Spirit. The Spirit is God's creative power in the creation of the world. "In the beginning God created the heavens and the earth. The earth was without form and void, and darkness was upon the face of the deep; and the Spirit of God was moving over the face of the waters" (Gen. 1:1f.). In the Father and through the Son, the Holy Spirit fills the inhabited earth (cf. Wisdom of Solomon 1:7).

(31) Because of the misuse of our human freedom, the power of evil invaded creation. In contrast to the Holy Spirit, source of life for the world, the *power of evil* seeks to ruin and destroy the creation. Because of sin, the whole life of creation and humanity is engaged in the bitter struggle between the power of darkness and the power of the light.

(32) The power of evil constantly urges human beings to desire to put themselves in God's place in relation to the creation, with a view to its destruction. "All these I will give you, if you will fall down and worship me" (Matt. 4:19). Humankind, which succumbs to this temptation and forgets God as the true source of life, is the cause of

its own misery. Unillumined by the Holy Spirit, human beings can dominate the creation, but not themselves. They can conquer outer space, but not themselves. They can change social systems, but remain incapable of changing themselves. They can master many things in the laboratory, but are unable to master themselves.

(33) In contrast to the power of evil, the Holy Spirit, permeating the universe, preserves for the creation the hope of deliverance from destruction (Rom. 8:21). The Spirit spoke through the prophets, therefore, to announce the coming of the Messiah and the Spirit's own descent at Pentecost. By the mouth of the prophets, the Lord declared: "And it shall come to pass afterward, that I will pour out my spirit on all flesh... Even upon the menservants and maidservants in those days, I will pour out my spirit" (Joel 2:28f.).

(34) *In the power of the Holy Spirit*, the incarnate Son dealt the power of evil a fatal blow on the cross. "The people who sat in darkness have seen a great light, and for those who sat in the region and shadow of death light has dawned" (Matt. 4:16). In this light of the Holy Spirit, humanity discovers the meaning of its life outside itself, namely, in Christ whose divine light shines into all the depths of human life and who, with his body and blood, delivers us from evil. "It is no longer I who live, but Christ who lives in me" (Gal. 2:20). The Holy Spirit makes us partakers of Christ. He is the power whereby Jesus becomes present and the fruits of his life and death accessible to us. The Spirit causes the gifts of bread and wine to become for us the bread of life and the cup of salvation and in this way we are cleansed from our sins and sanctified by Christ's sacrifice on the cross. The Holy Spirit makes the scriptures of the Old and New Testaments "spirit" and not just "letter", so that they *bear witness* to the action of the triune God in history and summon us to faith. The Holy Spirit awakens in individual Christians charismata for the benefit of Christ's body, the church.

(35) In the light of the Holy Spirit who shines in the church through the gospel and the sacraments, Christ himself triumphs over the power of evil in each Christian and restores us again to our likeness to God. "We all, with unveiled face, beholding the glory of the Lord, are being changed into his likeness from one degree of glory to another; for this comes from the Lord who is the Spirit" (2 Cor. 3:18).

12. (36) The sphere of the new life given us by the triune God is the *church*, the people elected by the Father, the body of Christ and the temple and the instrument of the Holy Spirit. In his power it is the *one*, holy, catholic and apostolic church. We can say all that together, in the hope that as we listen to the word of God we also mean the same things. It is the *one* church because it is "the people united by the unity of the Father and the Son and the Holy Spirit". The one baptism, the one holy scripture of the Old and New Testaments, the Creeds of the ancient church and common prayer point towards this unity. And one day, we hope, the one eucharist will unite us all. It is the *holy* church, for "Christ loved the church and gave himself up for her, that he might sanctify her, having cleansed her by the washing of water with the word" (Eph. 5:25f.; cf. Heb. 13:12). When the life of Christians is strong in faith, firm in hope and persistent in love, they reflect this holiness and point the way to the unity which God wills. It is the *catholic* church, for "where Jesus Christ is, there too is the catholic church", i.e. where Jesus Christ is, there the church is present through the power of his spirit as the fullness of divine truth and of divine salvation, and there, in all ages, she makes people participants in his salvation, without respect to sex, race or position. The catholicity of the church is demonstrated in her worldwide mission (Matt. 28:19), as

well as in the diversity and ordering of spiritual gifts (Rom. 12; 1 Cor. 12). Finally, it is the *apostolic* church, built indeed "upon the foundation of the apostles... Christ Jesus himself being the chief cornerstone..." (Eph. 2:20). It preserves and transmits the gospel received by the apostles in their meeting with the risen Christ and through the outpouring of the Holy Spirit.

(37) By our life, of course, we repeatedly deny what we affirm about the church in faith and what has been given us indefeasibly. The *divided state* of the church permits only a fragmented experience of its Christ-based unity, holiness, catholicity and apostolicity. The painfulness of this comes home to us with special poignancy in our inability any longer and yet again to share the one loaf and the one cup at the one Lord's Table. In this distress we beseech God not to weary of us but to help us to see more clearly how, together, we may obey Christ's will that his own might all be one, as he prayed in his high-priestly prayer. At the same time, we thank God for having already enabled the churches to take significant steps towards one another, particularly in our interpretation of scripture, and also incipiently in our understanding of the eucharist and its liturgical practice.

(38) Historically and materially, the one confession of faith in the triune God is rooted in the liturgy of the one *baptism*, which we celebrate in all our churches and which unites us at a profound level, especially since we are united in our mutual recognition of it across all confessional boundaries. In baptism, God incorporates those baptized into the one body of Christ and in this way delivers them "from the dominion of darkness and transfers us to the kingdom of his beloved Son, in whom we have redemption, the forgiveness of sins" (Col. 1:13f.). Baptism and the faith which issues in the confession of faith belong together. When we recite the Creed, alone or in common worship, we renew our acceptance of baptism, encourage our sisters and brothers to enter into the faith and to join in its confession, and affirm the message which will shape our life and be the standard by which it is measured.

(39) The people of God to which we belong by faith and baptism and by our place at the "Lord's Table", traverses the ages. Filled with hope, it travels towards its own and the whole creation's fulfilment in God, so that for eternity he may be all in all. It is his will therefore to be for us all *life in all its fullness*. We look in hope therefore for the resurrection from the dead and for the life of the world to come. We realize that this patient expectation of the new creation does not exonerate us from working with others for the establishment of a more just and human world. Indeed this hope liberates us for this task. Although the New Jerusalem does indeed come down out of heaven from God (Rev. 3:12, 21:2), we are nevertheless confident that nothing of what we have done in expectation of that Holy City will be lost. This gives to our labours a new, indeed an eternal, significance. The courage to live has its source in the hope of eternal life. When we bear witness to the good news of the final victory of life over death and "account for the hope that is in us" (1 Pet. 3:15), we are serving the world which suffers from its fear of longing for death. In the Holy Spirit, who is the earnest of eternal glory, we may already here and now join in the "voice of a great multitude in heaven": "Hallelujah! For the Lord our God the Almighty reigns. Let us rejoice and exult and give him the glory" (Rev. 19:6f.).

IV.
The Study Programme
"Towards the Common Expression
of the Apostolic Faith Today"

1. TOWARDS THE COMMON EXPRESSION OF THE APOSTOLIC FAITH TODAY
Lima Report, 1982

This document of the Faith and Order Commission welds into a single statement the findings of two earlier conferences. At the invitation of the Ecumenical Patriarchate in Constantinople, a small consultation was held in the Orthodox Centre in Chambésy, near Geneva, from 28 June to 3 July 1981, for the purpose of producing an outline plan for the project on the apostolic faith. The report of this consultation[1] is taken up mainly with the consideration of three themes: (1) recognition of the Nicene Creed as the ecumenical symbol of the apostolic faith; (2) the explication of this ecumenical symbol in the contemporary situations of the churches; (3) some implications of the common recognition of the ecumenical symbol of faith.

In Odessa in October 1981 a second consultation examined the ecumenical importance of the Nicene-Constantinopolitan Creed. A number of points and questions concerning "sufficiency" and the relation of Bible and Creed were taken from the report of this consultation and embodied in the Lima report.[2]

At the Faith and Order Commission meeting in Lima, Peru, from 2 to 16 January 1982, a working group concentrated its attention on the theme "Apostolic Faith Today". Its task was to produce an overall plan for the future course of this project in the light of the preliminary work of the Chambésy and Odessa consultations. The report of the working group was adopted unanimously by the Commission in Lima on 14-15 January 1982. The following is an outline of its contents:

Introduction: The importance of this study as an ecumenical project

I.   Towards the common recognition of the apostolic faith as expressed in the ecumenical symbol of that faith: the Nicene Creed

II.   Towards the common explication of this apostolic faith in the contemporary situations of the churches

III. Towards a common confession of the apostolic faith today

Recommendations

---

[1] "Towards the Common Expression of the Apostolic Faith Today", FO/81:9, August 1981.
[2] "The Ecumenical Importance of the Nicene-Constantinopolitan Creed: the Odessa Report", FO/81:17, November 1981.

This document provides the basis for the implementation of the entire project on the apostolic faith today.

● Text in "Towards Visible Unity. Vol.II: Study Papers and Reports," ed. M. Kinnamon, *Faith and Order Paper No. 113*, Geneva, 1982, pp.29-46.

Introduction: the importance of this study as an ecumenical project

1. In our present divided state, visible unity cannot be restored unless each church becomes aware of the painful situation of our divisions and takes decisions to overcome our disobedience to the will of Christ as expressed in his prayer for unity (John 17:1-26). These decisions will be genuine only to the extent to which they imply a resolve to do what the re-establishment of communion demands: conversion through a constant return to the source which is God as revealed in Jesus Christ through the Holy Spirit. Such a conversion requires an effort to express the content of the faith in such a way that the life of the community is consonant with the word of God.

2. At its Fifth Assembly in Nairobi in December 1975, the World Council of Churches, after its discussion of "conciliar fellowship", adopted the following recommendation:

> We ask the churches to undertake a common effort to receive, reappropriate and confess together, as contemporary occasion requires, the Christian truth and faith, delivered through the apostles and handed down through the centuries. Such common action, arising from free and inclusive discussion under the commonly acknowledged authority of God's word, must aim both to clarify and to embody the unity and the diversity which are proper to the church's life and mission (Section II,19).

The same assembly, in revising "The Constitution of the World Council of Churches", adopted the following statement as the first of the purposes of the Council:

> (i) To call the churches to the goal of visible unity in one faith and in one eucharistic fellowship expressed in worship and in common life in Christ, and to advance towards that unity in order that the world may believe (Art. III,1).

The intention of the Faith and Order Commission in formulating the following project is to help the World Council to fulfill its recommendations, and so to advance towards the realization of its first purpose.

3. A primary assumption of this project is the recognition of the special rank and function of the Nicene Creed.[1] For, together with a growing convergence in our understanding of baptism, eucharist and ministry, the appeal for a common expression of the apostolic faith belongs to the movement towards the unity of the Church. In the attempt to work out such a common expression, it is impossible to disregard the special place of the Nicene Creed. It is the one common creed which is most

---

[1] Throughout this paper the reference is always to the Creed commonly believed to be of the Second Ecumenical Council at Constantinople in 381 A.D., although various customary terms are used, such as "the Nicean Creed" "the Nicene Creed", "the Creed commonly called Nicene", "the Nicene Symbol", "the Ecumenical Creed", etc.

universally accepted as formulation of the apostolic faith by churches in all parts of the world, where it primarily serves as the confession of faith in the eucharistic liturgy.[2]

4. The *koinonia* of the eucharistic community, which is united to Christ by baptism, is grounded on the apostolic proclamation of the crucified and risen Christ which is documented in the scriptures, summarized in the creed of the church and is served by the minister who presides over the eucharistic celebration. The common understanding of the apostolic faith was expressed by the ancient Church in the Ecumenical Creed of Nicea (325), complemented at Constantinople (381) and solemnly received at Chalcedon (451) as the authentic symbol of the Christian faith, witnessing to the fullness of the Christian faith and life and authoritative for the entire Church.

5. The eucharist builds up the Church and visibly manifests its unity. The apostolic faith, fruit of the Holy Spirit, is the ground of that unity. The outward expression of this intimate relationship of faith and eucharistic celebration is therefore essential to the visible unity of the Church, so much so that without common recognition of the Nicene Creed as the ecumenical symbol of the apostolic faith, it is difficult if not impossible to understand how we are to advance "to the goal of visible unity in one faith and in one eucharistic fellowship expressed in worship and in common life in Christ... in order that the world may believe" (WCC Constitution III, 1). Thus, together with a growing convergence in our understanding of baptism, eucharist and ministry, the appeal for common expression of the apostolic faith of the one, holy, catholic and apostolic Church as expressed in its Ecumenical Symbol of faith belongs to movement towards the unity of the Church.

6. It should be remembered how well this Creed has served millions of Christians, with whom we are also bound together in the unity of the Church, in the past. Its brief statement of the essential faith has provided at least formally a thread of unity down through the centuries. In one form or another, this Creed has been used by the Orthodox churches, by the Roman Catholic and Anglican churches, and by most of the churches of the Protestant Reformation, and in all parts of the world. It has helped the churches to affirm their fundamental belief in God, in the Lord Jesus Christ and his saving action, in the Holy Spirit and the Church, and in the life of the kingdom to come. Some have used it as a baptismal confession, others as a central standard of doctrine. It has been read and sung at the eucharist and other liturgical services and has been used as a statement of belief at the ordination of church ministers. As the product of a council received by the churches in a time of great confusion and strife, it has stood as a model of ecumenical confession, both in the method of its formulation and in the content of its definition. As such, it has inspired theologians, hymn writers, preachers and artists in all ages. It seems appropriate, therefore, to ask the churches, when they try to express their common understanding of the apostolic faith today, to recognize this Creed from the time of the early Church as the ecumenical expression of the apostolic faith which unites Christians of all ages in all places.

---

[2] Thus, the Faith and Order Conference in Lausanne in 1927 referred to its members as "united in a common Christian faith which is proclaimed in the holy scriptures and is witnessed to and safeguarded in the Ecumenical Creed, commonly called Nicene, and in the Apostles' Creed" (Sect. IV).

7. Such recognition would call each church to examine its beliefs and actions today in relation to that Ecumenical Creed and so to express and interpret its meaning today theologically, ethically, liturgically, socially in terms understandable in that church's everyday life and in society.

8. We are convinced that any real progress among the divided churches towards the common expression of the apostolic faith today will require a twofold movement, towards unity in faith with the early Church, and towards unity in mission with the Church of the future. The word "towards" is important: both movements are actually, from our present divided situation, movements towards the future. Our hope then is that we can initiate a threefold study project, aiming:

a) to ask the churches to make a common recognition of the apostolic faith as expressed in the Ecumenical Symbol of that faith: the Nicene Creed (Chapter I);
b) to ask the churches how they understand its content today in their own particular situations of worship, fellowship and witness (Chapter II); and
c) to ask the churches "to undertake a common effort to confess together, as contemporary occasion requires, the Christian truth and faith, delivered through the Apostles and handed down through the centuries" (Chapter III).

9. We believe that this project will guide the churches to confess Christ in their life, and lead them towards the common celebration of the eucharist where "we proclaim the Lord's death until he comes" (1 Cor. 11:26).

I. Towards the common recognition of the apostolic faith as expressed in the Ecumenical Symbol of that faith: the Nicene Creed

10. Our hope is that all the churches will recognize the Symbol of Nicea-Constantinople as the common expression of the faith of the Church because:

(a) The Nicene Creed over the centuries has been, and is now very widely acknowledged as, the ecumenical symbol of the apostolic faith, a fact of fundamental significance for an ecumenism which seeks the unity of the Church "in all places and all ages" (New Delhi statement). We therefore plead with those churches that do not acknowledge it, or, while acknowledging it in reality disregard it, that they ask themselves whether for the sake of unity they might agree to reconsider their attitude.

(b) While the act of confessing the contemporary meaning of the apostolic faith has to be done again and again in different situations and in different forms, and this life of contemporary confessing and witness must never be interrupted, nevertheless we consider that designing a new creed, intended to replace the Nicene Creed as the Ecumenical Symbol of the apostolic faith, is not appropriate.

(c) The World Council of Churches is not authorized to propose a new creed.

(d) Proposing an ecumenical symbol of the apostolic faith clearly presupposes the authority of an ecumenical council. Such a council would have as an essential purpose the confession of the apostolic faith on behalf of the whole Church in the situation of its own present day. Among the important preparatory steps for just such an event would be what this project calls for: a wider recognition among the churches of the Ecumenical Symbol of Nicea.

11. The plurality and variety of documents which occur in the act of confessing in particular situations do not imply that each new creed or symbol binds the whole

catholic Church. It is true that Christian witness should always aim to express the whole faith of the one Church; but the whole Church is not thereby bound to each particular act of confessing. These various acts and documents of confession rather apply the one apostolic faith to particular situations, and are to be judged, therefore, by the criterion of their consonance with that apostolic faith as confessed in the Ecumenical Creed of the Church.

12. How shall we understand the relation of scripture and the Creed? This, of course, is a principal question to be studied ecumenically in the project we are proposing. Here we can only indicate some points to be considered in that study.

(a) Christian identity is rooted in the acceptance of God's revelation of himself through Jesus Christ and the Holy Spirit. Initiated in creation, witnessed to in the Old Testament, this revelation of God's identity was fully manifested in the mystery of Jesus Christ. Transmitted in the power of the Holy Spirit by the preaching of the apostles, it is the great gift of God to humanity. And the Christian community has the mission to keep it and transmit it to all humankind.

(b) It is this revelation, already understood and lived out in various ways by the first Christian communities, that the scriptures record. It is significant, however, that already in the documents of the New Testament we can see the need for some brief statements in which at least the main elements of the revelation are brought together in such a way that they help the Christian communities to test the consonance of their beliefs with what God did and said in the Holy Spirit by Jesus Christ.

(c) The creeds of the first centuries, in a more elaborated form, tried to continue this service. Their language was, indeed, dependent on the culture, the needs, the situations of their time. But they were intended to convey a summary of the central teaching of the scriptures. Their authority, however, comes from the consonance of their content with the revelation itself. They are instruments for its acceptance by faith, and its proclamation in the life of the Christian community.

13. It is sometimes asked whether the Nicene Creed can be considered "sufficient" to express the Christian faith for contemporary Christians. It is pointed out that some biblical themes and concepts, indispensable for Christian life and thought, are not explicitly treated in the Creed. Again it is noticed that there are many contemporary questions and issues which are urgent for Christian obedience today, but which were simply not actual when the Creed was written.

(a) It is, of course, true that not everything is said explicitly in the Creed, and that certain affirmations came into focus for historical reasons. The Creed is also historically conditioned in its language, its concepts, its thought forms. Moreover, the Creed aims to fulfill particular functions, and its language is sometimes doxological, sometimes dogmatic.

(b) The question of the Creed's "sufficiency", however, leads to the authority of the Creed, and it must be clearly said that the Creed's authority for contemporary Christian life and thought does not lie in the extensiveness with which it treats either the biblical witness or contemporary questions, but in its consonance — claimed and recognized in the Church — with the testimony of the apostles to God's revelation in Jesus Christ. The urgent question for Christian witness is, "Who is Jesus Christ for us today?" This question has been faced and answered in all ages, and the adequacy of any answer, however relevant to its age it may appear to be, ultimately is grounded in its participation in the authority with which the apostles and the early Church bear witness to the revelation of God in Jesus Christ.

(c) But the element of mystery must be noted, both in the Creed and in any attempt to verbalize the Christian faith. When the word was made flesh, the inexpressible became expressed. Words can express the mystery, yet it remains a mystery, and the words used to express it must respect the fullness of it. Every creed and all our attempts to formulate or explicate our faith have their limits before the mystery of what they try to express. In that perspective, it is wrong to expect either too much or too little, also from the Creed.

14. In order to rediscover the unity of faith, therefore, it would be an important step if the churches would remind themselves again of the significance of the Nicene Creed as Ecumenical Symbol of the one, apostolic faith, implying as it does temporal as well as geographical universality. As such it is not merely to be considered as a first stage in the development of definitions of the faith, but also as intimately connected with the unity of the one, holy, catholic and apostolic Church.

15. Therefore, the World Council of Churches might ask the churches to recognize anew that integral unity of the Christian faith expressed in the Symbol of Nicea-Constantinople, to reconsider the status of their own teaching in its light, to affirm its content as the basis of more comprehensive church unity, and to strengthen its place in the liturgical life of the churches wherever necessary and possible under circumstances of pastoral responsibility.

16. In view of research and recent proposals concerning the *filioque* clause in the Faith and Order Commission, we propose for purposes of this study to use the original Greek text of the Nicene Creed, without thereby prejudging in any way the theological views of the churches on this issue,[3] as follows:

And we believe in the Holy Spirit,
  the Lord and Giver of life,
  who proceeds from the Father,
  who with the Father and the Son together is
  worshipped and glorified,
  who spoke by the prophets.

II. Towards the common explication of this apostolic faith in the contemporary situations of the churches

17. The content of this apostolic faith, although it is the ground in itself for Church unity and contemporary witness, finds its context in the divided state of the Church and the alienation of humankind. This ground can only become effectual as, given time and opportunity, we appropriate it for ourselves in our times, seek to grasp and understand its meaning in our own language and attempt to share and bear its witness in ways which others in turn can understand. Authoritative in itself, it manifests its authority in the midst of that divided state of the Church and that alienation of humankind, as it asks for and empowers contemporary interpretation of its meaning in the countless particular languages, cultures and crises of today.

---

[3] See "Spirit of God — Spirit of Christ: Ecumenical Reflections on the Filioque Controversy", ed. Lukas Vischer, *Faith and Order Paper No. 103*, London, SPCK, and Geneva, WCC, 1981.

18. This was already the case, for example, when the Council of Chalcedon (451 A.D.) reaffirmed the Creed of Nicea, even as it proceeded to formulate its own definition, more than a century afterwards, of the doctrine of Christ. The procedure was repeated as the Reformers reaffirmed the Apostles' Creed and the Creed of Nicea, and in so doing confessed their recognition of the relation between apostolic faith and their context of sixteenth century questions about justification and sanctification. And it appears likely that ecumenical renewal today will once again open our eyes to the authority of the Creed and our communion with those who assembled at Nicea. At the same time, it can open our eyes to our vocation to explicate the power and meaning of that faith in the many diverse fields of contemporary Church life and witness.

19. The place of the Creed itself in making such a contemporary interpretation will be matter for study and debate, owing to the differing status it is accorded in different churches. In some traditions, the expression of the faith today is quite inconceivable without giving a central and decisive role to the Creed itself, not only in its substantial contents but even in its wording. Others would see themselves as more or less urgently bound by the substance of the Creed but would be more willing to attempt modern statements of the heart of the faith. Still others might value the Creed above all as a procedural model for a task which needs to be accomplished ever anew, namely the confession of the faith in particular circumstances and with the conceptual and linguistic tools available at the time. Even those churches which do not use the Nicene Creed, or indeed any other creed, are usually ready to acknowledge that the Creed deals with matters that are vital for Christian confession.

20. A common expression of the apostolic faith today will necessarily involve some attempt to relate Creed to contemporary situation and contemporary situation to Creed in such a way that each throws its distinct light on the other. "The unity of the Church is a sign of the coming unity of humankind" (Uppsala, I), and it is the apostolic faith which unites us for the renewal of human community.

21. What kind of questions would such a contemporary explication of the Nicene faith need to address? In the following we offer some tentative examples of such questions. Other clearer formulations of such questions would need to be developed in the study itself. These examples pose questions not only of a social and personal character in the context of our alienation and divisions as women and men but also pose questions of an ecclesial nature in the divided state of the Church.

(a) The Ecumenical Creed confesses faith in one God. How do we explicate that over against tendencies to absolutize today's finite realities, aspirations, historical situations? What does faith in one God mean for human community torn by poverty, militarism, racism?

(b) The Ecumenical Creed confesses faith in the triune God, Father, Son and Holy Spirit. How do we explicate that to those of other faiths or of no faith who charge us with having surrendered the unity of God?

(c) The Ecumenical Creed confesses that this one God created all things. How do we explicate that to persons who consider God to be a human creation, a projection of human wishes and realities?

(d) The Ecumenical Creed confesses faith in one Lord, Jesus Christ. How do we explicate that to contemporaries in a myriad of cultural and religious situations who, venerating Jesus, understand him to be a mere human being? Or who refuse to see his lordship in social, economic, political life?

(e) The Ecumenical Creed confesses Jesus Christ, God's only begotten Son, to be "of one essence" with the Father. How do we explicate today this claim that human salvation and liberation cannot be real without our participation in what is divine and eternal? How are we to understand such a term as "essence" today as a way of speaking about God?

(f) The Ecumenical Creed confesses that God's own Son has become human. How do we explicate to present-day men and women in the many relationships of their lives that it is this incarnation that provides meaning for human life? How does this faith in the incarnate God illumine our understanding of human creation as well as human redemption? Of human community and the cosmos as well as the human self?

(g) The Ecumenical Creed confesses that Jesus Christ was crucified for us under Pontius Pilate. How do we make clear to our contemporaries that salvation has historical character, that it is no mere cosmological speculation, but a matter of divine election and mission to all humanity? How do we proclaim God's coming into human suffering in the cross, strengthening and empowering as well as consoling those who are oppressed by sin and evil?

(h) The Ecumenical Creed confesses that on the third day Jesus Christ arose according to the scriptures. How do we make clear in our twentieth century world that this cross and this resurrection lie at the roots of a new life, liberate and reconcile us, and stand at the centre of all we can say about God's love and justice for God's creatures.

(i) The Ecumenical Creed confesses faith in the Holy Spirit. How can we explain the many ways in which we discern the life, the truth, the communion, the morale in which the Spirit creates the life of God in us in the everydayness of our locations and predicaments? At the same time, how does that same Spirit come to us with prophetic authority? By what means do we recognize that it is the same Spirit who is speaking today who spoke through the prophets? What does the discernment of the Spirit mean for the common recognition of the teaching function of the Church, not only in the church authorities but in the inter-relatedness of the contemporary theological enterprise?

(j) The Ecumenical Creed confesses one, holy, catholic and apostolic Church. How can we bear witness individually, corporately and representatively to the reality of this community of faith as a liberating and reconciling people of God, confessing one faith and one baptism, sharing one table, and hospitable to all, especially to each other's members and ministers?

(k) The Ecumenical Creed confesses one baptism for the forgiveness of sins. How can we strive towards the recognition of that one baptism in each other's churches today? How can we more closely relate baptism and the experience of our forgiveness before God and neighbour? How can we today share in a reconciliation and redemption among women and men, among persons of all races and classes, which is appropriate to the costliness of God's forgiveness of us all in Christ?

(l) The Ecumenical Creed confesses the life of the age to come. How can we explain to twentieth century neighbours an understanding of life which transcends death, yet can be lived now? How can we explicate a Christian hope, rooted and grounded in eternal life with God, which addresses urgent human problems, which illumines human suffering and persecution, which clarifies and judges human utopias in the light of God's coming kingdom? How can we attest the unity in this hope and eternal life which we share with the saints, the ancestors, the church of other ages?

22. It is obvious that such contemporary explication will generate much diversity in confessing the faith. Is that consonant with the common expression of which the WCC recommendation speaks?

23. We believe that it is. We believe that diversity is a necessary feature of any serious attempt to recognize and explicate the one apostolic faith today. The one faith is for all. It is universally relevant. But that means it is for each one, each relationship, each family, each group, each class, each culture, each nation. The Christian gospel entered Greco-Roman culture, and the Church accepted the pluralism which that meant for Christian *koinonia* and witness.

24. Nevertheless, although the Creed of Nicea is widely used by churches all over the world, many Christians are asking legitimately whether confessing the faith of the Creed of Nicea means being bound to ancient Greco-Roman forms of thought and speech. Recognizing this, we nevertheless believe that participation in this project could help all churches to receive their common tradition, and link them with other Christians in other parts of the world and in all time.

25. To speak about "the common expression of the apostolic faith", then, does not necessarily mean a single verbal formulation. Faith may be common even where wordings differ. The immediate task is to move towards mutually recognizable expressions of faith. This does not exclude the possibility that a growing mutual understanding could eventually lead to the widespread acceptance of one expression of faith, without abandoning other congruous forms that exist already or could later be formulated. None of this entails the replacement of the Nicene Creed as the Ecumenical Symbol of the apostolic faith.

III. Towards a common confession of the apostolic faith today

26. *The need for and meaning of "common confession":*
  (a) Interpreting the Creed of the church is not the same thing as actually confessing the faith expressed in the Creed. The act of confession is always personal, even if it is done in community. It is personal also in the sense that it finally relates to the person of Jesus Christ and to the personal reality of the triune God. It means taking sides with Jesus (Luke 12:9) for the truth and love he proclaimed. This also involves assertions concerning who Jesus is, but those assertions are subservient to the intention of acclaiming Jesus as Lord and of joining in his mission to humanity and in his proclamation of the kingdom to come.
  (b) Confessing Jesus Christ is a communal event, because after Easter it is the apostolic Church in which Jesus is present and which proclaims who Jesus is. To confess Jesus Christ now means to share in the Church's acclamation of Jesus as Lord (Rom. 10:9) through the Holy Spirit (1 Cor. 12:3), and in the profession of the apostolic faith (1 John 4:2-3). Therefore the personal confession of individual Christians is embedded in the community of the Church, even when it occurs in particular situations and is expressed in specific ways. In his or her personal

223

confession, the individual Christian is supported and encouraged by the confessing community. The common confession of the Church does not preclude individual modifications according to specific situations, provided that it is the same faith that comes to expression. Unity is not uniformity. In fact, uniform repetition of the Creed of the Church can become a device in evading a personal confession to Jesus Christ in an actual situation.

(c) The normal place for confessing the Creed in the life of the Church is its liturgy. Here all Christians are united in praise and glorification of their Lord. Thus they devote themselves to the Lord so that they may share communion with him in the eucharistic meal.

(d) This common confession in the liturgy is expressed in a language of glorification of Jesus Christ and of the triune God and of hope for participation in that glory. It also includes narrative elements that serve to identify the Jesus of history and his relation to the Father and to the Spirit. It is based on repentance, because a conversion to God is required, turning to God from bondage to a world that separated itself from God. Only by way of such conversion can Christians share in God's salvation.

(e) If confession means participation in the unity of the body of Christ by joining the acclamation of Jesus as Lord, it must overcome the inherited divisions among the faithful. Therefore the element of repentance and conversion in the act of confession also applies to the separation and division of the churches. Our separations are against the will of the Lord. It is important for the apostolic faith to be confessed by the churches as one and the same faith, so that when the individual shares in the liturgical confession of the Church, he or she will be assured of turning to the one Jesus Christ. The very fact that the act of confession is communal, therefore, obliges the churches to overcome their divisions and to seek a common confession of the apostolic faith that would enable them to enter again into conciliar fellowship.

(f) A common confession of faith is also required in view of the challenges arising from contemporary experience which extend to all Christian churches alike, although their focus may be different in different situations. As every form of confession to Jesus Christ involves repentance, conversion and renewal on the part of the confessing person, so also a common confession of the churches responding to the challenges of the time must involve conversion and renewal in the human community. This applies in the first place to community within the Church and among churches, a community of women and men across all barriers of races, classes and cultures. But it also extends to the human community at large, to its economic and political conflicts in the national as well as international context, because the Church witnesses to the kingdom of God, the goal of all human community. The Church is called to be a symbol of that eschatological community of justice and peace. But it lives up to this function only to the degree that the community of the Church itself is truly united through the love of Christ.

27. The Creed as criterion for a common confession of the apostolic faith:

(a) The challenges of the present world, as well as a widespread feeling that these challenges are not answered in the wording of the traditional creeds and other confessional documents of the churches, have given rise to a wide range of contemporary statements of the Christian faith. They come from entire churches as well as from individuals and groups. Besides, there are confessional documents of the past that are cherished by particular churches as expressing the faith of their fathers. How is this variety of confessional documents and traditions related to the unity of the Christian faith and to the task of a common confession of that faith? The unity of the apostolic faith is expressed in the Ecumenical Creed, proclaimed on behalf of the entire Church as a summary of the central teaching of the scripture and therefore serving as a criterion for the unity of other statements of faith with the teaching of the Church. In relation to the Ecumenical Creed later confessing documents, including those from the present age, will be evaluated as to their witness to the same Lord, expressing the same Spirit that unites the Church in the same faith. But the Creed will also be read with different eyes in new situations so that its assertions may reveal new insights.

(b) When on the basis of the Ecumenical Creed later confessional documents are evaluated, the churches may also rediscover in that Creed the basic unity of the faith which they have in common in spite of their separation. The more they come to evaluate their particular confessional traditions in the light of the Creed, the more they may learn to understand other traditions as expressing the same faith under different circumstances and in different situations. While each church should be ready to interpret its own confessional heritage in the light of the apostolic faith as summarized in the Ecumenical Creed, it might also be able to accept other churches and their confessional heritage on the same basis.

(c) In such a process of interpreting the confessional positions of one's own church on this basis, it might become possible to overcome condemnations (anathemas) that have been formulated and understood in the past to exclude the teaching of other churches. Without necessarily dissociating themselves from these judgments as such, the churches might discover that they do not apply to those other churches as they are at present. Perhaps particular condemnations never applied to the basic intentions of those positions that occasioned them. This is not to say that the Church can always avoid condemning false teaching and disciplining its adherents. This expresses an element which is essential to the act of confession as taking sides with Jesus in situations where his claim is disputed. But whether this condemnation actually applies to a particular opponent remains open to reconsideration.

28. *On the way to a common confession:*

(a) A specific challenge that requires the confession of the Church to Jesus Christ and to the triune God emerges in the encounter with other faiths and ideologies, especially as they influence the mind of the Christian people. But other faiths and ideologies are not simply opposed to Jesus Christ. They can contain many elements of truth which the Christian Church should acknowledge and even appropriate to its own life and understanding. Even explicit rejection of the Christian proclamation may often be conditioned by partial misrepresentations of the truth of the gospel by the churches themselves.

(b) Elements of a common confession to Jesus Christ and the triune God are implicit in many documents of ecumenical dialogue, especially in "Baptism, Eucharist and Ministry", but also in many bilateral agreements between particular churches. They should be taken into consideration when the churches move towards confessing together the apostolic faith in the context of the challenges of the contemporary world and on the basis of their common heritage.

(c) A common confession of the apostolic faith today will exhibit the potential of the Creed as a summary of the apostolic teaching to illumine the experience of

Christians and of their churches in a secularized world and in the particular context of their different cultures. It will help to transform those experiences through the power of the life-giving Spirit by responding to the challenges of the time and thus reassuring the Christian conscience of the truth of the apostolic faith.

Recommendations

I. We recommend the pursuit of the theme "Towards the Common Expression of the Apostolic Faith Today" as one of the main study projects of the Faith and Order Commission in the years to come.

II. We recommend the constitution of a steering group, to be appointed by the Standing Commission, which would be responsible for the performance and coordination of the different aspects of the study, such as:

A. Concerning the recognition of the Nicene Creed
1) To get information from the churches about the place the Nicene Creed has in their specific tradition and present life.
2) To work on the implementation of the Klingenthal recommendations on the *filoque* clause.
3) To work for a common wording of the Creed in the various languages, so that all churches using the same language should also employ the same wording of the Creed.
4) To make concrete proposals for the use of the Creed in liturgy, especially in the celebration of baptism, in the eucharist, in catechesis and spirituality, and in hymnology.
5) To clarify the relation of the Nicene Creed to other creeds in widespread liturgical use, such as the so-called "Apostles' Creed".
6) To study the authority, reception and use of the Nicene Creed in the course of the centuries and its role for the unity of the Church.

B. Concerning the contemporary explication of the apostolic faith
1) To work towards a substantial theological interpretation and explanation of the Nicene Creed, e.g. with regard to its trinitarian theology, christology, anthropology and the doctrine of the Spirit.
2) To work towards integrating into that explication the relevant issues of the study on the Community of Women and Men in the Church.
3) To clarify the relation of modern confessions of faith to the apostolic faith as expressed in the Nicene Creed.
4) To clarify the meaning of the term "apostolic faith" in relation to the scriptures and to the early Church.

C. Concerning the common confession of the apostolic faith today
1) To get information from the churches about contemporary statements of faith which they use officially or unofficially.
2) To relate to this study the results of the study on "Giving Account of the Hope" (Louvain-Bangalore 1971-78).

3) To consider the results of the New York/Princeton consultation on "Baptism, Eucharist and Ministry" and the implied statements of faith of the "Baptism, Eucharist and Ministry" document.
4) To study the confessions of faith which arose in key stages of church history, e.g. the fourth, sixteenth, nineteenth, and twentieth centuries.
5) To consider the use of the Nicene Creed and such biblical summaries of the faith as Ephesians 1:3-14 in ecumenical gatherings.
6) To get information from the churches about mutual recognition of confessions of faith.

III. We recommend, with regard to methods and levels of the study:
A. The preparation and distribution to the churches of sufficient information about this new Faith and Order study, and asking them for participation in it as a long-term study.
B. The cooperation with regional bodies and ecumenical institutes, e.g. the Societas Œcumenica, and with the bilateral dialogues.
C. The formation of regional working groups in Asia, Africa, Latin America, Europe and North America for the different aspects of the study on the Nicene Creed and on contemporary confessions of faith.
D. The preparation of input on this theme for the Vancouver Assembly of 1983.
E. The preparation of a 1987 Faith and Order World Conference involving this theme.

IV. We recommend the following publications among others in connection with the study:
A. "The Ecumenical Importance of the Nicene Creed."
B. Continuation of the series: "Confessing our Faith around the World."
C. "Towards the Common Expression of the Apostolic Faith Today." A handbook for this study with texts from Lausanne 1927 to Lima 1982, and outlines for further study.

V. Work to be done until the first meeting of the Steering Group:
A. To take steps to inform the churches and the organs of the World Council of Churches about the Lima decision concerning the apostolic faith study and to ask them for participation in the project.
B. Publication work as mentioned under IV.
C. If financially possible, to prepare a consultation on "The Apostolic Faith in the Scriptures and in the Early Church".

2. THE COMMUNITY STUDY AND APOSTOLIC FAITH
Lima Memorandum of the Working Group
on the Community of Women and Men
in the Church, 1982

The four-year study programme on "The Community of Women and Men in the Church" was brought to a provisional conclusion at the plenary Faith and Order Commission meeting in Lima, Peru, in January 1982. As a way of making the theological insights gained in this study programme fruitful for other Commission projects, the following memorandum was produced by a small working group in Lima. It was received by the Commission and its recommendations approved. It has the following structure:

Preamble
Reflections on the contents of the Nicene Creed
Exploration of contemporary confessions of faith in relation to Nicea
Recommendations to the Steering Committee on apostolic faith
Recommendation 3 is as follows: "That women (should) play a full part in the study process and make their contribution to answering the question of the possibility of the churches' common recognition of the Nicene Creed."

● Text in "Towards Visible Unity. Vol.II: Study Papers and Reports", ed. M. Kinnamon, *Faith and Order Paper No. 113*, Geneva, WCC, 1982, pp.47-50.

Preamble

Both the provenance of the historical creeds and the contemporary confessions of faith have in some way to do with threats to the community of faith. One of the intentions of creeds is to enable the community to be maintained in the face of threats, whether from heresy or from other ideologies. Thus, community is a basic notion in understanding the function of credal confessions; there would be no need for creeds apart from the need to maintain the community in the truth. We need to ask, therefore, what role the creeds play — through their language, thought patterns and images — in uniting and keeping together the community of men and women in the Church. Are the language, thought and imagery of the Nicene Creed sufficiently inclusive to keep together the community of women and men, a community whose members are created and redeemed in the image of God? The study on apostolic faith should consider the picture of a renewed community of women and men which has been articulated by the Community of Women and Men in the Church Study as a contribution to understanding the context in which their investigations need to be carried out.

In its work on the Nicene Creed, the study will inevitably deal with the relation of the Nicene Creed to scripture, "Tradition and traditions", both in the sense of traditions within the confessional families as well as the various cultural traditions. Already the Community Study has provided insights in these areas which deserve consideration at the relevant points in the discussion (as various papers and reports from the Sheffield consultation demonstrate). The Community Study has had much to say on the place of the inclusive community in the interpretation of scripture and tradition. This should be taken seriously in the formation of any working groups in this project. No meetings should be held without the adequate representation of women, so that the community of women and men can become a part of the groups that explicate the Nicene Creed and contribute towards the answering of the question posed by the Study: Is it possible for churches to accept the Creed? The question might be rephrased: Is it possible for the community of women and men, the earthly form of the body of Christ, to accept the Nicene Creed?

Reflections on the contents of the Nicene Creed

The Community Study has direct implications for every item of the Nicene Creed. In particular we ask that special attention should be given to the following:

1. The notion of God as Creator needs further work, especially the understanding of this in relation to the creation of women and men as set forth in the two Genesis accounts of creation and interpreted in the preaching and teaching of the Church.

2. The trinitarian language of the Creed needs particularly careful investigation. How far are the terms Father, Son and Holy Ghost/Spirit, which safeguard the distinctiveness of persons, still adequate today to describe the Trinity? How far should the contention of many women that this language excludes them from the community of the body of Christ be taken seriously and lead us towards discussing new terms for confessing our belief in the Holy Trinity?

3. The confession that Jesus became man *(anthropos)* needs to be investigated to explicate the relation between the Jewish man Jesus and the risen, ascended, glorified Christ. Is maleness central to our perception of Christ? Many women are suggesting that the implication that maleness has been taken into the Godhead profoundly affects their understanding of their redemption. If the incarnation is thought of, as one speaker in Lima expressed it, as "enmalement" and not "enfleshment", then the implications of a male saviour are impossible for women to bear. An investigation also needs to be made on the way this affects our understanding of the representation of Jesus Christ by the celebrant of the eucharist.

4. The phrase "born of the Virgin Mary" raises important questions about the place and role of Mary in the life of the community today. Should we seek ways of discovering a new and truly catholic Mariology which is neither a foreign imposition on evangelical thought nor an intolerable break in the continuity of Roman Catholic and Orthodox thought? What significance can we give to the fact that these churches which affirm and venerate Mary are the churches that do not ordain women, while those who do ordain women have little or no place for Mary in their spirituality?

229

5. What is the meaning of being men and women in the kingdom of God beyond time? Is there a new reality which transcends biological and sexual distinction? This is a complex area and needs to be investigated sensitively.

6. How does an eschatological vision of the community of women and men affect our ecclesiology today?

Exploration of contemporary confessions of faith in relation to Nicea

Particular attention should be taken to note the ways in which contemporary confessions of faith challenge Nicea's understanding of Creator, Trinity, incarnation, the place of Mary, eschatology, ecclesiology, pneumatology. At those places where they do offer a challenge to the understanding of Nicea, what criteria do we use to evaluate such a challenge? Would it be sufficient that, while not going directly through Nicea, they were consonant with one of the New Testament traditions or New Testament "trajectories"? In this case, how important is the judgment of the community of women and men in affirming such beliefs?

Recommendations to the Steering Committee on apostolic faith

1. That they take seriously the picture of a renewed community of women and men articulated by the Community Study.

2. That they use as background materials the insights of the Community Study on scripture, "Tradition and tradition".

3. That women play a full part in the study process and make their contribution to answering the question of the possibility of the churches' common recognition of the Nicene Creed.

4. That in the reflective process of this study we hope that the understanding of the tradition that emerges will, in its turn, interact with the insights which have come through the Community Study.

3. THE FILIOQUE CLAUSE
IN ECUMENICAL PERSPECTIVE
Klingenthal Memorandum, 1979

Theologians from both Eastern and Western church traditions met in the Schloss Klingenthal near Strasburg, France, from 26 to 29 October 1978 and from 24 to 27 May 1979 for two small consultations on the filioque *question which has for so long been a point of dispute between the Eastern and Western churches. The* filioque *is a Western addition to the Third Article of the Nicene Creed whereby the words "and the son" were inserted after the word "Father" in the clause: "We believe in the Holy Spirit... who proceeds from the Father." This addition not only tampered with the text of the Nicene Creed adopted by the Fourth Ecumenical Council of Chalcedon in 451; it also gave rise to different understandings of the doctrine of the Trinity. The following memorandum was produced at the two consultations, then submitted to a number of expert theologians for their comments and finally, in Taizé in August 1979, recommended by the Standing Commission on Faith and Order for transmission to the churches. It is in six parts:*

  I.   Introduction
  II. The Nicene Creed and the filioque *clause*
  III. The Trinity and the procession of the Holy Spirit
  IV. Theological aspects of the filioque
  V.   The relevance of the question
  VI. Recommendations

The memorandum ends by recommending "that the original form of the Third Article of the Creed, without the Filioque, *should everywhere be recognized as the normative one and restored" and "that the different churches should respond to these suggestions in ways appropriate to their own historical and theological situations".*

● Text in "Spirit of God, Spirit of Christ: Ecumenical Reflections on the Filioque Controversy", ed. L. Vischer, London, SPCK, and Geneva, WCC, 1981, *Faith and Order Paper No. 103*, pp.3-18.

Preliminary note

The following memorandum has been drawn up by a group of theologians from eastern and different western traditions who met at Schloss Klingenthal near Strasbourg, France, 26-29 October 1978 and 23-27 May 1979. An initial draft was composed after the first meeting and circulated for comment to a number of other specialists. At the second meeting, the document was revised and expanded in the light of their reactions. A large number of specially prepared papers was presented at these meetings.

I. Introduction

The Niceno-Constantinopolitan Creed, often called simply "the Nicene Creed", which dates from the fourth century, has for over 1500 years been regarded as a primary formulation of the common faith of the Christian people. It has been used in many ways in the worship and teaching of different churches throughout the world, and holds a unique place as the Creed which is most widely received and recognized throughout the various Christian traditions.

There have, however, been significant differences between churches in the use that they have made of this Creed and in the authority they have ascribed to it. In the Eastern Orthodox churches it displaced all other credal formulations and came to be seen as *the* authoritative expression of the faith. In the western Church it only more gradually came into regular use alongside other, distinctively western formulae: the so-called Apostles' and Athanasian Creeds. At the Reformation, many of the Protestant churches (including the Anglican) continued to use it, or made reference to it in their own confessions of faith, though some have in effect ceased to make any use of it at all.

Alongside these variations in attitude and practice, there is a further contrast between the broad eastern and western traditions. In the West the wording of the third article was expanded by the addition of the "*filioque* clause". This supplemented the description of the Holy Spirit as "proceeding from the Father" with the Latin *filioque*, "and (from) the Son". In the background to this lay certain differences between the eastern and western approaches to understanding and expressing the mystery of the Trinity. The clause itself was one of several principal factors in the schism between East and West in the Middle Ages, and has continued to the present day to be a matter of controversy and a cause of offence to the Orthodox churches. So the Nicene Creed has come to be a focus of division rather than of unity in common faith.

Three distinct issues may be recognized in this situation. First, there is the divergence of approach to the Trinity. Second, we are presented with the particular problem of the wording of the Creed and the *filioque*. Third, the question needs to be faced of the standing and potential ecumenical significance of the Nicene Creed itself. All of these matters have taken on a new urgency and relevance in our present time. There is a widespread feeling that, especially in the West, the trinitarian nature of God needs again to be brought into the centre of Christian theological concern. The new ecumenical climate of recent years poses afresh the question of a reconciliation between East and West — a question which inevitably involves that of the *filioque*. This in turn gives a new sharpness to the question whether the Nicene Creed itself can again be received and appropriated afresh as a shared statement of the Christian faith. These questions are a challenge to all the churches; they are placed on the agenda by our present theological and ecumenical setting; and they deserve to be widely and seriously considered.

II. The Nicene Creed and the filioque clause

A. THE HISTORY AND RECEPTION OF THE NICENE CREED

In spite of its name, this Creed is not in fact that of the Council of Nicea (A.D. 325). In the form in which it has been handed down, it dates from the Council of Constantinople in A.D. 381, though it does include the main emphases of the original formulation of Nicea, if not always in exactly the same words. The full text of the Creed was reproduced by the Council of Chalcedon in A.D. 451, and since then it has been seen as the classical and definitive expression of the orthodox Christian faith as developed and articulated in the controversies of the fourth and fifth centuries.

In the Eastern Orthodox churches, this same Creed was also seen as the heir and beneficiary of the instruction made by the Council of Ephesus (A.D. 431) that no other Creed than that of Nicea should be used. The force of this regulation was primarily directed against any return behind the affirmations of the Council of Nicea concerning the full divinity of Jesus Christ, but it came in the East to have a further significance as ratifying the sanctity of the Creed framed at Constantinople, which was seen as possessing the same authority, and with it, the same exclusive status.

In the West, by contrast, the process of "reception" of this Creed was a slower one in the sense that while its canonical authority was not questioned, its actual use in the life and teaching of the church was for many centuries distinctly limited. The western Church already possessed and continued to use the various local forms of the Old Roman Creed, from which in the eighth century the "Apostles' Creed" finally evolved; and also the "Athanasian Creed", which is not in any way connected with Athanasius, but dates from sixth century Gaul. The use of the Nicene Creed spread gradually through the western Church, and it was as late as ca. 1014 that its singing was introduced into the liturgy of the mass in Rome itself. It was at the same time that the addition of the *filioque* was sanctioned by the Pope.

B. THE ADDITION OF THE FILIOQUE

Although the *filioque* was officially added to the Creed throughout the western Church only in the eleventh century, its history runs back very much further. As early as the fourth century, some Latin writers spoke of the Holy Spirit as "proceeding from the Father and the Son", or "from both", or in other similar ways directly linked the person of the Son with the procession of the Spirit. This understanding was developed further by Augustine in the early fifth century, and between his day and the eighth century it spread throughout the West. What may be called "*filioque* theology" thus came to be deeply anchored in the minds and hearts of western Christians. This represents the first stage of the development and the necessary background to what followed.

The next stage was the appearance of the *filioque* in official statements — e.g. the Canons of the Council of Toledo in A.D. 589 — and in the Athanasian Creed. At that time there was no apparent intention thereby to oppose the teaching of the Church in the East. (Many scholars have thought that the main concern was to counter western forms of Arianism by using the *filioque* as an affirmation of the divine status of the Son.)

By the end of the eighth century the *filioque* had come in many places in the West to be added to the Nicene Creed itself — one of these places being the court of the Emperor Charlemagne at Aachen. Charlemagne and his theologians attempted to persuade Pope Leo III (795-816) to ratify the alteration; but Leo, though seeming to agree with the theology of the *filioque*, refused to sanction an addition to the wording of the Creed which had been drawn up by an Ecumenical Council and reaffirmed by others. The expanded form of the Creed continued, however, to be widely used in the West; and two centuries later Pope Benedict VIII (1012-1024) finally authorized and approved it. Since then the western form of the Creed has included the *filioque*.

Attempts were made at the Councils of Lyons (1274) and Florence (1439) to impose the *filioque* on the East. These attempts were unsuccessful, however, and their effect in the long run was to intensify the bitterness felt in the eastern Church at the unilateral action of the West — not least because of the *anathema* which Lyons laid on those who rejected the clause. Eastern and western theologies of the Trinity and of the procession of the Holy Spirit came very much to stand over against each other, and the differences in approach which the *filioque* problem highlighted hardened into what were felt to be mutually exclusive positions.

While the Reformers were very critical of many of the developments in medieval theology, the question of the *filioque* was not seriously raised in the sixteenth century. Most Protestant churches accepted the clause and its underlying theology and continued to subscribe to both. It has only been much more recently that a new perspective has opened up. The last hundred years have brought many fresh contacts between East and West and enabled a new dialogue between them — a dialogue that is still growing today. The question of the *filioque* is now being discussed in a climate very different from that of the medieval Councils.

In this new climate, the possibility of returning to the original wording of the Creed has suggested itself to more than one western Church. The Old Catholic churches already began to make this change in the nineteenth century; the Lambeth Conference of 1978 has asked the churches of the Anglican Communion to consider doing the same; other churches too are exploring the question. It is our hope that yet more will give it serious consideration. Even those which make relatively little (or even no) use of the Nicene Creed have an interest in the matter in so far as they too are heirs of the western theological tradition and concerned both with the issues involved in the *filioque* and the progress of the ecumenical movement.

III. The Trinity and the procession of the Holy Spirit

The *filioque* question demands some consideration of the relation between the doctrines of the Trinity, of the "eternal procession" and of the "temporal mission" of the Holy Spirit. This is offered in the following four sub-sections which deal in turn with the Church's faith in and experience of the triune God (A), with biblical reflections upon the Spirit and the mystery of Christ (B), with the implications of the Spirit's temporal mission for relations between the persons of the Trinity (C), and with the way in which the Church always has to do with the Father, Son and Holy Spirit (D).

A. From its beginnings in the second and third centuries, the doctrine of the Trinity was intended to be a help for Christian believers, not an obstacle or an abstract intellectual superimposition upon the "simple faith". For it was in simple faith that the early Christians experienced the presence of the triune God; and it was in that presence that were gathered and held together the remembrance of the God of Israel, the presence within the congregation of the crucified and risen Christ and, from Pentecost, the power to hope in God's coming Kingdom which is the future of humankind.

This perception, celebrated in worship, strengthened and renewed by word and sacrament, and expressed in the individual and corporate lives and actions of believers, was not "dogmatic" or "conceptual" in the sense of enabling them to distinguish between "the advent of the risen Christ", "the presence of the Spirit" and "the presence of the Father". Their experience was — as it still is today — of the unity of the triune God. Both their prayerful acceptance and their rational under-standing of this gift of God's presence, however, were articulated in terms of his triune life and being. This enabled the early Church — as it enables the Church today — to see itself as belonging within the story which God began with Abraham and Sara, which culminated in the coming, teaching, suffering, death, resurrection and ascension of Jesus Christ, and which marks out the way of the Church ever since Pentecost.

It was for this reason that the early Fathers gave witness to God's activity in Israel, his speaking through the prophets, in Jesus of Nazareth, and in the apostolic Church, as the activity of the triune God. They did not deduce their theological conclusions from a preconceived trinitarian concept. So, too, today in any reconsideration of trinitarian concepts as they have come to be developed, it is desirable that we should retrace and follow through the cognitive process of the early Church. The communion of the Church as articulated in ecclesiology seems to be the appropriate theological starting point for re-examining the function of trinitarian thought in the Church's faith, life and work. God is received, thought of and praised in the Church as God in his triune life: as Creator and God of Israel, as God the Logos and Son, as God the Spirit. It is this insight which preserves the biblical and historical roots of Christian faith in the living God.

B. The most personal Christian experience grafts us into the very heart of the mystery of Christ; sharing in the work of salvation, we are introduced into the divine life, into the heart of the deepest trinitarian intimacy. It is thus that, through the whole experience of the Church, the mystery of Christ is realized in a trinitarian perspective of salvation. New life in Christ is inseparable from the work of the Spirit. In its depths, the Church is nothing other than the manifestation of the risen Lord, whom the Holy Spirit renders present in the eucharistic community of the Church. There is a profound correspondence between the mystery of the Church and of Christian life on the one side, and the earthly life and work of Jesus himself on the other. It is thus not possible to speak of the mystery of Christ, of his person and work, without at once speaking not only of his relation to the Father, but also of the Holy Spirit.

In the earthly life of Jesus, the Spirit seems to be focused in him. The Spirit brings about his conception and birth (Matt. 1:18, Luke 1:35), manifests him at his baptism in the Jordan (Mark 1:9-11 and par.), drives him into the desert to be tested (Mark 1:12-13 and par.) empowers him in his return to Galilee (Luke 4:14) and rests in fullness upon him (Luke 4:18). It is thus in the permanent presence of the Spirit that Jesus himself lives, prays, acts, speaks and heals. It is in the Spirit and through the Spirit that Jesus is turned totally towards the Father, and also totally towards humankind, giving his life for the life of the world. Through his passion, his sacrifice on the cross "through the eternal Spirit" (Heb. 9:14), and his resurrection by the power of the Spirit (Rom. 8:11, etc.), it is in the Spirit that henceforth Jesus comes to us in his risen body, penetrated and suffused by the energies of the Spirit, and communicating to us in our turn power from on high. The humanity of Christ, full of the Holy Spirit, is real and authentic humanity; and it is by the Holy Spirit that we, too, become a new creation (John 3:5), sharing in the humanity of Christ (Eph. 2:15). We are "christified", "made christs", in the Church by the indwelling in us of the Holy Spirit who communicates the very life of Christ to us, who in Christ makes us the brothers and sisters of Christ, and strengthens us in our new condition as the adopted children of the heavenly Father.

The Spirit thus appears in the New Testament at once as he who rests upon Jesus and fills him in his humanity, and as he whom Jesus promises to send us from the Father, the Spirit of Truth who proceeds from the Father (John 15:26). The Spirit therefore does not have an action separate from that of Christ himself. He acts in us so that Christ may be our life (Col. 3:4), so that Christ may dwell in our hearts by faith (Eph. 3:12). The Spirit, who proceeds from the Father, is also therefore the Spirit of Jesus Christ himself (Rom. 8:9, Phil. 1:19) who rests in him (Luke 3:22, John 1:32-33), in whom alone we can confess Jesus as Lord (1 Cor. 12:3), the Spirit of the Son (Gal. 4:6). These and many other New Testament passages reflect the Church's deep experience of the Spirit-filled and Spirit-giving being of Jesus himself. Here can be seen a full and constant reciprocity of the incarnate Word and the Holy Spirit, a reciprocity whose depths are further revealed in the fact that the sending of the Spirit had as its result the formation of the mystical body of Christ, the Church. This reciprocity must be emphasized as a fundamental principle of Christian theology. It is from this interaction, at once christological and trinitarian, that the divine plan for the salvation of the world is to be viewed in its continuity and coherence from the beginning of creation and the call of Israel to the coming of Christ. Further, all the life of the Church, indeed all Christian life, carries the imprint of this reciprocity from the time of Pentecost till the final coming of Christ. If it loses that vision, it can only suffer grievously from its lack.

C. The points of the Holy Spirit's contact with God's people are manifold. While one might be inclined to connect the coming of the Spirit exclusively with Pentecost, it must be remembered that any such limitation tends towards Marcionism in its patent neglect of the Old Testament witness to the presence and activity of the Spirit in Israel. Moreover, the Spirit is confessed to have been instrumental in the coming of Christ ("conceived by the Holy Spirit"), and to have been the life-giving power of God in his resurrection. Jesus during his ministry promised the sending of the Spirit, and the earliest Christians understood the pouring out of the Spirit at Pentecost to be the fulfilment of that promise. Thus the Spirit *precedes* the coming of Jesus, is active *throughout* his life, death and resurrection, and is *also sent* as the Paraclete by Jesus to the believers, who by this sending and receiving are constituted the Church. This chain of observations suggests that it would be insufficient and indeed illegitimate to "read back" into the Trinity only those New Testament passages which refer to the sending of the Spirit by Jesus Christ.

In the New Testament, the relation between the Spirit and Jesus Christ is not described solely in a linear or one-directional fashion. On the contrary, it is clear that there is a mutuality and reciprocity which must be taken into account in theological reflection upon the Trinity itself. The "eternal procession" of the Spirit of which trinitarian theology speaks as the ground which underlies and is opened up to us in his "temporal mission" cannot be properly characterized if only one aspect of the latter is taken into account. This raises certain questions about the *filioque*. Does it involve an unbiblical subordination of the Spirit to the Son? Does it do justice to the necessary reciprocity between the Son and the Spirit? If its intention is to safeguard the insight that the Holy Spirit is truly the Spirit of the Father in *Jesus Christ*, could other arguments and formulations defend that insight as well or even better? Is it possible that the *filioque*, or certain understandings of it, may have been understandable and indeed helpful in their essential intention in the context of particular theological debates, but yet inadequate as articulations of a full or balanced doctrine of the Trinity?

In approaching these questions it is imperative to remember that any reference to the Trinity is originally *doxological* in nature. This is all the more important in our own time, when talk of God is so severely challenged and trinitarian thinking so obviously neglected. Doxology is not merely the language of direct prayer and praise, but all forms of thought, feeling, action and hope directed and offered by believers to the living God. Doxological affirmations are therefore not primarily definitions or descriptions. They are performative and ascriptive, lines of thought, speech and action which, as they are offered, open up into the living reality of God himself. Trinitarian thought in the early Church originated within that doxological context, and only within it are we able to speak of the "inner life" of the triune God. Further, as fathers like Athanasius and Basil made clear, all such doxological references to that inner life must be checked by reference back to the biblical message concerning God's activity and presence with his people.

D. Conceptual distinctions between the "economic" and "immanent" Trinity, or between "temporal mission" and "eternal procession" should not be taken as separating off from each other two quite different realities which must then be somehow reconnected. Rather, they serve the witness to the triune God as the living God. In calling upon God, we turn and open ourselves to the God who is none other than he has revealed himself in his Word. This calling upon his name is the essential expression of doxology, that is, of trust, praise and thanks that the living God from eternity to eternity was, is and will be none other ("immanent Trinity") than he has shown himself to be in history ("economic Trinity").

In our calling upon him, the mystery of the Trinity itself is actualized. So we pray with Christ and in the power of the Spirit when we call on God his Father as *our* Father. So too we have a share in the joy of God when we allow ourselves to be told again that "for us a child is born". So too we pray in the Holy Spirit and he intercedes in us when we call on the Father in the name of the Son. In the calling upon the Father, the Spirit who proceeds from the Father, and we who worship in the Spirit, witness to Jesus Christ (John 15:26-7). The Spirit who proceeds from the Father of the Son is he whom the risen and ascended Christ sends, and by whose reception we are made the children of God.

IV. Theological aspects of the filioque

A. THE APPROACHES OF EASTERN AND WESTERN TRINITARIAN THEOLOGY

In its origins the Latin tradition of the *filioque* served as an affirmation of the consubstantiality of the Father, Son and Holy Spirit, and also gave expression to the deeply-rooted concern in western piety to declare that the Spirit is the Spirit of the Son. The theology of Augustine marked a definite stage in the development of this tradition by articulating with particular clarity its fundamental concern for the oneness of the divine being, and by setting out on that basis to conceive of the Trinity in terms of a dialectic of oneness-in-threeness and threeness-in-oneness. In subsequent interpretation and application, this approach crystallized into a formal system which became the standard western teaching, and to which all the authority of the name of Augustine himself was attached. The introduction in the West of the logical procedures of medieval scholastic theology brought this form of trinitarian thinking to a new level of definition. One result of this development was to make dialogue with the East increasingly more difficult: hence arose the polemical frustrations of medieval controversy.

The eastern tradition of teaching about the Holy Trinity had from the beginnings somewhat different emphases. A central concern from the time of the Cappadocians in the late fourth century has been to affirm the irreducible distinctiveness of each of the divine hypostases (or, in the term more familiar in the West, "persons") of the Father, Son and Holy Spirit and at the same time, the uniqueness of the Father as the sole principle (ἀρχή), "source" (πηγή) and "cause" (αἰτία) of divinity. Thus, while Greek theologians could and did use such expressions as "from the Father through the Son", they could not accept the western "from the Father and the Son" as a suitable formulation for describing the procession of the Holy Spirit. This difference in emphasis, combined with the virtual absence in the East of the scholastic methods developed in the medieval West, made it difficult for the eastern Church to appreciate the western attitude. The controversies of the ninth century between Constantinople and the West — controversies, it must be said, which were as much political as theological — were the occasion of a further definition of the eastern position in the teaching of Patriarch Photius and his famous formula, "the Spirit proceeds from the Father *alone*". This tradition was continued and further developed by the work of Gregory the Cypriot and Gregory Palamas. Both these writers sought to respond to the controversy with the West by distinguishing between the *procession* of the Spirit from the Father and an "eternal *manifestation* of the Spirit through the Son".

What is striking is that, despite the evident differences between East and West before the eleventh century, communion was maintained between them. The two traditions of trinitarian theological teaching, though divergent and at times in friction with each other, were not considered to be mutually exclusive. In the seventh century indeed, a notable attempt to explain and reconcile them was made in the work of Maximus the Confessor, a Greek Father who spent a large part of his life in the West. Only after the eleventh century did the two traditions come to be felt to be altogether irreconcilable.

B. TWO CENTRAL ISSUES

In the debate between East and West about the *filioque,* two sets of questions can be seen as central. The first has to do with the traditional eastern insistence that the

Spirit proceeds from the Father "alone"; the second with the western concern to discern a connexion between the Son and the procession of the Spirit.

1. Procession from the Father "alone"

According to the eastern tradition, the Holy Spirit proceeds from the Father *alone* for the following reasons:

a) The Father is the principle and cause of the Son and the Holy Spirit because it is an "hypostatic" (or "personal") property of *the Father* (and *not* of the shared divine nature) to "bring forth" the other two persons. The Son and the Holy Spirit do not derive their existence from the common essence, but from the hypostasis of the Father, from which the divine essence is conferred.

b) On the ground of the distinction between *ousia* ("being" or "essence") and hypostasis — which corresponds to the difference between what is "common" or "shared" and what is "particular" — the common properties of the divine nature do not apply to the hypostasis, and the distinctive properties of each of the three hypostases do not belong either to the common nature or to the other hypostases. On account of his own hypostatic property, the Father derives his being from himself, and brings forth the Son and the Holy Spirit. The Son comes forth by γέννησις ("generation" or "begetting"), and his hypostatic property is to be begotten. The Holy Spirit comes forth by ἐκπόρευσις ("procession"), and that is his own distinctive hypostatic property. Because these hypostatic properties are not interchangeable or confused, the Father is the only cause of the being of the Son and of the Holy Spirit, and they are themselves caused by him.

c) In no way does the Father communicate or convey his own particular hypostatic property to either of the other two persons. Any idea that the Son together with the Father is the cause of the Holy Spirit's "mode of existence" (τρόπος τῆς ὑπάρξεως) was felt in the East to introduce two causes, two sources, two principles into the Holy Trinity. It is of course impossible to reconcile any such teaching with the divine μοναρχία ("monarchy") of the Father, that is, with his being the sole "principle" (ἀρχή).

d) In asserting in its theology, though not in the wording of the Creed, that the Spirit proceeds from the Father alone, the eastern Church does not believe that it is adding to the meaning of the original statement of the Creed. It holds, rather, that it is merely clarifying what was implicit in that original wording but had come to be denied by the West.

From a western point of view, which at the same time appreciates the concerns of the eastern tradition, it may be said that neither the early Latin Fathers, such as Ambrose and Augustine, nor the subsequent medieval tradition ever believed that they were damaging the principle of the Father's "monarchy" by affirming the *filioque*. The West declared itself to be as much attached to this principle as were the eastern Fathers. But by describing the Son as the "secondary cause" of the procession of the Holy Spirit, the doctrine of the *filioque* gave the impression of introducing "two principles" into the Holy Trinity; and by treating the Son in his consubstantiality and unity with the Father as the origin of the person of the Holy Spirit, it seemed to obscure the difference between the persons of the Father and the Son.

Nonetheless, an important fact remains. Quite apart from the — more or less happy or unhappy — formulations of the *filioque* advanced in western theology (which one must be careful not to treat as dogmas), and even if western Christians are prepared simply to confess in the original terms of the Creed that the Holy Spirit "proceeds from the Father" (without mentioning any secondary causality on the part of the Son), many would still maintain that the Holy Spirit *only proceeds from the Father as the Father is also Father of the Son*. Without necessarily wishing to insist on their own traditional understanding of a logical priority of the generation of the Son over the procession of the Spirit, they believe nonetheless that the trinitarian order (or, in Greek, τάξις) of Father-Son-Holy Spirit is a *datum* of revelation confessed by the Creed itself when it declares that the Spirit is to be "worshipped and glorified together with the Father and the Son". Thus they might indeed be ready to confess that the Holy Spirit proceeds "from the Father alone"; but by this they would not mean, "from the Father in isolation from the Son" (as if the Son were a stranger to the procession of the Holy Spirit), but rather, "from the Father alone, who is the only Father of his Only-begotten Son". The Spirit, who is not a "second Son", proceeds in his own unique and absolutely originated way from the Father who, as Father, is in relation to the Son.

2. *The place of the Son in relation to the procession of the Holy Spirit*

The Creed in its original form does not mention any participation of the Son in the procession of the Spirit from the Father, nor does it indicate the relationship between the Son and the Spirit. This may be because of the conflict with various current heresies which subordinated the Spirit to the Son, and reduced him to the level of a mere creature. However this may be, the absence of any clear statement on the relation between the Son and the Holy Spirit faces dogmatic theology with a problem which the West in the past attempted to solve by means of the *filioque*. In the Creed's lack of clarity on the point lies at least one of the roots of the divergence between later eastern and western theology of the Trinity. This means that even if agreement were reached on returning to the original wording of the Creed, that by itself would not be enough. In the longer term an answer must be given to the question of the relation between the Son and the Holy Spirit.

The observations which follow are advanced as a suggestion on the way in which western theology might move forward towards a closer understanding with the East, while still maintaining its concern to link the persons of the Son and the Spirit:

a) The Son's participation in the procession of the Spirit from the Father cannot be understood merely in terms of the *temporal mission* of the Spirit, as has sometimes been suggested. In other words, it cannot be restricted to the "economy" of the history of salvation as if it had no reference to, no bearing upon and no connexion with the "immanent" Trinity and the relation within the divine life itself between the three consubstantial persons. The freedom of God in his own being and as he acts in history must alway be respected; but it is impossible to accept that what is valid for his revelation of his own being in history is not in some sense also valid for his eternal being and essence.

b) There is a sense in which it is correct to say that the Holy Spirit proceeds from the Father *alone* (ἐκ μόνου τοῦ Πατρός). This "alone" refers to the unique procession of the Spirit from the Father, and to his particular personal being (ὑπόστασις or *hyparxis*) which he receives from the Father. But it does not exclude a relationship with the Son as well as with the Father. On the one hand, the procession (ἐκπόρευσις) of the Spirit must be distinguished from the begetting (γέννησις) of the

Son; but on the other hand this procession must be related to the begetting of the Son by the Father alone. While the Holy Spirit proceeds from the Father alone, his procession is nevertheless connected with the relationship within the Trinity between the Father and the Son, in virtue of which the Father acts *as Father*. The begetting of the Son from the Father thus qualifies the procession of the Spirit as *a procession from the Father of the Son*.

c) From this fundamental thesis, two things follow. *First, it should not be said* that the Spirit proceeds "from the Father and the Son", for this would efface the difference in his relationship to the Father and to the Son. *Second, it should be said* that the procession of the Spirit from the Father presupposes the relationship existing within the Trinity between the Father and the Son, for the Son is eternally in and with the Father, and the Father is never without the Son. Eastern theology has traditionally emphasized the first of these two conclusions. The Latin Fathers were already exploring the implications of the second long before the *filioque* had finally been clarified and introduced into the Creed.

d) Along these lines, western trinitarian theology could come to understand the procession of the Holy Spirit in the way suggested by such patristic formulations as "the Spirit proceeds from the Father and receives from the Son". This underlines the fact that the Son is indeed not alien to the procession of the Spirit, nor the Spirit to the begetting of the Son — something which has also been indicated in eastern theology when it has spoken of the Spirit as "resting upon" or "shining out through" the Son, and insisted that the generation of the Son and procession of the Spirit must be *distinguished* and not *separated*. Differences certainly remain still in this area, for eastern theology is not easily able to agree that there is any *priority* of the generation of the Son over the procession of the Spirit, and desires rather to emphasize the "simultaneity" of the two, and to see the one as "accompanying" the other. Nonetheless, there does open up here a field for further exploration. So far as western theology is concerned, the Spirit could then be seen as receiving his complete existence (hypostasis) from the Father, but as existing in relation to both the Father and Son. This would follow the principle that because the Father is the source of divinity, the Spirit does proceed from him "alone". At the same time, however, it would express what that principle alone and by itself cannot: the relation of the Spirit as a person within the Trinity to the Son as well as to the Father. The *filioque*, on this suggestion, would have valid meaning with reference to the relationship of the three hypostases within the divine triunity, but not with regard to the procession of the complete and perfect hypostasis of the Spirit from the Father.

e) These suggestions raise the further question of whether new or at least alternative formulations might be found which could express what the *filioque* validly sought to convey. Several old-established expressions have been mentioned in this section of the memorandum, viz.:
— the Spirit proceeds from the Father of the Son;
— the Spirit proceeds from the Father through the Son;
— the Spirit proceeds from the Father and receives from the Son;
— the Spirit proceeds from the Father and rests on the Son;
— the Spirit proceeds from the Father and shines out through the Son.
These and possibly other formulations as well deserve to be given attention and consideration in future discussion.

V. The relevance of the question

These ancient controversies about what at first sight seems to be a strictly limited point of doctrine have, we believe, an unexpectedly urgent relevance. The study of the *filioque* question can be the point of entry into a wider exploration of the person and work of the Holy Spirit, of the relation of the Spirit to Jesus Christ, and indeed of the whole of trinitarian theology. The feeling that in all the western traditions something has been lacking in our experience and understanding of the Holy Spirit has grown rapidly in recent years. This tendency has carried with it a sense that the doctrine of the Trinity as such has come to appear remote and abstract to many, indeed very many Christian people. As Lesslie Newbigin writes: "It has been said that the question of the Trinity is the one theological question that has been really settled. It would, I think, be nearer the truth to say that the Nicene formula has been so devoutly hallowed that it is effectively put out of circulation."[1] In the western Christian world, while the churches continue to repeat the trinitarian formula, the trinitarian experience seems distant from many ordinary Christians. To them the word "God" is more likely to evoke thoughts of a supreme Monad than of the triune being of the Father, the Son and the Holy Spirit.

In the course of our discussions, we have realized that the question of the Trinity is one which is very far from being "settled". We have found in this fact not only a source of difficulties which have still to be tackled and overcome, but also at the same time a source of hope. In many different quarters it seems as if these basic articles of the Christian faith were coming to be the centre of new enquiry and fresh reflection. While we have not been able to agree as to how far the addition of the *filioque* clause was the cause of the differences between East and West on this whole subject, we have come to see that at least it has become a sign or indication of an underlying difference in theological approach. For the first ten centuries of the Christian era this difference was contained within a unity of faith and sacramental communion; since then it has been one of the primary causes of the continuing division between Orthodoxy on the one side and the Roman Catholic, Anglican and Protestant churches on the other. Within the last century, however, this situation has begun to change. First among the Old Catholics, then amongst Anglicans and others, the position of the *filioque* clause in the Creed has come under question. The whole matter of trinitarian theology has begun to be approached afresh. It has seemed to many that the balance and fullness of trinitarian doctrine, the reciprocity of the action of the Son and the Spirit, have been to some extent obscured in the West. It is not at all easy to trace the links of cause and effect in such areas. We do not say that the doctrine of the *filioque* was the cause of these developments. It may be that they have other origins. But certainly there is an interaction between one point of doctrine and others, between teaching and faith, between doctrinal formulations and the growth of Christian life.

In our discussion two points in particular have been suggested as opening up the wider bearing of the *filioque* debate. Both have figured especially in modern discussion of the issue. As they arise out of the concern to see the doctrine of the Trinity in connexion with the experience and practice of the Church, we must take them seriously into account.

---

[1] *The Open Secret*, Grand Rapids, Mich., Eerdmans, 1978, p.30.

A. On the one hand, it can be argued that the *filioque* underlines the fact that the Holy Spirit is none other than the Spirit of Jesus Christ; that this understanding of the Spirit is fundamental to the New Testament witness; and that the *filioque* is a necessary bulwark against the dangers of christologically uncontrolled "charismatic enthusiasm", dangers against which the churches today need to be on guard.

In no way would we wish to underplay the significance of this concern. At the same time, the Spirit too must not be "quenched" (1 Thess. 5:19). Justice can be done to both sides of the matter only if in our speaking of the relation between the Spirit and the Son we do not give the impression of a one-sided dependence of the Spirit upon Christ, but express the reciprocity between them mentioned above in Section III B.

B. On the other hand, it can be maintained that the *filioque* subordinates the Holy Spirit to Christ; that it tends to "depersonalize" him as if he were a mere "instrument" or "power"; and that this tendency can also encourage a subordination of the Spirit to the Church in which the Church itself becomes hardened in authoritarian institutionalism.

This warning, too, must be taken seriously. It is admittedly an open question whether and how far connexions of this kind can be historically demonstrated in the development of the western Church. Nevertheless, this danger too can only be met and countered on solid theological ground by the recognition of the reciprocity and mutual interaction of the Son and Holy Spirit.

VI. Recommendations

We therefore recommend:

A. That the new possibilities of discussion about the meaning of our faith in God, Father, Son and Holy Spirit, which are now opening up, and which we have begun to explore in this memorandum, should be pursued by all the churches; and that there should be a deeper effort to see how this faith is to be expressed in the forms of Christian worship, in the structures of the Church, and in the patterns of Christian life, so that the Holy Trinity may be seen as the foundation of Christian life and experience. This will require in particular a new sensitivity to the person and work of the Holy Spirit as the one who in his fullness both rests upon Jesus Christ and is the gift of Christ to the Church, the Lord and Giver of life to humankind and all creation.

B. That the original from of the third article of the Creed, without the *filioque*, should everywhere be recognized as the normative one and restored, so that the whole Christian people may be able, in this formula, to confess their common faith in the Holy Spirit:

And we believe in the Holy Spirit,
    the Lord and Giver of life,
    who proceeds from the Father,
    who with the Father and the Son together is
      worshipped and glorified,
    who spoke by the prophets.

C. That the different churches should respond to these suggestions in ways appropriate to their own historical and theological situations. For some, this will involve a more living appreciation of formulae whose authority has never been questioned. For others, it will mean a wholly new appreciation of the value and significance of this ancient ecumenical confession of faith. For some in which the Creed is constantly used in public worship, it will imply liturgical changes which will need to be introduced step by step. In all these various ways a renewed reception of the Nicene Creed can play a vital role in the growing together of the separated Christian traditions into the unity of faith.

4. THE ECUMENICAL IMPORTANCE
OF THE NICENE-CONSTANTINOPOLITAN CREED
Odessa Report, 1981

At the invitation of the Russian Orthodox Church, a consultation was held in the Orthodox seminary and the Dormition monastery in Odessa from 9 to 15 October 1981, the jubilee year of the adoption of the Nicene-Constantinopolitan Creed sixteen centuries earlier. Three main themes were addressed:

1. The historical and theological interpretation of the Creed, with special reference to the Holy Spirit

2. Responses to the Klingenthal memorandum ("The Filioque Clause in Ecumenical Perspective") from various confessional traditions

3. God's three-in-oneness in the light of the Bible and the Nicene Creed

The Odessa report concentrates on the first and third themes and has the following outline:

I. The consultation at Odessa

II. The importance of the Nicene-Constantinopolitan Creed at the present stage of the ecumenical movement

III. The ecumenical "sufficiency" of the Nicene-Constantinopolitan Creed

IV. The Nicene-Constantinopolitan Creed and the Bible

V. The Nicene-Constantinopolitan Creed and the common expression of the apostolic faith today

VI. Recommendations

Among the recommendations is "that the member churches of the World Council of Churches be asked in an appropriate way whether they would see the possibility of accepting the Nicene-Constantinopolitan Creed as their common ecumenical basis from the time of the ancient church, understanding this as a first step on the way to the common expression of the apostolic faith today".

● Text in FO/81:17, November 1981.

I. The consultation at Odessa

From 9 to 15 October 1981 the WCC Commission on Faith and Order held in Odessa (USSR) a consultation on "The Ecumenical Importance of the Nicene-Constantinopolitan Creed". Retrospectively this consultation may be seen as beginning to repair the lack of a thorough study of trinitarian doctrine ever since the mention of "the Father, the Son and the Holy Spirit" in the membership basis of the World Council of Churches at the New Delhi Assembly in 1961. Prospectively, the attention given to the Nicene-Constantinopolitan Creed is to be viewed as part of the developing project of Faith and Order concerning "The Common Expression of the Apostolic Faith Today". Detailed treatment had already been afforded one contentious question in relation to the Nicene-Constantinopolitan Creed, namely the difference between East and West over the *filioque*. Studies and recommendations on this point can be found in the Klingenthal Memorandum, published as part of "Spirit of God — Spirit of Christ".

The Odessa consultation brought together some twenty participants. They came from Africa and America, from Lebanon, India and Japan, as well as from several European countries and the Soviet Union itself. Christians from the Orthodox, Roman Catholic, Armenian, Syrian, Lutheran, Reformed, Baptist and Methodist traditions were present.

The consultation took place in a land where the Church is looking forward to the thousandth anniversary of the coming of Christianity to Russia (988-1988). It took place in a year in which many churches throughout the world have been responding to the call by the Ecumenical Patriarch to commemorate the 1600th anniversary of the Second Ecumenical Council held in Constantinople in 381; and it is generally thought that the Council of Constantinople played a decisive part in giving to the Church the Symbol which is often known as the Nicene-Constantinopolitan Creed.

The participants in the Odessa consultation greatly appreciated the spiritual atmosphere of the Dormition Monastery and the adjoining seminary. It was impressive to hear the Creed sung by the entire people both during the Sunday liturgy at the monastery church and at a festival service in the metropolitan cathedral of Odessa. His Eminence Sergius, Metropolitan of Odessa and Kherson, exercised generously the apostolic virtue of hospitality. His Eminence Filaret, Metropolitan of Kiev and Galich and Exarch of the Ukraine, gave a substantial theological address, in which he recognized that "while the divine origin of the Church remains unchangeable in its fulness and self-identity, the human nature of the Church lives and develops in history":

> The development of the Church in history consists in the clarification and realization of its eternal, divine, supra-historical beginning. The human expression of the unchangeable divine content reflects the language, the way of thinking and the culture of this or that epoch. In the process of history the Church perceives, through her human nature, the God-revealed truth and receives life eternal from God. In this sense one may and must speak about dogmatic development, since there can be neither stagnation nor standstill in the life of the Church. The human nature of the Church is manifested in the dogmatical development and in the dogmatical definitions of the Ecumenical Councils in particular, since all the actions connected with the human nature of the Church are being done by man and for man, and this is inevitably linked with human limitedness. From this limitedness springs the necessity of the historical development of the dogmatical definitions which are realized by the means of this or that epoch and which therefore reflect the character of this very epoch.... The dogmatical formulations have a historically conditioned character, but this by no means diminishes the significance of the contents of these formulations. All this

testifies to the fact that the Church, in principle, has a possibility of new dogmatical formulations and definitions: but by their contents they should remain self-identical to the one divine Truth kept by the Church and existing outside and beyond history.

The Odessa consultation concentrated on the pneumatological section of the Nicene-Constantinopolitan Creed. It allowed for provisional, unofficial reactions to be voiced concerning the Klingenthal Memorandum and the *filioque* question. Wider discussion of the Creed's teaching on the Holy Spirit led to trinitarian questions and finally to consideration of the Creed's authoritative status and its value in the search for unity in the faith.

The following papers were presented and discussed:

— "The mystery and the expression of the faith in the early Church and today" (N. Lossky);
— "The historical and theological development between 325 and 381" (G. Konidaris);
— "The importance of the affirmations concerning the Holy Spirit in the third article of the Creed for our trinitarian understanding of the Spirit" (T. Hopko);
— "The filioque clause in ecumenical perspective — reactions to the Klingenthal Memorandum from various traditions" (Oriental Orthodox: Bishop Ashjian; Eastern Orthodox: L. Voronov; Roman Catholic: R. Girault; Lutheran: M. Seils; Reformed: J. Smolik);
— "The transition of the Christian faith from the New Testament-Jewish context to the Nicene-Hellenistic context and its relevance for the contextualization of the Christian faith today" (E. Flesseman-van Leer);
— "The trinitarian understanding of the Christian God in relation to monotheism and polytheism" (V.C. Samuel).

In the rest of this report, sections III, IV and V are to be seen as the record of a discussion and as indication of matters needing further treatment, rather than as agreed solutions to problems. Section VI offers unanimous recommendations for continuing work in Faith and Order on questions connected to the Nicene-Constantinopolitan Creed. Where the phrase "the Creed" stands on its own, the intended reference is to the Nicene-Constantinopolitan Creed.

II. The importance of the Nicene-Constantinopolitan Creed at the present stage of the ecumenical movement

We are convinced that for many reasons the Nicene-Constantinopolitan Creed has special importance in the movement for Church unity. It has, first of all, served at least formally as a brief statement of the essential faith of millions of Christians through the centuries down to the present day. In one form or another this Creed has been used by the Orthodox churches, by the Roman Catholic and Anglican churches, and by most of the churches of the Protestant Reformation. It has also been used by many churches in Asia, Africa, and Latin America.

This Creed has helped the churches to affirm their fundamental belief in God, in the Lord Jesus Christ and his saving action, in the Holy Spirit and the Church, and in the life of the Kingdom to come. It has been a forceful reminder of the Christian heritage which has united believers in different times, places, cultures and earthly conditions.

It has been used by some as a baptismal confession of faith and by others as a central doctrinal statement of the faith of the Church. It has been read and sung at the eucharist and other liturgical services and has been used as a statement of belief at the ordination of church ministers.

As the product of a council received by the churches in a time of great confusion and strife, the Nicene-Constantinopolitan Creed has stood as a model of ecumenical confession, both in the method of its formulation and in the content of its definition. As such, it has inspired theologians, hymnwriters, preachers and church artists in all ages.

In addition to these general reasons for affirming the ecumenical importance of the Nicene-Constantinopolitan Creed, we judge that there are three more particular reasons why this symbol of faith may prove helpful in the movement for Christian unity, and more especially in the WCC Commission on Faith and Order.

First of all, the Creed provides the churches which use it, in whatever ways, with the opportunity of examining their beliefs and actions today in relation to it, and so to interpret its meaning (theologically, ethically, liturgically, socially...), showing how it may be implemented in our time in the everyday life of church and society. It also affords the opportunity for the churches which do not use it, or any creed, to express their convictions in relation to the issues which are raised by its examination.

Secondly, the study and evaluation of the Nicene-Constantinopolitan Creed provides a present opportunity for the churches to expose their beliefs and practices to the judgment of the Bible which all Christians hold as basic to their life and teachings. When we study the Creed, we are compelled to compare its language and content with that of the Scriptures. When we do this, we not only encounter many issues concerning the Bible, but many issues concerning Christian tradition, theology, worship and mission which are of critical importance within the movement for unity among the churches today.

Thirdly, the examination of the Nicene-Constantinopolitan Creed has particular significance for Christians, especially within the Faith and Order Commission, as we labour together to facilitate the common expression of the apostolic faith for our time. The study of the Creed urges us in all churches to examine the similarities and differences in our credal statements and doctrinal confessions, and our uses of creeds in liturgy, catechetics and mission; and it compels us to decide whether our creeds, or lack of creeds, are expressive of genuine differences of faith and conviction between the churches, or are merely differences of words and expressions.

We are called upon today to witness to the one apostolic faith in different ways, in different circumstances. The examination of the Nicene-Constantinopolitan Creed can be of great service to all of us towards this end, as separate churches and in common as one Christian family seeking perfect unity in our Lord.

The preliminary attempt at such an examination made in Odessa led to the raising of the following issues and questions for further study and discussion:
— the ecumenical sufficiency of the Nicene-Constantinopolitan Creed (III);
— the Nicene-Constantinopolitan Creed and the Bible (IV);
— the Nicene-Constantinopolitan Creed and the common expression of the apostolic faith today (V).

III. The ecumenical sufficiency of the Nicene-Constantinopolitan Creed

On several occasions the question was raised whether or not the Creed can be considered "sufficient" to express the Christian faith, or even as "perfect" for that purpose. It then proved useful to distinguish between, on the one hand, a *qualitative* sufficiency (and perfection), which would imply that the Creed provides the necessary general foundation on which to stand (cf. later confessional articles "stantis et cadentis ecclesiae"), and, on the other hand, a *quantitative* sufficiency, which, if it were maintained in the case of the Creed, would suggest a very limited and stereotyped formulation of faith. Such a distinction between qualitative and quantitative sufficency could allow one to maintain that the Creed contains the basis — and yet many important issues of Christian faith and life are not mentioned at all.

At least two important questions are then raised in that regard:

— Are there *biblical themes and concepts* which are indispensable for Christian theology and which are left out from the Creed? If so, does that amount to a qualitative insufficiency of the Creed, or could such themes and concepts be taken as implied in what is already said in the Creed?

— Are there *contemporary questions* to which the Creed cannot be said to relate, or in any way address itself, not even indirectly or implicitly, so that the Creed from this point of view would have to be considered insufficient or even irrelevant, not only then quantitatively, but also qualitatively?

The following observations are pertinent to the answering of those two types of question:

a) Not everything is said explicitly in the Creed. This Creed is not, nor is any other creed, a "summa theologica" trying to respond to all issues.

b) In the composition of the Creed, certain things came into focus for current historical reasons; no particular attention was devoted to other matters.

c) The Creed had particular functions to perform, both negatively (against heresies) and positively (as a baptismal confession of faith, etc.).

d) What had to be said *then* might not be emphasized *now* — even though it is basic to faith both then and now. Contrariwise, other things could *then* be taken for granted, or were not controversial, but might *now* need to be explicitly stated.

e) The Creed is historically conditioned in its language, its concepts, and its presupposed ontology.

f) Although not all churches use the Creed, it tries to express in forms of its time an indispensable content of Christian faith, suggested in these four points: (i) faith in God, (ii) the incarnation and redemption of the Son, (iii) the Holy Spirit and the Church, (iv) the Christian hope.

g) If the Creed is regarded as a sufficient formulation of faith, this sufficiency does not mean that the Creed cannot be interpreted, applied, explicated, and even expanded on — as long as proposed consequences or additions cannot be understood as contradictory to the Creed. How far is it possible to regard the dogmatic decisions of later Ecumenical Councils as following the inner logic (*die innere Folgerichtigkeit*) of the Creed? How far may modern "reinterpretations" be stretched without going counter to the original meanings?

h) Even though the Creed may not address certain contemporary issues, its importance is not diminished in matters which it does address. It may even be discovered to shed at least an indirect light on certain of today's questions (see paragraph V below).

i) Some appear to consider that the Creed uses not only outdated language but even an erroneous underlying ontology. Even though they would not themselves affirm the Creed, not all of them would press for the abandonment of its use, considering it to be an interesting and even important historical document.

j) Distinctions must be recognized between doxological language, dogmatic language, and the language of a particular theology; but it is hard to see how one could with integrity use all three without intending the substantial identity of what is said in all of them.

k) Finally the element of mystery must be noted, both in the Creed and in any attempt to verbalize the Christian faith. When the Word was made flesh, the inexpressible became expressed. Words can express the mystery, yet it remains a mystery, and the words used to express it must respect the fulness of it. Every creed and all our attempts to formulate or explicate our faith have their limits before the mystery of what they try to express. In that perspective, it is wrong to expect either everything or nothing, too much or too little, also from the Creed.

These considerations reflect points made in the Odessa papers and discussions. The group as a whole was not of a mind to pass judgments on the theological value of the Creed. It was seeking rather to understand the Creed in its own historical context and to express some problems and questions that are raised from various standpoints today — all of this with a view to the place which the Creed might occupy in the efforts "towards the common expression of the apostolic faith today".

IV. The Nicene-Constantinopolitan Creed and the Bible

1. The relationship between the Creed and the Bible is seen in different ways by Christians informed by different traditions:

a) The Creed is seen by many as an adequate Symbol of the biblical faith:

God lives in a light too bright for human eyes to behold. And yet God makes himself known. The Logos has become flesh. The divine mystery is expressed in words and images. Theology is possible. Words "adequate to God" can be uttered with authentic meaning. This is God's gift to creatures in his Son and Spirit.

Words "adequate to God" are never "closed" words. They never contain or exhaust the reality and mystery of God. They are not ends in themselves. They point beyond themselves to the Living God himself. This is true of all proper words, biblical, doxological, credal, theological.

Many consider the Nicene-Constantinopolitan Creed an "adequate" symbol of the apostolic faith — in so far as any "symbol" can be adequate. They may even consider it "perfect" in the sense that it "brings together" the "essentials", clearly and concisely. They may consider it to be "inspired" in a manner similar to the Bible, though none would place it on the same level with the scriptural word of God.

Those who consider the Creed to be "adequate, perfect, sufficient and inspired" consider it to be thoroughly biblical. They claim that except for the phrase "homoousion to Patri", virtually all the words of the Symbol are literally scriptural; and they defend this phrase as a "God-befitting" expression needed to defend and protect the biblical message.

They also contend that the Creed, like the Bible, must be interpreted and explained. They see the *Sitz im Leben* for biblical and credal "exegesis" as being the "lived tradition" of the Church, primarily manifested in worship: *Lex orandi est lex credendi*. They do not generally see the Creed as only a "hermeneutical tool" for interpreting the Bible, but rather as itself in need of interpretation in scriptural light.

They also generally claim that the Creed is not merely a "summary" of the faith which is biblically revealed and liturgically celebrated, but is rather a symbolic (i.e. gathered together) testimony to the living faith and spiritual experience of the believers, particularly the saints, who know God directly through the glorified Christ in the Spirit in the Church. The Creed is thus taken as a testimony to living and contemporary faith, and not merely as an ancient statement of faith. And it is not considered to be in any sense "philosophical".

The Creed says nothing about *what* God is in himself. It rather speaks about *who* God is, and *how* God is. It is silent about the content of God's innermost being. It is oblivious to any separation or opposition between the so-called "functional" or "relational" in regard to God, on the one hand, and the "ontological" on the other. It bears witness to God as he is known in his activity in and towards the creatures which he creates, redeems and sanctifies by his Son and his Spirit.

b) The Creed is seen by many as an inadequate Symbol of the biblical faith:

It has been argued that the Creed is an inadequate symbol of the biblical faith because it is *one-sided*. It draws out just one line of New Testament christological thinking from among several. Only with the Gospel of John can one speak of a clear conception of Christ's personal pre-existence and a clear doctrine of incarnation. A christology of pre-existence, however, is not the only one that can be found in the New Testament. Indeed, in most New Testament writings one does *not* find a christology of incarnation, but one for which the designation "Son of God" has its *Sitz im Leben* in the events of the passion/resurrection/exaltation of Jesus the Christ. Even the conceptions of "virgin birth" and "pre-existence" may be related to different christologies. According to some scholars, the various christologies can be harmonized; but others do not consider that to be the case.

If the Creed is seen as so "selective" in respect to biblical contents, how can the Creed itself, and also the World Council of Churches confession of Christ "as God", be said to be "according to the Scriptures"? Should one not perhaps say that they are "according to one particular interpretation of the Scriptures"?

The Creed is also said by some to be inadequate as a symbol of the biblical faith because of a certain *shift* that has taken place between the Bible and the Creed. This shift has been variously described as one

— from "functional" to "ontological" terms, from the person of Jesus Christ as seen in his works and words to his "essential nature";

— from relational to substantial categories, not only in christology but also in soteriology, i.e. from the understanding of salvation as fellowship with God to the thought of divinization, the sharing of the divine "nature";

— ultimately from God *pro nobis* to God's being, from the economic trinity to the immanent trinity, from the God who is known through his works performed in his history with his people to the immovable, unchangeable, impassible Deity.

If it be replied that these shifts are more apparent than real, or that they even depend on a misreading of the Bible or of the Creed's affirmations, those who detect such shifts would insist that it is impossible to miss at least a significant change of emphasis between Bible and Creed, a new accent which raises important questions.

Western scholars who have compared the Bible and the Creed during the past few centuries have often expressed, particularly on the Protestant side, their uneasiness about the "Hellenization" of the Christian faith. Today such uneasiness is expressed in rather a differentiated way:

— One would have to raise not only the question of the "Hellenization" of the gospel but also the question of its "Jewishness". Raising this question drives home the point that we never have the gospel "chemically pure". The gospel is always incarnate in a given culture and needs to be transposed for different cultures.

— The meeting of the Semitic and the Greek minds can already be observed in that period of Judaism in which the Scriptures of the New Testament were written. It would be wrong to think that the process of Hellenization started only after the New Testament period and only outside the Jewish culture.

— One recognizes today more clearly than some earlier scholars did that the Fathers suspected of "Hellenization" were rather aiming at a synthesis of "Israel" and "Hellas" in which Plato (the philosophers) and the Old Testament did not by any means enjoy equal standing.

— There is, however, another point to be raised when one considers the possible "Hellenization" of the biblical faith through the Creed. It is a radical question, important for some and judged inappropriate by others. Is not the step from a confession of God, who acts in history and manifests himself in the realm of the flesh and in his works on earth, to a statement about God's immanent being a departure from the Jewish belief in the mystery of God? More pointedly: Is it not a transgression of the commandment not to make an image of God?

Finally, the view that the Creed has proven to be an inadequate symbol of the biblical faith has to do not only with the experience of Christians in the passing of time (each generation experiences its own "front" where confession needs to be made): it has to do with *the nature of the biblical faith itself*. Not only in later centuries, but already within the New Testament period itself, faith needed to be confessed (a) in a personally responsible fashion ("Who do *you* say that I am?" Mark 8:29) and (b) in a "contextualized" form, e.g. in the Palestinian-Jewish context primarily in terms of "Messiah", "Son of Man" etc., in the Hellenistic context primarily as "Lord", "Son of God" etc. The New Testament writings themselves bear witness to an ongoing process of tradition and its reinterpretation. "The gospel needs to change in order to remain the same." The question, though, might be: How much can the Church of all ages confess together (because the gospel remains the same, cf. Gal. 1:8) *and* How do we need to express our confession today? If there was *a constant process* of the formulation and reformulation of the faith in the New Testament period, why does one think that this process could be stopped, frozen as it were, at any point in history, or why should the confessions of one generation have greater dignity than those of another?

252

2. Different views of the relationship between the Creed and the Bible pose *questions which it is important to try to answer together*.

The question of the Nicene-Constantinopolitan Creed itself is important, but beyond it conversations about the Creed and its meaning for the churches lead to weighty theological questions which bear directly on the way in which we "do" theology in our own confessions and ecumenically. Two such questions may be indicated here:

a) The Faith and Order Commission has already devoted a period of study to the question of "Scripture and Tradition". Now it seems imperative to address the question of biblical hermeneutics in view of the different understandings of the relation that exists between the Creed and the Bible.

— Is the Creed a hermeneutical key to be used in our interpretation of Scripture, and if so, how?

— How do we respond to the question of unity and diversity in the New Testament, especially in the matter of christology? Conversations at Odessa showed that it still needs to be faced squarely in connection with the study of the Creed, and in a way which does not ignore the various understandings of biblical inspiration and authority. This concrete hermeneutical question has direct consequences for ecumenical conversations about a trinitarian theology; and it is equally important for our preaching and witness today.

b) The second major question raised by consideration of the relation between Creed and Bible concerns exactly the fresh reflection on trinitarian thinking that seems to be required in our time.

Although it is difficult at this stage to express this concern adequately and clearly, a few hints may point in the direction in which one might be looking for a contemporary statement of a trinitarian concept of God:

— Are the terms *ousia, hypostasis, persona* adequate today?

— If we are agreed that one proceeds from the "economic" trinity to the "immanent" trinity, how is this to be done properly today?

— Is the divine reality better expressed in metaphysical categories of being and essence or in a "narrative theology"? Why did Jesus speak about God in parables and not in abstract terms? Simply because he was a good pedagogue or because it is more adequate to God's reality when we tell a story about him than when we try to "define" him?

— How do we relate today the "historical" and the "metaphysical", the "temporal" and the "eternal" concretely: Jesus of Nazareth and the eternal Son? What is the significance of the fact, as one scholar expresses it, that throughout the New Testament "the resurrection of Christ is recognized as marking a not-yet in Jesus' own becoming"? This observation runs counter to the view that the divine-human person of Jesus was constituted once and for all from the very outset of the incarnation. If that had been the case, then the history and activity of Jesus, and above all the cross and the resurrection, would no longer have the constitutive meaning which the New Testament ascribes to them. "Then", as another recent writer on christology puts it, "the death of Jesus would be no more than the completion of the incarnation. The resurrection would be no more than the confirmation of his divine nature. That would mean a diminution of the whole biblical testimony." The question gets even more complicated when the eternal

253

Spirit and his work must not be thought of apart from the work of the Son accomplished in time and space.

The putting of such questions expresses a recognition that a dialogue about the Trinity can reveal fundamentally different worlds of thought and of spiritual and liturgical experience in which and from which we speak when we try to communicate with one another and seek to share our deepest convictions about God, Jesus Christ and the Holy Spirit.

The Odessa group was in fact convinced that a serious effort towards a faithful restatement of the truth contained in the Creed and treasured by the Church throughout the centuries will be helpful, and that such a faithful restatement may speak by itself through its winsome content.

V. The Nicene-Constantinopolitan Creed and the common expression of the apostolic faith today

The purpose of striving "towards the common expression of the apostolic faith today" is twofold: the aim is both to make possible the unity of all Christians in the one faith and also to ensure that it is truly the apostolic faith which is being proclaimed in and to the world. The reconciliation of the churches in the common faith will be part of the Church's testimony to the gospel, while in turn the united proclamation of the gospel before the world will strengthen the churches in their common faith.

To speak about "the common expression of the apostolic faith" does not necessarily mean a single verbal formulation, the one undisputed expression of the common faith. Faith may be common, even where wordings differ. The immediate task is to move towards mutually recognizable expressions of faith. This does not exclude the possibility that a growing mutual understanding could eventually lead to the widespread acceptance of one expression of faith, without abandoning other congruous forms that exist already or could later be formulated. None of this entails the *replacement* of the historically unique Nicene-Constantinopolitan Creed.

Nevertheless, the place of the Nicene-Constantinopolitan Creed in such a process is controversial, owing to the status it is accorded in different churches. In some traditions, the expression of the faith today is quite inconceivable without giving a central and decisive part to the Creed itself, not only in its substantial contents but even in its very wording. Others would see themselves as more or less urgently bound by the substance of the Creed but would be more willing to attempt modern statements of the heart of the faith. Others again might value the Creed above all as a procedural model for a task which needs to be accomplished ever anew, namely the confession of the faith in particular circumstances and with the conceptual and linguistic tools available at the time. Even those churches which do not use the Nicene-Constantinopolitan Creed, or indeed any other creed, are usually willing to recognize that that Creed touches matters that are vital for Christian confession.

The approach "towards the common expression of the apostolic faith today" may be made from at least two directions. One may begin scripturally and historically with an attempt to describe the apostolic faith. In connection with the Creed, that raises the kind of questions indicated above in paragraph IV. Otherwise one may start from the social and cultural contexts of today in which the Christian faith has to be expressed. To the extent that the Creed receives positive evaluation as an expression of the apostolic faith, it may be called on to shed light on contemporary issues. It may be that these new demands made of the Creed help to bring the Creed to life for those who have not been accustomed to see its relevance to some of the concerns which engage them. While the Creed has never had the function of supplying a detailed social ethics, it may provide a theological frame of reference — through its teaching on creation, incarnation and salvation — for the treatment of many current issues.

Take, for example, the theme of "life" proposed for the Vancouver Assembly of the WCC:
— The Creed proclaims the Creator, "maker of heaven and earth". This is a basis from which to expand on the good creation, the resources for a good life, man's responsibility for good stewardship in an environmental crisis, and so on.
— The Creed confesses the humanity of a God who gets involved in the world's affairs, being born of a woman, suffering crucifixion, rising from the dead.
— The Creed celebrates the Holy Spirit as "the Giver of Life". Here is a basis on which to treat matters of personal ethics and life-style, love and solidarity, peace and liberation.

VI. Recommendations

Whereas the report has so far been raising questions which need to be faced, without a unanimous support or negation of particular theses, the Odessa group now wishes to make the following recommendations in the name of the whole group for submission to the Faith and Order Secretariat and to the Plenary Commission on Faith and Order meeting in Lima:

1. We recommend the pursuit of the theme "Towards the Common Expression of the Apostolic Faith Today" as one of the main study projects of the Faith and Order Commission in the years to come (we also bear in mind "Baptism, Eucharist, Ministry" and "The Unity of the Church and the Unity of Humankind").

2. We recommend the continuation, on different levels, of the work on "the ecumenical importance of the Nicene-Constantinopolitan Creed". In a more detailed perspective we face the following tasks:
a) to ask for official church reactions to the Klingenthal Memorandum;
b) to come to an agreement concerning the *filioque* clause in the Creed (at the level of doctrinal history and systematic theology, we are prepared to support the proposal of the Klingenthal Memorandum to delete the *filioque* clause from the Creed, provided the positive reasons which led to its inclusion be appreciated; at the level of scriptural exegesis and hermeneutics, the questions raised in part IV of our report remain to be treated more carefully);
c) to work for a common wording of the Creed in the various languages, so that all churches using the same language may also employ the same wording of the Creed;
d) to give a substantial theological interpretation of the Nicene-Constantinopolitan Creed, especially with regard to its third article, and an interpretation of its trinitarian theology;
e) to consider whether the Nicene-Constantinopolitan Creed should be more used in the liturgies and worship services, especially in eucharistic celebrations;
f) to consider whether the Creed should be brought more into use in the catechetical teaching of the churches;

g) to find ecumenically acceptable melodies for singing the Creed, taking into consideration those that already exist;

h) to clarify the relation between the more Eastern-rooted Nicene-Constantinopolitan Creed and the more Western-rooted Apostles' Creed and *Quicunque vult* in an ecumenical perspective;

i) to ask the WCC member churches, in an appropriate way, whether they could see the possibility of accepting the Nicene-Constantinopolitan Creed as their common ecumenical basis from the time of the ancient Church, understanding this as a first step on the way to the common expression of the apostolic faith today.

3. We recommend the initiation of more detailed studies for developing the ecumenical importance of the Nicene-Constantinopolitan Creed and for arriving at the common expression of the apostolic faith today. Specifically this would include scientific and other work on the ways faith was confessed:

a) in the Scriptures, especially for clarifying the question: What is precisely meant by the expression "apostolic faith"?;

b) in various stages of history, for instance: in the ancient Church; in the sixteenth century; and in our twentieth century, with special regard to confessing the faith in the various cultural and social situations.

5. THE APOSTOLIC FAITH IN THE SCRIPTURES AND IN THE EARLY CHURCH
Rome Report, 1983

At the Faith and Order Commission meeting in Lima, one of the decisions made was to organize a consultation on the theme: "The Apostolic Faith in the Scriptures and in the Early Church".[1] At the invitation of the Roman Catholic Church, this consultation took place in Rome from 1 to 8 October 1983. It concentrated on three main aspects of the theme. Detailed consideration was given not only to the fundamental New Testament sources but also, aided by discussions with a Jewish scholar, to the Old Testament Judaic roots of the Christian faith. Ways in which the faith was expressed in prayers, doxologies and liturgies of the ancient church were also studied.

The pattern of the Rome report is as follows:

Introduction

I.   The Hebrew scriptures: some points made and issues raised

II. Confession of faith in the New Testament: some points made and issues raised

III. Apostolic faith in the early church: some points made and issues raised

Conclusion: Some implications of our discussion for the development of a convergence statement: "Towards the Common Expression of the Apostolic Faith Today"

Appendix: A preliminary working definition of the terms "faith" and "apostolic faith"

The report concludes with the suggestion for regional and local groups that they should investigate "the role of various contextual factors in the process of shaping and transmitting the apostolic faith... in the early centuries... Similar investigations are needed concerning the contemporary situation. Such studies ought to illuminate the factors operative in the explication of the apostolic faith and its confession today."[2]

● Text in "The Roots of Our Common Faith: Faith in the Scriptures and in the Early Church", ed. H. G. Link, *Faith and Order Paper No. 119*, Geneva, 1984, pp.9-20. Also in *The Ecumenical Review*, Vol. 36, No. 3, July 1984, pp.329-37.

---

[1] "Towards Visible Unity", Vol. II, p.46.
[2] *The Ecumenical Review*, Vol. 36, 1984, p.336.

Introduction

The Nairobi Assembly asked "the churches to undertake a common effort to receive, reappropriate and confess together, as contemporary occasion requires, the Christian truth and faith, delivered through the apostles and handed down through the centuries". As a help in the response to that challenge, the Commission on Faith and Order launched the project "Towards the common expression of the apostolic faith today". The enterprise had already been placed by the Nairobi Assembly under "the commonly acknowledged authority of God's word". At its Lima meeting in 1982, the Commission on Faith and Order acknowledged a special place to the Nicene-Constantinopolitan Creed as an expression of the apostolic faith. The "reception", "reappropriation" and "confession" listed by the Nairobi Assembly were then formulated as follows:

1. Towards the common *recognition* of the apostolic faith as expressed in the ecumenical symbol of that faith, the Nicene Creed.
2. Towards the common *explication* of this apostolic faith in the contemporary situations of the churches.
3. Towards a common *confession* of the apostolic faith today.

This triple goal appears to demand a fourfold working method. There is, first, the *exegetical* task of determining by means of the scriptural witness the Christian faith concerning God, Christ, the Spirit, the Church, the present life of believers, and the world to come. Second, there are the *historical* tasks of tracing how and why that faith came to find expression in the Nicene Creed, and of determining the relations between that Creed and other formulations of the faith. Third, there is the *hermeneutical* task of reading Scriptures and Creed in our present situations in such ways that the one faith may illuminate our contemporary world. Fourth, there is the ecumenically *constructive* task of finding means and forms by which the faith may today be confessed before our fellow human beings. The Rome consultation showed that these four aspects will be mutually involving. More attention was devoted to the first two, though the third kept reasserting itself and even the fourth was not totally absent.

The following report indicates some of the issues we have begun to tackle and whose settlement will require further and more detailed reflection. The three main sections reflect the concentration placed on the Scriptures and the Early Church. The conclusion seeks to point some implications for the further course of the study "Towards the common expression of the apostolic faith today". An appendix gives a preliminary working definition of the terms "faith" and "apostolic faith".

I. The Hebrew Scriptures: Some Points Made and Issues Raised

A. Confession of Faith in the Hebrew Scriptures

1. The Hebrew Scriptures set a structure of faith as an existential act and attitude of believing. Faith is directed towards a God who represents himself and addresses a person; who evokes the response of worship and the following of his call (Gen. 12,15,17,22; Ex. 20:2; Josh. 24). His covenant is freely and graciously given ("You will be my people") in the expectation that the people so blessed will acknowledge him as Lord ("I will be your God"). He requires *trust* and *obedience*, subsumed in an all-embracing *love* (Deut. 6:5). Trustful and obedient love of God implies the *knowledge* of this God who so promises, acts, and commands.

2. The substantial content of faith is determined by the God who promises, acts, and commands. God creates all things, provides for his creatures and delivers his people, and the Creator, Provider and Deliverer continues to be praised and invoked as such by the faithful, even in slavery and in exile, under the attack of enemies and in the face of personal adversity. God's blessings to Abraham concern descendants and a land. The God of Abraham, Isaac and Jacob, the God who spoke to Moses, is the only God. God's gift of Torah became an object of deep thankfulness, meditation and action; in it God pointed out to his people the way to love in faithfulness to him and in loyalty to the covenant he had made with them. In mercy, God seeks out even an erring people for forgiveness and restoration.

3. In the Hebrew Scriptures, confessions of faith often occur in the contexts of worship. The example of Deuteronomy 26:5-11 may be noted, where the oral confession accompanies an act of offering. Again, Psalms 105, 106 and 136 show the clear marks of liturgical composition and use. The word *higgid* (LXX *exhomologeis-thai, an-angellein*) often introduces confessions of faith, which gratefully proclaim the Name of God, his character, his creative power and his redemptive acts. God and God's deeds are told before God and before the world, all for the glory of God. Such confession is a means by which individuals and generations enter into the history of God's relationship with the people.

4. The sacred writings of Israel nourish to this day the faith of Jews who through the vicissitudes of history have continued to worship the one God who made himself known to their ancestors.

B. The Hebrew Scriptures in Christian Use

1. The sacred writings of Israel were Scripture to Jesus. The New Testament writers used them to interpret the life, death and resurrection of Jesus, and Jesus Christ in turn became the first Church's key for understanding those Scriptures of Israel which became and remained the Church's "Old Testament". This Christian claim has been controversial from the beginning. From the start it was necessary to face the question of continuity and discontinuity between Israel and the Church. In what sense is the New Covenant of Christian faith new?

2. Jesus himself endorsed the Shema (Deut. 6:4f.: "Hear, O Israel: the Lord is our God, the Lord alone. You shall love the Lord your God with all your heart, all your soul, and all your might") as the first commandment and as the way to eternal life (Mark 12:29; Matt. 22:37; Luke 10:27). With a significant christological inclusion, this confession underlies 1 Cor. 8:5-6, which appears in turn to have been one of the formative influences upon the Christian creeds. The affirmation of the Shema by Jesus and its adoption by the apostle to the Gentiles mean that the Church's faith is directed towards the one God whom Israel worships.

3. The earthly concreteness of the blessings God gave to Israel teaches Christians also to rejoice in "every good and perfect gift which comes from the Father of lights" (James 1:17). When the creation of God is received with thanksgiving, it is sanctified (1 Tim. 4:4-5). The present blessings get their full significance in light of the eschatological expectation concerning the resurrection of the body and the life of the age to come. For the Christian, confidence in the end time is based on Jesus, "who was put to death for our sins and raised for our justification" (Rom. 4:25).

4. Abraham appears as "the father of the faithful" (cf. Rom. 4:11). With appeal to Genesis 15, Paul in Romans 4 argues that Abraham was justified before God by his simple trust in the promise of the One who, Paul elaborates, calls things into being that were not and has the power to raise from the dead. Christians believe that by the resurrection of Jesus a new creation has already been inaugurated, into which one is brought by a baptism of repentance and faith into the crucified and risen Christ.

5. Both continuity and discontinuity between Israel and the Church are recognizable also in the various responses of the early Christian communities (and their writings) to the Law of Moses: according to Matt. 5:17-20 Jesus came not to abolish but to fulfil the Law, and what that meant is illustrated in the whole Sermon on the Mount (Matt. 5-7) and in such further passages as Matt. 22:34-40; the Johannine understanding of Jesus and the Law (John 1:17; 15:25) and the understanding presented in the letter to the Hebrews (chs 7-10) underline newness and discontinuity rather than continuity; Paul's dialectical view of the Law (Rom. 3:31; 10:4) seems related to both the positive and the negative (at least limited) functions that Paul ascribes to the Law (Gal. 3:19ff; Rom. 7:1-8:4).

6. The faith of Israel contained from the beginning an orientation towards the future. When the promises of God had already received fulfilment, such fulfilment itself served as the ground for hope that the divine promises would continue to be implemented, even when historical events appeared to threaten them; and indeed a new fulfilment would exceed the earlier (Jer. 23:5-8; 31:31-34; cf. Is. 43:14-20). Christians believe that such a greater fulfilment has taken place in Jesus the Christ (2 Cor. 1:20). Even so, and yet again, the hope persists for the return of Jesus and the visible establishment of God's kingdom.

7. Such issues of continuity and discontinuity between Israel and the Church need fresh attention, since it is in any case certain that the Christian confession cannot be made without regard to the Jewish people — because of the historical origin of Christianity; because of the ongoing history of the Jewish people, which claims "the Old Testament" as Scripture; because of the continuing witness of the Jewish faith to the one God; and because of the hope held by the apostle Paul for the people of Israel.

II. Confession of Faith in the New Testament: Some Points Made and Issues Raised

1. According to the synoptic gospels, Jesus comes announcing the kingdom of God, and by his exorcisms, healings, and acts of forgiveness he even appears as the agent of its dawning. In this context, the confession or rejection of Jesus determines a person's position in the final judgment (Mark 10:32f=Luke 12:8f; Mark 8:38=Luke 9:26). Confession of Jesus involves taking up the cross in following him. Jesus warns that "not everyone who calls me 'Lord, Lord' will enter the kingdom of heaven, but only those who do the will of my heavenly Father" (Matt 7:21). While oral confession is not sufficient, it must be asked whether it is not necessary. Or is it possible without it to do the will of the One whom Jesus called Abba and enter the kingdom?

2. Continuing confession of Jesus raises the questions of the relations between the faith of Jesus himself, the faith of his hearers and followers during his earthly ministry, and the faith of early and later believers after his death and resurrection. The Proclaimer became the Proclaimed. What does that mean for continuing response to his teaching and behaviour? That question arises both in the ethics and in the

fundamental content of the faith. What do Jesus' solidarity with all humanity and his partiality for the poor and outcast mean for the profession of a Christian? What is the relation between the parable told by Jesus concerning the publican and the pharisee and the belief that justification comes through faithful response to the death and resurrection of Jesus? Continuing confession of Jesus must deal also with the continuity of the transmission of faith, already at the different stages of the New Testament writings. In what ways are second and later generations of believers dependent on the first apostles?

3. Confession of the Christian faith can only come by a gift from God: "No one can say that Jesus is Lord except by the Holy Spirit" (1 Cor. 12:3). That applies not only to the act of confessing but also to the content: the Holy Spirit guides the believers into all the truth (John 16:13). The Holy Spirit appears as the divine power in baptism (John 3:5; 1 Cor. 12:13; Tit. 3:5), and the Holy Spirit gives the life (John 6:63; 2 Cor. 3:6) which is nothing other than participation in God (2 Cor. 13:(13)14; 2 Pet.1:4).

4. The New Testament writings exhibit diversity in the formulation of the faith confessed concerning Jesus. There are four gospel books to proclaim the one gospel. Epistles stem from the questions that are being addressed; but a positive variety of thought and formulation must also be ascribed to the abundant character of the faith and to the mystery of the person being confessed, both of which find a doxological expression. Questions arise as to whether the diversity amounts to internal contradictoriness. While individual Christians and scholars have sometimes considered this to be the case, the churches have maintained the unity and coherence of the scriptural canon whose establishment owed much to the use of these writings, all these writings, and no other writings in the gradually settled worship of the Early Church. Tensions among the various accepted writings permit mutual correction and enrichment. What variety of confession is thereby allowed and encouraged in the later Church and in the contemporary situation? In what does the unity of the Christian faith consist?

5. Within the writings of the New Testament, a prominent place falls to Paul, who remains the one apostle about whose understanding of faith we know most. For Paul, "faith" is expressed in obedience to the message of the Gospel (Rom. 1:5). As the "word of faith" (Rom. 10:8), the gospel has a liberating and transforming power (Rom. 1:16); it draws the believer into a life of trust in, and commitment to, Jesus as the Christ and Lord (Phil. 3:8-12). Paul is eager to practise such faith himself and also to elicit and to foster the faith response among all people, especially the Gentiles to whom he is sent.

As faith is exercised in a personal relationship to the living Lord, the content of faith is, for Paul, Jesus Christ himself and all that this name stands for: "... Christ Jesus, whom God made our wisdom, our righteousness and sanctification and redemption" (1 Cor. 1:30). The "for us" character of God's work in Christ is already confessed in the pre-Pauline tradition of the Church (1 Cor. 11:24; 15:3) with which Paul shares the essential elements of the kerygma. Paul continues to expound the Christ "for us", concentrating on the significance of the cross and the resurrection of Christ. In his *apologia* of faith over against Judaizers and Gnostics, Paul clarifies the nature of faith in distinction from their understandings of "works" and "knowledge".

1 Cor. 8:6 seems to have played an important role in the development of the Creed. A detailed comparison of Paul's letters and the Nicene Creed calls for reflections on Paul's pneumatology and especially his christology: how does Paul conceive of Christ

as pre-existent (e.g. 1 Cor. 8:6; 10:4), as obedient to God (Phil. 2:8), as exalted Lord (e.g. Rom. 10:9; Phil. 2:9-11), as "God" (perhaps Rom. 9:5), and as Son submitting to God the Father (1 Cor. 15:28)?

6. Concerning the later writings of Paul or his followers, we find God in 1 Tim. 6:15-16 called "the blessed and only Sovereign, the King of kings and Lord of lords, who alone had immortality and dwells in unapproachable light". In Col. 1:16 we read that all things in heaven and on earth were created in, through and for Christ. In the Lucan infancy narrative (as in the Matthaean), Jesus is conceived by the Holy Spirit (without human father) in the womb of the virgin Mary; and so alongside his status as son of David, he is Son of God in a unique sense. In the book of Acts, the Spirit is portrayed as the main agent in Church history, guiding at every main crisis the Church faces. The concept of "the Church", universal, all holy, the Body of Christ, emerges very prominently in Colossians and Ephesians and becomes a goal of the salvific mystery: "Christ loved the Church and gave himself up for her" (Eph. 5:25). The Pastoral Epistles imply the importance of the apostolic lineage. 2 Thess. 2 portrays a major onset of evil at the end of times challenging Christ, and yet warns against allowing the coming future to paralyze Christian life.

7. The letter to the Hebrews cites many Old Testament figures who exemplified a faith that "is the assurance of things hoped for, the conviction of things not seen" (11:1). In 12:1-2 Jesus is the forerunner or pioneer and perfecter of our faith, enduring the cross because of the joy set before him; and so we are exhorted to run the race with perseverance.

8. In the Gospel and Epistles of John, faith is the all-subsuming, necessary response to Jesus, and it has a necessary content: one must know that he has come from heaven, sent by the Father into the world: "This is eternal life, that they know you, the only true God, and Jesus Christ whom you have sent" (John 17:3). The Word of God, through whom all things were created (John 1:3), became flesh as Jesus Christ (1:14) who is Lord and God (20:28). He receives all things from the Father (5:19ff; 7:16; 8:28), so the Father is greater than he (14:28); and yet he is so one with the Father (10:30) that whoever sees him sees the Father (14:9). In chapters 14-16 of the Gospel, the personal Paraclete, who proceeds from the Father, is to Jesus as Jesus is to the Father: he is the ongoing presence of Jesus (from whom the Paraclete receives all he teaches) when Jesus has departed, dwelling in everyone who loves Jesus and keeps his commandments. Judgment takes place as we face the light come into the world (John 3:19), so that those who believe in Jesus already have the eternal life of God (John 17:3) and are God's children in water and Spirit (John 3:5), nourishing their life through the food of Jesus' flesh and blood (John 6:51ff).

9. The New Testament writings contain evidence (quotations and traces) of early formulaic expressions of the Christian faith. It will be helpful to trace the motives which led to the coining of such brief formulae. They often seem to carry the stamp of liturgical origin and use. The New Testament writers sometimes employ them to make a polemical point of belief or to offer ethical exhortation.

III. Apostolic Faith in the Early Church: Some Points Made and Issues Raised
1. Verbal Formulas: Occasions and Needs

Ever since apostolic times there has been occasion and need to express the Christian faith in verbal formulas. Such expression was required by catechesis, which would draw on the material of preaching and prayer. At baptism itself, candidates made a brief confession of faith, whether directly or in answer to the minister's questions. The eucharistic assembly proclaimed over bread and wine the Lord's death and resurrection. Martyrs at their trial often confessed their faith in words received from tradition. Definitions were needed to defend the faith against heretical distortion.

2. Content and Structure of the Confessions

At the centre of Christian believing, teaching and confessing stood, from the start, Jesus, through whom God is working for the world's salvation. The early formulas therefore include both predications of Jesus' dignity (such as Messiah, Son of God, Lord) and also a recital of his way from birth to cross, resurrection, exaltation and on to his expected return. This style of formulation can already be seen in the New Testament (e.g. 1 Cor. 15:3f) and in Ignatius of Antioch. The model for its articulation to the confession of the Father may be seen in 1 Cor. 8:6: "For us there is one God, the Father, from whom are all things and for whom we exist, and one Lord, Jesus Christ, through whom are all things and through whom we exist." The baptismal command of Matt. 28:19 brings near also the thought of the Spirit who had worked and was working in the history of salvation, and verse 20 may even have suggested the inclusion and place of the Church and of the last things in the more developed confessions of faith: "Go therefore and make disciples of all nations, baptizing them in the name of the Father and of the Son and of the Holy Spirit, teaching them to observe all that I have commanded you; and lo, I am with you always, to the close of the age" (cf. 1 Cor. 12:1-7, 12-13).

3. The Defence and Intelligibility of the Faith

In the second century, the fundamental Christian assumption of the unity of the one God who made the world, called the patriarchs and prophets of the Old Testament, and sent his Son as redeemer, needed to be maintained and defended against doctrines which so separated creation and redemption that the unity of God was lost, and thereby also the connexion between the Old and New Testaments. In that situation, the formulas of faith were elaborated to underline the indivisible unity of God and of the history of salvation (Irenaeus of Lyons).

At the same time, this story of redemption had to be made intelligible to people of different cultures and backgrounds in such ways that they could accept the gospel as a message of salvation (Tertullian at Carthage; Clement in Alexandria).

Both these tasks called for a theology which was not afraid to make positive and critical use of the intellectual tools and the thought forms available at the time. Some theological essays remained long under debate and were finally abandoned, and yet they furthered the insight of the Church into truth (Origen).

4. The Scriptural Basis and Test

The basis of the whole process of teaching and learning in the struggle to preserve, transmit and commend the apostolic faith remained the Scriptures, even though the complete settlement of the canon took time. Every formula of faith had to be measured against the Scriptures. The early formulas of faith do not narrate the stories of the Holy Scriptures but rather presuppose them. They do not aim to replace the scriptural accounts of the gospel but to state its truth in a sharp and summary form. In so far as they succeeded, they were not only faith's response to the apostolic message but became themselves one form of expressing the gospel. They became a norm of doctrine under the supreme norm of the Scriptures, whose riches no formula of faith can exhaust. A formula faithful to the gospel was seen to share in the gospel's power to bind and loose (cf. already 1 John 4:2ff).

5. The Nicene Expression of Faith: a Model for Content and Method

The formula of the Early Church which has pre-eminently received ecumenical acceptance down the centuries is the Nicene-Constantinopolitan Creed. In the Arian controversy, it was a matter of maintaining the unity of God who in the Holy Spirit makes of it a new creation. At stake was not just a part but the whole of the apostolic faith. The form, at least, of the question was new in comparison with the time of the apostles; the answer could not avoid taking into acount the form in which the question was raised. The first method of argument used in the debate was the exegesis of Scripture. While the Nicene fathers would have preferred to keep to scriptural language in the expression of the true faith, they were prepared to adopt other terms from another conceptuality (notably the *homoousios*) where fidelity to the profound tendency of the Scriptures and to the continuing Christian faith appeared to require it. The various parties in the fourth-century controversy appealed also to the liturgical life of the Church: the argument which maintained the Nicene conviction rested particularly on the appeal to baptism in the name of the Father, the Son, and the Holy Spirit (Matt. 28:19), the saving agent in baptism being necessarily God.

In our own project we shall inevitably face questions posed by the Father's ways of interpreting Scripture and by the ways in use in the churches today.

6. Apostolic Faith in the Prayer and Worship of the Church

a) From the start, apostolic faith has shaped the prayer of the Church. That God has redeemed the world through his Son and has sent his Spirit into the hearts of believers — that is the ground on which Christians call on God as Father. The risen Christ, exalted "at the right hand of the Father" and present "in the midst of those gathered in his name", is for the early Church both the mediator of all prayer and himself receives praise and adoration (cf. already 2 Pet. 3:18; Rev. 1:5f; 5:13). Athanasius could in turn appeal to the Church's worship of Christ, strictly understood, as part of his argument against an Arian understanding of the Son. Doxology has, in any case, always been one form of confessing the faith.

b) The Lord's Supper, too, the Church's eucharist, is a form of the apostolic faith and a testimony to it. The service, of course, included preaching. In face of the Gnostics, the Fathers saw in the meal itself a confession of the unity of creation and redemption: the earthly, created gifts of bread and wine become by Christ's word and the Holy Spirit the body and blood of Christ which already bring us into God's kingdom. The ancient eucharistic prayer celebrated in manifold form the memorial of Christ's saving way, giving praise and thanks for God's creative and redemptive work. The eucharistic *anamnesis* substantially echoed the confession of faith made at baptism.

c) As the liturgies evolved, further links were made between liturgical forms and the apostolic faith, sometimes even to the point of obscuring the original connexions. Since the fifth century in the East, and at later periods also in the West, the whole structure of actions and prayers at the eucharist is seen as a dramatic portrayal of Christ's way to the cross and resurrection. The apostolic faith was always expressed also in hymns and acclamations; but sometimes formulas have been interpreted or introduced with polemical intent. The Nicene Creed itself started to find its way locally into the eucharistic liturgy in the sixth century, and this use gradually spread into wide regions of the Church. Its point there is not simply to ward off heresy but, as an expression of apostolic faith, to express fellowship among the churches and to offer a positive invitation to right prayer and right worship.

Conclusion
Some Implications of Our Discussion for the Development of a Convergence Statement: "Towards the Common Expression of the Apostolic Faith Today"

The work of this consultation has presupposed the Lima prospectus for the Apostolic Faith Study as well as the proposal by Faith and Order officers that the primary focus of the study should be the attempt to produce a convergence statement along the lines outlined at Lima, and that the study should aim to make a significant contribution to the proposed Fifth World Conference of Faith and Order (1987 or 1988). In that context, the present consultation provided a preliminary exploration of some of the questions which will need to be faced in the production of such a convergence statement. What are some of the implications of our discussions for this project?

1. Our discussions repeatedly underlined the importance of adequately distinguishing yet holding fast together the three main points of the Lima prospectus: (1) "recognition", (2) "explication", and (3) contemporary "confession" of the apostolic faith. Any adequate understanding of what the "apostolic faith" means requires attention to all three aspects.

2. Accepting that threefold concern as indissoluble, this consultation (as Lima asked to do) emphasized the importance of Scripture for the development and understanding of the Niceno-Constantinopolitan Creed, and therefore for further work on this project. Our discussions made it abundantly clear that the fullness of that apostolic faith which the Creed symbolizes can only be discerned and understood in the light of the Scriptures, as both are opened up to contemporary understanding.

3. Of particular significance in our work was the realization of the importance of the Old Testament for our study. We are convinced that the relation of Church and Jewish people is an essential aspect of the apostolic faith, and that any convergence document must deal adequately with this relation.

4. We have realized afresh the importance of clarifying the authority, significance and use of the Nicene Creed. Moreover, it will be essential to clarify quite specifically what it means to recognize this creed as "ecumenical symbol" of the apostolic faith.

5. We have encountered persistent difficulty in clearly distinguishing points two and three of the Lima mandate: the "explication" of the Creed in relation to contemporary questions about its meaning, and "the contemporary confession" of the apostolic faith. Further work must clarify whether these two points refer to one task or two.

6. We have come to the strong conviction that the right point of entry for making a beginning on Lima's threefold task is to attempt to "explicate" the Nicene Creed in relation to contemporary questions about its meaning (the Lima prospectus, *Towards*

Visible Unity, §21, makes a tentative beginning in formulating some of those questions), and in relation to the scriptural witness of the apostolic faith. This effort at "explication" can open doors for the other aspects of Lima's threefold task.

7. While we do not give it explicit attention in our report, we wish to record our suggestion that an effort be made, perhaps in some regional or local groups, to investigate how an historiography especially sensitive to social and political analysis would view the role of various contextual factors in the process of shaping and transmitting the apostolic faith, and the development of credal authority in the early centuries of the Christian era. We have in mind such questions as cultural, social and political factors in the rise of various heresies and divisions, and in the efforts to realize ecclesiastical and political unity; the relations between imperial authority and credal authority, and imperial ritual and Christian liturgy. Similar investigations are needed concerning the contemporary situation. Such studies ought to illuminate the factors operative in the explication of the apostolic faith and its confession today.

Appendix: A Preliminary Working Definition of the Terms "Faith" and "Apostolic Faith"

1. Faith

The term "faith" indicates at the same time a decisive act and a continuing attitude of believing *(fides qua creditur)* as well as a set of beliefs and convictions *(fides quae creditur)*. The Old and New Testaments witness that faith in God is expressed by an existential, personal and communal act and attitude of acceptance, decision, trust, confidence, confessing, hope, and obedience. This *fides qua* can never be without or separated from the content of faith *(fides quae)*. Otherwise the act of faith would be an empty or a purely self-generated act. The content of faith is determined by the One towards whom it is directed. The *fides quae* can be expressed in a great plurality of forms, ranging from short biblical affirmations such as "Jesus is Lord" to massive theological expositions.

2. Apostolic Faith

The term "apostolic faith" as used in this study does not refer only to a single fixed formula or a specific moment in Christian history. It points to the dynamic, historical *(geschichtlich)* reality of the central affirmations of the Christian faith which are *grounded* in the witness of the people of the Old Testament and the normative testimony of those who preached Jesus in the earliest days ("apostles") and of their community, as attested in the New Testament. These central affirmations were further *developed* in the Church of the first centuries. This apostolic faith is expressed in various ways, i.e. in individual and common confession of Christians, in preaching and sacraments, in formalized and received credal statements, in decisions of councils and in confessional texts. Ongoing theological explication aims at clarifying this faith as a service to the confessing community. Having its centre in the confession of Jesus as Christ and of the triune God, this apostolic faith is to be ever confessed anew and interpreted in the context of changing times and places in continuity with the original witness of the apostolic community and with the faithful explication of that witness throughout the centuries.

C.
APPENDICES
Background Material

1. TOWARDS THE COMMON EXPRESSION OF THE APOSTOLIC FAITH TODAY

Report of the Standing Commission
on Faith and Order, Crete 1984

I. The mandate

1. Nairobi 1975

Section II "What Unity Requires" made the following first recommendation concerning our study: "We ask the churches to undertake a common effort to receive, reappropriate and confess together, as contemporary occasion requires, the Christian truth and faith, delivered through the apostles and handed down through the centuries. Such common action, arising from free and inclusive discussion under the commonly acknowledged authority of God's word, must aim both to clarify and to embody the unity and the diversity which are proper to the church's life and mission."[1]

2. Bangalore 1978

At the meeting of the Plenary Commission on Faith and Order in Bangalore in 1978 three actual requirements for the unity of the church were agreed upon:
a) consensus in the apostolic faith;
b) mutual recognition of baptism, the eucharist and the ministry;
c) structures making possible common teaching and decision-making.[2]

3. Lima 1982

At the following plenary meeting in Lima in 1982 the Commission unanimously adopted an outline of the whole project which contains the three basic aspects of recognition, explication and confession of the apostolic faith today. The first recommendation reads: "We recommend the pursuit of the theme 'Towards the Common Expression of the Apostolic Faith Today' as one of the main study projects of the Faith and Order Commission in the years to come".[3]

4. Vancouver 1983

The Fifth Report (1983) of the Joint Working Group between the Roman Catholic Church and the World Council of Churches proposes for future work with regard to its study "The Way Towards Unity": "The Joint Working Group shall maintain close

---

[1] *Breaking Barriers: Nairobi 1975*, London, SPCK, and Geneva, WCC, 1976, p.66.
[2] "Sharing in One Hope", Bangalore 1978, *Faith and Order Paper No.92*, Geneva, WCC, 1982, p.243.
[3] Lima Report, Recommendations I.

contact with the work of the Commission on Faith and Order, especially in the area of a common expression of the apostolic faith and in the deepening of agreement on the understanding and practice of baptism, eucharist and the ministry."[4] Accordingly, the Issue Group 2 report of the Vancouver Assembly, "Taking Steps Towards Unity", stresses as the second step "we can take now towards this goal" to "clarify the meaning of 'a common understanding of the apostolic faith' ".[5] The programme guidelines note under the first priority for the future WCC work: "Further work is needed on the common understanding of the apostolic faith as a presupposition of effective steps towards unity."[6] Finally the recommendations from Issue Group 2 read "concerning the common understanding of the apostolic faith that the Faith and Order Commission continue to give priority to its study, 'Towards the Common Expression of the Apostolic Faith Today', as outlined at Lima (1982), and that this study be closely linked with the 'Baptism, Eucharist and Ministry' process of reception, of which it is, indeed, the presupposition."

These quotations indicate beyond any doubt the high priority which is given by the WCC to this study.

II. Content

The *Lima outline* of the study focuses on the three main emphases: recognition, explication and confession of the apostolic faith.

1. Recognition

In order to rediscover the bases of faith binding for all Christians, the project goes back to the Nicene Creed in its version of 381 (Nicea-Constantinople), for this Creed stems from the time of the one undivided church. Moreover, it has the advantage of having been approved by the first councils of the early church (Nicea 325, Constantinople 381) and of having been recognized as a summary of faith by virtually the whole church (Chalcedon 451). In the course of the centuries it served innumerable Christians as a norm of their faith; it was taken up in many worship formulae and up to the present time is the most widespread confession of faith among Christians.

"Therefore, the World Council of Churches might ask the churches to recognize anew that integral unity of the Christian faith expressed in the symbol of Nicea-Constantinople, to reconsider the status of their own teaching in its lights, to affirm its content as the basis of more comprehensive church unity, and to strengthen its place in the liturgical life of the churches wherever necessary and possible under circumstances of pastoral responsibility."[7]

Such a common official recognition of the Nicene Creed will strengthen the links with the faith of the early church and the *oikoumene* through the centuries.

2. Explication

Contextual explication and appropriation of the Christian faith are necessary in order not to be limited merely to a formal act of recognition of the Nicene Creed. It is a question of actualizing the classic themes of confessions of faith as well as responding to contemporary challenges to the Christian faith.

---

[4] *The Ecumenical Review*, Vol. 35, No. 2, 1983, p.211.
[5] *Gathered for Life*, report of the WCC Sixth Assembly, Vancouver 1983, Geneva, WCC, 1983, p.48f.
[6] *Ibid.*, p.253.
[7] Lima report, §15.

In view of the articles of faith in the *Nicene Creed* for example, the consequences of the confession to the one God for the unity of Christians and their relation to Judaism and Islam will have to be clarified. The second article requires an answer to the question: "Who is Jesus Christ for us today?" for our contemporary situations. In connection with the third article there is the contemporary understanding of the Holy Spirit and the overcoming of the so-called *filioque* controversy between Eastern and Western traditions. We must give "special attention to the nature and mystery of the Church of God, since the confession of the one, holy, catholic and apostolic church belongs to the apostolic faith".[8] On the whole, the gain or loss of a contemporary trinitarian understanding of God is at stake with an explication of the Nicene Creed today.

Especially the situations in the third world pose *new challenges* to the Christian faith, be it the relations to other religions and to nature in Asia or the question of justice and liberation in Latin America or the relations to ancestors and the family of God in Africa. The call for an incarnation of faith in various cultures, regions and societal contexts cannot be ignored and waits for authentic answers. Questions of common actions of Christians belong to the contemporary challenges of faith as well.

At Crete the Standing Commission adopted the recommendation of the Rome consultation on apostolic faith questions to begin with this task of explication. "We have come to the strong conviction that the right point of entry for making a beginning on Lima's threefold task is to attempt to 'explicate' the Nicene Creed in relation to contemporary questions about its meaning (the Lima report, §21, makes a tentative beginning in formulating some of those questions), and in relation to the scriptural witness to the apostolic faith. This effort at 'explication' can open doors for the other aspects of Lima's threefold task."[9]

3. Confession

Finally everything is related to undertaking steps which enable the divided churches increasingly to recognize themselves as members of the one body of Christ "in order that the world may believe". This means first of all to overcome church-dividing condemnations (anathemas) from the past, such as they are formulated in Canon I of Constantinople 381 and in some articles of the Augsburg Confession from 1530.[10] Another step would be the study, in relation to earlier formulations of the apostolic faith, of specific statements of faith in different church traditions, e.g. the "Theological Declaration of Barmen" (in Germany), 1934, or "The Basis of Union" (in South India), 1941.[11] Finally, there is also the concern to possibly find common answers to vital challenges of our present time, e.g. the increasing worldwide nuclear arms race or the relationships between poor and rich people, churches and nations.[12]

III. Purpose

What is the *concrete result* the study is aiming at?

1. The project does *not* aim to present a *new ecumenical creed* which the WCC is not, in any case, authorized to do. "Proposing an ecumenical symbol of the apostolic

---

[8] *Gathered for Life, op. cit.*, p.48f.
[9] Rome Report, October 1963, Conclusion, No. 6.
[10] Cf. Lima report, §27c.
[11] Cf. Lima report, §27a,b.
[12] Cf. Lima report, §26f.

faith clearly presupposes the authority of an ecumenical council. Such a council would have as an essential purpose the confession of the apostolic faith on behalf of the whole church in the situation of its own present day."[13]

2. *Instead*: "The purpose of the whole study project would be to prepare for a kind of 'preliminary plateau' of common confessing that would be necessary and sufficient to convene a universal ecumenical council".[14] "...Such an event can be hoped and prayed for, and the project 'Towards the Common Expression of the Apostolic Faith Today' offers *a beginning* towards such an event."[15]

3. At Crete the Standing Commission adopted the decision of the officers at their meeting in Rome (January 1983) that "the basic *instrument* for the project to be focussed on is a substantial *convergence document*, dealing with the three main aspects of the project: (1) recognition, (2) explication, (3) confession of the apostolic faith today" (Decisions, II).

Note: A review of the study process so far is appended as Appendix 1, and the relation of this study to two other major study concerns in the WCC is appended as Appendix 2.

IV. Relation to other Faith and Order studies

1. Relation to "Baptism, Eucharist and Ministry"

As it was already clearly pointed out in the quoted statements (cf. I,4), this apostolic faith study is profoundly related to the convergence document on "Baptism, Eucharist and Ministry" and its reception process in the churches. Baptism, eucharist and ministry theologically belong into the wider horizon of the apostolic faith and it is the apostolic faith that the churches are being asked to discern and respond to in their responses to "Baptism, Eucharist and Ministry". On the long pilgrimage of ecumenical encounter towards visible unity the apostolic faith project is the next step which is to be undertaken. In connection with the reception process of "Baptism, Eucharist and Ministry" also the third step of the priority list from Bangalore (cf. I,2) will have to be taken up again, the development of "structures making possible common teaching and decision-making".

2. Relation to the "Unity and Renewal" study

The endeavour to express the apostolic faith *today* asks the kind of questions which the unity/renewal study is designed to articulate and discuss. It focuses upon the complex relationship of the contemporary quest for visible church unity and problems of contemporary human community. The apostolic faith study needs to face exactly those problems in order to do justice to its theme. In this way, the interrelation of the three major present Faith and Order studies is essential for each one of them.

---

[13] Lima report, §10d.
[14] Annecy Minutes, *Faith and Order Paper No. 106*, 1981, p.48.
[15] *Gathered for Life, op. cit.*, p.48.

V. Next steps

1. International consultations

In order to provide sufficient input for the next Plenary Commission meeting three international consultations are planned for 1984 and 1985. These consultations will focus on the explication of the apostolic faith, especially the Nicene Creed. They will seek to respond to the question, to which degree and in which form can the main thrust of the three articles of the Creed, in the wider context of the apostolic faith, be commonly understood and expressed by churches of different confessional identity and living in different cultural, social, political and religious contexts.

Concerning themes the consultations will be very specific along the lines indicated. They cannot make an attempt at explicating the apostolic faith for our time and contemporaries with regard to all possible challenges. This is the task of proclamation and theological reflection in each church. But they should render a significant ecumenical contribution to this task.

Two or three members of the Steering Group, members of the Plenary Commission and a strong representation of people from the region in which the consultations take place should be invited.

A report is expected from each consultation.

Between 1986 and the World Conference on Faith and Order 1988/89 three international consultations on the common expression and confession of the apostolic faith should be foreseen.

2. Meeting of the Steering Group

A meeting of members of the Steering Group on Apostolic Faith should take place around the end of May 1985 (with one or two consultants). On the basis of the results of the consultations, its own reflections and some preliminary drafting work, the aim of the meeting would be:
— to prepare an annotated outline of a statement on the explication of the apostolic faith;
— to give already some more content to the section on the third article of the Creed — the Holy Spirit and the church (because here more Faith and Order material will be available as a basis).

3. Plenary Commission meeting

The meeting of the Plenary Commission foreseen for summer 1985 would give special emphasis to this study. It would aim at a statement on specific aspects and would provide theological input and orientation for further work. The annotated outline of the Steering Group and other papers would be the basis for the work. In addition a major paper should summarize and evaluate the work already done before 1984 and suggest lines of an ecumenical convergence for a common *recognition* of the apostolic faith. This could be taken up as an introduction for a statement on the explication of the apostolic faith.

4. Local study groups

a) The Standing Commission endorses the setting up of local study groups on apostolic faith questions.

b) A letter will be sent to local group leaders inviting them to concentrate the group work in a first round on the two questions: (1) What are for you the main challenges to the confession of the Christian faith today? (2) How do you respond to these challenges? Responses before 1 May 1985 would be helpful for the preparation of the Plenary Commission meeting in August 1985.

c) The idea is to send the preliminary draft of the explication of the apostolic faith after the Plenary Commission meeting to local groups for study and comments beginning an intensified stage of dialogue between the Commission on Faith and Order and grassroots all over the world. The revision of the study guide for local group work will facilitate the process of local participation in the apostolic faith study.

5. Regional conferences

Regional conferences should be held on specific regional experiences, challenges and essentials in relation to the apostolic faith. It would be helpful for the future development of the whole study to have such conferences in as many regions as possible prior to the World Conference foreseen for 1988/89. The following members of the Standing Commission take responsibility for exploring the possibilities for such a conference in their region: Africa, Mercy Oduyoye; Asia, Yeow Choo Lak; Caribbean, H.O. Russell; Eastern Europe, Ulrich Kühn; North America, Jeffrey Gros; Western Europe, Mary Tanner.

6. Collaboration with other WCC sub-units

At Crete the Standing Commission once more emphasized Faith and Order's readiness to cooperate with other WCC sub-units, whenever possible and appropriate. Whereas the BEM process relates to different sub-units from Unit III and the unity/renewal study to the Sub-unit on Church and Society, the most appropriate partners for the apostolic faith study seem to be the study on "Gospel and Culture" (CWME) and the study on "Theological Significance of Other Living Faiths" (DFI) (cf. Appendix 2). More detailed cooperation between these projects should include:

a) mutual exchange between the respective staff persons in Geneva;

b) mutual distribution of documentation concerning the ongoing progress of the above-mentioned studies;

c) invitation for participation of representatives from CWME and DFI in the three international consultations (at the expense of the sub-unit concerned);

d) a more intensified way of collaborating will take place after the next Plenary Commission meeting, especially concerning part III (confession) of the apostolic faith study.

7. Letter to Christian World Communions

A letter will be sent to the secretaries of the Christian World Communions asking for short and precise information about:

1) the status of the ancient creeds;

2) the role of specific historical confessional traditions;

3) the use of contemporary statements of faith;

4) mutual recognition of confessions of faith;

within and between the different confessional families. Responses are required by 1 April 1985.

8. Contact with the churches

The Standing Commission approved sending to the churches and other appropriate bodies a letter (together with a description of the apostolic faith study) informing them about the project and inviting them to participate in this long-term study.

9. Publications

Because of the importance of the study, the Standing Commission asked for continued and qualified intensified publications of apostolic faith themes.

a) The handbook of texts for study shall be published with the help of national publishers, as far as possible also in French, German, Greek and Spanish.
b) The series "Confessing Our Faith Around the World" will be continued.
c) A new series of booklets with materials from the international consultations will be initiated under the heading: "The Nicene Creed in contemporary contexts". The reports of the three consultations will be available at the Plenary Commission meeting in August 1985 in all WCC working languages. The presentations and other material from the consultations will be published at least in English on a local basis according to the meeting places.
d) The preliminary draft text of the explication of the Nicene Creed will be published after the Plenary Commission meeting for further study and comment.

10. Convergence document

a) The principal instrument for the apostolic faith project should be a convergence document, like the BEM text.
b) The Standing Commission asked the Steering Group to prepare a preliminary draft text of the explication of the Nicene Creed for the next meeting of the Plenary Commission in August 1985.

11. Timetable

1984
— Contacts with Christian World Communions, local group leaders and others interested in the study
— Information to churches
— First international consultation on Second Article (17-24 November, South India)

1985
— Second international consultation on Third Article (parallel to consultation on unity/renewal, 3-10 January, Chantilly, France)
— Third international consultation on First Article (14-22 March, Kinshasa, Zaire)
— Meeting of Steering Group (28-31 May, Crêt-Bérard, Switzerland)
— Plenary Commission (13-26 August, Stavanger, Norway)
— Editing and communication of results of the Plenary Commission

1986-88
— Three international consultations on the common expression/confession of the apostolic faith today.

Appendix 1: Review of the study process

Here are only listed the major conferences; more detailed descriptions of the "history" of the study project and of related "activities" are available in the Secretariat's file on apostolic faith documents.

1. 1927-1978
a) *Lausanne 1927*, First World Conference on Faith and Order — Subject IV: The Church's Common Confession of Faith, cf. the final report, in *Proceedings of the World Conference Lausanne 1927*, p.466f.
b) *Aarhus, Bristol, Geneva, Addis Ababa 1964-1971* — Four consultations between representatives of Oriental and Eastern Orthodox Churches on Christological questions. Cf. the four agreed statements, in *Does Chalcedon Divide or Unite? Towards Convergence in Orthodox Christology*, 1981, pp.1-16.
c) *Louvain, Accra, Bangalore 1971-1978* — Study project and statement on "A Common Account of Hope", in "Sharing in One Hope: Bangalore 1978", *Faith and Order Paper No. 92*, 1978, pp.1-11.

2. 1978-1983
a) *Venice 1978/Le Louverain 1979* — Two consultations on apostolic faith questions, sponsored by the Faith and Order Commission and the Joint Working Group; cf. the document: "Towards a Confession of the Common Faith"; *Faith and Order Paper No. 100*, 1980.
b) *Klingenthal 1978/79* — Two consultations on the *filioque* controversy. Elaboration of the memorandum: "The filioque clause in ecumenical perspective", in "Spirit of God — Spirit of Christ: Ecumenical Reflections on the Filioque Controversy", *Faith and Order Paper No. 103*, 1981, pp.3-18.
c) *Chambésy 1981/Lima 1982* — Consultation and Plenary Commission meeting. Elaboration of an outline on "Towards the Common Expression of the Apostolic Faith Today", in "Towards Visible Unity, Vol. II, Lima 1982", *Faith and Order Paper No. 113, pp.28-46*.
d) *Odessa 1981* — Consultation and report on "The Ecumenical Importance of the Nicene Creed".
e) *Rome 1983* — Consultation and report on "The Apostolic Faith in the Scriptures and in the Early Church", in "The Roots of Our Common Faith: Faith in the Scriptures and in the Early Church", *Faith and Order Paper No. 119*, 1984.

Concluding the study process since 1978 one can say that besides the time-consuming elaboration of a frame for the whole study project, the work concentrated on three special aspects: the *filioque* controversy between Eastern and Western Christianity, the ecumenical importance of the Nicene Creed and the biblical roots of the Christian faith.

Appendix 2: Relation to "Gospel and Culture"
and "Theological Significance of Other Living Faiths"

Such a broad and deep project as the apostolic faith study goes naturally far beyond the responsibility of one sub-unit within the WCC.

a) The Commission on World Mission and Evangelism (CWME) plans a special programme on "Gospel and Culture". The Vancouver programme guidelines state that the WCC should "help member churches in developing and understanding of the relation between evangelism and culture in respect of both the contextual proclamation of the gospel in all cultures and the transforming power of the gospel in any culture".[16] As the provisional description of this programme says "the breadth of this study will require close cooperation with other sub-units, e.g. ... Faith and Order ...".[17]

b) The Commission on Dialogue with People of Living Faiths and Ideologies (DFI) foresees a study on the "Theological Significance of Other Living Faiths". This programme "will help the growth in churches' own self-understanding" encountering people of other living faiths. It will also be carried out "in cooperation with the Faith and Order Commission and the Commission on World Mission and Evangelism".[18]

Both programmes are relevant for the explication as well as for the confession of the apostolic faith today.

---

[16] *Ibid.*, p.254.
[17] Paper for the WCC Executive Committee, February 1984.
[18] Paper for the WCC Executive Committee, February 1984.

2. STUDY GROUPS ON APOSTOLIC FAITH TODAY
Proposals and Questions

I. Proposals

1. Size: We suggest informal study groups of 5-10 interested persons.

2. Composition: Various confessions should be represented in the groups and women and men, lay and ordained, young and old, should work together.

3. Meetings: Each group should meet regularly over an appropriate period of time. Existing ecumenical groups, congregational seminars or other groups could take up the theme.

4. Procedure: Study could progress in three stages:
a) determining group members' own interests and questions;
b) individual and group reading of relevant texts;
c) discussion on the content of these texts and their relation to individual experiences, interests and questions.

5. Selection: Each group should select only one or two themes related to the interests of its members in order to reflect on these in more depth.

6. Additional materials: In addition to the texts in this volume, we refer groups to the list of publications of the Commission on Faith and Order concerning "Apostolic Faith Today" (see Appendix 3).

7. Contact with the Secretariat on Faith and Order: The Secretariat of the Commission on Faith and Order (150 route de Ferney, CH-1211 Geneva 20, Switzerland) would be grateful to receive information as soon as possible on:
a) planned or already existing groups and their composition;
b) the selected topic(s);
c) the existence and use of contemporary statements of faith (texts are welcome).

8. Group findings: It would be appreciated if the groups would send the Faith and Order Secretariat the results of their work, in whatever form they wish.

9. Exchange of experiences: We hope that, on the basis of the group work, it will be possible to have an exchange of experiences and results at the regional and international levels.

10. Goal: The work of local study groups should contribute to a better and richer understanding of our common faith and its implications for Christian life. It should at the same time contribute to the Faith and Order study on "Towards the Common Expression of the Apostolic Faith Today".

II. Questions

1. On the importance of the study theme
a) What is the significance for you of dealing with the topic of the common expression of the *apostolic faith today*?
b) For "expressing" the Christian faith how do you understand the relationship between *words and acts* in faith?
c) In what way do the common *eucharistic* celebration and the common expression of the *apostolic faith* belong together?
d) Do you consider the three *goals* of the study project as ecumenically significant and necessary: (1) recognition of the Nicene Creed by the churches; (2) explication of the apostolic faith in and for contemporary situations; (3) common confession of the Christian faith by the churches today? Which of these three goals do you consider most important?
e) What *efforts* are required to bring the life within the churches as much as possible into harmony with the content of faith?

2. On the role of the Nicene Creed
a) What role does the *Nicene Creed* play in your church today? Is it used in worship and teaching?
b) What *other* traditional confessions are used in your church?
c) How do you determine the relationship between *scripture* (Old and New Testament) and *creed*? Do you think the new formulation of confessions of faith is necessary or are you content with reference to the scripture?
d) Do you consider the Nicene Creed a *sufficient* expression of the Christian faith today? If not, what is lacking?
e) Could you imagine that the churches in your region would *recognize* afresh the Nicene Creed and examine their own understanding of being Christian in its light? What consequences would such a process have for the relationship between the various churches?

3. On the explication of the Christian faith today
a) Which *themes* are especially important for you?
b) What consequences does confessing the *one God* have for the relationship between different confessional churches?
c) How do you answer the central *Christological* question: Who is Jesus Christ for us today?

279

d) In what way can you recognize in your own church the one, holy, catholic and apostolic *church*?

e) On which of the topics would you like to develop a short, contemporary *explication* of faith with your group?

4. On the confession of the Christian faith today

a) Which contemporary *statements of faith* are in use in your region or church, officially or unofficially? (The Secretariat on Faith and Order would be grateful to receive texts.)

b) Which contemporary *challenges* are especially urgent for you in view of: (1) the attitude of the Christian churches; (2) the encounter between cultures, religions and ideologies; (3) the situation of humankind as a whole?

c) What possibility do you see for handling the *condemnations* (anathemas) of other Christian convictions and/or groups (e.g. Arians, Anabaptists) as they are formulated, e.g. in Canon 1 of the Second Ecumenical Council of 381 in Constantinople and in Articles 1, 2, 5, 8, 9, 12, 16, 17 of the *Confessio Augustana* (1530), in such a way that they no longer obstruct a mutual recognition of the churches as members of the one body of Christ?

d) Which themes, viewpoints and findings do you consider *indispensable* for a common expression of the apostolic faith today (cf. the old principle: *quod requiritur et sufficit* — what is necessary and sufficient)?

e) In which fields (e.g. combating racism, developing a positive relationship between Christians and Jews, advocating peace and justice) do you see the contemporary need for a *confessional stance* by Christians?

3. RECENT PUBLICATIONS OF THE COMMISSION ON FAITH AND ORDER CONCERNING APOSTOLIC FAITH TODAY

"Towards a Confession of the Common Faith", P. Duprey and L. Vischer eds, *Faith and Order Paper No. 100,* 1980.

"Confessing Our Faith Around the World I", C.S. Song ed., *Faith and Order Paper No. 104,* 1980.

"Spirit of God, Spirit of Christ: Ecumenical Reflections on the Filioque Controversy", L. Vischer ed., *Faith and Order Paper No. 103,* 1981.

Does Chalcedon Divide or Unite? Towards Convergence in Orthodox Christology, P. Gregorios, W.H. Lazareth and N.A. Nissiotis eds., 1981.

"Towards Visible Unity. Commission on Faith and Order, Lima 1982. Vol. I: Minutes and Addresses", Section V: Towards the Common Expression of the Apostolic Faith Today, M. Kinnamon ed., *Faith and Order Paper No. 112,* 1982, pp.90-100.

"Towards Visible Unity. Commission on Faith and Order, Lima 1982. Vol. II: Study Papers and Reports", Part I: Towards the Common Expression of the Apostolic Faith Today, M. Kinnamon ed., *Faith and Order Paper No. 113,* 1982, pp.3-119.

"Confessing Our Faith Around the World II", H.-G. Link ed., *Faith and Order Paper No. 120,* 1983.

"The Roots of Our Common Faith: Faith in the Scriptures and in the Early Church", H.-G. Link ed., *Faith and Order Paper No. 119,* 1984.

"Confessing Our Faith Around the World III: the Caribbean and Central America", H.-G. Link ed., *Faith and Order Paper No. 123,* 1984.

"Confessing Our Faith Around the World IV: South America", H.-G. Link ed., *Faith and Order Paper No. 126,* 1985.

All available from the WCC Publications Office.